Colonial Subjects

Colonial Subjects

Essays on the Practical History of Anthropology

EDITED BY
PETER PELS
AND
OSCAR SALEMINK

Ann Arbor

THE UNIVERSITY OF MICHIGAN PRESS

First paperback edition 2000
Copyright © by the University of Michigan 1999
All rights reserved
Published in the United States of America by
The University of Michigan Press
Manufactured in the United States of America
♾ Printed on acid-free paper

2002 2001 2000   4 3 2

No part of this publication may be reproduced, stored in a retrieval system, or transmitted in any form or by any means, electronic, mechanical, or otherwise, without the written permission of the publisher.

A CIP catalog record for this book is available from the British Library.

Library of Congress Cataloging-in-Publication Data

Colonial subjects : essays on the practical history of anthropology
   / edited by Peter Pels and Oscar Salemink.
     p. cm.
   Includes bibliographical references.
   ISBN 0-472-11017-9 (alk. paper)
   1. Ethnology—History. 2. Ethnology—Developing countries—Field work. 3. Europe—Colonies—History. 4. Developing countries—Colonial influence.   I. Pels, Peter.   II. Salemink, Oscar.
   GN308 .c66   1999
   301'.09—ddc21   99-6129
                                                                          CIP

ISBN 0-472-08746-0 (pbk. : alk. paper)

Contents

Preface and Acknowledgments   vii

Introduction: Locating the Colonial Subjects
of Anthropology   1
Peter Pels and Oscar Salemink

The Fetish of Civilization: Sacrificial Blood and
Monetary Debt   53
William Pietz

The Rise and Fall of the Indian Aborigines: Orientalism,
Anglicism, and the Emergence of an
Ethnology of India, 1833–1869   82
Peter Pels

The Illusion of Consent: Language, Caste, and
Colonial Rule in India   117
Gloria Goodwin Raheja

The Crimes of Colonialism: Anthropology and the
Textualization of India   153
Nicholas B. Dirks

Hopi Snakes, Zuñi Corn: Early Ethnography in the
American Southwest   180
Curtis M. Hinsley

White Man's Flour: The Politics and Poetics of an
Anthropological Discovery   196
Patrick Wolfe

The Making of Traditional Bali: Colonial
Ethnography and Bureaucratic Reproduction   241
Henk Schulte Nordholt

Ethnography as Martial Art: Ethnicizing Vietnam's
Montagnards, 1930–1954   282
Oscar Salemink

Constructing Racial Landscapes: Africans,
Administrators, and Anthropologists in Late
Colonial Northern Rhodesia   326
   Lyn Schumaker

Contributors   353

Name Index   355

Subject Index   359

Preface and Acknowledgments

This volume is the result of a process that started when Hans Sonneveld, director of the Amsterdam School for Social Scientific Research, conceived the excellent idea of introducing its editors—then both research students at the School—to each other in 1992. This meeting produced, first, a seminar, "Colonial Ethnographies: Writing, Cultures and Historical Contexts," which was held at the Amsterdam School for Social Scientific Research in June 1993. This seminar was made possible by the generous support of the Amsterdam School, the Royal Netherlands Academy for Arts and Sciences (KNAW), the University of Amsterdam's Fund for Development Cooperation (FUOS), the Directorate-General for International Cooperation (DGIS) of the Dutch Ministry of Foreign Affairs, the Society for Scientific Research in the Tropics (Treub-Maatschappij), and the Amsterdamse Universiteitsvereniging. The seminar resulted in a collection of essays, the majority of which had been presented at the seminar (*Colonial Ethnographies*, special issue of *History of Anthropology* [vol. 8, 1994]). We again thank FUOS for support in the production of that volume, and Nicholas Thomas and Christopher Pinney for their support and advice in preparing it. Special thanks should go, as far as this phase of the process was concerned, to the Centre for Asian Studies Amsterdam, which, as part of the Amsterdam School, generously hosted our activities. This project would not have been possible without the support of its director, Jan Breman, and the administrative genius of Iet de Groot.

However, we felt that some of the ideas aired in this volume deserved wider distribution. There are excellent texts on the anthropology of colonialism that also discuss anthropology's place in the processes of colonial expansion (such as Nicholas Dirks's *Colonialism and Culture* [1992], Nicholas Thomas's *Colonialism's Culture* [1994], and Frederick Cooper and Ann Stoler's *Tensions of Empire* [1997]). George Stocking has produced a collection of essays that covers the same terrain as that targeted in this book (*Colonial Situations* [*History of Anthropology* 7, 1991]). However, one has to go back to Talal Asad's *Anthropology and the Colonial Encounter* (1973) to find an attempt at systematic coverage of the possible consequences, for the history and practice of anthropology, of a study of anthropology's colonial roots. Despite the depth and range of both the analysis and historical ethnography displayed by the other contributions to this book, we do not claim to have succeeded in this; as the introduction makes clear, much remains to be done. However, we feel that this volume can, at least partly, fill the lacunae we have come up against when trying to teach the history of anthropology from the point of view of its social embeddedness in the situations where ethnographic knowledge was actually coproduced.

We thank, again, Christopher Pinney for his advice in proceeding with the second phase of this project. We also gratefully acknowledge permission to reprint essays previously published elsewhere: Harwood Academic Publishers, for permission to reprint, only slightly modified, the essays by Patrick Wolfe and Henk Schulte Nordholt from our previous collection of essays in *History and Anthropology* 8 (1994); and the American Anthropological Association for permission to reprint an enlarged version of Gloria Raheja's essay in *American Ethnologist* 23, no. 3 (August 1996). Three of the papers published here were originally presented at the "Colonial Ethnographies" seminar (Hinsley, Schulte Nordholt, and Wolfe). Three papers were specifically written for this volume (the introduction, Pels, and Salemink). William Pietz, Nicholas Dirks, Gloria Raheja, and Lyn Schumaker present substantial reworkings of materials published elsewhere, and we thank them for joining in and enriching this project further. We thank Susan Whitlock for her editorial work, three anonymous readers of the University of Michigan Press for their acute comments, and Ingrid van den Broek and Annette Jansen for help in processing this into a legible manuscript.

Finally, we gratefully acknowledge the financial support for this publication by the Faculty of Political, Social and Cultural Sciences of the University of Amsterdam.

Introduction
Locating the Colonial Subjects of Anthropology
Peter Pels and Oscar Salemink

1. Introduction

Despite the initiative of George Stocking Jr. and others in the 1960s, and the impressive amount of historical scholarship that has developed since, the historiography of anthropology is still marked by a certain "whig" interpretation. Its "principle of abridgment" (Stocking 1982:3) is to project the self-image of twentieth-century academic anthropology onto all ethnographic activities that played a role in the formation of the discipline. The history of anthropology therefore still concentrates largely on ideas, on the formation and background of the theories and methods that are supposed to constitute anthropology's core. For a large number of its practitioners, the "real" history of anthropology commenced only at the time that theoretical and research expertise were fused in the person of the professional fieldworker. This implies, more often than not, that ethnographic practices by nonprofessionals are measured against anachronistic standards, insufficiently set within their historical contexts, or written out of the discipline's history altogether. As a result, important moments in the development of anthropology are ignored. The following collection of essays aims to question this distinction between academic anthropology and other ethnographic practices and thereby to unsettle the comfortable boundary of professionalism that this distinction maintains around the former.

We hope to do this by providing a number of examples of ethnographic practices under colonial rule, practices that suggest alternative interpretations of anthropological commonplaces in past and present: different genealogies of "fetishism," "virgin birth," or "Balinese character"; different constructions of the "native point of view" or the "field"; other, nonacademic roles for linguistics or anthropometry; and, as a result, more room for indigenous authorities, gatekeepers, and informants, for middlemen, and for traders, settlers, missionaries, and colonial administrators, than is usually allowed for within disciplinary history.

Since "practice" and "history" have been welcomed as twin pillars of anthropological theory since the 1980s (Ortner 1984), it is remarkable that such an approach toward the history of anthropology has not yet been developed systematically; that, in other words, reflexive theorizing by anthropologists has made rather less use of the notions of "practice" and "history" than Ortner's diagnosis would lead one to expect. This can at least partly be explained by the hierarchical relationship between "pure" and "applied" anthropology that has dominated the discipline since World War II. The very use of the term *applied* suggested the existence of a "pure" disciplinary core that was relatively autonomous from historical circumstance or practical use. In a review of anthropology outside the academy, Susan Wright has criticized such implicit hierarchies of "pure," "applied," and "no longer" anthropologists, the latter being those who are trained as anthropologists but find employment outside the academy (1995). The latter were for quite some time assumed to be "lost to the profession," implying that the anthropological discipline and its identity were thought to be exclusively located within the academy. However, from the 1970s onward more and more anthropologists work in nonacademic settings, and their demands for representation on professional platforms are increasingly heard (Fluehr-Lobban 1991; Goldschmidt 1979; Wright 1995).

The academic disavowal of practical application is, of course, an odd strategy of professionalization when compared to other professions. Medical doctors, lawyers, or psychologists do not lose their professional credentials when, after their academic studies, they start to work as general practitioners or therapists. In Anthropologyland, however—as in allied disciplines like sociology—those who are not exclusively preoccupied with the construction of academic knowledge, but are involved with its "application," are often considered a lesser breed of scholars. The implicit and, as Wright argues, unfounded assumption is that "applied" work does not lead to the higher-rated achievement of formulating theory (Wright 1995:72)—showing again that theory-formulation from something like clinical or experimental practice, as in medical or psychological therapy, is assumed to be impossible. If one starts from such an assumption, the history of anthropology can, indeed, be nothing but a history of ideas and methods.

A historical perspective shows that this hierarchy of "pure," "applied," and "no longer" anthropologists has only recently become hegemonic: Malinowski's definition of "the average practical man" as someone incapable of good ethnography (1922:5) only became influential during the second quarter of this century, at about the same time that the Boasian school achieved a similar academic autonomy in the United States. "Pure science" did not become a high-water mark of professional anthropology until after World War II, when academic appointments boomed and decreased the necessity for anthropologists to advertise their practical utility. The New Left's distaste of the practical uses of anthropology in colonial and neocolonial situations in the 1960s and 1970s often reinforced this identification of anthropology with the academic profession, using anthropology's assumed (neo-)colonial complicity as the scapegoat of a newly emancipated academic professionalism, that in its turn proceeded to fashion the history of anthropology in its own image (Pels and Nencel 1991; Pels and Salemink 1994).

Like the classical anthropology it criticized, this new professionalism often relied on a juxtaposition of a positive, emancipated, and academic core of ideas with a negative past of colonial practice, an image of emancipation through science and literature that was as old as colonial policy itself (Viswanathan 1989). This was not the only way in which anthropology remained entangled with colonial subjects. Since the 1960s, the critique of anthropology severely damaged the *dyadic* image of anthropology, one that isolated the relationship between a detached and "pure" scientific observer and "his" informants. Instead, it was argued that this view of the anthropological relationship ignored its situatedness in a history of global inequality, perpetuated by the unequal power relations between a universal anthropological subject and his "local" coproducers of knowledge. The triple sense of our use of the term *colonial subjects* reflects this critical consciousness. First, the colonial subjects of anthropology are the "detached" *observers* who welded power to knowledge by claiming universality for the latter, a claim that could serve to distract from their position in a field of local colonial interests. The second set of colonial subjects are the topoi of colonial discourse, the rhetorical commonplaces that organized the intellectual containment of the practical anxieties of colonial rule and became sufficiently entrenched in academic discourse to survive decolonization. Last, the colonial subjects of anthropology are its "subject peoples": the "races," "tribes," or "ethnic groups" targeted by both colonial states and anthropologists as future citizens. It is within this triangle of discursive strategies, of universal subject, colonial commonplace, and global and local citizenship, that anthropology found, and still finds, its proper locus.

It is, however, insufficient to restrict this inquiry to the realm of discursive strategies: practical anthropologies are not mere rhetorical constructions. It is necessary to locate discursive strategies in the contexts of their use, in the tactics of specific relationships of power and exchange that actualize and determine the value of these discursive strategies.[1] Most discursive strategies of anthropology extract the subject—the ethnographer—from such contact zones and deny that ethnographer and ethnographized once stood in a relationship of coevalness, in which the knowledge later authorized by the former was coproduced by the latter (Fabian 1983; Pratt 1992). Throughout its history, the writing of ethnographies and anthropological reflections required authors to distance themselves from the relationships within which their experience of human difference was formed. As many critics of orientalism, colonial discourse, anthropology, or social science in general now agree, they did this by essentializing selected traits of observer and observed, producing dehistoricized representations of either subject, or object, or both, that obscure, obliterate, or transform the relationship negotiated in practice.

Perhaps the most obvious illustration of this intellectual movement from relation to essence is the way in which historical relationships of geographical location, based on the practice of travel from Europe, have been transformed into objects of study like the "Indian," "Oriental," or "African." Whether the relevant relationship was one of travel or trade, of conquest or conversion, the essentialized definitions of self and other arising out of these historically specific locations of ethnography generally bear the traces of the relationship in which they were defined: "Indians" were produced as a result of the European search for riches along the Western route; "Orientals," of its crusades, conquests, and commerce along the Eastern; "Africans," particularly when essentialized as a black race, by the European slavery practiced on the Western and Eastern coasts of the continent. But the relationships that made Indians, Orientals, and Africans into objects of desire as well as contemplation were denied in order to emphasize the Europeans' self-image of distanced, "universal" observation.

Once one treats the history of anthropology along the lines previously sketched, taking account of the practical relationships between observers and observed, and their subsequent transformation by the representations of ethnography, this history multiplies into colonial situations, intellectual genealogies, and practical anthropologies (Stocking 1991:4). The essays that follow work, each in its own way, toward novel syntheses, but cannot be expected to draw together a field in which so many accepted generalizations, once analyzed historically, turn out to rest

---

1. The distinction between strategy (implying a "proper" locus, or subject position outside the targeted group) and tactic (a bricolage of political calculations in which subject and target are coeval) is gleaned from de Certeau (1984:xix; for an application to the history of ethnography, see Byrnes 1994). In this particular case, it is congruent with Foucault's distinction between "discourse" and "discursive practice" (1972:200).

on shaky foundations, and in which so much remains to be discovered. We shall, therefore, try to situate these essays in some of the major colonial relationships that Europeans have forged in the nineteenth century (section 6), and attempt to suggest how this approach affects our understanding of the history of twentieth-century professional anthropology (sections 7 and 8). But before we can thus contextualize the essays in this book, we first need to unpack the arguments that we only addressed in skeleton form: first, the specific historical location of "pure" academic anthropology (section 2); second, the movement from colonial relationship to essentialized subject and object (section 3); and third, the context of formation of anthropology's colonial subjects (section 4), and the way these strategies fragment once they are analyzed against the background of the colonial relationships from which they emerge (section 5).

2. Disciplinary Anthropology and the Colonial Encounter

If anthropology is viewed as a discipline, it is identified with an academic location, which implies that the most important intellectual events in anthropology's history are deemed to have taken place in scientific societies or at universities in Britain, France, the United States, Germany, and perhaps some other centers in the West. Obvious though the identification of anthropology and academy may seem at present, it is very much a product of anthropology's self-conception (in the double sense of "self-image" and "self-production"). This becomes clear when we consider the career of the volume *Anthropology and the Colonial Encounter*, edited by Talal Asad (1973).

At the time of its publication, *Anthropology and the Colonial Encounter* was taken up in a heated debate about the extent to which British anthropologists had been engaged in "aiding and abetting British colonial policy in Africa" (Scholte 1975:45), a debate following on the denunciation of the involvement of anthropologists in U.S. counterinsurgency projects in Latin America and Southeast Asia (Wolf and Jorgensen 1970).[2] Asad's volume was interpreted as making precisely the point that anthropologists had been the handmaidens of colonial rule (Loizos 1977:137; Ortner 1984:138), despite Asad's insistence that the crucial issue was not whether anthropologists were complicit with colonialism or not, but how anthropology emerged from the colonial context (Asad 1973:18–19). Since then, the (denial of the) colonial complicity of individual anthropologists loomed large in discussions of the relationship between British anthropol-

---

2. For the rest of the discussion, see Diamond 1974; Gluckman 1974; Leach 1974; and Scholte 1974.

ogy and colonialism (Goody 1995:7–9; Kuklick 1991:183; Kuper 1983:116). Even though others sometimes echoed Asad's intentions with the book (e.g., Kuper 1983:117), the majority of anthropologists seem to have concurred in the judgment of a later, second wave of critics, who included *Anthropology and the Colonial Encounter* in their dismissal of the 1970s critique as caricatural, immoderate, and superficial (Clifford 1986:9; Marcus and Fischer 1986:35; Ortner 1984:138).

Disciplinary politics explains, at least partly, why the book was so unevenly appreciated. The 1970s generation of critics had a material interest—academic distinction—in presenting the work of the previous generation as politically suspect, and in the process, the distinction between "pure" aspirations and its derivative "application" shifted to one between an explicit emancipatory politics (which could be "applied" in "action-research") and a hypocritical "value-free" science (that masked its "real," but in fact assumed, complicity with colonial practice). There was a clear continuity, therefore, between the self-conceptions of classical anthropologists and their radical critics of the 1970s: while the former repudiated complicity with colonialism in the name of science in general (Evans-Pritchard 1946), the latter denounced it for political reasons. Of course, "action-research" and related concerns still urged attempts to change power relationships rather than academic political allegiance. However, this threat to the integrity of anthropological professionalism was domesticated by a second wave of critics: some of the theorists of the literary turn of the 1980s toned down the "immoderate" critique of the 1970s, substituted for it the reading of hegemonic texts, and thereby re-entrenched criticism in the academic context (Stocking 1991:4).

Of course, this is by no means the whole story of postwar academic anthropology and the criticism it generated in the 1970s and 1980s. But this simplified version is meant to emphasize that the issue of the colonial *complicity* of *academic* anthropologists has come to dominate the historical study of the constitution of the discipline in relation to the colonial context. The academic critics of the involvement of anthropologists with neocolonial domination and counterinsurgency in the projects Camelot (Latin America) and Agile (Vietnam) tended to equate the situation in the 1970s, when the anthropological profession had been firmly established in the academy, with colonial situations where the profession had not been defined as such, or not in the same way.

Under the cross fire of critique, few people noticed the paradox that most studies of the complicity of anthropology and colonialism focused on a place and period—Africa and late British colonialism—that witnessed a concerted attempt by anthropologists to *extricate* themselves from colonial patronage systems. Malinowski and Radcliffe-Brown stand out in the history of anthropology as scholars who succeeded in redefining anthropological research as—maybe: reducing it to—a dyadic relationship between observer and observed. Their strategy was mainly successful because Rockefeller funding enabled them to do away with the colonial patronage coveted by a previous generation of anthropologists, who saw their work as located in the triad between "subject peoples," colonial administration, and anthropological expertise.[3] Malinowski and his colleagues needed to portray colonial administrators and missionaries as anthropologically inept "practical men," and this goes a long way in explaining the undeniable friction that existed between the three groups in the 1930s and 1940s (James 1973; Kuklick 1991:182ff.).

The existence of this friction implies that the image of a "pure" academic anthropology was partly constituted in a direct struggle with nonacademic ethnographic traditions that largely emerged from colonial practice. Of course, nonacademic predecessors of anthropology have been recognized in Greek and Roman writers like Herodotus and Tacitus (Voget 1975:5–20; Honigmann 1976:11–40), and in traders like Marco Polo or missionaries like Las Casas and Lafitau (Haddon 1934:103; Hodgen 1964:94; Pagden 1986). But these studies concentrate on a history of "ethnology" (Voget 1975), on "anthropological ideas" (Honigmann 1976) or "theories of culture" (Harris 1968), that is, on the logos rather than the practice of ethnography. Since Malinowski, the ethnography produced by nonacademics has been reinvented as a *protoethnography*, measured against the telos of professional ideas.

We submit that, in order to follow up on Asad's admonition to study the location of anthropology in the colonial encounter, it is necessary to free the study of colonial ethnographies of disciplinary bias and to treat them sui generis, not in thrall to an academic idea. One should reverse the point of view of disciplinary history and regard academic anthropology as only a specific instance of a much broader field of ethnographic practice, in which professional methods emerged in direct competition with extra-academic ethnographies (Pels and Salemink 1994:5). Because of that competition, and in spite of the methodical distinction that Malinowski *cum suis* successfully introduced, there are clear continuities between the rhetoric of academic ethnography and the "manners and customs" genres that preceded it (Fabian 1983; Pratt 1985). Many academic descriptions take their cue from ethnicities, social structures, and ethnographic traditions defined and materially constructed under colonial rule. Not all ingredients of academic anthropology have been produced at academic locations.

---

3. See, for example, Rivers 1917. This is worked out in more detail in section 7.

Moreover, the identification of "pure" anthropology with the academy, characteristic of the disciplinary view, needs to be questioned. Even when restricting our analysis to the professionalism of the twentieth century, we have to acknowledge that academic anthropology, too, was made by "practical men" like colonial administrators and missionaries (Clifford 1982; Fortes 1974; West 1994). Of course, anthropology in the metropoles has always acknowledged the existence of a museum anthropology as an important link in the institutionalization of the discipline, but has simultaneously depicted it as past, and material culture studies as of little consequence (until recently: see Stocking 1985b). Nowadays, this hegemony of the disciplinary view is challenged not only by the increasing number of anthropologists employed outside the academy that we mentioned before. Academic monopolies on ethnographic representation are also undermined by the fact that those represented are increasingly able and anxious to represent themselves. We want to add to this questioning of academic hegemony by including those situations in which ethnography and anthropology were institutionalized in missionary rather than scientific societies, colonial rather than metropolitan bureaucracies, commercial rather than intellectual economies, and military rather than research engagements.

We suggest treating the academy as just one location of ethnographic activity among many, and its production of knowledge as bearing the stamp of that location. We feel it is necessary for anthropologists to make a break with academic experience, in order to

> question the presuppositions inherent in the position of an outside observer, who, in his preoccupation with *interpreting* practices, *is inclined to introduce into the object the principles of his relation to the object* ... (Bourdieu 1977:2; emphasis added)

Academic anthropologists tend to transform their relation to the people studied—a relation based on the distancing attitude of interpretation—into a definition of the "essence" of their object. In Bourdieu's reasoning, this explains why they usually define their object, "culture," as a "map" or set of "rules," that is, as an *ideal* model for behavior. Moreover, they define their own essence as subject in a similarly idealistic way, in terms of the theories and methods that were supposed to determine the making of academic anthropology itself.

Indeed, *method* was the term employed to formulate a relationship between observer and observed that was supposed to be emptied of localized interpretations and material interests. By thus reducing the relationship between observer and observed to an abstract method, positive "facts" were thought to be channeled to a "pure" academic anthropology that could subsequently distill them into the essences of "universal" theory. Although this idealism has been discarded by the majority of practitioners, it still lingers in their historical self-conceptions. This idealism can now be identified as the product of a *specific location,* that is, of an *academic* relationship with the outside world in which scientific distinction is attained through the construction of "pure" knowledge. It will be profitable to consider how such transformations of practical relationships into definitions of subjective and objective essence work in other locations, where ethnographies aimed at more "practical" targets.

3. From Relation to Essence: The Example of "Fetishism"

A genealogy of the idea of the fetish, as set out in a brilliant series of essays by William Pietz (1985, 1987, 1988, 1993, this vol.), brings out several of the points that this book in general, and our introduction in particular, wants to make: the importance of other-than-academic locations for the genealogy of central anthropological concepts; the transformation of the practical problems of relationships with different people into a discourse on their essential difference; and the way in which an ethnographic tradition, despite this erasure of the relations of contact, often retains a link between the concept and the hybrid locality in which it was first formulated.

The origin of the idea of the fetish has usually been sought in the application of the medieval Portuguese word *feitiço,* "charm," to African religious objects in the course of the first explorations of the West African coast. As standard accounts have it: after feitiço had been transformed into a doctrine of "fetishism" in the late eighteenth century, "fetish" gained a wide currency during the nineteenth, to disappear from most anthropological theorizing during the first half of the twentieth century. This disappearance seems to be related to the (seldom explicitly addressed) idea that "fetishism" was somehow a wrong, ethnocentric translation of what Africans "really" thought.[4] Pietz departs from this idealist history in insisting that the idea of the fetish was a novel concept (instead of a preexisting, and misapplied, European idea) that emerged

---

4. Two recent examples of the ethnocentricity argument are MacGaffey 1994 and Pool 1990. The disappearance can partly be explained by the victory of anthropological professionalism over museum anthropology and material culture studies (see Stocking 1985a): the former had, given the idealism noted above, little need for a concept of untranscended materiality. In recent years "fetishism" is once more en vogue, largely through the theoretical traditions of Marx and Freud, which, however, are closer to the ethnographic tradition started by de Marees and Bosman than most scholars realize (see Apter and Pietz 1993; Bhabha 1994; Ellen 1988; *Etnofoor* 1990; Mbembe 1992; Spyer 1998; Taussig 1980).

from and had practical value in the hybrid relationships of trade on the West African coast.

The novelty of *fetisso*, the pidgin word used on the African coast, lay in the fact that the original notion of feitiço "did not raise the essential problem of the fetish: the problem of the social and personal value of material objects" (Pietz 1987:35). Feitiço was conceived in the context of a medieval Christian doctrine of idolatry, in which a material object could only be treated as a passive medium for the relations between spiritual agents. Like theology's emphasis on idolatry, it designated venerated objects in terms of a paradigm of linguistic revelation, of verbal prophecy and scripture, that had no room for the divine power of material objects as such. It was precisely the latter aspect that was novel in the use of the pidgin *fetisso*, and it is significant that it was not derived from the term *idolo* (the common designation of a heathen god), but from *feitiço*, which still retained a link to the material manufacture of witchcraft items, a link that gave it "greater descriptive accuracy" in the African context than the former concept (Pietz 1987:37). Pietz suggests that the "untranscended materiality" of the *fetisso* (in contrast to the transcendent spirituality of the idol) was developed in particular in the hybrid intercultural world of the *tangomaos*, the Portuguese-speaking middlemen living on the Guinea mainland, for whom the wearing of both Christian sacramental objects (such as rosaries) and fetissos was important for establishing their identity as mediators in the European-African trade. But because texts by these middlemen are lacking, this process can only be reconstructed through the reading of subsequent European texts (1987:39).

The most important among these were written by Dutch Calvinist merchants who ousted the Portuguese from the West African trade in the first half of the seventeenth century. Pieter de Marees and Willem Bosman, in particular, introduced and popularized the term *fetish* in Northern European languages and further removed it from the horizons of Christian thought. Iconoclastic Calvinism dismissed material objects from "true" religion, but more importantly, the traders' interests in the West African context made material objects paradigmatic in creating and understanding economic relationships.

Such material objects included (marine) technology, native objects classifiable as commodities, and entities without economic value but potentially dangerous or useful for Europeans within the relationship of trade with Africans (Pietz 1987:40). All these objects were necessary for the trade relationship, but they also fed the confusion that marked its hybridity: the products of European technology, embodying the true understanding of causality, were interpreted as fetish by Africans; important African commodities could be exchanged for beads and other "trifles" that had no value in European eyes; and lastly, the necessary use of fetishes in the oath-taking that ensured permanent and reliable trade relationships gave these objects a political importance that was hard to understand for these Dutch champions of law and commercial order.

Willem Bosman, in particular, developed the idea of the worship of fetishes on the basis of the mercantile valuation of normal and abnormal exchange. The fetish came to be defined as an object valued by the African's "capricious fancy" and opposed to the rational merchant's true technological and commercial values. This "caprice" explained why Africans chose "trifles" to trade for valuables, because anything that took their fancy or struck them as out of the ordinary might become a fetish, just as the products of European technology were interpreted as magical. It also provided a source for a theory of African politics, because the African's "caprice" could only be tamed by the fear of the fetish, exploited by a class of fetish priests who had similar if perverted material interests in mind as did the European traders themselves (Pietz 1987:39–42; 1988:117).

Thus, Bosman formulated the prerequisites of the Enlightenment conception of fetish religion, a materialistic cult incommensurable with Christian categories, conceived "as the worship of haphazardly chosen material objects believed to be endowed with purpose, intention, and a direct power over the material life of both human beings and the natural world" (Pietz 1988:106). This religion was thought to be the central institution of African culture and society (1988:105). In such a way, observations crucial for creating and maintaining trade relationships on the West African coast were transformed into a definition of the essence of African society. Moreover, Bosman's supposition of the moral value of material interest turned African society into a perverted version of his own (1988:106). This defined the subject in its rational, mercantile essence. Subject and object were essentialized in a single discursive move.

Enlightenment philosophers did not adopt Bosman's assumption of the moral value of material interest (Pietz 1988:106). Charles de Brosses's *Du culte des dieux fétiches* (published 1760) inaugurated an intellectual process of redefining the untranscended (and un-Christian) materiality of the fetish in nonreligious, psychological, and aesthetic terms; a process that ended up, in the second half of the nineteenth century, by subsuming the untranscended materiality of the fetish under a secular doctrine of spiritual causation (like medieval theology had subsumed feitiço under idolo). While Auguste Comte still retained "fetishism" as a materialistic stage of religion preceding polytheism and monotheism, Edward Tylor reduced it to a subordinate category of the general term *animism*, stipulated that it was an empowering spirit and not a powerful material object that defined the fetish, and remarked that fetishism imperceptably grades into idolatry. Similarly, while Marx retained a notion of fetishism as a materialistic religion (Pietz 1993), Freud translated it, like Tylor, into a doctrine of a subconscious misrepresentation of reality (Freud 1950). All these reworkings of the concept departed from the trading relationships in which Bosman found himself, and grounded it in intellectual relationships instead.

In a sequel to the essays previously discussed, Pietz shows (in this volume) how the trading relationships in the original West African contact zone were transformed by the military and legal requirements of colonial rule, and how this affected the notion of "fetish." Yet, all these shifts and changes did not completely destroy the continuity between "fetish" and the mercantile valuations of a trading relationship. Even Edward Tylor retained the doctrine of "trifles" and "abnormal curiosity" that is opposed to European conceptions of material value, and thought the best information on fetishism came from Africa (Tylor 1873, II:144–45). Apparently, the ethnographic tradition started by de Marees and Bosman tenaciously retained some of the links with the relationship within which they formulated it. This becomes particularly clear with Mary Kingsley, who followed up on Bosman, de Brosses, Comte, and Tylor by treating "Fetish" as "the African form of thought" (1982:429). She also actively defended the traders and middlemen—who embodied her relationship with the West Africans she studied in 1893–94—against the contempt of missionaries and colonial officials. "All I know that is true regarding West African facts, I owe to the traders," wrote Kingsley (1982:7). Two hundred years earlier, Willem Bosman might have said the same.

Pietz's genealogy of fetishism shows that it is possible to trace the transition from a specific relationship between groups of people to a definition of their essential difference, if we conceive of ethnography as a *practical process* rather than an ideal method or a text. It is in this sense that we argue for the study of the *locations* of ethnography—"location" in the active sense, of a "production of locality" (Appadurai 1996). Elsewhere, we have argued that an ethnographic process can be (analytically) divided into three phases: *préterrain*, ethnographic occasion, and ethnographic tradition (Pels 1994:322; Pels and Salemink 1994:14–15). Here, we want to take Pietz's genealogy of fetishism as an opportunity to systematize and develop this analytic as a guide in the study of ethnography.

The *préterrain* (literally "fore-field") is defined by James Clifford as "all those places you have to go through and be in relation with just to get to your village or to that place of work you will call your field" (1992:100).[5] It is made up of the hybrid spatiotemporal relationships that precondition the work of ethnography: mercantile, colonial, or academic discursive practices that define the possibility and necessity of going "out there"; means of transport; forms of residence; power relationships with and within the societies the ethnographer shall describe; the modes of production and reproduction of these relationships. The préterrain is hybrid not just because two "cultures" meet (this opposition is, in itself, an essentialization) but because the "cultures" that meet are themselves fragmented, multiple, and contradictory.

The préterrain obtains its coherence from certain dominant forms of relationship: in the case of fetishism, the dominant relationship was trade and its attendant exchanges and interpretations of objects. But the dominance of the trading relationship also required other mediating relationships: the middleman or *tangomao* articulating identity on religious objects like rosaries and fetissos; the sexual and domestic relationship between European men and African women, who "fetished" their men by ornamenting themselves (or so European observers thought; Pietz 1988:111); or the relationship with members of the West African elite (kings, "fetish priests") who monopolized benefits of European trade at the expense of their countrymen.

The constitution of the préterrain is historically contingent, and major revolutions in the interpretation of ethnographic commonplaces occurred because colonial relationships shifted, for instance, from a predominantly legal and textual relationship to a labor or an agricultural regime (Pels, this vol.), or from a rural to an urban construction of the "field" (Schumaker, this vol.). However, the example of Mary Kingsley shows that there can be remarkable historical continuities between a specific préterrain (that is, West African trade) and certain ethnographic traditions (the discourse on "fetish"). Even in professional anthropology, where the dominant relationship is academic, it is important to study the composite nature of the préterrain: whereas the help that professional ethnographers receive from administrator, storekeeper, plantation manager, or missionary may not make them share the assumptions of the latter, "[they are] often led to examine these assumptions more carefully than otherwise [they] would" (Firth 1977:146–47).

The *ethnographic occasion* can now be identified as the situation of contact between ethnographer and those to be described, in which they coproduce the knowledge that is to be written down in terms of essences

---

5. A term borrowed, with some change of meaning, from Georges Condominas (1973:9–10; for the change of meaning see Pels 1994:322, and Salemink, this volume).

of self and other. In professional anthropology, it is called the "field," and its construction is a long-neglected aspect of the history of anthropology (but see Schumaker, this vol.). In the case of fetishism, the ethnographic occasion has to be reconstructed by coupling an analysis of dominant relationships pertaining within the préterrain with a critical reading of ethnographic texts, to allow for the conclusion that trade, indeed, produced "fetishism." Here, we can only guess at the specific occasions (contacts with *tangomao?* with native concubines? with kings and priests?) that historically determined how a politics of presenting oneself (then and there) was transformed into a (timeless) representation of self- and otherness. Such a process of historical reconstruction will often be necessary, for the average ethnography contains little information about informants and the situations in which they were encountered.

Other ethnographic occasions, however, can be unequivocally identified: in the "indirect" administration of the Uluguru mountains of Tanganyika, it was the *baraza,* a meeting of the colonial administrator with a selected number of indigenous leaders, from which some other powerful men and all of the leading women of the district were excluded. In this way, the performance of the baraza simultaneously reformed indigenous politics and redefined it in terms of a Luguru "tribe," the topos of subsequent ethnographies of Uluguru (Pels 1994; 1996). This shows the importance of singling out the ethnographic occasion (if only analytically), because it emphasizes the moment at which the object of an ethnographic tradition was defined *and* brought into being. When one can identify, for example, the moment at which "fetishism" was redefined in terms of human sacrifice (Pietz, this vol.), or Bali was turned into a "theatre state" (Schulte Nordholt, this vol.), one has located an ethnographic occasion as both the origin of the commonplaces of an ethnographic tradition, of its empirical "proof," and of its practical, mediating value in colonial relationships.

The analysis of the texts of an *ethnographic tradition,* therefore, should never only focus on the intertextual, but incorporate the inter*con*textual (Appadurai 1996:187), and this can partly be done by including préterrain and ethnographic occasion in the analysis. Often, however, these texts are the most important vehicle through which we can reconstruct préterrain and ethnographic occasion: the texts tend to obscure what contextualizes them. It is therefore crucial to see an ethnographic tradition as itself a practical process, in order to see to what extent a continuity of préterrain, ethnographic occasion and ethnographic tradition has persisted (as in Mary Kingsley's ethnography in relation to West African trade), or whether major shifts in préterrain and ethnographic occasion have altered the meaning of the topoi or commonplaces that mark the tradition.

Such translations are apparent, for instance, in the shift from the *fetisso* of the *tangomao* to the Dutch Calvinist's *fetish*, which is not just a change of name but also a change of object. Similar shifts occurred where the interpretation of "caste" in India went through a major reinvention because the colonial regime increasingly relied on racialist forms of ethnological classification (Pels, this vol.; see also Dirks 1992). This shift in the understanding of caste also produced modifications in the ethnography of proverbs (Raheja, this vol.) and made anthropometry increasingly relevant to colonial policing (Dirks, this vol.). Similarly, a novel missionary and military engagement with West African courts produced a new understanding of "fetish" that centered on blood sacrifice (Pietz, this vol.); while a correspondence between ideas about ignorance of paternity in the metropole, and ethnocidal state-formation in Australia, produced a blossoming of the former in terms of the "virgin birth" controversy (Wolfe, this vol.).

In other words, one should be wary of the nature of the "persistence" of an ethnographic tradition: the repetition of a commonplace may hide a redefinition of it. Such shifts are often the result of a change in genre, as when the "fetish" of Bosman's travelogue was transformed in the "fetishism" of de Brosses's study in comparative religion. Commonplace and genre may define an ethnographic tradition, but in analysis turn out to be themselves constantly redefined under the influence of changing préterrains and ethnographic occasions.

4. Art of Travel, Art of Government: European Strategies of Observation

We used *fetishism* to illustrate the transformation of practical relationships into ethnic essences, a translation that produced our triumvirate of colonial subjects. We still need to specify, however, what we mean by *colonial*. As Pietz's contribution to this book shows, "fetish" played an important role in West African colonial administration. But if Dutch traders never conquered and settled West Africa, to what extent can the fetish be said to emerge from "colonial" relationships? We will not be able to answer such a question with the terminological rigor of a definition, since that would entail a comparison with ethnographies produced in Hellenic, Roman, Arab, or Mughal colonial empires that is beyond our scope and powers. Moreover, our interest in ethnography implies we are more concerned with the cultural organization of colonial power than with the exercise of this power as such. When we talk of "colonial," we think of specific forms of *modern* colonialism, and particularly of its organization of ways of observing and ordering the world. These strategies of observation did much to give "European" or "Western culture" its aura of universality and were therefore central to the constitution of the anthropological subject. Their development depended on the simultaneous transformation of the "art of travel" (Stagl 1990, 1995) and the "art of government" (Foucault 1979). As we shall see later, this transformation was very much indebted to de Marees, Bosman, and their fellow merchants, which serves to show that "European" or "Western culture" was *not* produced in Europe or the West only.

European trade paved the way for modern colonialism partly because travels of trade and exploration were important in establishing European concepts of nationality: Camões's *The Lusiads* and Hakluyt's *Principal Navigations of the English Nation* stand out as representations of a travel relationship in which definitions of others led also to definitions of self, in terms of Portuguese or English "nationhood." They are not only related to the work of Bosman and others through maritime practice (discussed later) but also by their common background in merchant capitalism: the mercantilist classic of Thomas Mun (*England's Treasure by Foreign Trade*, published 1664) redefined Hakluyt's account to such an extent that the diligence, thrift and worldly knowledge of merchants came to stand for their ability—contrasted to that of England's actual, aristocratic, leaders—to properly govern the nation. Like Bosman, Mun made the traders' mercantile valuations define the world of "normal" behavior. And while travel and trade led, in Enlightenment thinking, to a distinct anti-imperialist tendency,[6] it also contributed to the redefinition of "economic" government that would be crucial to modern "governmentality" (Foucault 1979)—including colonial rule.

From the sixteenth century onward, the practice of travel in and from Europe shifted from pilgrimage, through the "Grand Tour" of young noblemen, to Enlightenment expeditions (Stagl 1990, 1995). This shift was accompanied by changing conceptions of time and space: the "incorporating" cosmology characteristic of crusade, pilgrimage, and mission, which was essentially directed inward at a center (Rome or Jerusalem), was transformed and gave way to a "distancing" cosmology of explorations starting from a center in the here and now to discover the unknown "then" and "there" (Fabian 1983:27). To be sure, trade relationships and the lure of gold and spices were also important for early Portuguese travelers with a "crusading" mission (such as the discovery of "Prester John" in India in order to close in on the infidel occupying the Holy Land), but Bosman and his predecessors inherited more of the former than the latter disposition. This is reflected in their "distanced" view of African religion,

---

6. As witnessed by Adam Smith's chapter "Of Colonies" in *The Wealth of Nations*; on Camões and Hakluyt and their successors, see Helgerson 1992.

which described it in the positive terms of African trade rather than as the negative object of a Christian mission.

The *ars apodemica* or art of travel codified cultural patterns of traveling, earlier presented orally or in handwriting, by disseminating travel manuals in print to the reading public (Stagl 1990:319; 1995:51–52). Under the influence of the philosopher Petrus Ramus (1515–72) and his "natural method" for the organization of all knowledge, such manuals acquired encyclopedic status and became the paradigm for later anthropological questionnaires such as Degérando's *Considérations sur les méthodes à suivre dans l'observation des peuples sauvages* (published 1800; Moore 1969) and the Royal Anthropological Institute's *Notes and Queries on Anthropology* (first published 1874, but preceded by similar forms since the 1830s). The Ramist method of storing knowledge invited, above all, a metalanguage of classification, in which all knowledge should be particled to fit the slots of Ramus's ubiquitous tree diagrams. This "diagrammatic reduction" of knowledge to singular phenomena created reports that were "far removed from the experience of the traveller" (Fabian 1983:116; Stagl 1990:322). This was not just a "denial of coevalness" carried over into anthropology (Fabian 1983) but also a precondition for the "collection" of "objects" basic to the development of both museum and statistics.

The movement of the art of travel toward a conception of knowledge as "things" to be "collected" in a classificatory grid can also be associated with the development of mercantilism and the changing technologies of statecraft. This link is perhaps best expressed by the metaphor of the ship. The vessel of trade and exploration, the ship was not only the material embodiment of relations between Europeans and their "others," but also the major object of the development of insurance, the predecessor of "political arithmetic" and statistics (Hacking 1990:16). The ship was not just the carrier of Admiralty expeditions and their questionnaires, it was also the dominant metaphor used in treatises on the art of government (Foucault 1979:11) and, as such, provided it with a conception of "economy" that could function as an alternative to the family model used previously.

Thus, shipping and trade provided alternative models that redefined government from a discourse of sovereignty that stressed the government of "territory," to government as the "right disposition of *things,* arranged so as to lead to a convenient end" (La Perrière, quoted in Foucault 1979:10; emphasis added). Government became, therefore, in itself a form of classification (the latter being the intellectual corollary of material "disposition" and "arrangement"), and the "convenient ends" it strove to attain were not simply the protection of sovereignty and territory, but a plurality of responsibilities that came to the fore once the "economy" was no longer conceived on the model of the management of the family, but as the management of "population" (even if only a ship's population)—a quantity now to be expressed in a novel form of state intelligence: statistics.

The Enlightenment period further matured these new technologies of observation and statecraft, and it is important to stress that some of the crucial steps in their development were not made in the metropoles, but at colonial, non-European locations.[7] We have already seen how West African trade produced generalizations about the proper and improper "disposition of things" characteristic of European trader and African, respectively. But expeditions like Cook's, which were sent out by the Admiralty in a "governmental" spirit, were also in a very practical way centered on the exchange of "things": not only was the barter for goods necessary to keep the ship's economy going, "curiosities" and the proper method of their collection also created intellectual authority for those scholars who joined these expeditions to obtain them (and distinguished them from those who traveled and collected without the proper philosophical interest; Thomas 1991:141).

Moreover, colonial locations and voyages of exploration contributed directly to the formulation of the discipline of statistics (*Statistik* or "statecraft"). The census was primarily developed in the colonies, above all by William Petty's 1679 census of Ireland, that accompanied the pillage of that, also in other ways paradigmatic, colony (Hacking 1990:17). Whereas much statistical material was gathered in Europe itself, it remained either secret, for the use of the monarch, or it was done by amateurs whose work the state only recognized as valuable in the first half of the nineteenth century (Hacking 1990: chaps. 3, 4). The academic discipline of statistics was outlined, in the late eighteenth century, by scholars at Göttingen in Germany, many of whom had been employed by, or were inspired by employees of, the Russian empire, which, under Catherine the Great, sent them out on expeditions into the vast territory it had acquired east of Moscow. Around 1770, these scholars also coined the term *ethnography* (Slezkine 1994; Vermeulen 1992).

Statistics acquired its present quantitative meaning during the first half of the nineteenth century (Cullen 1975). That means that, initially (and for quite some time afterward), statistics and ethnography were

---

7. This is impressively demonstrated by Richard Grove, who shows that colonial expansion, tropical island environments, and non-European botanical knowledge together produced modern environmentalism (1995). It also suggests that we take Foucault's dictum—that it is not society that is penetrated by the state, but the state that, from the sixteenth century onward, becomes increasingly "governmentalized" from the *outside* (1979:20)—as literal, historical fact, if the "outside" is interpreted as the colonial, non-European world.

closely allied because both relied on a discourse of typification and classification, and statistical surveys listed much information we would now class as "ethnographic." Sir John Sinclair, who introduced statistics into the English language with his *Statistical Account of Scotland* (published 1798), included "much information about lifestyles" in his account.[8] Quantification played a role in early statistics, but primarily by the assumption of enumeration that lay at the heart of its central concept, "population." The word *population* meant the *number* of a state's inhabitants, the measure of its power. But *measure*, though inspired by enumeration, was also a qualitative and classificatory notion, and it is this sense of measure that was used by Johann Gottfried Herder when he formulated the idea that nations had their own natural history, the direction of which could not be assessed by "external measures" but only "internally" (Fink 1993:53–57).[9] By assimilating the quantitative aggregate of "population" to an identity of type, he laid the groundwork for the scientific conceptions of race and culture.

5. Colonialism, Resistance, and the Locations of Ethnography

We have sketched some of the major strategies of observation that came to define the European or Western subject, but it should be apparent that this is only a part of the préterrain of European ethnography. These strategies still had to be actualized on foreign terrain, that is, to be tactically deployed in the process of producing ethnography. If the colonial subjects of anthropology were partly determined by modern transformations of travel and government, this should not persuade us of the existence of a "colonial governmentality" that somehow managed to become globally hegemonic (Bhabha 1994:70). Such an assumption of hegemony would confuse the presumption of universal self-realization of the colonial subject (in the first sense in which we use it) with its practical capacity to contain resistance and obstruction, whether in the form of direct confrontation or of everyday avoidance and transformation of so-called hegemonic forms (Guha 1989:228; de Certeau 1984). By distinguishing préterrain,

---

8. About the fishwives of Fisherow in Inveresk, for instance, Sinclair included the following ethnographic remarks: "[These are] women who take the dominant role in their family and the community, swear much but, according to their minister, otherwise sin seldom, who play golf on Sundays and have football matches between the married and unmarried women, the former of whom invariably win" (Hacking 1990:26). It shows that, in this case at least, Sinclair's ethnographic occasion was the interview with the congregation's minister.

9. Herder did this in a critique of August Schlözer, Göttingen's foremost *Statistiker* and the author of the concept of *ethnographie* (Vermeulen 1992), building upon the language work of an important amateur statistician, J. P. Süssmilch (Hacking 1990:21).

ethnographic occasion, and ethnographic tradition, one can analyze ethnographic texts as both signs and sites of struggle between the hegemony aspired to by colonizers and the subaltern voices that they have been able, or attempted, to silence. By setting the texts of an ethnographic tradition against the background of its préterrain and ethnographic occasions, one is forced to consider the combinations of coercion, persuasion, collaboration, and resistance that make up the latter two, combinations that are always radically contingent (Guha 1989:229–31).

This implies that, if we speak of the constitution of colonial subjects in the sphere of governmentality, we cannot assume anything like a coherent ensemble of strategies. We can only expect a certain *redundancy* between the strategies of modern governmentality, as different elements of them are deployed at different times, in widely differing fields of tactical negotiation. Even if the redundancy of colonial strategies reinforces colonial power in ways that such strategies could not effect on their own, still this does not allow one to speak of a "colonial project" or a "colonial discourse" in the singular (Thomas 1994). As we already indicated, even where the topoi and genres of an ethnographic tradition give it a semblance of unity, an analysis of its préterrain and ethnographic occasions may show that its locations are multiple.

This can also be put differently: the analytical sequence of préterrain, ethnographic occasion, and ethnographic tradition is a genealogy of colonial subjects read forward, that allows for a restoration of agency to voices muted or silenced in the process of ethnographic production. In anthropology, the possibility that subordinate voices are "muted" by structures of dominance, to the extent that they are never inscribed in the public record, was first theorized in the context of power relations between men and women (Ardener 1975). "Muted" voices may be distinguished from voices that were heard and recorded, but subsequently silenced by a process of writing up or "entextualization" that deprived them of any message of resistance they carried (Raheja, this vol.). In anthropology, feminist and neo-marxist perspectives have emphasized the existence of muted voices by, among other things, stressing that "cultures" are divided by gender and class differences. This approach may be coupled with a historiographical one—often associated with the Subaltern Studies group—of reading ethnographic texts "against the grain" for the contrapuntal voices that, despite the hegemony of certain narrative sequences, can still be identified in these texts.

Ethnographers' subalterns are, of course, their "native informants," or, more generally, the persons with whom ethnographers produced knowledge about the society in question at specific ethnographic occasions. An increasing number of studies documents the divergence of interests and political programs between "native informants" and ethnographers. In late nineteenth-century Northern India, a research assistant's belief in "progress" could be contradicted by his superiors' practice to picture India as "traditional" and stagnant (Amin 1994:45). In colonial Africa, the political programs of research assistants complicated the ethnographer's production of "tribal" or "African" identities (Forster 1994). At a later stage, African research assistants' nationalism could become a problem in the academic anthropologist's relationships with the colonial administration (Schumaker, this vol.).

In fact, the position of the indigenous expert is a major indicator of different phases in the history of a colony: in late-eighteenth-century British India, the reign of orientalism was partly predicated on the necessity for Indian mediators to translate and comment upon Sanskrit texts. In the early decades of the nineteenth century, however, it was to be superseded by an ethnology of India that, in emphasizing personal observation, greatly reduced the necessity—at least in theory—of such mediators (Pels, this vol.). At a later stage, the "native point of view" became once more important in Indian ethnology, but this time it was domesticated by a specific entextualization of proverbial wisdom that silenced it politically (Raheja, this vol.). Simultaneously, a parallel tradition of naturalist, anthropometric observation existed that could almost completely dispense with the role of the native mediator (Dirks, this vol.). Thus, each ethnographic tradition has its own implicit sociology of preferential relationships between ethnographer and informants.

"Native informants" clearly demonstrate the necessity of incorporating the préterrain in the analysis of ethnography, because many of them were recruited from from an indigenous elite (Brahmin scholars in orientalist India, educated Africans in late colonial Rhodesia). This elite had its own agenda and relationships with the less privileged of their society. Other power relationships that made up préterrain and ethnographic occasion were constituted by distinctions between public and domestic spheres that were inherent in practices of travel and residence. If the Dutch traders on the West African coast lived together with African women, we may well presume that they gained cultural competence "on the pillow," while their idea that African women "fetished" their Dutch men also suggests that this was a situation fraught with conflict. For an anthropologist like Richard Burton, sexual contact was part of his "field," even though at home, his ethnographies of sexual mores could only be published in private and in Latin (Brodie 1967).

The mutual constitution of "home" and "field" is well brought out by the complaint that the coming of European women to the colonies increased its racism, a complaint that—as Ann Stoler has shown—masks a colonial strategy for reinforcing a color bar by reducing the contact between European men and indigenous women (Stoler 1992). In many colonial administrations and Christian missions, the field, symbolized and embodied by the administrator's or missionary's *safari*, his tent or rest house, and his caravan and retinue, was a predominantly masculine world, often modeled on comparable establishments like the public school, the army, or the hunting camp (Pels 1994; Schumaker, this vol.; West 1994). This male gendering of ethnographic occasions greatly contributed to the underrepresentation of women's roles in the societies described (Pels 1994:332; Risseeuw 1988; Salemink 1991:254 and this vol.). It will not always be possible to reconstruct the voices muted or silenced in the process of ethnographic production, and usually the analyst will have to speak for them. But the deconstruction of the texts of an ethnographic tradition by means of the reconstruction of its préterrains and ethnographic occasions at least attunes us to the multiplicity of possible ways in which ethnography was located by these forms of resistance, avoidance, or obstruction.

6. Colonial Relationships and Ethnographic Traditions

Having outlined our analytical approach and situated our object historically, we want to conclude this introduction by spelling out some consequences for the history of anthropology, by touching upon some novel directions that the essays in this volume open up, and by pointing to some of the lacunae still to be filled. In the next section, we hope to address the tensions that developed when anthropology's colonial heritage was partly assimilated, partly transformed, and partly set aside by the professionalism that developed under the aegis of the welfare state; the emphasis of that discussion will be on the twentieth century. In this section, we try to assess some of the dominant nonacademic relationships that helped produce the colonial subjects of anthropology. Here, the emphasis will be on the nineteenth century, the time that some of the most persistent and enduring identifications of anthropology's colonial subjects took place: of the observer, through, for instance, the (further) development of colonial empiricism (Ludden 1993); of subject peoples, by the state boundaries drawn during the heydays of imperialism; and most of all, by the development of commonplaces about tribes and castes, religions, forms of political and agricultural organization, nomadism and the relative ranking of all these, topoi that would endure into the present, to be taken up, modified, or criticized by academic anthropologists.

We need to stress again that historians of anthropology have not taken sufficient account of the forging of such identities because its *disci-*

plinary focus marginalized the ethnographic work going on in colonial practice. That does not mean, however, that (anthropology as a) science was equally peripheral to such ethnographic production. Scientific endeavors were often explicitly *inter*national rather than limited to a specific empire (Pratt 1992:15–16). This international network of scientists—botanists, medical doctors, lawyers, and language experts in the service of a navy, army, colonial bureaucracy, or missionary organization—was one of the main conduits for the global circulation of the ethnographic commonplaces of colonial intelligence. One cannot, therefore, simply disengage the developments in one colonial or metropolitan ethnographic tradition from those in others. The whole system of colonial intelligence of the early British Indian administration was applied to Java by Raffles and his surgeon John Crawfurd (who later became president of the Ethnological Society of London) during the British interregnum (1811–16) and was subsequently copied by the Dutch when they resumed control. Conversely, the Dutch "Indology" courses were an important example for ethnographically minded British colonialists in the late nineteenth and early twentieth centuries (when even Malinowski praised their work); while the Dutch *adatrecht* school inspired Afrikaner nationalism through someone like J. Holleman senior, who settled in Stellenbosch after a career as Indologist at the Batavia law school.[10]

These relationships crosscutting the different colonial traditions themselves fell victim to anthropological disciplinary amnesia. To this day, such amnesia is part of the resistance one encounters among anthropologists and orientalists against the idea that their discipline was nurtured in colonial circumstances. A regular critique of the work of Edward Said (1978, 1989) has been that Said ignores German orientalism because it doesn't fit his theory of orientalism as an apparatus of colonial control. Such critics, however, ignore that the tradition that produced the German orientalists (like von Humboldt, Bopp, and others) goes back to the colonial intelligence produced by British administrators (Alexander Hamilton in particular), to the British expeditions under Cook, through his naturalists Johann and Georg Forster, and to the immense experience of colonial rule and military expeditions gathered by Germans employed by the Russian empire and the Dutch East India Company, an experience that led to the formulation of the tandem concepts of *Ethnographie* and *Statistik* at the University of Göttingen in the late eighteenth century (Grove 1995: chap. 7; Rendall 1982; Slezkine 1994; Vermeulen 1992). By their "purely scientific" work, the brothers von Humboldt, Bopp, and others maintained the momentum of a tradition of colonial intelligence in a country

---

10. We owe the last example to the comments of an anonymous reader of this volume.

without colonies. This tradition was immediately applicable when newly united Germany joined the scramble for Africa in the late nineteenth century and explains why it quickly outstripped the other colonial powers in the quality and organization of its colonial intelligence.

In the following, we try to emancipate some of the colonial locations of ethnography from the disciplinary perspective on the history of anthropology. However, our classification in terms of military, administrative, missionary, and settler relationships is only provisional and needs to be revised. It concentrates too exclusively on "governmental" relationships and ignores other locations of ethnography like hunting, trading, or tourism.[11] Even worse, the discreteness of the categories is illusory, and even ethnocentric. Our classification takes European "governmental" strategies for granted and fails to consider what they would look like from the societies studied. Moreover, it does not sufficiently engage with the argument about muted and silenced voices of the previous section. We still present this preliminary outline of préterrains and ethnographic occasions because the argument that specific colonial projects produce their own colonial subjects is so central to our approach, and because it has so rarely been dealt with systematically.

Military and Other Expeditions

War is a neglected ethnographic occasion in the study of modern colonial discourse, perhaps because it often implies a (violent) negotiation of territories and identities. Warlike relationships lack the kind of stable boundaries required for the application of a statistical panopticism. Tolstoy's *War and Peace* brings out that warlike relationships are often more dependent on tactical bricolage than on strategic planning, on an exchange of blows with, rather than the imposition of a violent discipline on, one's opponent. Wars of colonial conquest typically took the form of the (military) expedition, which, by settling the boundaries of a unit of territory and population, often provided both the ethnographic occasions and the préterrain from which an ethnographic tradition could emerge. This relatively "unsettled" character of ethnographic categories is equally characteristic of geographical expeditions that, like military ones, depend on the horizontal relationships of negotiation and tactical exchange with indigenous informants or opponents, rather than the vertical ones of observation and discipline.

This horizontality of military relationships is brought out well by the work of Colin Mackenzie, a surveyor of the British East India Company.

---

11. For hunting, see Mackenzie 1987; trading relationships have at least partly been dealt with in the genealogy of fetishism given previously; for tourism, see Hinsley (this vol.).

Mackenzie was involved in the battle of Seringapatam, the successful conclusion of which enabled the Company to become the major territorial power in India. Nicholas Dirks has shown how Mackenzie was both engaged in creating an archive of Oriental manuscripts (on which many Orientalists and ethnologists later relied) and in making a "visual ethnography" of the Indian landscape by means of self-produced and commissioned drawings. The interesting thing about his "picturesque" relationship with India is that it marks an aestheticization of India that also had military goals: his sketches of Seringapatam "pointed the way" to the final overrunning of the fort, especially where they served to determine artillery positions (Dirks 1994). Mackenzie's colonial knowledge, therefore, was partly based on a horizontal "view toward" rather than a vertical "overview." Likewise, because of the necessity for support and guidance by knowledgeable inhabitants of the country explored, geographical expeditions depend on the tactical, horizontal relationship of the explorer to indigenous uses of space (Byrnes 1994; Noyes 1994).

Of course, there are many military and geographical relationships that do not start from a tactical relationship and from mutual dependence: military discipline, for instance, is a crucial element of established colonial rule, and the vast network of surveying work that followed on Mackenzie's in India, for instance, was closely tied to the panoptic view of the statistical survey. This, however, shows that the initial horizontal relationship evolves into a vertical one: war into policing, reconnaissance into overview. This shift is often called *pacification*, and its importance for present-day anthropological categories is brought out, for example, by Northern Nigeria, where the units of "indigenous" political organization established by Frederick Lugard's "indirect" rule during his conquest of the area in the late nineteenth century, still form the basis of the classification of tribes and states today (Sharpe 1986; see also Salemink, this vol.).

But there are many more commonplaces in present-day anthropology that go back on military relationships. Traces of formerly horizontal relationships are evident in the romantic visions of "martial tribes" (or "races") that picture former valiant enemies as respected soldiers of colonial armies (such as the Nepalese Gurkhas in British India, the Karens in Burma, the Rhadé in Vietnam, the Ambonese in the Netherlands Indies, or the Senegalese in French West Africa; see Enloe 1979; Salemink, this vol.) or as freedom-loving warriors who should be left in peace (such as the Nagas in the India-Burma border area; West 1994). Conversely, military buildup or intervention requires a *Feindbild*, which provided the background, for instance, for the reformulation of "fetishism" in terms of blood sacrifice (Pietz, this vol.). Military intelligence has always been an important source of ideas and methods for anthropology: important and gifted ethnographers like Richard Burton (Brodie 1967) and Snouck Hurgronje (Wertheim 1972) worked as spies for the British and Dutch armies, and the image of the spy still plays an important role in the construction of professional ethnography, in the sense that it was fundamental to conceptions of unethical conduct of anthropologists (Fluehr-Lobban 1991). But if the spy was a *Feindbild* for professional ethnographers, they often cannot escape being associated with him. The link may not always have been as obvious as with Colonel Creighton, the boss of Kipling's Kim, who acted openly as the head of the ethnological survey of India, and covertly as the leader of the "Great Game" of oriental espionage against the Russians. But the bond between anthropology and war has always been a tight one: whether an anthropological tradition was set up by, for instance, the military ethnographers of the Bureau of American Ethnology (Hinsley 1979 and this vol.); whether anthropologists were despised because they helped American counterinsurgency tactics in Vietnam (Salemink 1991; this vol.; Wolf and Jorgensen 1970); or whether their military intelligence work was condoned, as during World War II (Yans-McLaughlin 1986).

Administration: Census, Law, Economy, and Police

Modern governmentality assured the proper disposition and arrangement of its population and property through—among other things—the apparatuses of law, economy, and police. It realized vertical relations between a colonial subject (in the first sense in which we use it) and its "subject peoples" (our third sense). While this shaped the most fundamental distinction of colonial discourse—the racist one of white observer and nonwhite observed (Stoler and Cooper 1997)—other differences among "subject peoples" were usually felt to be needed for adequate control, and we have already indicated how much colonial administration relied on such classificatory regimes. Whether cultural, geographical, linguistic, physical, or political criteria were used, the common administrative need was to produce "things" to be ruled: discrete and static ethnic groups inhabiting a clearly delimited territory.

Thus, colonial administrations often tribalized and ethnicized a field of fluid and multilayered ethnic interrelations into a mosaic of discrete, static, and singular identities (Condominas 1966; Ranger 1983; Salemink, this vol.). These ethnic distinctions, often arising from such practical needs as having to deal with a "representative" chief or council, were subsequently laid down in statistical surveys and censuses, which have been an object of the study of colonial ethnography by a number of scholars (Anderson 1991; Cohn 1987; Pinney 1990a; Rafael 1994; see also Pels, this vol.). These distinctions were often the source of the ethnographic traditions into which professional ethnographers arrived in the "field"; in fact, they often made up the definition of the "field" itself.

This is not to say that a single administrative subject position existed—defined, for instance, by the census—that was able to control the operations of all administrative apparatuses simultaneously. Legal, economic, and police relationships developed at different moments in a colony's history, shaped by the different subaltern agencies in the field to which they apply, by the historical context of the colonizer's initiative, and by the way in which the establishment of one sector of a colony's administration precedes the establishment of another. Henk Schulte Nordholt shows (in this volume) how such a process, in which different ethnographic occasions produce different images of the indigenous population that are subsequently carried by bureaucratic reproduction, took place on Bali. Initially pictured as fierce soldiers, the Balinese were, at later ethnographic occasions, transformed (both in text, and by the administrative measures of colonial rule) into the ritualists obsessed by order and "theatre" that we know from the anthropologies of Bateson, Mead, and Geertz.

In British India, the establishment of a legal apparatus contextualized the development of other sectors of colonial governmentality. The fixing of a "rule of property" in India (Guha 1963) was conditioned by a préter-rain consisting of earlier initiatives in "dual government," of the desire to reduce the corruption of an earlier mode of British rule, of the budding Orientalism in Britain, and of a tradition of contact with an Indian intellectual élite. Through the work of Sir William Jones and his fellow members of the Asiatic Society of Bengal, a specific ethnographic occasion was privileged: the exchange and translation of *texts* among British rulers and Indian intellectuals. The ethnographic tradition that evolved from this colonial location was, of course, the Indological variety of orientalism, and its importance for the further development of colonial discourse in the colony and in the metropoles has been extensively documented (see Dirks, Pels, and Raheja, in this volume, for the relevant references).

What needs to be stressed here is the fact that all legal relationships in modern colonialism presupposed a specific relationship between colonizers and colonized that was mediated by textualization and codification. "Customary law" was often the first, and always one of the foremost, synecdoches of ethnography that transformed a specific historical relationship of legal textualization into the essence of local social order, whether through *adat* in the Netherlands East Indies (Ellen 1976), through the *coutumier* of French administrators in Indochina (Salemink, this vol.), or through the idea, in Indirect Rule, that tribal institutions made up a tribal "constitution" (Pels 1994, 1996).[12] The effect of textualization was usually to fix regularities of social practice and complicate a situation by adding a more rigid and "traditional" dimension to colonial relationships, thereby reinventing social regularities at the same time that it determined their ethnographic description (Pels 1996). This is well illustrated by the *coutumier rhadé* in French Indochina, which was presented as their almost forgotten "traditional" law code, but which was a transformation of their reconciliation chants into a body of rules sanctioned by a colonial law court. At a later stage in the development of the ethnographic tradition, this coutumier has been identified by anthropologists and modernized Rhadé alike as embodying their "traditional" culture itself (Salemink 1991 and this vol.).

The legal fixing of social practices, however, can often be interpreted as an obstacle to further developments of colonial rule. In British India, the incorporation of Hindu and Muslim legal texts by Orientalist discourse implied a recognition of the mediating role of Indian knowledge that was often resented by other colonizers, and particularly those that, in fixing revenue assessments, felt a need to bypass Orientalist and Indian authorities to deal directly with the peasant (Ludden 1993). Thus, the felt need for the "Improvement" of both the indigenous population and the colonial economy could militate against ethnographic traditions that a previous phase of colonial rule had produced, pitting conservative colonialists against more progressive ones (see Pels, this vol.).

This management of the colonial economy required direct dealings with existing leaders at the village level and gave rise to the concept of the (peaceful, timeless) "village community" that characterized colonial relationships throughout Asia (Breman 1987; Kemp 1987; Pels, this vol.; Schulte Nordholt, this vol.). Through the work of Henry Maine, this topos was central to the formulation of the anthropological notion of "primitive society" (Kuper 1988). It also fed the juxtaposition of Asian tradition and Western modernity that informed Boeke's famous essay on economic dualism of colonial Indonesian society (Boeke 1930, 1953) and recurred in much anthropological writing, whether it takes a classical perspective, a Marxist one, or a moral economy approach. (Labor issues could also lead to ideas about "traditional" labor and economic dualism. They are further discussed later in the section "Settlers, Slaves, and Workers.")

It is only recently that the role of colonial policing in the emergence of anthropological commonplaces has become an object of study. While the

---

12. In the latter case, the argument could also be that the essence of tribal society necessitated postponing codification (as was said in Tanganyika in the late 1920s), but even then the relationship with textualization remains central, despite its being denied. On "synecdoche," see the section "Colonial Ethnography and the Making of a 'Pure' Anthropology."

work of law was articulated on textual relations, and economic surveying on the land and its produce, policing was mainly articulated on the surveying of bodies and their movement. In British India "criminal tribes" became an ethnic category in those cases where territorial boundaries were violated by migrating peoples (Nigam 1990a, 1990b; Tolen 1991), and the most famous colonial ethnographer in this field was Colonel William Henry Sleeman, the suppressor of "Thuggee." It is significant that Sleeman was a military man, because policing, like "pacification," can be seen as the transformation of warlike relationships into state security, and of the horizontal relationship of battle into the vertical one of disciplining state citizens. Its articulation on the body implies that, here, physical anthropology was most useful, and the importance of the colonial location for anthropology is manifest from the way in which Bengal police practice contributed to the development of fingerprinting by Francis Galton (Herschel 1916). Another ethnographic tradition that owed much to colonial policing was ethnographic photography, as iconic representations lend themselves directly to certain forms of typification and measurement of bodies (Pinney 1990b). The topic is discussed in much more detail by Nicholas Dirks (this vol.).

In this context, "policing" should not be regarded merely as the work of the police: one of the more important forms of policing—of "biopolitics," in Foucault's words—was the field of medical relationships: the recognition of disease and the development of hygiene (see Fabian 1990; Thomas 1994:118ff.), in which again the military, particularly in the development of medical statistics, played an important role. But anthropology also owed much to the colonial network of medical doctors, who regarded physical anthropology and psychopathology—two major features of nineteenth-century anthropology—as their province, and who, as prominent members of colonial scientific societies, often provided incentives toward the production and collection of ethnographic information.

Missionary Observations

Christian missions are far older than modern colonialism, and much missionary ethnography bears the imprint of that history. Early missions were part of the travel practices of an "incorporative" cosmology, directed inward at a center like Rome or Jerusalem. On the basis of that heritage, many missionaries subordinated ethnological discrimination (making different) to Christian assimilation (making same). In a sense, therefore, the relationship of missionaries with potential converts was less conducive to "*ethno*graphy," if we take that to imply the definition of essential ethnic difference. The degradation that the lack of knowledge of the Gospel had brought had to be rectified, and customs that stood in the way of that rectification eradicated. Given that they therefore wanted to promote and enlarge what was good, and to eradicate what was evil, missionaries were less inclined toward a unified conception of essential otherness and often adopted a selective rather than holist attitude toward indigenous society (Pels 1994; Thomas 1994:129).

But if Christian missionaries were often less prone to essentialize human difference in terms of ethnic wholes, their relationship with potential converts required its management. Plunged in a foreign society without resources, missionaries often had no choice but to create a niche in local polity by adapting to local customs. It is hardly surprising that missionaries were often the first to practice something resembling present-day ethnographic fieldwork, and to produce more or less systematic accounts of indigenous societies. The quality of the knowledge about China and India, for instance, that the Jesuits sent home in the sixteenth and seventeenth centuries still stands out as a remarkable achievement. But even those missionaries who had little or no tolerance toward "other" customs had to communicate the Gospel, and to learn another language to do so. Learning a language also implies learning the cultural competence to speak it. Thus, from Matteo Ricci's sixteenth-century proficiency in Chinese, to the prominence of missionary linguists in the journal *Practical Anthropology* in the 1950s, missionaries probably contributed more to the bulk of anthropological knowledge than any other single group of ethnographic specialists.

Modern colonialism forged major changes in this admittedly older tradition of managing human difference. When states no longer regarded mission as an essential part of their colonization, missions more and more became mass movements relying on public (moral and financial) support, and missionary publications for a European audience increasingly stressed the difference between civilized Christianity and depraved and barbarian "savages" in order to cultivate sympathy with the hardships endured by the missionaries and underscore the urgency of their work of salvation. At the same time, the practice of modern colonial rule gave missionaries a specific, novel relationship to their potential converts: the increasingly secular mission of education toward citizenship. Christian teaching required the secular activity of learning to read and write, and the gospel of labor and commerce added arithmetic, together the "three R's" that were taught alongside the Christian message. Indeed, while citizenship and Christianity were often hard to distinguish in Europe itself, the colonial situation itself, with its problems of missionizing among adherents to another, strongly entrenched, world religion like Hinduism or Islam, produced some of the first secularizing tendencies within education (Viswanathan 1989). On the one hand, this implied introducing and developing the individualizing tendencies of educational discipline in the mission area, with its attendant ethnographic emphasis on personal names and individual life cycles (Pels 1994). On the other, the necessity to communicate in and teach a language made missionary education one of the major factors in the production and reification of the ethnicities associated with those languages (Ranger 1989; Dirks 1995).

Moreover, there is reason to assume that a missionary background (also as a preliminary to conferring social rights and duties upon new citizens) was, historically speaking, crucial for the emergence of ethnology. The emergence of comparative ethnology has been traced to the work of Spanish and French missionaries and their intellectual establishment (Pagden 1986). The emergence of British ethnology, at least, was dependent on two missionary initiatives: in Britain, on the partly dissenting, partly humanitarian one of the Aborigines Protection Society, and in British India, on the drive toward "anglicizing" education among missionaries in British India (Rainger 1980; Pels, this vol.). Anthropology's professionalization in Britain was enabled by the missionaries who founded the International African Institute and gave Malinowski the opportunity to obtain Rockefeller funds and dispense with colonial patronage (see the following section). And after World War II, the new secular mission that went under the name of "development" probably provided more job opportunities to anthropologists than ever before. In other words, the assimilative tendency of the missionary relationship, based on an ethnography of a past Other, and his present or future conversion (van der Veer 1995), stood at the basis of the overarching temporal schemes of ethnology and anthropology.

Settlers, Slaves, and Workers

Like missions, settler colonies predate modern colonialism, and some ethnographic traditions still bear their stamp. Whereas missionary relationships were primarily articulated on disciplining the bodies of individual converts and translating their language, settlement is predicated on land. The older traditions of settlement discourse therefore include doctrines of land occupation, *terra nullius*, and a politics centering on the question of rights to land (by aboriginality, conquest, or possession by virtue of cultivating "virgin" land). Much writing deriving from settlement relationships, therefore, stressed the *absence* of an indigenous population, by ignoring its existence, by theorizing its lack of claim to the land because it wasn't cultivated properly, by theorizing its future extinction, or by theorizing on successive waves of migrations or settlement that would justify the last and ultimate migration—by Europeans (see Pels, this vol.; Wolfe, this vol.). While ignoring the existence of an indigenous population can hardly be called "ethnographic," there nevertheless is a direct relationship between settler colonization and the development of British ethnology, because the Ethnological Society's parent organization, the Aborigines Protection Society, aimed at defending aborigines from being exterminated by aggressive settlers in New Zealand or Australia. "Salvage" ethnography, such as formulated by the APS, depended for much of its urgency on colonial policies that aimed at creating *terra nullius* by ethno- and genocide. Thus, the importance of the settlement relationship for the development of anthropology is also apparent from the fact that a discourse directly antagonistic to settler interests, that of salvage ethnography, was so important for anthropological identity as to accompany it throughout its career.

Among the more obvious ethnographic traditions that arose from a settlement relationship were those that postulated the extinction of an ethnic group. Whether this result was to be achieved by active policy, that is, outright killing or ethnocidal eugenics, or by simply waiting for the last of the Mohicans or Tasmanians to expire, it was very often essentialized as the inevitable outcome of the character of the natives, which made them incapable of withstanding the onslaught of modernity. Similar essentializations of aboriginal character rationalized another important element of modern settler polities: the use of African labor on plantations was justified by doctrines of the essentially slavish character of the negro (for which the political elements of the idea of fetishism provided additional confirmation; Pietz 1988:112). This ethnographic tradition influenced the history of anthropology in the 1860s, when the controversy between polygenists and monogenists often turned around taking sides in the American Civil War, for or against slavery (Haddon 1921; Stocking 1987:63). African labor was used because native American labor did not appear a viable possibility or actually died out in the process; hence the idea that some "races"—apart from Africans, predominantly Asians—were by nature more fit for European labor discipline or "industry."

In early modern times, settlers often controlled the government of colonies, and we have already recorded that in that capacity, particularly in the development of the census, settler governments made crucial contributions to the development of the intelligence apparatuses of modern governmentality. But a fully developed modern governmentality implied a separation of economic and administrative concerns as much as it separated church and mission from the state. Settlers, with their particular interest in land and labor, often created circumstances that militated against colonial security or propriety, which had strategic interests in defending (sectors of) indigenous society against overly rapacious or violent forms of economic expropriation. As a result, the initial conflict of interests characteristic of the Aborigines Protection Society's attitude toward settlement, with its perceived tendency toward ethnocide, became a regular feature of the colonial state's weighing of political strategy against economic "improvement." In this way one can interpret the antagonism between the (anthropologically inclined) indirect rulers of a strategic colony like Tanganyika and the settler polity of Kenya (Pels 1996); similar conflicting political and economic interests characterized many other colonies, like French Indochina (Salemink 1991). In the modern period, settlement relationships often influenced anthropology by default, by showing anthropologists how indigenous people should *not* be treated.

The cultural provenance of indigenous laborers was, to some extent, of no concern: because it was their present or future performance that counted, labor recruiters sometimes couldn't care less about the ethnography of the society from which they recruited. Labor power could be conceptualized in purely physical terms, as decontextualized, deculturated bodies, for which ethnic identity was only important where it served the maintenance of racial distance between white settlers and colored workers. The "deculturization" of workers must be taken literally, as it was often based on physically removing them from their cultural background. African slaves, like other imported laborers (Indians in Fiji, Chinese in the Dutch Indies, or in British Malaya), were usually not regarded as requiring the ethnographic investigation that governments otherwise lavished on the "indigenous" populations. Yet, resistance to colonial labor regimes often provoked an investigation of its causes and produced ethnographic speculations about the indigenous organization of labor. Such ethnographic speculations long underpinned the legitimations of forced labor by colonial administrators and settlers in Africa. Yet, when resistance to forced labor by both Africans and the United Nations became too insistent to ignore, colonial governments often turned to anthropological experts to study how—given this incompatibility of modern labor regimes and African customs—"development" could be implemented (Cooper 1996:369ff.).

There is another way in which paying attention to settler polities leads to a better understanding of the practical development of anthropology: settlers, by defining the colony as "home," invited a number of measures that contrasted sharply with the anthropological (but also military, administrative, and missionary) identification of a "field" (away from home). Wherever the highly gendered practices of "field" and "home" were contiguous—as among settlers—the definition of colonial subjects acquired dimensions that were less salient among those who had to travel to their "field" in order to work there. In places with a sizable European population, while European "homes" were usually coproduced by European women and their indigenous domestic servants, this cooperation was often produced across racial and sexual barriers meant to "protect" white men and especially white women from the "contagious" contact with others. Many of these assumptions also informed ethnographic statements, even if only written for the "home" audience of settlers themselves (Stoler 1992). Again, if the distinction of "field" and "home" enabled many anthropologists to be more relativist than these settlers and their households, it is important to remember that they often could not do without them. In fact, it was the persuasive character of such racially inflected colonial discourse and praxis in French Indochina in the 1940s that led the French anthropologist Georges Condominas to coin the term *préterrain* (Condominas 1973), which we have put to so much use in this essay.

7. Colonial Ethnography and the Making of a "Pure" Anthropology

The standard self-conception of disciplinary anthropology as centered on holism and intensive fieldwork is commonly thought to be a product of academic innovators, who replaced an earlier approach involving questionnaires drawn up by armchair scholars with a later one that fused theoretical and research expertise in the professional fieldworker (for a recent example of this view, see Urry 1984a). This view neglects the practical necessity of having to construct the anthropological "field" in colonial circumstances, even where the anthropologist concerned was, in theory, an independent professional—an issue that, as Lyn Schumaker shows (this vol.), is best approached by the "field science approach" of historians of science. It also does not take account of the *historical* necessity for the budding profession of anthropology to set itself off from (and thereby engage with) preexisting "holist" and "fieldwork" practices in colonial ethnography.

Some form of holist representation can be identified in most colonial ethnographies, and the rhetoric of ethnographic holism was not invented by professionals, although they made a powerful contribution to the genre. All fieldworkers have to assume that social wholes can be understood and described by concentrating on certain key elements of society: institutions like the Kula, Azande witchcraft, or initiation, or methodical constructs like kinship genealogy or social structure, are all synecdoches, parts of social relationships that are taken to be representative of the society as a whole (Clifford 1983:129–30). Because "social wholes cannot be directly perceived by a single observer" (Thornton 1988:288), the synecdoche is crucial in establishing the ethnographic object (a "social whole"), establishing its subject as an outsider not implicated in it (the "observer"), and erasing the relationships that practically connect the two. Thus, for Willem Bosman, the fetish could come to stand for African society in general, effacing that it had been defined in a particular trade relationship. Throughout Asia, an agricultural relationship based on the extraction of revenue conceptualized the "village community" as a microcosm of society as a whole (Pels, this vol.; Schulte Nordholt, this vol.). While the choice of synecdoche—indigenous texts, bodies, languages, political institutions—depended on the practical relationship between colonial ethnographer and people studied, the wider question—which of these synecdoches most adequately typified society as a whole—could lead to a discussion about ethnographic methods in colonial circles (Pels, this vol.).

This shows that, in our approach, "method" is not the abstract, extrahistorical road to objective knowledge that positivist approaches to social science hope it will be. "Method," to us, is a representation of the practical relationship between ethnographer and people described. Each method has a practice and a politics proper to its historical background. Thus, calls for textual critique or empiricism had specific connotations of national or colonial control when applied to Scottish folklore or Indian colonial ethnography (Dirks 1996; Ludden 1993). In a scientific setting, that meant that "method" was deployed to transform the relationship of ethnographer and people described into one in which no specific coalition of interests (except the scientific or academic one) could interfere with the pure subjectivity of the observer and the objectivity of the observed.[13]

Methodical discussion was, as we have already indicated, basic to the development of modern techniques of observation, and in particular to the development of the subject position of the statistical observer and his definition of the categories within which "things" measured could be slotted. In British India, colonial ethnographers were self-conscious about their development of an ethnographic survey based on personal observation and felt that these methods rivaled those of metropolitan anthropology (Risley 1890). Indeed, not only was the ethnographic survey developed (though not instituted) in India before Alfred Haddon deployed it in United Kingdom in 1892 (see Urry 1984b:87), but the systematic use of proverbs in Indian ethnography preceded and accompanied the rise of metropolitan folklore studies in the 1880s (see Raheja, this vol.), while the development of anthropometry (fingerprinting in particular) was the product of a dialectic between Indian colonial rule and the policing of British society (see Dirks, this vol.).

13. As Stanislaw Andreski has observed: "Method is prophylactic in its essence" (1974:115), that is, it defends the "pure" subject and object against contagion or fertilization.

If, therefore, holism and method were prefigured and promoted in colonial ethnography, one may well ask to what extent the invention of academic "fieldwork" was indebted to colonial examples. The story is best told by placing developments among British anthropologists—whose conception of "fieldwork" became globally hegemonic after being popularized by Bronislaw Malinowski and Margaret Mead—against the background of other national traditions. In this development, the *dirigiste* type of fieldwork (Kuper 1988:103) characteristic of Tylor's relations with A. Howitt and L. Fison, and of Frazer's with W. B. Spencer and F. Gillen, was of relatively minor importance as compared to the coalition between Cambridge physical anthropologists and psychologists and representatives of the Indian survey tradition. Represented, in particular, by Alfred Cort Haddon, William H. R. Rivers, Herbert Hope Risley, and Richard Carnac Temple, these scholars urged for an institutionalization of anthropology in the academy on the lines of the bureaucrats produced by Dutch Indology courses and the military ethnographers of the U.S. Bureau of American Ethnology (see Hinsley, this vol.; Schulte Nordholt, this vol.). In the process, however, the British (Indians) developed a emphasis on "intensive work" that differed from these foreign exemplars. By borrowing from colonial administrative discourse about desirable contact with the colonized, these scholars tried to make academic anthropology into a necessary element of the préterrain of colonial ethnography—a movement consonant with the growing demand for social engineering by welfare state experts.

While, since the 1870s, a distinction between scientific experts and colonial ethnographers had been increasingly stressed in British anthropology, it by no means dominated the thoughts of all ethnographers and academics. The Indian survey tradition kept its own momentum throughout the late nineteenth and early twentieth centuries, and Dutch and American models of institutionalizing anthropology were also predicated on specific fusions of anthropological and administrative expertise. While the Dutch were the first to found an Asiatic Society (Batavia, 1778), the initiative was quickly taken over by the British. The Asiatic Society of Bengal (1784) and the Colleges of Fort William (Calcutta, 1800) and Haileybury (1804) inspired the institutionalization of training courses for Dutch colonial administrators up to the 1850s. Then, Dutch ethnology regained the initiative by appointing the first professor of ethnology at Leiden (P. J. Veth, 1877), while the Dutch "Indology" courses became a model for the institutionalization of anthropology in Britain up to the 1920s, together with the example of the Bureau of American Ethnology under John Wesley Powell (see Ellen 1976; Fasseur 1993; Hinsley 1979).

Both Dutch Indology and the Bureau of American Ethnology

employed a "survey" model comparable to that of existing Indian ethnography, although they owed more to orientalism (in the Dutch case) and military ethnography (in the American) than the British. What was most enviable to the British, however, was that these establishments of ethnological expertise were promoted and funded by the colonizing state. In their desire to achieve something similar, British anthropologists and retired Indian administrators started to emphasize the necessity for method in colonial ethnography—and consequently, of the training of colonial administrators by anthropological experts proficient in these methods. To this end, they employed a discourse about "tact" and "sympathy" with native peoples that was directly derived from colonial administrative circles and their assessment of the qualities of the administrative officer.

"Sympathy" in dealing with natives was the "root principle of Applied Anthropology," a form of tact "born of intuitive anthropological knowledge," and this knowledge should therefore be taught to probationers of the colonial services, future missionaries, and traders (Temple 1914:25, 37; see also Haddon 1921). At the same time, the Cambridge anthropologists and their administrative allies elaborated their ideas about "intensive work"—also inspired by the examples of zoological fieldwork (Haddon) and the psychological laboratory (Rivers)—from the ground mapped by the South Asian colonial administration. With Rivers among the Todas, Seligmann among the Veddas, and (Radcliffe-)Brown among the Andamanese, methodological innovation in British anthropology strongly concentrated on the most curious (and therefore best studied) ethnic anomalies of South Asia, at sites chosen on the basis of problems defined by colonial ethnography and its survey tradition. Later, in French Indochina, Marcel Mauss played a similar role by giving intellectual direction to the ethnographic and linguistic survey of Indochina (1903) after the foundation of the *Ecole Française d'Extrême-Orient* in Hanoi (1898), while stressing the need for more intensive fieldwork during a later phase of his career. The French research tradition, however, diverged from the British in the twentieth century, and was never completely dominated by the British model (Salemink, this vol.).

William Rivers was in agreement with the former head of the Ethnographic Survey of India, Herbert Risley, about the relations between colonial survey and academic intensive work (Risley 1911; Rivers 1913). Both anthropologists and (former) administrators thought the institutionalization of anthropology should take place within the triangle of academic anthropology, colonial administration, and "subject peoples": anthropologists were to teach administrators, and administrators were to do research among "subject peoples" on the basis of this training (see Rivers

1917). This cooperation between anthropologists and colonial administrators influenced the development of Cambridge anthropology up to the 1950s (see West 1994).

This lobby for an institutionalization of anthropology in the service of the colonial establishment did not change shape until the 1920s, when Malinowski claimed that "practical men" were incapable of gathering correct ethnographic information (1922:1–25) but nevertheless needed this information to "help the white man to govern, exploit, and 'improve' the native with less pernicious results to the latter" (Malinowski 1926:xi). In this way, the colonial administrator disappeared from the definition of anthropological research, and the models of Dutch Indology and the Bureau of American Ethnology (the latter already partly superseded by Boasian "culturalism") lost their relevance to British anthropology. Malinowski was able to gain—through his plea for a "practical anthropology" (Malinowski 1929)—Rockefeller funding for the International African Institute and his research students (Stocking 1985a), thus dispensing with the immediate need to pursue colonial patronage.

Although Malinowski's own engagement with the problems of colonial rule remained intense, he had gained a position from which a "pure" scientific anthropology could be emancipated from its colonial applications. In this, he was responding to the growing demand for experts of the emerging welfare state: the London School of Economics, in particular, was set up as their training ground and at the same time provided much of the early support for the Cambridge anthropologists' initiatives toward anthropological institutionalization. In France, Durkheim and Mauss defined society as a "thing in itself," claiming theoretical status for the sociology that was about to study it; while in the United States, Boas's pupils were engaged in carving out a place for "culture" in an academy they felt was threatened by the scientific racism of eugenics. The holist visions of functionalism and culturalism could unite with the professional emphasis on "intensive" work, to produce a form of expertise that, in its application to problems of "indirect rule" and indigenous minorities, fitted a need for qualitative typification that the new quantitative form of variational statistics—applied to "home" societies rather than "others"— lacked (see Asad 1994). Even in the Netherlands, when, after World War II, the necessity for change of the former "Indology" courses could no longer be denied, the training for colonial administrators in the East Indies was transformed into education toward development expertise in other parts of the world (Kloos 1992).

If the call for an "applied" colonial anthropology was superseded by the development of a "pure" scientific one, the latter also had a practical agenda. For example, students of Rivers and Malinowski set up academic anthropology in India and Africa, often developing ethnographic traditions that had arisen from colonial practice on the spot (Parkin 1990; Vidyarthi 1977). But apart from these scientific missions, "pure" anthropology also created a subject position from which a critique of colonizing "practical men" was made possible, a critique that was often ill at ease with the necessity to treat colonizers as clients of anthropological expertise. While, on the one hand, the anthropologist posed as a culture broker handing the necessary data for government to the administrator, on the other, he relished "the feeling of power given by the sense of control of human reality through the establishment of general laws" (Malinowski 1930:406).

In all early-twentieth-century reflections on "practical" or "applied" anthropology, one can discern a tension between the professed objective to let "government and industry" fashion "out of the present whatever future they desire" and the simultaneous claim that only anthropological experts can tell whether a colonial policy "is possible of application to given conditions" (Wilson 1940:46, 51). Thus, anthropologists exemplified the dilemma of welfare state experts, hesitating between the "neutral" brokerage supposedly provided by a *freischwebende Intelligenz* and the desire to plan and legislate for society from the lofty heights of their expert position. This paradoxical position remained relevant—for advice about the position of minority groups, ethnic conflict, neocolonial counterinsurgency, or development work—for as long as the welfare state and the development regime thought it had to rely on such trained experts for its own intelligence practices. There are many reasons to suppose, however, that, with the demise of the welfare state, this position is becoming increasingly difficult to uphold.

8. Histories of the Present: About This Book

The essays that follow provide histories different from "the" history of anthropology (singular) that has—often tacitly—made up the disciplinary canon, and we feel the alternatives they suggest are necessary because of changes in present-day anthropology. We have tried to conform, on the one hand, to George Stocking's plea to avoid "presentism" (1982:11), by an attempt to outline some of the essentializing moves of the stereotype conceptions on which anthropology as a discipline, and ethnography as a writing practice, were historically based. Yet we have also tried to go beyond this historicizing move by insisting that the notion of "history" itself, as it was enshrined in the narratives of linear progress that characterize standard accounts of "the" history of the discipline, needs to be diversified by an awareness of the cultural differences that manifest themselves in the different locations of anthropology and ethnography. As Nicholas Dirks has argued, "history" and "culture" stand in a "supplementary" relationship: because they are necessary for each other, each "proclaims the essential inadequacy" of the other (Dirks 1996). The anthropology of colonialism is one of the developments that shows that the disciplinary boundaries between anthropology and history are increasingly difficult to maintain (Dirks 1992; Thomas 1994). Similar ruptures and encroachments occur on the boundaries between anthropology and other humanities and social sciences. Yet it may be more important that these reconfigurations are not restricted to the academic realm.

We are also in need of different histories of present-day anthropology, because its "history" (in the singular) was based on a boundary between "pure" academic and practical anthropologies that is no longer self-evident. The professional self-conception of anthropology narrowly focused on the constitution of this bounded "academic" realm. It constituted itself by the invention, by Malinowski, Radcliffe-Brown, and others, of the dyadic relationship between the ethnographer and "his" people, an invention that defined colonial rule as external to the relationship of ethnographer and informants. This was, of course, a fiction, but an effective one, since it supported a claim to scientific independence that was needed in the postwar buildup of anthropology departments. The radical critiques of the 1960s and 1970s once more restored the continuity between anthropology and the welfare state governmentality that was developed under (late) colonial rule, although it exaggerated the complicity of anthropologists and tended to ignore the independence from the state that welfare state experts (also) claimed.

In recent years, such continuities between academic, colonial, and postcolonial governmentalities have been increasingly studied. On the one hand, it turns out that orientalism and (functionalist) anthropology supplied some of the core images of anticolonial nationalism (Berman and Lonsdale 1991; Chatterjee 1989; Forster 1994; Ludden 1993:270–71). On the other, we have come to realize that colonial governments instituted a "development" regime that could be directly transferred to newly independent governments (Cooper 1996:110ff.; Ludden 1992). The ambivalent relationship between anthropologists and colonial bureaucracies that characterized the late colonial period can also be discerned in postcolonial circumstances, if fractured and increasingly complicated: nationalist intellectuals and governments often dismissed anthropology as a colonial science (see, for example, p'Bitek 1970); some anthropologists critically monitored any government's treatment of "their" tribes (now usually "indigenous minorities") from an independent academic position; others collaborated with Western or newly independent governments, or both, in development work or counterinsurgency projects.

While such studies indicate the extent to which the academic independence of anthropology was (or was not) fictional, others show that the dyadic image of ethnographic research is no longer as hegemonic as it was around 1970. The primary responsibility of anthropologists toward the people studied, as canonized by the first article of the AAA's Principles of Professional Responsibility in 1971, is no longer taken for granted by anthropologists in extra-academic employment (Fluehr-Lobban 1991). Others criticize the assumption that a practical anthropology does not generate theory, and they make a plea for studying through policy (Wright 1995). Cultural difference has imploded into the political and economic realms by ethnic wars and peacekeeping missions, Asian factory discipline and economic performance, new diasporas and multiculturalisms that have left many anthropologists panting to keep up. These developments suggest fundamental changes in the préterrains of ethnography and anthropology: shifts, in the art of government, toward a culture of the market in which everything and everyone becomes a "product" to be sold and no country can escape the clutches of liberalism; and in the art of travel, toward tourism, global migration, and the virtual destinations of mass media and cyberspace.

Such shifts in préterrains and ethnographic occasions may explain why the role of the anthropologist as academic welfare expert is increasingly delegitimized and replaced by the exhortation to do relevant research that pays itself back; why people studied—like their newly independent governments in the 1960s—increasingly resist being objectivized as such; and why the commonplaces imposed by colonial ethnography have become the rallying cries of large-scale political movements. Thus, the practices within which the colonial subjects of anthropology were formulated, and from which its current disciplinary identity was culled, change shape and shift to other positions in the global economy. We are convinced that the reinvention of anthropology that, in response to these changes, has been going on since the 1970s (Hymes 1974) needs a better awareness of the practices on which the discipline was built. The essays in this volume, therefore, are histories of and for the present, providing alternatives for the history of anthropology that show the fictions of academic purity as well as the dangers of practical commitment, and that may warn against our pending loss of academic independence as much as they enable us to contemplate alternative practices of anthropology in the future.

The essays have been set in a roughly chronological order, as chronicle rather than history. They mostly deal with nineteenth- and early-twentieth-century anthropology, and although we have made the attempt to break the bonds of the history of anthropology's dominant regional focus, the number of essays that deal with colonial ethnography outside the Anglo-Saxon traditions is limited, for the simple reason that there are few historians of Russian, German, French, and Dutch colonial ethnography even when one does not restrict oneself to those writing in English with a similar anti-orientalist analytic as we use (but see Salemink, this vol.; Schulte Nordholt, this vol.). However, even within the historiography of this hegemonic tradition one can explore hitherto unknown regions. This is reflected in the large number of contributions about India, which provide an alternative to the commonplace focus, in discussions about anthropology and colonialism, on the example of British anthropology in Africa.

Given the central role of the example of fetishism in this introduction, we are very happy that William Pietz's sequel to the story we summarized directly follows it. More important is, however, that his essay sets the stage within which much of the subsequent development of anthropology and ethnography needs to be seen. By following the nineteenth-century career of "fetishism," Pietz shows some crucial moments in the emergence of Europe's colonial subject position—that of "civilization"—and the topos that was used to provide it with a project and object—slavery. Shifts in the préterrain from trade to colonial conquest provoked shifts in the conception of "fetish" toward a new location: the "fetish shrine" where African tyrants sacrificed the blood of their dependents. This enabled postabolitionist imperial ideology to turn slavery from a predominantly capitalist practice (now abolished) into a "savage" institution. It is significant that T. F. Buxton, the founder of the Aborigines Protection Society—the parent organization of the Ethnological Society of London—*both* successfully concluded the abolitionist campaign *and* coauthored the conception of fetishism as blood sacrifice. Pietz not only shows how this ideological distance between civilization and savagery was formulated and deployed in relation to the changing préterrain of West Africa, and how intimately it was connected to the emergence of British ethnology. He goes much further by brilliantly suggesting a language for comparison (in terms of "debt" and "fetishism") that may uncover the infrastructure of the political and economic conflict on which these developments were based.

The next three essays provide an alternative to the history of anthropology's tendency to concentrate on British colonialism and Africa. The critique of orientalism has produced an impressive number of studies of colonial ethnography in India, and the essays in this volume extend this inquiry to the interrelationship between ethnology in India and in Britain. Peter Pels argues that the orientalist methodology of textual commentary was transformed into a more racialist methodology of naturalist observation and philological analysis by certain (Christian and secular) missionary projects. Missionaries have, since Malinowski, been defined as the "others" of anthropologists, coming to teach rather than to learn (Pels 1990). Contrary to that twentieth-century notion of a missionary-anthropological antagonism, both Pels and Pietz show how essential the civilizing mission was to the emergence of ethnology.

While Pels argues for the recognition of Indian ethnology as an important location for the development of anthropology, Gloria Goodwin Raheja shows the specificity of the Indian ethnographic tradition by zooming in on the way it provided an illusory consent of the Indian population with British colonial rule through the entextualization of proverbial speech. She thereby recovers a conception of the "native point of view" that was eclipsed by Malinowski's more influential twentieth-century formulation and restores to folklore studies something of its original importance in the history of anthropology. Moreover, it shows the colonial activities of the three most influential administrators in British anthropology around the turn of the century: William Crooke, Herbert Risley, and Richard Carnac Temple, whose role in promoting anthropological professionalism was outlined in the previous section of this introduction.

Nicholas Dirks's essay provides an excellent counterpoint to the two previous essays with a sustained argument why they (as well as the other essays in this volume) need to be read as histories of the present in anthropology. He directs himself against the nervousness that assails anthropologists when they are forced to consider their history as something more than incidental to their present practice, arguing that the texts of the Indian ethnographic tradition on caste were themselves material contributions to a process of constructing "criminal castes." He shows how the texts of an ethnographic tradition themselves became part of a préterrain of colonial policing in late-nineteenth-century Madras, and thus became pretexts of a situation in which "culture was a violent imposition before it became the sine qua non of anthropology." He points out the mutual implication of historical and anthropological knowledge in colonial governmentality and insists that we need to unravel their contribution to the colonial archive in order understand the knowledge we take with us to the "field" today.

Curtis Hinsley and Patrick Wolfe extend our understanding of high imperial anthropology beyond India. Hinsley zooms in on a situation of internal colonialism in the North American Southwest, where two important actors in the production of North American anthropology turned

Pueblo Indian societies into a space of otherness from the background of a tradition of military ethnography. The potential relativism of the military relationship (also dealt with, in this volume, by Oscar Salemink) shows in the way in which John G. Bourke and Frank Hamilton Cushing prepared the ground for a cultural imposition on Southwestern societies of a romantic imagery that, despite its critical potential, was also predicated on a denial of history vital to the growth of tourism in the region. Thus, anthropology became a pretext that turned Hopi and Zuñi into "sites of consumption."

Patrick Wolfe's detailed reflections on the theories and ethnographies of "virgin birth" show that this seemingly esoteric anthropological commonplace was in fact dialectically engaged with a process of high imperial state formation in Australia. In a sophisticated analysis of the musings on "virgin birth" by British high imperial anthropologists and the Australian ethnographers whose material they used, he lays bare a cultural logic shared by evolutionism's fantasies of savagery and the assimilationist policies of the Australian state toward the indigenous inhabitants of the continent. By thus uncovering an unexpected alliance between ethnographic occasions provided by settler colonialism, and an ethnographic tradition maintained in the metropole, his history of our present provides a necessary relativization of "one of relativism's most celebrated examples."

The last three essays direct our attention to préterrains and ethnographic occasions that directly helped to constitute what in the disciplinary history of anthropology counts as its "professional" phase. Henk Schulte Nordholt outlines the transformations that produced what professional anthropologists like Mead, Bateson, and Geertz have described as "traditional" Bali, one of the most celebrated commonplaces of twentieth-century anthropology. He charts some of the ethnographic occasions that changed Balinese from redoubtable warriors into the custom-bound, ritual-loving inhabitants of a "theatre state," actors on a stage of professional anthropology that turns out to have been constructed by Dutch colonial rule. Oscar Salemink similarly shows how military policies in the Vietnamese Central Highlands created an ethnic category of "Montagnards," producing the essential requirements of a cultural relativism that later informed the professional work of anthropologists like Gerald Hickey and Georges Condominas. Thus, like Patrick Wolfe, they show how these showpieces of professional anthropology's cultural relativism were actually constituted in a process of intense colonial interaction. They enrich our understanding of these processes, however, by moving them into préterrains different from that of settler colonialism: Schulte Nordholt emphasizes the role played in this process by bureaucratic reproduction in the colonial administration, while Salemink stresses the contingencies of decades of military engagement with the peoples of the Indochinese Highlands.

Lyn Schumaker provides a fitting—if necessarily provisional—conclusion to this volume by shifting our attention from the historical constitution of the ethnic categories of professional anthropology, to the construction, in a particular situation, of one of its central methodical concepts, the "field." *The field* and *fieldwork* are terms that professional anthropologists often used to reify their ethnographic occasions and the work that went into constructing them. Schumaker shows that the history of anthropology still has a lot to learn from the research principles established among historians of the "field sciences" and elaborates on this by showing how, by paying attention to the material practices of constructing a field of research, we can bring out that the distinction between the internal ("disciplinary") development of a science and the external situations to which it applies itself is artificial. Her analysis of the intense involvement of the scholars of the Rhodes-Livingstone Institute with their African "fields" does away with simplistic assessments of anthropologists' colonial complicity, while at the same time showing what, in this case, is "African"—and we might add, "colonial"—about anthropology.

In this way, reflecting on Schumaker's essay turns us full circle, back to the issue of the practical history of anthropology with which we started this introduction. Both Schumaker and Salemink start to show some of the implications of momentous shifts in the préterrains of anthropology that occurred in the 1950s and 1960s: the rise of African nationalism and the Vietnam war are just two of the developments "out there" that helped to rescript the parameters of anthropology's professionalism. As we have argued, the professionalism of the 1960s—with its tense conjunctions of cultural relativism and Western intellectual hegemony, of a critical engagement with as well as dependence on Western policies of development and welfare—is now under siege. While the préterrains and ethnographic occasions of anthropologists are shifting from state to private sponsorship at "home" (Wright 1995), and from passive subjects to indigenous pressure groups in the "field" (Albert 1997), changes in the art of government and the art of travel "deterritorialize" our homes and fields to such an extent that the distinction between home and field—and with it, much of classical anthropology's understanding of its own practices—is, perhaps irrevocably, upset (Appadurai 1996). Maybe these changes in our practices have created the historical possibility for the renewed reflection on the practical history of anthropology that we have tried to put forward in this volume. With it, we hope to show, in any case, that such historical reflections are necessary in order to re-create anthropology's relevance in the present.

REFERENCES

Albert, Bruce. 1997. "'Ethnographic Situation' and Ethnic Movements. Notes on Post-Malinowskian Fieldwork." *Critique of Anthropology* 17:53–65.
Amin, Shahid. 1994. "Cataloguing the Countryside: Agricultural Glossaries from Colonial India." *History and Anthropology* 8:35–54.
Anderson, Benedict. 1991. *Imagined Communities.* 2d enlarged ed. London: Verso.
Andreski, Stanislav. 1974. *Social Sciences as Sorcery.* Harmondsworth: Penguin Books.
Appadurai, Arjun. 1996. *Modernity at Large. Cultural Dimensions of Globalization.* Minneapolis and London: University of Minnesota Press.
Apter, Emily, and William Pietz, eds. 1993. *Fetishism as Cultural Discourse.* Ithaca and London: Cornell University Press.
Ardener, Edwin. 1975. "Belief and the Problem of Women." In S. Ardener, ed., *Perceiving Women*, 19–27. London: Dent.
Asad, Talal, ed. 1973. *Anthropology and the Colonial Encounter.* London: Ithaca Press.
Asad, Talal. 1994. "Ethnographic Representation, Statistics and Modern Power." *Social Research* 61:55–88.
Bayart, Jean-François. 1993. *The State in Africa: The Politics of the Belly.* London and New York: Longman.
Berman, Bruce, and John Lonsdale. 1991. "Louis Leakey's Mau Mau. A Study in the Politics of Knowledge." *History and Anthropology* 5:205–32.
Bhabha, Homi K. 1994. *The Location of Culture.* London and New York: Routledge.
Boeke, J. H. 1930. *Dualistische economie.* Leiden: Van Doesburg.
———. 1953. *Economics and Economic Policy of Dual Societies, as Exemplified by Indonesia.* Haarlem: Tjeenk Willink
Bourdieu, Pierre. 1977. *Outline of a Theory of Practice.* Cambridge: Cambridge University Press.
Breman, Jan. 1987. *The Shattered Image: Construction and Deconstruction of the Village in Colonial Asia.* Amsterdam: Centre for Asian Studies Amsterdam.
Brodie, Fawn M. 1967. *The Devil Drives: A Life of Sir Richard Burton.* Harmondsworth: Penguin Books.
Byrnes, Giselle. 1994. "'The Imperfect Authority of the Eye': Shortland's Southern Journey and the Calligraphy of Colonialism." *History and Anthropology* 8: 207–36.
Chatterjee, P. 1989. *Nationalist Thought and the Colonial World: A Derivative Discourse?* London: Zed Books.
Clifford, James. 1982. *Person and Myth: Maurice Leenhardt in the Melanesian World.* Berkeley: University of California Press.
———. 1983. "On Ethnographic Authority." *Representations* 2:118–46.
———. 1986. "Introduction: Partial Truths." In J. Clifford and G. Marcus, eds., *Writing Culture: The Poetics and Politics of Ethnography.* Berkeley: University of California Press.
———. 1992. "Traveling Cultures." In L. Grossberg, C. Nelson, and P. Teichler, eds., *Cultural Studies.* New York and London: Routledge.
Cohn, Bernard S. 1987. "The Census, Social Structure and Objectification in South Asia." In *An Anthropologist Among the Historians and Other Essays.* Delhi: Oxford University Press.
Condominas, Georges. 1966. "Classes sociales et groupes tribaux au Sud-Vietnam." *Cahiers Internationaux de la Sociologie* 40:161–70.

———. 1973. "Ethics and Comfort: An Ethnographer's View of His Profession." Distinguished lecture, American Anthropological Association. *Annual Report, 1972.* Washington, D.C.: American Anthropological Association.

Cooper, Frederick. 1996. *Development and African Society. The Labor Question in French and British Africa.* Cambridge: Cambridge University Press.

Cullen, M. J. 1975. *The Statistical Movement in Early Victorian England.* New York: Harvester Press.

De Certeau, Michel. 1984. *The Practice of Everyday Life.* Berkeley: University of California Press.

Diamond, Stanley. 1974. "End Games of Empire?" Letter to the editors. *New York Review of Books* 17–10–1974, 37–38.

Dirks, Nicholas B. 1992. "Castes of Mind." *Representations* 37:56–78.

———. 1994. "Guiltless Spoliations: Picturesque Beauty, Colonial Knowledge, and Colin Mackenzie's Survey of India." In Catherine B. Ascher and Thomas R. Metcalf, eds., *Perceptions of South India's Visual Past.* New Delhi: Oxford University Press.

———. 1995. "The Conversion of Caste: Location, Translation and Appropriation." In P. v.d. Veer, ed., *Conversion to Modernities: The Globalization of Christianity,* 115–36. New York and London: Routledge.

———. 1996. "Is Vice Versa? Historical Anthropologies and Anthropological Histories." In T. McDonald, ed., *The Historic Turn in the Human Sciences.* Ann Arbor: University of Michigan Press.

Ellen, Roy. 1976. "The Development of Anthropology and Colonial Policy in the Netherlands, 1800–1960." *Journal of the History of the Behavioral Sciences* 12:303–24.

———. 1988. "Fetishism." *Man,* n.s., 23:213–35.

Enloe, Cynthia. 1979. *Ethnic Soldiers: State Security in Divided Societies.* Harmondsworth: Penguin Books.

Etnofoor. 1990. Special Issue on Fetishism. *Etnofoor* 3 (1).

Evans-Pritchard, Edward E. 1946. "Applied Anthropology." *Africa* 16:92–98.

Fabian, Johannes. 1983. *Time and the Other: How Anthropology Makes Its Object.* New York: Columbia University Press.

———. 1990. "Religious and Secular Colonization: Common Ground." *History and Anthropology* 4:339–55.

Fasseur, C. 1993. *De Indologen. Ambtenaren voor de Oost, 1825–1950.* Amsterdam: Bert Bakker.

Fink, Karl. 1993. "Storm and Stress Anthropology." *History of the Human Sciences* 6:51–71.

Firth, Raymond. 1977. "Whose Frame of Reference? One Anthropologist's Experience." *Anthropological Forum* 4:145–67.

Fluehr-Lobban, Carolyn. 1991. "Ethics and Professionalism: A Review of Issues and Principles within Anthropology." In C. Fluehr-Lobban, ed., *Ethics and the Profession of Anthropology. Dialogue for a New Era,* 15–35. Philadelphia: University of Pennsylvania Press.

Forster, Peter G. 1994. "Politics, Ethnography and the 'Invention of Tradition': The Case of T. Cullen Young of Livingstonia Mission, Malawi." *History and Anthropology* 8:299–320.

Fortes, Meyer. 1974 [1953]. "Social Anthropology at Cambridge since 1900." In R. Darnell, ed., *Readings in the History of Anthropology.* New York: Harper and Row.

Foucault, Michel. 1972. *The Archeology of Knowledge.* New York: Harper and Row. (orig. French 1969.)

———. 1979. "Governmentality." *Ideology and Consciousness* 6:5–21.

Freud, Sigmund. 1950. "Fetishism." In *Collected Papers,* vol. 5, ed. J. Strachey. London: The Hogarth Press.

Gluckman, Max. 1974. Report from the Field. Letter to the editors, *New York Review of Books* 28-11-1974, 43–44.

Goldschmidt, Walter. 1979. "Introduction: On the Interdependence between Utility and Theory." In W. Goldschmidt, ed., *The Uses of Anthropology.* Washington: American Anthropological Assocation, special publication no. 11.

Goody, Jack. 1995. *The Expansive Moment: Anthropology in Britain and Africa, 1918–1970.* Cambridge: Cambridge University Press.

Grove, Richard. 1995. *Green Imperialism. Colonial Expansion, Tropical Island Edens and the Origin of Environmentalism, 1600–1860.* Cambridge: Cambridge University Press.

Guha, Ranajit. 1963. *A Rule of Property for Bengal: An Essay on the Idea of Permanent Settlement.* Paris and The Hague: Mouton.

———. 1989. "Dominance without Hegemony and Its Historiography." *Subaltern Studies* 6:210–309, ed. R. Guha. Delhi: Oxford University Press.

Hacking, Ian. 1990. *The Taming of Chance.* Cambridge: Cambridge University Press.

Haddon, Alfred Cort. 1921. *The Practical Value of Ethnology.* Conway Memorial Lecture. London: Watts and Co.

———. 1934. *History of Anthropology.* London: Watts and Co.

Harris, Marvin. 1968. *The Rise of Anthropological Theory: A History of Theories of Culture.* New York: Thomas Y. Crowell.

Helgerson, Richard. 1992. "Camões, Hakluyt, and the Voyages of Two Nations." In Nicholas B. Dirks, ed., *Colonialism and Culture.* Ann Arbor: University of Michigan Press.

Herschel, Sir William J. 1916. *The Origin of Fingerprinting.* London: Humphrey Milford/Oxford University Press.

Hinsley, Curtis. 1979. "Anthropology as Science and Politics: The Dilemmas of the Bureau of American Ethnology." In W. Goldschmidt, ed., *The Uses of Anthropology,* 15–32. Washington D.C.: American Anthropological Association.

Hodgen, Margaret T. 1964. *Early Anthropology in the Sixteenth and Seventeenth Centuries.* Philadelphia: University of Pennsylvania Press.

Honigmann, John J. 1976. *The Development of Anthropological Ideas.* Homewood, Ill.: Dorsey Press.

Hymes, Dell. 1974. *Reinventing Anthropology.* New York: Vintage Books.

James, Wendy. 1973. "The Anthropologist as Reluctant Imperialist." In T. Asad, ed., *Anthropology and the Colonial Encounter.* London: Ithaca Press.

Kemp, Jeremy. 1987. *Seductive Mirage: The Search for the Village Community in Southeast Asia.* Amsterdam: Centre for Asian Studies Amsterdam.

Kingsley, Mary. 1982. *Travels in West Africa.* Reprint of the 1897 original. London: Virago.

Kloos, Peter. 1992. "Into Africa: Dutch Anthropology and the Changing Colonial Situation." *Antropologische Verkenningen* 11:49–64.

Kuklick, Henrika. 1991. *The Savage Within: The Social History of British Anthropology, 1885–1945.* Cambridge: Cambridge University Press.

Kuper, Adam. 1983. *Anthropology and Anthropologists: The Modern British School.* London: Routledge and Kegan Paul.
———. 1988. *The Invention of Primitive Society.* London and New York: Routledge.
Leach, Edmund. 1974. "Anthropology Upside Down." *New York Review of Books* 4-4-1974, 33-35.
Loizos, Peter. 1977. "Personal Evidence: Comments on an Acrimonious Debate." *Anthropological Forum* 4:137-44.
Ludden, David. 1992. "India's Development Regime." In Nicholas B. Dirks, ed., *Colonialism and Culture.* Ann Arbor: University of Michigan Press.
———. 1993. "Orientalist Empiricism." In C. Breckenridge and P. van der Veer, eds., *Orientalism and the Postcolonial Predicament.* Philadelphia: University of Pennsylvania Press.
MacGaffey, Wyatt. 1994. "African Objects and the Idea of Fetish." *Res* 25:123-31.
Mackenzie, John. 1987. *The Empire of Nature. Hunting, Conservation and British Imperialism.* Manchester: Manchester University Press.
Malinowski, Bronislaw. 1922. *Argonauts of the Western Pacific.* London: Routledge and Kegan Paul.
———. 1926. *Crime and Custom in Savage Society.* London: Routledge and Kegan Paul.
———. 1929. "Practical Anthropology." *Africa* 2:22-38.
———. 1930. "The Rationalization of Anthropology and Administration." *Africa* 3:405-23.
Marcus, George, and Michael Fischer. 1986. *Anthropology as Cultural Critique. An Experimental Moment in the Human Sciences.* Chicago: University of Chicago Press.
Mbembe, Achille. 1992. "Provisional Notes on the Postcolony." *Africa* 62:3-37.
Moore, F. T. C. 1969. *The Observation of Savage People (by J.-M. de Gérando).* With preface by E. E. Evans-Pritchard. Berkeley: University of California Press.
Nigam, Sanjay. 1990a. "Disciplining and Policing the Criminals by Birth, Part 1: The Making of a Colonial Stereotype—The Criminal Tribes and Castes of North India." *Indian Economic and Social History Review* 27 (2): 131-64.
———. 1990b. "Disciplining and Policing the Criminals by Birth, Part 2: The Development of a Disciplinary System, 1871-1900." *Indian Economic and Social History Review* 27 (3): 257-87.
Noyes, John. 1994. "The Natives in their Places: 'Ethnographic Cartography' and the Representation of Autonomous Spaces in Ovamboland, German South West Africa." *History and Anthropology* 8:237-64.
Ortner, Sherry. 1984. "Theory in Anthropology since the Sixties." *Comparative Studies in Society and History* 26:126-65.
Pagden, Anthony. 1986. *The Fall of Natural Man. The American Indian and the Origins of Comparative Ethnology.* Enlarged paperback edition. Cambridge: Cambridge University Press.
Parkin, David. 1990. "Eastern Africa: the View from the Office and the Voice from the Field." In R. Fardon, ed., *Localizing Strategies.* Edinburgh and Washington: Scottish Academic Press/Smithsonian.
p'Bitek, Okot. 1970. *African Religions in Western Scholarship.* Nairobi: Kenya Literature Bureau.
Pels, Peter. 1990. "Anthropology and Mission: Towards an Historical Analysis of

Professional Identity." In R. Bonsen, H. Marks, and J. Miedema, eds., *The Ambiguity of Rapprochement: Reflections of Anthropologists on Their Controversial Relationship with Missionaries.* Nijmegen: Focaal.

———. 1994. "The Construction of Ethnographic Occasions in Late Colonial Uluguru." *History and Anthropology* 8:326–51.

———. 1996. "The Pidginization of Luguru Politics. Administrative Ethnography and the Paradoxes of Indirect Rule." *American Ethnologist* 23:738–61.

Pels, Peter, and Lorraine Nencel. 1991. "Introduction: Critique and the Deconstruction of Anthropological Authority." In L. Nencel and P. Pels, eds., *Constructing Knowledge: Authority and Critique in Social Science.* London: Sage Publications.

Pels, Peter, and Oscar Salemink. 1994. "Introduction: Five Theses on Ethnography as Colonial Practice." *History and Anthropology* 8:1–34.

Pietz, William. 1985. "The Problem of the Fetish, I." *Res* 9:5–17.

———. 1987. "The Problem of the Fetish, II. The Origin of the Fetish." *Res* 13:23–45.

———. 1988. "The Problem of the Fetish, IIIa: Bosman's Guinea and the Enlightenment Theory of Fetishism." *Res* 16:105–23.

———. 1993. "Fetishism and Materialism: The Limits of Theory in Marx." In E. Apter and W. Pietz, eds., *Fetishism as Cultural Discourse.* Ithaca and London: Cornell University Press.

Pinney, Christopher. 1990a. "Colonial Anthropology in the 'Laboratory of Mankind.'" In C. A. Bayly, ed., *The Raj. India and the British.* London National Portrait Gallery Publications.

———. 1990b. "Classification and Fantasy in the Photographic Construction of Caste and Tribe." *Visual Anthropology* 3:259–88.

Pool, Robert. 1990. "Fetishism Deconstructed." *Etnofoor* 3:114–27.

Pratt, Mary Louise. 1985. "Scratches on the Face of the Country, or: What Mr. Barrow Saw in the Land of the Bushmen." *Critical Inquiry* 12:119–43.

———. 1992. *Imperial Eyes. Travel Writing and Transculturation.* London and New York: Routledge.

Rafael, Vicente. 1994. "White Love: Census and Melodrama in the United States Colonization of the Philippines." *History and Anthropology* 8:265–97.

Rainger, Ronald. 1980. "Philanthropy and Science in the 1830s: The British and Foreign Aborigines' Protection Society." *Man*, n.s., 15:702–17.

Ranger, Terence O. 1983. "The Invention of Tradition in Colonial Africa." In E. Hobsbawm and T. O. Ranger, eds., *The Invention of Tradition.* Cambridge: Cambridge University Press.

———. 1989. "Missionaries, Migrants and the Manyika: The Invention of Ethnicity in Zimbabwe." In L. Vail, ed., *The Creation of Tribalism in Southern Africa.* London, Berkeley, and Los Angeles: James Currey/University of California Press.

Rendall, Jane. 1982. "Scottish Orientalism: From Robertson to James Mill." *Historical Journal* 25:43–69.

Risley, Herbert Hope. 1890. "The Study of Ethnology in India." *Journal of the Anthropological Institute* 20:235–63.

———. 1911. "Presidential Address: The Methods of Research." *Journal of the Anthropological Institute* 41:8–19.

Risseeuw, Carla. 1988. *The Fish Don't Talk About the Water: Gender Transformation, Power and Resistance among Women in Sri Lanka.* Leiden: Brill.

Rivers, William H. R. 1913. "Report on Anthropological Research Outside America." In W. H. R. Rivers, A. E. Jenks, and S. G. Morley, *Reports upon the Present Condition and Future Needs of the Science of Anthropology*. Washington: Carnegie Institution.

———. 1917. "The Government of Subject Peoples." In A. C. Seward, ed., *Science and the Nation*. Cambridge: Cambridge University Press.

Said, Edward. 1978. *Orientalism*. London: Routledge and Kegan Paul.

———. 1989. "Representing the Colonized: Anthropology's Interlocutors." *Critical Inquiry* 75:205–25.

Salemink, Oscar. 1991. "*Mois* and *Maquis*. The Invention and Appropriation of Vietnam's Montagnards from Sabatier to the CIA." In G. W. Stocking, ed., *Colonial Situations: Essays on the Contextualization of Ethnographic Knowledge*. Madison: University of Wisconsin Press.

Scholte, Bob. 1974. "Insult and Injury." Letter to the editors, *New York Review of Books* 18–7–1974: 42–43.

———. 1975. Reply. Letter to the editors, *New York Review of Books* 23–1–1975: 45.

Sharpe, Barrie. 1986. "Ethnography as a Regional System. Mental Maps and the Myth of States and Tribes in Northern Nigeria." *Critique of Anthropology* 6:33–65.

Slezkine, Yuri. 1994. "Naturalists versus Nations: Eighteenth-Century Russian Scholars Confront Ethnic Diversity." *Representations* 47:170–95.

Spyer, Patricia, ed. 1998. *Border Fetishisms. Material Objects in Unstable Spaces*. New York and London: Routledge.

Stagl, Justin. 1990. "The Methodising of Travel in the 16th Century. A Tale of Three Cities." *History and Anthropology* 4:303–38.

———. 1995. *A History of Curiosity. The Theory of Travel, 1550–1800*. Chur: Harwood Academic Publishers.

Stocking, George W. 1982 [1968]. *Race, Culture and Evolution: Essays in the History of Anthropology*. New York: The Free Press.

———. 1985a. "Philanthropoids and Vanishing Cultures: Rockefeller Funding and the End of the Museum Era in Anglo-American Anthropology." In G. W. Stocking, ed., *Objects and Others. Essays on Museums and Material Culture. History of Anthropology*, vol. 3. Madison: University of Wisconsin Press.

———. 1985b. (Ed.) *Objects and Others: Essays on Museums and Material Culture. History of Anthropology*, vol. 3. Madison: University of Wisconsin Press.

———. 1987. *Victorian Anthropology*. New York/London: Collier Macmillan/The Free Press.

———. 1991. Preface. In G. W. Stocking, ed., *Colonial Situations: Essays on the Contextualization of Ethnographic Knowledge. History of Anthropology*, vol. 7. Madison: University of Wisconsin Press.

Stoler, Ann Laura. 1992. "Rethinking Colonial Categories: European Communities and the Boundaries of Rule." In N. B. Dirks, ed., *Colonialism and Culture*. Ann Arbor: University of Michigan Press.

Stoler, Ann Laura, and Frederick Cooper. 1997. "Between Metropole and Colony: Rethinking a Research Agenda." In F. Cooper and A. L. Stoler, eds., *Tensions of Empire: Colonial Cultures in a Bourgeois World*. Berkeley: University of California Press.

Taussig, Michael. 1980. *The Devil and Commodity Fetishism in South America*. Chapel Hill: University of North Carolina Press.

Temple, Sir Richard Carnac. 1914. *Anthropology as a Practical Science*. London.
Thomas, Nicholas. 1991. *Entangled Objects. Exchange, Material Culture and Colonialism in the Pacific*. Cambridge: Harvard University Press.
———. 1994. *Colonialism's Culture. Anthropology, Travel and Government*. London: Polity Press.
Thornton, Robert J. 1988. "The Rhetoric of Ethnographic Holism." *Cultural Anthropology* 3 (3): 285–303.
Tolen, Rachel. 1991. "Colonizing and Transforming the Criminal Tribesman: The Salvation Army in British India." *American Ethnologist* 18:106–25.
Tylor, Edward Burnett. 1873. *Primitive Culture*. 2 vols. 1924 reprint. New York: Brentano's.
Urry, James. 1984a. "A History of Field Methods." In R. Ellen, ed., *Ethnographic Research: A Guide to General Conduct*. London: Academic Press.
———. 1984b. "Englishmen, Celts, and Iberians: The Ethnographic Survey of the United Kingdom, 1892–1899." In G. W. Stocking, ed., *Functionalism Historicized: Essays on British Social Anthropology. History of Anthropology*, vol. 2. Madison: University of Wisconsin Press.
Van der Veer, Peter. 1995. Introduction. In P. v. d. Veer, ed., *Conversion to Modernities: The Globalization of Christianity*. New York and London: Routledge.
Vermeulen, Han. 1992. "Footnotes to the History of Anthropology: The Emergence of 'Ethnography', ca. 1770 in Göttingen." *History of Anthropology Newsletter* 19 (2): 6–22.
Vidyarthi, L.P. 1977. "The Rise of Social Anthropology in India (1774–1972): A Historical Appraisal." In K. David, ed., *The New Wind. Changing Identities in South Asia*. The Hague: Mouton.
Viswanathan, Gauri. 1989. *Masks of Conquest. Literary Study and British Rule in India*. New York: Columbia University Press.
Voget, Fred W. 1975. *A History of Ethnology*. New York: Holt, Rinehart and Winston.
Wertheim, Wim F. 1972. "Counter-insurgency Research at the Turn of the Century. Snouck Hurgronje and the Acheh War." *Sociologische Gids* 19:320–28.
West, Andrew. 1994. "Writing the Nagas: A British Officers' Ethnographic Tradition." *History and Anthropology* 8:55–88.
Wilson, Godfrey. 1940. "Anthropology as 'Public Service.'" *Africa* 13:43–61.
Wolf, Eric, and Joseph Jorgensen. 1970. "Anthropology on the Warpath in Thailand." *New York Review of Books* 15, 19–11–1970: 26–35.
Wright, Susan. 1995. "Anthropology: Still the Uncomfortable Discipline?" In C. Shore and A. Ahmed, eds., *The Future of Anthropology*. London: Athlone.
Yans-McLaughlin, Virginia. 1986. "Science, Democracy and Ethics: Mobilizing Culture and Personality for World War Two." In George W. Stocking Jr., ed., *Malinowski, Rivers, Benedict and Others: Essays in Culture and Personality. History of Anthropology*, vol. 4. Madison: University of Wisconsin Press.

The Fetish of Civilization
Sacrificial Blood and Monetary Debt
William Pietz

> No more the palms with ghastly trophies wave,
> The boughs from weight of murder now have ease,
> The daily human sacrifices cease,
> For blood no longer the fetish tyrants crave.
>
> —Rev. H. D. Rawnsley, "In Memory of Acting Consul-General Phillips, and those who perished with him near Benin City, January 1897" (1898)

The most sensational revelation to emerge from British adventures in West Africa during the nineteenth century was surely the City of Blood. On February 18, 1897, a British punitive expedition captured Benin City in retribution for the killing of acting Consul-General James R. Phillips. For six years Phillips had been urging Oba Overami, the king of Benin, to do two things: to open his country to free trade (he had been exercising a monopoly over the flow of goods from the north and east whose custom was coveted by British merchants of the Royal Niger Company), and to abolish the practice of human sacrifice (the king had signed a British treaty to this effect in 1892 but had not enforced it). Six weeks after the ambush of Phillips's party, British troops entered Benin City. What they found, in the words of the new Consul-General, was

---

This essay continues a line of inquiry begun in two earlier essays: "The Spirit of Civilization: Blood Sacrifice and Monetary Debt," *Res* 28 (autumn 1995): 23–38; and "The Death of the Deodand: Accursed Objects and the Money Value of Human Life," *Res* 31 (spring 1997): 97–108. The ideas developed in these essays were first presented in very rough form in the Angel of History lecture series of the Department of Anthropology at Columbia University on October 11, 1993, and in the Ethnohistory Workshop at the University of Pennsylvania on October 20, 1994. I am grateful for the supportive criticism I received from Michael Taussig, Elaine Coombs-Schilling, Nancy Farris, Webb Keane, Achille Mbembe, Lee Cassanelli, Molly Roth, and the other participants in these two events. Thanks also to Felix Asiedu for generously giving me a copy of his essay "Ritualized Executions and Concepts of Sacrifice in XIXth Century Asante," to Jay Geller and Wyatt MacGaffey for helpful remarks, to Francesco Pellizzi for his unflagging encouragement, and to Peter Pels and Oscar Salemink for useful comments on earlier drafts of this essay.

appalling evidence of "the absolute terror of the fetish and Ju-Ju of the King" (Burns 1929:174). A British captain summarized the spectacle:

> Altars covered with streams of dried blood . . . Huge pits, forty to fifty feet deep, were found filled with human bodies. . . . Everywhere sacrificial trees on which were corpses of the latest victims—everywhere, on each path, were newly sacrificed corpses. On the principal sacrificial tree, facing the main gate of the King's Compound, there were two crucified bodies, at the foot of the tree seventeen newly decapitated bodies and forty-three more in various stages of decomposition. . . . The same sights were met with all over the city. (Boisragon 1898:187)

While such accounts would later prove somewhat exaggerated, the undeniable fact of large-scale human sacrifice was memorialized in photographs of crucifixion trees and headless corpses snapped by British kodaks. Books by participants in the sack of the City of Blood, as it came to be known, revealed to the British public the terrifying truth of African fetishism (Bacon 1897; Boisragon 1898; Roth 1903). Those who cared most about the great cause of Livingstone's three C's—commerce, Christianity, and civilization—exulted. "We have just destroyed another stronghold of Fetishism in West Africa," trumpeted the Christian journal *The Living Age* (April 3, 1897:62). What more viscerally compelling proof could there be that the cause of civilization was just and good than this City of Blood where, in the words of a poem by a friend of Phillips's family, there were "daily human sacrifices" for blood-craving "fetish tyrants"? Not even the day's great literary figure of evil, a blood-drinking monster from the East European aristocracy—Bram Stoker's *Dracula* was published the same year—could rival the real fetishism of West Africa. The latter, as Richard Burton had said of the fetishism of Dahomey back in the 1860s, was nothing other than "the old path of blood" (1966:299).

Such was the British image of African fetishism—human sacrifices, a savage logic of blood—during the period of the scramble for Africa. As a religion, fetishism was understood to be the worship of deified material objects. But this most primitive of superstitious delusions was able to function as the general system organizing African societies because its rituals contained a kernel of real power: the terror induced in the local population by the practice of human sacrifice. Writing nine years after the sack of Benin City, Major Arthur Glyn Leonard expressed a familiar and widely held opinion when he said of the Ibo of eastern Nigeria that human sacrifice was "the substance, spirit, and practice of their religion" (1968:441). The fact that human sacrifice was the core ritual of African fetishism in turn explained its connection to the indigenous institution of slavery: both expressed an utter disregard for the value of human life. Speaking of a town in his own colony's pagan hinterlands, a British Consul-General for Liberia explained:

> Life is held to be cheap there, as it often is in barbaric Africa, and human sacrifices are enacted. Large quantities of slaves are bought and sold.... I saw seven slaves who were secured by the leg in wooden stocks. They had been in that position for some months. One of them told me that he had been kept thus for two years.... I noticed an empty grave, which it appeared had been used for the purpose of burying a man alive as a sacrifice; and I was informed in a most matter of fact way, and as if the occurrence was a quite ordinary one, that the unfortunate victim's body had been lately exhumed to obtain certain potions for the purpose of manufacturing fetish medicines. (Wallis 1910, quoted in Orr 1911:283)

The scant value placed on human lives was witnessed in the routine cruelties of the slave trafficking and ritual killing that characterized the regime of Fetish. Yet this identification of African fetishism with slavery and human sacrifice was a fairly recent development in the four-century-long discourse about African fetish worship. The main historical concern of this essay is to trace how this identification came about. As I will discuss, the notion that the truth of fetishism was revealed when "fetishes" were made from the dismembered pieces of "sacrificed" human beings was grounded in the historical experience of British colonials: British belief in the terrorist essence of fetishism was fixed in the fearful image of a colonial governor who had himself suffered the ultimate horror of being transformed into a multiplicity of fetish objects. While the idea of fetish underwent a fundamental shift when it subsumed this novel referent, the extensive ideological elaboration of "fetishism" was the work of a number of social forces active in Victorian England.

During the nineteenth century, *fetishism* came to stand as the polar opposite of *civilization*. What precisely was meant by these terms? My thesis is this: the novel identification of African fetishism with human sacrifice and with slavery was established in British public discourse in the 1840s at the same time that *civilization* came to name a specific, proactive policy. *Civilization* (at least, in reference to Africa) meant the replacement of human sacrifice with Christianity and the replacement of slave dealing with what was called "legitimate commerce"—a phrase coined during the campaign to abolish slavery referring to trade that was both legal and moral, as opposed to the immoral and now illegal traffic in human beings.

Thus construed, these terms helped forge an activist discourse that appealed to the highest of moral principles: the universal right of people to life. Fetishism, with its ritual killing and its trafficking in human flesh, represented the ultimate violation of the fundamental human right to life: as a religious system, it depended on the destruction of innocent individuals; as an economic system, it recognized the value of people only through their potential price as slaves. Civilization, on the other hand, uniquely upheld the value of human life: its Christianity respected the infinite value of each human soul; its free trade (in everything except human beings) recognized the value of people by the price set on the labor of free men. The Victorian discourse about the right and the value of human life explained the difference between African fetishism and European civilization by contrasting the barbaric logic of blood sacrifice with the civilized order of free trade, whose own logic, as I will discuss, was that of monetary debt.

As my title indicates, this opposition between savage fetishism's medium of sacrificial blood and modern civilization's one of monetary debt is the theoretical subject of this essay. By examining certain historical concepts of fetishism and of debt, I want to explore the issue thematized by this contrast: the value of human life. My approach is to ground the abstract idea of a fundamental "right to life" in different cultures' concrete procedures for determining the material value of a human life. The problem of the value of human life is raised most concretely by two sorts of negations of the basic right to life: those in which life is taken through intentional violence (war, murder, criminal execution, human sacrifice) and those in which the morally significant cause of death is more obscure and might or might not involve a culpable intentionality (sudden illness, lethal collisions, errant projectiles, toxic pollution). In regard to the latter, any society must have some method of forensic reasoning for determining liability and, when death is deemed wrongful or unnatural, for arriving at a material valuation of the life that has been lost (Douglas 1992:5–14, 22–34). In cases of what modern law terms fatal accidents, the meaning of the civil right to life is expressed in the remedy of a certain monetary value that becomes a debt owed by the party who has been judged liable. In Britain, this modern method for determining liability and the debt-value of human life was established in a statute of 1846 called the Fatal Accidents Act. It was by this law that death (at least, accidental death) was "civilized," in the original sense of the word. That is, cases of unintentional killing were transferred from the criminal law, in which the state was the complainant, to the civil law, in which an injured private party sued. This statute of the 1840s for the first time in British history made the value of human life directly quantifiable: damages were determined by estimating the likely lost future wage earnings of the deceased. It was also in the 1840s that British policy first took a proactive stand on the most horrific intentional violation of the value of human life: the practice of human sacrifice in Africa. Both the new law of fatal accidents and the much-publicized policy for the suppression of human sacrifice were characteristic expressions of the rising force of political liberalism in Britain.

As I will discuss, this new focus on human sacrifice had functional value in the context of the British conquest of African societies. Conquest, in turn, opened the way for the imposition of the legal framework of "civil society" (including the law of fatal accidents). That is, British colonialism introduced a new social method for valuing human life, having justified its own violent conquest as a defense of the value of human life. But what interests me more than the familiar ideological significance here is the truth in the contemporary argument that civilization meant the replacement of a cultural logic of sacrificial blood by one of monetary debt. My suggestion is that these two logics for valuing human life might both be viewed as forms of fetishism, that is, as competing social modes of material valuation.

Debt, Fetishism, and Anthropology

Let me begin with some general remarks on the nineteenth-century discourse about fetishism. It is helpful, I think, to distinguish between the theory of primitive fetishism that was an object of criticism for the emerging academic discipline that settled on the name *anthropology* in the 1870s and the pragmatic discourse about African fetishism that had functional significance in Afro-European relations. Only in the latter was the idea of fetishism explicitly related to capitalist notions of monetary debt as the true principle of any civilized social order. (I am assuming that by *anthropology* one means the work of a specific group of social theorists who originally distinguished themselves in the 1860s against the legal historicism of Henry Sumner Maine. For Maine, who had no interest in theories of the religious fetishism of non-European primitives, laws of debt were an important index of the difference between ancient status-based societies and modern contract-based ones [Maine 1963:311–12].)

Theories of fetishism are not usually thought to concern the problem of debt. The term itself was first formulated in the late 1750s by the Burgundian parliamentarian and anticlerical intellectual Charles de Brosses. *Fetishism* was defined as the worship of mere earthly, material objects to which supernatural powers had been superstitiously attributed. Although de Brosses spoke of "fetish-gods," fetishism was a religion that lacked any theistic belief in transcendent divinities. By the end of the eighteenth century, the term had become the generally accepted name for the religion of ancient Egyptians and contemporary Africans. Moreover, as one of the day's great authorities on the history of religion, Christoph Meiners, stated, "It cannot be denied that fetishism is not only the oldest, but also the most universal worship of gods" (Müller 1882:62, n. 1). Meiners was following the view expressed in 1764 by his own teacher, Philipp Christian Reinhard, that "pure fetishism" was "the origin of all religion" ("reiner Fetischismus als Ausgangspunkt aller Religion" [Gruppe 1921: 105]). This opinion had come to German scholars through the letters of the Grimm-Diderot group; soon after the appearance of de Brosses's book, Diderot had declared fetishism to be the "primordial religion" of humankind (Tourneux 1878:231). By the end of the century, the African fetish had become an accepted type of religious object in popular handbooks of ancient mythology (Bell 1790:I, 311–12). General theories of fetishism similar to Meiners's were current in a number of influential books of the first decade of the nineteenth century (Bastholm 1818; Böttiger 1808). However, the claim that fetishism, with its utter lack of theistic belief, was the "primordial" religion of humankind proved unacceptable to other authorities, such as the ethnologist James Cowles Prichard, who believed that religion originated from a universal human intimation of a transcendent divinity. For the latter, fetishism was not the primordial religion but rather a subsequent degeneration of humankind's original theistic intuitions (Stocking 1995:208).

The acceptance of fetishism as a distinct type of religion transformed the traditional narrative of the history of religion by establishing a new general category. As such, it was used by nineteenth-century census-takers, geographers, philosophers, and historians of religion as a taxonomic pigeonhole comparable to monotheism and polytheism. Despite its dubious scientific status, the term was widely used during the century in the sense indicated by Heli Chatelain in an article on "African Fetishism" published in 1894.

> A geography published two years ago divided the religions of the world into the following classes: monotheism (including Christianity, Judaism, and Islam), polytheism, and fetishism. The latter term was defined as the worship of inanimate objects, such as stones, trees, and so on; and all the African negroes were said to be fetishists. As monotheists believe and serve only one God, and polytheists several, so the fetishists were represented as actually possessing no other god or gods than the fetish-objects. (1894:303)

The Fetish of Civilization

The importance of fetishism as a religious category may seem odd given the definition of the term as the worship of often trifling material objects. Fetishism, wrote John Lubbock (1898:580), "could hardly be called a religion." The opinion of eyewitnesses such as the slave trader Archibald Dalzel (1979:vi) that fetishism could best be described as "a jumble of superstitious nonsense" was equally that of learned professors such as the philologist F. Max Müller (1882:65), who defined "fetishism proper" as "the superstitious veneration felt and testified for mere rubbish." Yet learned arguments about the historical status of cultures capable of worshiping trash could become quite intense, since what was at stake was the definition of religion and the explanation of its origin.

To appreciate the significance of the notion of fetishism in nineteenth-century academic culture one must place it in the context of the struggle waged by champions of the new human sciences against the established intellectual culture upheld by Christian state religions. Appropriating the explanatory apparatus of David Hume, de Brosses and other Enlightenment intellectuals had conceived fetishism as a primitive personification of the unknown forces that caused physical events. If, as critical historians like Meiners claimed, fetishism was the original form of religion per se, then religion did not ultimately derive from the sorts of beliefs treated by theology but rather from prescientific conceptions of the powers of material objects to produce desired outcomes. Religion arose, then, not from Kantian intimations of a supreme deity and the prospect of immortality arising in sublime moments of awe in which glimmered the idea of transcendent divinity, but from the worldly desires and mortal fears of people concerned with living their finite, earthly lives. The more radical implication was that all religion, including Christianity, could be explained within the nontheological framework of science. Indeed, the theory of fetishism had been formulated as an ideological weapon useful to radical philosophers in their struggle against the power that Christian clerics and biblical "truths" exercised over education and publishing. In the 1830s, Auguste Comte took the radical implication of the idea to its logical conclusion: a post-theological age of science must revive people's capacity for "pure" pre-theistic fetishism so that sociology could itself become a new religion, the "religion of humanity," in which the life-giving earth and great "positivist saints" were the objects of worship. Theological religion, including Christianity, must be relegated to the dustbin of history along with Aristotelian metaphysics, replaced by an enlightened fetishism that fused humankind's religious sensibility with scientific reasoning. This attribution of religious mission to the human sciences was unacceptable to less utopian scholars. Indeed, the materialist theory of fetishism was a hindrance to the establishment of the secular social sciences as respectable academic disciplines. Among British anthropologists, "fetishism" was dismissed as either "a common but unscientific term" (Lang 1897:31) or a real but incidental feature of the animist religion and totemic beliefs of primitives. Moreover, by "fetishism" they meant the belief that sacred objects contained an indwelling spiritual being, whereas de Brosses—and following him Comte and Marx—used the term to refer to devotional practices and causal beliefs that arose from people's direct apprehension of objects whose supernatural power resided in their own divinized materiality, not their housing of an immaterial spirit.

Scholarly theories of fetishism had little significance for Europeans who were engaging what they thought of as the real fetishism of Africa. What had been filtered out of de Brosses's theory of fetishism was the economic explanation of fetishism found in the travel accounts that provided the factual evidence for Enlightenment theories of primitive religion. Even though the most authoritative text on African fetish worship for Enlightenment intellectuals was written by a Dutch trader, Willem Bosman, the explanations of this religion that were informed by his mercantile worldview were systematically ignored. Among these was Bosman's differentiation of European and African cultures according to their conceptions of debt. In Bosman's view, the continual violence and disorder of "Guinea" flowed from this: "the greatest part of their Wars are chiefly occasioned by the recovery of Debts" (1967:176). As the second in command for the Dutch West Indies Company on the Guinea coast during the 1690s, Bosman had himself lost his job as the result of an ill-conceived decision by his superior to massacre a group of local women (subjects of a rival power) as they were coming to trade at a market that was under Dutch protection—an act that outraged Bosman as "contrary to Common Faith of Nations" (1967:39). Very much the intellectual offspring of Grotius, Bosman believed in the universality not of any religion but of "the Law of Nations." In accordance with Bosman's general explanation that the superstitious religion of fetish worshipers was based above all on "the Principle of Interest" (the self-interest of fetish priests and the kings they served), he explains the violence of Guinea in terms of primitive attitudes toward debt.

> At several places on the Coast, Debts are recovered in a very unjust and villainous manner, especially on those places where we have little or no Power, or in some of the Kingdoms. A Rascally Creditor in those places, instead of asking his Money of his Debtor, and summoning him before the Judges in case of refusal, seizes the first thing he can meet with [just as in their religion Africans were thought to make a fetish of the first object they happened to encounter in setting

about some project—WP], though six times of the value of his Debt, without any regard to who is the Proprietor . . . This is very extravagant Justice. (Bosman 1967:176)

Lacking the judicial apparatus for an individual creditor to bring a private lawsuit against an individual debtor, the creditor would make a public complaint among his people and rouse them to wage war against the debtor's people, "and thus from a trifle a War" (Bosman 1967:179). Like other Europeans, Bosman could not see in this an institutionalized set of procedures in which a creditor made appeal up a hierarchy of kinship-based authorities, who then seized a valuable good or kin-member of the debtor as bail until a judicial procedure could be convened at which the truthfulness of testimony was assured through oaths sworn upon sacred objects by those pious enough to believe in their sanctioning power. Differing from what Bosman believed to be the universal forms of debt obligation expressed in the secular "law of nations," such activities appeared to express nothing more than the capricious anarchy of self-interested savages.

Although the new social order of mercantile capitalism and monetary debt would come to be recognized as an important problem by antislavery activists—Granville Sharp had tried to remedy the evils produced by the slave trade by establishing Sierra Leone as a colony for repatriated former slaves where settlers would "renounce the evils of a monetary economy" and exchange goods solely according their labor value (Fyfe 1962:17)—this issue did not carry over into the writings of the theorists of the human sciences. Suffice it to say that the one European theorist for whom the new social order of capitalist debt idealized by Bosman was relevant was Karl Marx. Marx viewed the social order of capital as itself a form of religion, albeit a nontheistic one. What he had in mind, I think, was the notion that different historical societies objectify their ongoing collective existence by positing some sort of general social substance in a certain system of objects and practices that take on the status of material universals (Marx's historical-materialist version of the Hegelian Idea).

From this perspective, the Eucharist bread of Catholic societies and the interest-bearing money of capitalist societies may equally be viewed as "fetishes": universalized objects that express the particular mode of social valuation by which a given society conceives its own system of self-perpetuation. While money itself is no more a fetish than is a commodity, money and commodities become so within the totalizing representational system of capitalist accounting practices. Their fetishized status appears not in market exchange, when the value of goods is "realized" in the form of money (that is, "real" money, currency), but rather in the financial representation of economic objects as assets recorded on balance sheets according to their hypothetical market value. Monetary debt has a special status in capitalist accounting since it exists as both an asset (in the creditor's financial statements) and as a liability (that portion of the value of an economic entity that is owed to other economic entities). It is capitalized debt that forms the ongoing system of legally enforceable obligations linking the various economic agents that make up this sort of social world. Given all the puerile nonsense that has been written about "commodity fetishism" in the name of Marx, it is worth emphasizing that the logic of capitalism is not found in economic theories of commodity markets. These bear the same relation to the actual practices of capitalist accounting that astrology bears to concrete methods of astronomical observation. Capitalism expresses its own logic in the fundamental equation of accounting: Assets = Liabilities + Owners' Equity. The social world receives a totalizing representation in the form of monetarily quantified assets (anything capable of generating income that may be legally owned). The telos of this logic—the fiduciary duty of the economic actor—is to maximize owners' equity (the value of assets owned minus liabilities owed). But it is capitalized debt (those liabilities that are another's assets) that knits together various monetized obligations into a general system of social reproduction. The fetishism of capital is the belief that monetary value derives exclusively from commercial transactions (that is, from real and hypothetical market values) and the experience of monetary value in this sense as a social substance that circulates among laboring people, useful things, and financial instruments such as national currencies. Capital is the generalized mode of market valuation that fetishizes money as the material medium of social life.

Whether or not the reader will agree that this is what Marx meant by capitalist fetishism (Pietz 1993:119–51), it cannot be disputed that the British merchants and government officials of the nineteenth century judged Africa in monetized terms: the control of, say, Zanzibar was worth contesting with the Germans because its annual trade was estimated at two million pounds, and it was strategically located to affect the sea lanes to the lucrative colony of India (Pakenham 1991:282). It was routine for boosters of colonial adventures such as Henry Stanley to begin their books by indicating the enormous money value that could be realized from some region if only a few trade stations and a railroad were run in there. My point is simply that British colonialism required a capitalist monetary form. This was true not only because private British firms were monetized institutions whose reality was structured by the practices of capitalist bookkeeping, but because the governmental colonies and protectorates of British West Africa were themselves monetized entities that were required to maintain themselves through their own income from local fees and taxes. (Indeed, the first Protectorate in Nigeria was established by means of a loan from London that local colonial authorities were forced to pay off in the course of establishing the new governmental apparatus.) Attempts to do this through direct taxation of African populations caused great political resistance. But the ultimate juridical authority of British courts in resolving disputes placed power in the hands of those who could afford monetized court costs and lawyers' fees. The colonial legal system was itself an important vehicle for restructuring social relations in the form of monetary debt. But before considering the civilizing work of colonial law, I need to discuss the phase of military conquest that made possible these efforts to transform West African cultures into civil societies.

Human Sacrifice and the Spirit of Civilization

Were one to examine the notion of two sorts of debts—those arising from blood and those arising from money—in British ideology during the scramble for Africa, one might logically begin with two realities that not only tormented the "official mind" of the British empire but also sickened what I suppose one could call its "official stomach." On the one hand, we have the "ritually" severed head of the idolized General Charles Gordon stuck in the fork of a tree by the Mahdi's victorious forces in Khartoum; on the other, we have the less palpable but no less stubborn reality of the monstrous debt owed by the British-controlled government of Egypt to (mostly French) bondholders according to the terms established in 1876 by that early avatar of the European Union, the Caisse de la Dette Publique. Historically, these two horrible realities of 1885 were inextricably related to each other, and both would play a significant role in the subsequent conquest of the continent that had so inconveniently placed itself in the way of a clear sail to India. Of course, the monetary debt created by the capital investment required to fund the Suez Canal is theoretically incommensurable with the "debt of honor" created by the blood of Gordon (though one might calculate the money cost of the army required to settle the score in the Sudan). However, both sorts of debt—those thought of as proper to the metropolitan centers of capitalist civilization and those arising from blood shed in lands subject to the dark logic of savagery—were real and sometimes competing factors motivating the historical actions of individuals and states. A study of the interplay between these two sorts of debt in Afro-British relations during the nineteenth century far exceeds my own competence. Nor is it what interests me here. Rather, I want to consider ideas of blood sacrifice and monetary debt arising from

British involvement in West Africa insofar as these express the problem of conflicting modes for the valuation of human life. The shifting discourse about fetishism is my guide in this.

Apart from a few apologists for the Atlantic slave trade (Snelgrave 1754; Dalzel 1979), prior to 1839 African fetish worship was not pictured as being based on ritual killing. While one finds many discussions of fetishism in early-nineteenth-century texts such as Henry Meredith's *An Account of the Gold Coast in Africa* (1812) or the Landers' accounts of Nigeria in the 1830s, one does not find the implication that fetishism, conceived as the religion organizing all aspects of African social and political life, ultimately depended on the practice of human sacrifice. This is true even of the accounts of Thomas Edward Bowditch and Joseph Dupuis concerning Asante, later a principal example of the supposed reliance of fetishism on human sacrifice. While Dupuis mentions practices of routinized bloodshed in Asante, these were not yet identified with the ubiquitous phenomena of "Fetische" (as he spelled it). In a long footnote, Dupuis glosses the meaning of the word "so commonly in use with Europeans and Negroes in this part of Africa" (Dupuis 1966:107). Correctly identifying the word as "a corrupt relic of the Portuguese . . . adopted by Africans to accommodate to the understanding of their visitors, such things connected with religion, laws, or superstition, as could not be explained by the ordinary use of a few common-place expressions," Dupuis lists a fairly characteristic range of things designated by the term: "slight of hand, necromancy, invocations of departed spirits, and witchcraft"; "the religious laws of particular sects or cults"; "the talismanic charms and sentences from the Koran, worn about the body"; "generally whatever is held sacred, including trees, stones, rivers, or houses." Dupuis particularly emphasized the use of fetishes in the swearing of oaths for everything from the most solemn "religious observances" to "trivial affairs" (Dupuis 1966:107).

By the 1820s, when Dupuis wrote this, the discourse about fetishes that flourished along the Atlantic coast of Africa had retained its basic ideological content for some three centuries. This was a result of its pragmatic function in Afro-European cross-cultural trade. As historians of Africa have explained, during the sixteenth century "a body of Afro-European commercial custom came into existence, with patterns of exchange and cross-cultural behavior that were to be remarkably stable until the second half of the nineteenth century" (Curtin et al. 1987:244). The terminology of "fetish" had been a pragmatic device to enable cross-cultural commercial transactions, and the binding promises that facilitated them, between European traders and various peoples of West and Central Africa. It was a middleman's term, a pidgin word that expressed an immense, yet highly functional, misunderstanding. The distinctive idea of fetish objects that took shape in this context expressed the problem of incommensurable modes for the valuation of material objects. For Europeans, it expressed their impression that the false "religion" organizing African societies caused irrational distortions in Africans' economic valuations of material things. Moreover, Europeans forced to participate in solemn oath-taking rituals in order to formalize their relations with their African trading partners viewed such "fetish oaths" as a superstitious travesty of the laws of contract and forms of treaty-making found in civilized societies.

Fetish was thus a key word in the trade language used by African and Afro-European middlemen who mediated cross-cultural transactions. Various artifacts and sites, prescribed and proscribed behaviors, and norms for sanctioning new social relations were identified as fetish for the pragmatic purpose of furthering peaceful trade. As late as the 1850s, an acknowledgment of this functional context was made by a British governor of the Gold Coast, Brodie Cruickshank. Second to none in his contempt for African "fetishism," he nevertheless recognized that it functioned as a form of civil society, or, as he put, "an engine of civil government" (Cruickshank 1960:157).

> The local government on the Gold Coast must have the candour to acknowledge its obligations to Fetish, as a police agent. Without this powerful ally, it would have been found impossible to maintain that order, which characterized the country during the last twenty years, with the physical force of the government. The extraordinary security afforded to property in the most remote districts, the great safety with which packages of gold of great value are transmitted by single messengers for hundreds of miles, and the facility with which lost or stolen property is generally recovered, have excited the astonishment of Europeans newly arrived in the country. (160)

By the time Cruickshank wrote this unusual acknowledgment of the role that Fetish played in cross-cultural trade, the British discourse about African fetishism had undergone a fundamental change. While this occurred in the 1840s, its roots go back to the first efforts of British officials to establish civil jurisdiction over a West African population.

A new emphasis on human sacrifice in the discourse about African fetishism may be traced to accounts of the death of the British governor of Sierra Leone and the Gold Coast, Sir Charles MacCarthy, in 1824. A series of bad decisions led to his death in a battle with Asante. His secretary, who was spared, returned home with lurid accounts of his decapitated corpse, of having to spend nights in a hut with the severed heads of his comrades, of the uncannily lifelike appearance of MacCarthy's head, and of being forced to attend rituals where living prisoners were sacrificed to the "fetish" as the "death-drum" pounded (Beecham 1968:74–76). The governor's chief of staff, Major Ricketts, another survivor, reported that MacCarthy's "heart was eaten by the principal chiefs, that they might imbibe his bravery; his dried flesh and bones were divided among the Caboceers, who always carried them about as fetishes" (Beecham 1968:75). MacCarthy's severed head, according to an account of 1858, "has become their fetish which they worship to this very day" (Burton 1966:I, 168). Indeed, MacCarthy's skull (like those of the defeated leaders in other wars) did become a ritual object used for years in the *Odwira* ceremony, and a life-mask made from MacCarthy's face was attached to the Golden Stool, the ritual object of Asante national sovereignty. The public impression made by MacCarthy's death was subsequently exploited by government agents, missionaries, and spokesmen for commercial interests when Britain began its efforts to establish governmental authority on the Gold and Slave Coasts.

Historians usually take the year 1830 as the first stirring toward colonial activism in West Africa. On the Gold Coast, George Maclean became Council President at Cape Coast Castle; although in 1827 (in the wake of the MacCarthy fiasco) Britain had officially abandoned the idea of establishing a civil government there, Maclean began to establish an informal but real jurisdiction over nearby settlements (George 1968:321). In Nigeria, the expedition of the Lander brothers traced the course of the Niger River, the first navigable water route into the interior of Africa to be discovered by a European power. This was also the year that the power of steam came into its own with the opening of the world's first public railroad in England; two years later, the first steamboat appeared on the waters of the Niger (Headrick 1981:60–62). Despite the very limited resources the British government was willing to commit to adventures in West Africa, the mobile power of gunboats for the first time permitted the extension of British commerce and military power beyond the few trade forts that had clung to the Atlantic coast for several centuries. Moreover, as colonial agents such as the Landers were mindful even in 1830, the new technology of railroads represented possible conduits of trade that were superior and even more easily controllable than good rivers. All that was needed was a valuable commodity from the African side, and this was found in palm oil, a good with increasing market value due its usefulness as a lubricant in the locomotives and other machinery that proliferated with the Industrial Revolution.

The colonial efforts in West Africa begun in 1830 had taken on serious momentum by 1846 (the year that the problem of fatal train wrecks led to the passage of the Fatal Accidents Act in England). This was a significant year for all three social forces under whose name the colonial conquest of Africa would be justified: commerce, Christianity, and civilization. In regard to commerce, in 1846 John Russell's Liberal Party took power and Parliament passed the Sugar Act. This removed protectionist tariffs favoring the sugar produced by Britain's West Indian colonies and thereby dismantled what remained of the old slave-based Atlantic economic system (Schuyler 1945:151–57). The new commitment to "free trade" and "free labor" encouraged British merchants in West Africa to redouble their efforts to develop "legitimate trade" in palm oil. This more aggressive entrepreneurialism of British merchants and those whom local Africans called "black Europeans" (traders from the colony of Sierra Leone) began to displace traditional African middlemen in the Niger Delta as well as established merchants engaged in the slave trade on the coast.

As for Christianity, after slavery had been legally abolished in Britain's West Indian colonies in 1833, Christian antislavery and missionary movements began to focus on Africa. This was, of course, just one aspect of the religious politics of the 1830s in which antislavery evangelism reshaped the anticlerical discourse about the "rights of man" into a set of universal ideals, at once liberal and Christian, promoted by such organizations as the Aborigines Protection Society (founded in 1837). In 1839 Thomas Buxton founded the Society for the Extinction of the Slave Trade and the Civilization of Africa under the nominal leadership of Prince Albert (who, the following year, married Queen Victoria [Blackburn 1988:467]). In 1842, the Wesleyan Methodist Missionary Committee, headed by John Beecham (an active member of Buxton's African Civilization Society), sent their principal "colored" agent on the Gold Coast, Thomas Birch Freeman, to the Niger Delta where, in 1846, he established the first Methodist mission among the Yoruba (Newbury 1961:44–45).

Back in England, in support of these efforts, books on West Africa were published by Buxton (1967) in 1839 and Beecham (1968) in 1841. Both offered sensationalized pictures of West African culture as a blood-drenched barbarism based on human sacrifice (including long and horrifying accounts of the death of Governor MacCarthy). Such extreme images of West Africa were functional as a fund-raising tool. Each of the two years prior to Beecham's book, his Wesleyan Methodist Missionary Committee had run a deficit of some 10,000 pounds (Metcalfe, Introduction to Beecham 1968:iv). Missionary societies focused on the Pacific had recently done well in raising contributions by emphasizing the cannibalism of the Fiji Islands, and it was hoped that highlighting human sacrifice in West Africa would do the same. Such sensationalism was reinforced by the newspapers and magazines of this period, whose publishers found that true accounts of exotic atrocities greatly increased their sales. As Philip Curtin has discussed, it was in the 1840s that there first appeared books such as J. D. East's *Western Africa: Its Condition, and Christianity the Means of its Recovery* (1844) in which "popular ethnography could be combined with exhortation to support missions" (Curtin 1964:325–26). The connection of African fetishism to slavery and human sacrifice inaugurated by Buxton and Beecham particularly emphasized the sacrifice of slaves. For instance, in the book that opened the way for the distinctive genre of evangelizing ethnography, Thomas Buxton explains that the "fetish places" of Benin are "the depositories of the usual objects of worship. Many unfortunate slaves are sacrificed in front of these temples" (1967:231). Implicit in this is the identification of slavery and human sacrifice as ultimate violations of the value of human life and of African fetishism as the antithesis of both free trade liberalism and Christianity. It is particularly ironic that the reinterpretation of African fetishism promoted by humanitarian missionaries of the 1840s was the one previously confined to the writings of those they most condemned, British slave traders. My own impression (one can hardly prove such a thing) is that the new emphasis on human sacrifice in Africa afforded both fervently abolitionist churchmen and reluctantly abolitionist politicians an exotic locus into which to displace the national embarrassment of Britain's historical role in the Atlantic slave economy. In any event, it is remarkable how soon after the legal abolition of slavery in 1833 British public discourse begins speaking of slavery as a barbaric practice proper to primitive cultures and of the elimination of the cruelest customs of the latter (cannibalism and human sacrifice) as the special spiritual calling of their own commercial empire. That the moral passion unleashed by the abolition of slavery helped forge the imperialist ideology of civilization that justified the colonial conquest of those societies most victimized by the Atlantic slave trade is one of the great historical lessons in the public psychology of righteousness.

As for *civilization*, in the 1840s this term designated a concrete policy in relation to Africa: the encouragement of European-style commerce and cash crop production, especially in palm oil, and the active suppression of the slave trade (which still thrived in some West African ports during the 1840s, since slaves could be bought for ten or fifteen pounds and sold in Brazil for fifty to eighty pounds; Newbury 1961:38). The British government officially committed itself to fighting this activity in the Slave Trade Abolition Acts of 1842 and 1843. But the policy that expressed the spirit of civilization meant more than replacing the slave trade with free trade. It meant the proactive effort to reshape African societies themselves by abolishing human sacrifice. These first efforts to transform African cultures began in the 1840s, at first through minimally interventionist efforts at treaty-making. Human sacrifice was first abolished in British-controlled parts of the Gold Coast in 1844; a gunboat-enforced British treaty with Lagos first abolished human sacrifice in a Nigerian town in 1852 (Law 1985:78; Elias 1954:49).

The other great violation of the value of human life, slavery, was always a more difficult issue. In the early 1830s, the newly elected Whig government that had been swept into power on a wave of unprecedented public activism had only reluctantly bowed to the force of public opinion by abolishing slavery in the West Indies. On the Gold Coast, Maclean had interfered in African slavery not by opposing the institution itself but rather in individual cases involving "cruelty." A liberal distinction among instances of slavery according to a standard of physical cruelty may also be found among missionaries. Slavery was actively opposed when it seemed directly related to pagan practices of human sacrifice, as among the Ibo, or when connected to the old Afro-European Atlantic slave trade. In the absence of these, especially when traditional African slavery was seen to accommodate modern commerce, a different attitude could be taken, as a Basel missionary did in speaking of the Krobo of Ghana.

> In Kroboland slavery is not so repugnant as in other places. Human flesh and blood is not the main currency, but palm oil and other products of the country. The main reason for the shocking slave trade is thus absent.... Our missionaries hardly hear about the maltreatment of a slave. (Wilson 1990:295)

When the British government first established a formal jurisdiction over the Gold Coast in 1844, it ignored the issue of slavery while accepting the responsibility to suppress human sacrifice and "panyarring," the practice that Bosman so despised: the seizure of a member of a debtor's family by a creditor (Curtin 1964:307).

It was only in 1874 that slavery was legally abolished on the Gold Coast, and then in a manner that tried to guarantee that the existing labor force would remain in place. (By 1874, British institutions and ideology had been restructured to accommodate the principles of both liberal democracy and racial empire; while the expanded franchise of the Reform Act of 1832 first expressed itself in acts to abolish colonial slavery, the much expanded male franchise of the Reform Act of 1867 came in the wake of the elimination of democratic self-rule for the colony of Jamaica and the rise of a consensus on the unfitness of blacks for self-government [Hall 1994:3–29].) While panyarring was forbidden as a custom of criminally violent coercion, pawning (voluntarily placing a person in the hands of another person or family as security for an unpaid debt) was approved as an effectively nondisruptive substitute for slavery, one that also accelerated the use of capitalist monetary debt as a medium for social relations.

> The anti-slavery ordinances of 1874–1875 apparently had no diminishing effect whatsoever on the transfer of individuals from one household to another as security for debts. On the contrary, the laws appear to have sparked a trend in the opposite direction . . . This upsurge in pawning was also bound up with the spread of commercial capitalism. . . . With the great value placed on land and leases beginning in the late 1870s, as a result of mechanized gold mining, and expanding later in the era of cocoa farming, there was a spate of legal disputes, which together with spiraling debts for lawyer's fees and court costs added still further to the pawning tendency. (Dumett and Johnson 1988:94)

While the more extreme instances of pawning soon also came under attack by colonial governors, the historical evidence suggests that pawning played a transitional role in the replacement of those traditional forms of debt obligation that colonial law came to classify as "fetish practices" with the monetary debt relations that Marx characterized as capitalist fetishism.

African Fetishism and Blood Sacrifice

As I discuss in my concluding section, the idea of fetishism constructed by colonial law was not premised on the negative conception of savage blood sacrifice that informed the ideology of colonial conquest. Since my theoretical interest is the contrast between fetishisms of monetary debt and sacrificial blood, I must first consider the notion of a fetishism of blood.

I have already explained in what sense capital might be viewed as a totalizing social logic premised on the fetishism of monetary debt. But in what sense is there any truth in the idea that traditional West African societies had a comparable fetishism of sacrificial blood? Surely this is an idea that has been thoroughly debunked for many good reasons. Far from lacking any "gods" apart from their sacred objects, as the original theory of fetishism claimed, West African cultures have plenty of these. Popular notions of savage society as being based on Burton's "old path of blood" are expressions of a cultural pathology that may be significant for historians and psychologists studying colonialism but not for anthropologists studying the real cultures of non-European peoples. Moreover, European notions of "blood sacrifice" are a legacy of Christianity, and Christian ideas are poor guides for understanding West African religious practices. Nevertheless, again by examining the history of the discourse about fetish worship, I want to consider in what sense there might be an anthropological truth in the idea of a fetishism of sacrificial blood.

For some four hundred years prior to the period of colonial conquest, the idea of fetish gained its meaning from the incommensurability of African modes for valuing material objects and those of European merchants. While many sorts of objects and practices were designated "fetish," the paradigmatic instance of the fetish was some movable thing to which both sacramental and economic value was attributed by parties from very different cultures involved in a possible commercial transaction. "Fetish" in this sense existed as a social reality, not merely as a textual construct of European writers: its meaningful existence was dependent on its functional value within a pragmatic context. In this context of routinized cross-cultural relations, "fetishes" were as real as any other type of cultural object. During the period of colonial conquest, the context, meaning, and reality of fetish changed dramatically. When Afro-European relations shifted from commerce to war, the meaning of the principal material objectifications mediating these relations also changed. What was at stake in the cross-cultural reality of fetishes during the period of colonial conquest was not commerce in commodities but rather jurisdiction over populations. It was not the value and social reality of cultural objects that was at stake, but the existence and political control of cultural worlds.

This is exemplified in the early effort by Governor MacCarthy to establish effective governmental authority over the towns near Cape Coast Castle in Ghana. MacCarthy's initial success in doing this placed him in conflict with the Asante empire, which viewed these people as its subjects. In Ghana (and many other parts of West Africa) there existed a number of established institutional forms for translocal social relations. One of these was the practice of sealing obligations between strangers (that is, obligations not already prescribed by some kinship relation) through the swearing of oaths at sacred sites or by invoking their names. The sanctioning power of these "fetish oaths" included supernatural and juridical components. A person who died without having fulfilled such a sworn obligation might be judged to have been killed by the fetish for failing to settle the debt. A person owed some unperformed obligation by another might appeal to the individual exercising the authority of the fetish to enforce the unpaid debt. As MacCarthy established his authority over the Gold Coast population, oaths began to be taken on Cape Coast Castle and in the name of "Mankata" (as MacCarthy was called). This was both a challenge to the power of Kumasi and a source of conflict when the government of Asante failed to receive satisfaction from MacCarthy when people over whom he claimed authority failed to fulfill some obligation to a member of Asante society. One of these conflicts, in which agents of the Asantehene seized a debtor, led to the battle in which MacCarthy was killed. By transforming MacCarthy's head into a ritually empowered object belonging among the regalia of the royal lineage of Asante, the power and authority exercised by MacCarthy was being absorbed into that of the Asante sovereign.

During the period of colonial conquest, "fetishism" may best be located in the fetish shrines that were the material centers of those African political forces whose jurisdiction the British sought to supplant. Examples of these are the execution tree at Kumasi, the Dente oracle located on the Volta River that became the center of the Bron Confederation that arose after the fall of Asante to the British, the Yoruba oracle at Aro-Chuku called in pidgin "the Long Ju-Ju," and, of course, the shrines of Benin City, the City of Blood itself. Each of these fetish shrines was the center of a trade monopoly that blocked the expansion of British hegemony. While the Dente shrine ultimately fell within the sphere of German colonialism, the other three became targets of British military expeditions and were physically destroyed by the conquerors. Each of these would be characterized by the British as a "charnel house of fetish lore" (di Cardi 1901:52), a material locus of a "fetish power" that British soldiers and Foreign Office administrators took very seriously, despite their disbelief in "supernatural powers." For the conquering British, there was little doubt that the social regime of fetishism exploited a superstitious belief in supernatural powers among West African peoples by linking it to the real power of ritualized killing and the fear this created in the living.

Colonial ideology viewed "fetishism" as a form of state terror based on human sacrifice. Because of the obvious function of this ideology in the process of conquest, critics of colonialism may be tempted to disavow the historical fact of ritual human killing, rather in the way that Freudians choose to bracket out the significance of real child abuse in the formation of adult sexual psychology. But for anthropology to do this would be to abandon the problem of real history, as psychoanalysis does. For those unwilling to pay this price, how should the historical facts of human sacrifice, and more generally "blood sacrifice," be understood?

The thesis that human sacrifice in West Africa was essentially a form of state terror is not without foundation. The kingdom of Asante, for example, was founded in the late seventeenth century at the time that the Afro-European traffic in slaves and firearms began to transform West African societies. The importance of human sacrifice as a tool of imperial authority was communicated in the naming of the capital itself, Kumasi, after the tree under which criminals were executed—according to Rattray

(1969:156) the word derives from *kum*, to kill, and *ase*, under, meaning "under the kill tree," in reference to "a tree in the center of the town under which human sacrifices and executions took place"—and in the ritual decapitations associated with Bantama, the royal mausoleum (Rattray 1956:130–35). The horror and dread of such sanctions were expressed in Asante proverbs: "Because I fear to be killed I have made my neck short"; "When you lie, you fear Kumase" (Rattray 1969:148, 155). Such ritual occasions as the great *Odwira* ceremony, at which the leaders of subject peoples assembled in Kumasi and participated in the annual renewal of the sovereign power of the Asantehene, along with the Golden Stool itself, were institutional innovations of the first Asantehene, Osei Tutu, and his chief priest, Okomfo Anokye, that helped establish a royal state on a scale larger than the lineage-based social arrangements of Akan society could otherwise accommodate.

It is clear, as Robin Law has argued, that the practice of human sacrifice "expanded in scale in West Africa largely through its association with royal authority and with militarism" (1985:86). Adopting a rational choice model of social scientific explanation, Law argues that human sacrifice functioned to enhance royal prestige and assure popular subservience; the suppression of the slave trade itself explains the increase in human sacrifices in the late nineteenth century, since eliminating the alternate use of slaves (their sale to Europeans) caused a glut in the market that made prestige-enhancing ritual killings cheaper. Yet this argument ignores the fact that states such as Asante, Dahomey, and Benin, as innovative responses to the new situation created by the Afro-European slave trade, were developed out of the institutional and ideological structures of earlier West African societies. This raises the question of the relation of the human sacrifices practiced by these so-called gunpowder empires to those once performed in the more traditional "stateless" societies of the region. Elizabeth Isichei has argued that, while human sacrifice was "the most serious of religious rituals" in West Africa prior to the impact of the Atlantic slave trade, "in their original form, these practices were not necessarily a matter of horror and dread" (1973:57). That is, such practices were not essentially instruments of state terror.

How, then, does one understand the "traditional" meaning of human sacrifice within West African societies, many of whose key rituals entailed "blood sacrifice"? In a recent book on sacrifice, Nancy Jay has suggested that ritual blood sacrifice may be associated with the institutionalization of male power in patrilineal societies. Discussing the specific case of Asante, she finds that bloodless communion sacrifices were associated with that society's original matrilineal arrangements, while expiatory sacrifices involving blood were exclusive to the patrilineal royal superstructure invented in the seventeenth century (1992:61–76). Yet such a use of social anthropology's traditional emphasis on kinship systems for explaining social structure has proved unhelpful for understanding cultural conceptions of the genetic powers of material blood. For instance, claims by West African "informants" belonging to matrilineal cultures that blood comes from both parents, or "really" comes from the father, have sometimes been regarded as confusions caused by relatively recent changes in social structure that occurred during the colonial period (Fortes 1950:264, cited in Minkus 1975:240). But this has not proved to be the case. Wyatt MacGaffey, an anthropologist of Central African cultures, notes: "The expectation that matrilineal societies should have matrilineal blood is contradicted by most if not all Central African matrilineal societies, including the BaKongo, who regard the mother as a mere incubator of material received from the father" (personal communication, March 27, 1996).

The idea of sacrificial blood has recently been transformed by studies of the ritual meaning of menstrual blood (Buckley and Gottlieb 1988). Older Christian conceptions and related studies of "Semitic" cultures emphasized the sacrificial function of killing: the victim's blood expresses the idea of a life being offered either as a propitiatory gift to God or else as a scapegoat in substitution for the life of an individual needing expiation for a sin or a group needing communion to affirm social solidarity. But the release of menstrual blood is not an act of violence, of killing, but is part of the natural process of generating life. If one accepts, as I do, the materialist critique of structuralist anthropology developed by Knight (1991), then the component of killing in rituals focused on sacrificial blood originally expressed the killing of animals by Paleolithic hunters that was a necessary mode for producing the material life of humans and that was institutionalized in a mode of economic exchange, expressed in a cultural symbolism of blood, that gave rise to the human species itself. This was the exchange of animal meat by male hunters for sex with women whose class solidarity was expressed in cultural symbolizations of the supernatural power of menstrual blood.

I assume that Knight's work is still controversial, and I am hardly the person to try to defend its fundamental importance. Moreover, even for those of us who accept the truth of Knight's argument about the cultural importance of Paleolithic blood symbolism, this hardly explains the complex significance of sacrificial blood in traditional West African societies. Indeed, since I am in no position to speak about these cultures, let me simply propose in what sense sacrificial blood could be viewed as comparable to monetary debt.

Neither Christian notions of blood sacrifice nor structuralist notions of lineage blood are useful for understanding general West African conceptions of sacrificial blood. Whatever else they are, West African practices of blood sacrifice involve the killing of a living being in a manner in which the visible shedding of blood is itself the realization and dynamization of an otherwise invisible spiritual power. In the Yoruba tradition, sacrificial blood has the power called *àse*, "the power to bring things into actual existence" (Drewal and Drewal 1990:5–6). This is the spiritual power present in all people and things in a potential state; its activated power is visible in sacrificial blood and is visibly expressed in ritual objects by the color of blood, red (Thompson 1983:6). Sacrificial blood is the material form of the active spiritual power of life, of living existence, understood as the real substance of a society whose members include the living and the still active ancestral dead. In this sense, it is the general material form of a real social substance posited and experienced by the members of these cultures. Blood is different from the other material components of sacrificial acts because its visible materiality is the general form of an invisible spiritual-social substance. Blood as such no more is this substance than money as such is capital. But, in ritual, sacrificial blood is the realization in material form of this substance in the same sense that, in commercial exchange, money is the objective realization of the social value substance called capital.

If this is so, then human sacrifice in West Africa is best understood within a general logic of blood sacrifice that included (and indeed consisted primarily of) practices of animal sacrifice. Unnatural deaths and acts of violence were often conceived in these cultures as pollutions of the earth (the visible world of the living) by the spilled blood of members of a kinship group (Bascom 1969:37). If sacrificial blood may rightly be understood as the general form of spiritual power in these cultures, then it makes sense that the acts remedying wrongs that were both crimes and sacrileges involved ritual blood sacrifice. While the cultural significance of different sacrificial animals was determined by symbolic systems specific to particular cultures, the type and number of animals required to be sacrificed to remedy a given wrong is a quantitative value question. The more severe the violation, the greater the value of the required remedy. In cases of the most severe violations, sacrifices of the greatest value were required: the sacrifice of human beings. Since killing a kin member would shed blood that would itself cause further pollution, the only possible options were to sacrifice an alien captive or a slave, who did not bear the kin blood, or a condemned criminal, who had already been excommunicated from the life of the kin group. If this reasoning is correct, then Isichei is right in distinguishing the practices of human sacrifice of traditional, lineage-organized West African societies from those of royal states such as Asante and Benin where human sacrifice (in the form of criminal executions and rituals at royal funerals and commemorations of royal ancestors) functioned as a form of state terror to maintain the power of kingship.

Colonial Law and Remedies for Fatal Accidents

When conquest destroyed long-standing arrangements for cross-cultural trade, the new context of colonial rule transformed the practical meaning of "fetish." As soon as merchants aligned with British-style commerce gained significant power in an area, they or colonial government officials would set up petty debt courts and other judicial mechanisms for enforcing the monetary obligations entailed in this form of commerce. New judicial structures were also established in a manner that affirmed the ultimate sovereign power of Britain. When traditional institutions threatened neither modern commercial relations nor British sovereignty, the desire was to leave them in place as a mechanism for civil order. The formula that emerged for a dual judicial system of British and "customary" law was that local customary law would be enforced unless it was contradicted by current British law or colonial proclamation or unless it was "repugnant to natural justice, equity, and good conscience" (Elias 1954:13). (Variations may be found going back to 1856, when a Gold Coast Council Order gave the colonial Supreme Court that then existed the power to hear cases from settlements and "protected territories" without consulting local native authorities: "the Court was adjured to pay equitable regard to local customs, where these were not repugnant to Christianity or to natural justice" [Kimble 1963:198].)

By the 1870s, "fetish practices" were a recognized category for cases coming before colonial courts in West Africa; by the end of the century, colonial ordinances would include "putting a person in fetish" among the crimes coming under the jurisdiction of minor courts (Newbury 1961:84; Elias 1954:98). Indeed, these cases were primarily a struggle over jurisdictional authority. Local populations in towns tended to divide themselves into precincts where traditional associations performed necessary public works and rendered customary justice. The headquarters of these associations were identified as "fetish houses" by colonial authorities and were suppressed for forcibly requiring the membership of area residents or for requiring "fetish oaths" of allegiance that treasonously challenged British authority. Customary courts of British-approved chiefs would be similarly quashed if the traditional penalties (such as chaining a person to a log) were deemed cruel. Governor Griffith's campaign in 1887 against native courts in Gold Coast towns, according to David Kimble, condemned "especially their severe punishments for debtors," in which, declared Griffith in a memorandum to the Colonial Office, rulings were based "as much on fetish as on facts" (Kimble 1963:464).

Apart from issues of jurisdiction (that is, political power) and sentencing, cases reviewed as "fetish practices" usually concerned traditional adjudication by means of ordeals involving the accused's ingestion of noxious substances (Newbury 1961:84). While putting someone in fetish was also associated with practices of witchcraft in ordinary language, this was not part of colonial law. Witchcraft was a distinct category with which European jurists were thoroughly familiar: Britain had abolished criminal penalties for witchcraft in 1732. Cases involving witchcraft coming before colonial courts in Africa criminalized those who made accusations of witchcraft against others (or, in rare instances, those who claimed to be witches themselves) (Chanock 1985:85–102). In British law, the injury done by witchcraft derived from the accusation, not the practice, and was comparable to the injury done by acts of slander; the criminal aspect of such accusations, that is, the infraction falling under the police power of the state, was the threat of civil disturbance that might be caused by witchcraft accusations. (I might note that in West Africa, witchcraft tends to be conceived as the secret—usually nocturnal—eating of the spiritual life substance of the human victim.)

The practices criminalized as "fetishism" by colonial law in Ghana and Nigeria were those customary procedures for ordering civil society and rendering remedial justice that could not be reconciled with the requirements of colonial sovereignty, capitalist commerce, and Christian conversion. The latter issue arose when the native institutions permitted by indirect rule required Christian Africans to swear "fetish oaths." This led to the formation of a committee of colonial officials and missionaries that met in Kumasi in 1912 at which "fetish" oaths and rituals were declared distinguishable from merely ceremonial customary practices by the binding obligations they entailed (Kimble 1963:156).

Under colonial law, African "fetishism" might be best defined as a criminal method for establishing obligations and settling debts. From the perspective of this essay, this is an expression of the irreconcilability of the fetishism of traditional West African societies and that of liberal capitalist societies. This is evident in their different methods for remedying the wrongful loss of life in cases of "suspicious deaths" (as British law calls deaths whose suddenness or apparent unnaturalness requires some formal inquiry into their causes). The diverse methods for establishing the liability and debt arising from such deaths is a particularly vivid illustration of the workings of very different cultural logics for valuing human life.

What especially interests me about the debts arising from fatal accidents in capitalist society is that they are instances of the creation of money (in the sense of legally enforceable monetary obligations) falling outside the sphere of market activity that is usually assumed to be the sole origin of monetary values. The innovative solution to the puzzle this posed for liberal jurists, instituted in the Fatal Accidents Act of 1846, was to make the debt-value of human life calculable in terms of hypothetical future wage income. This radical solution also required a transformation of the coroner's inquest. For some six hundred years of English history, this had consisted of impaneling a jury of local citizens, who decided whether a wrong had occurred by viewing the body of the victim and listening to the story of what happened from witnesses. If the jury deemed the death wrongful, an amount of money equal to the value of the object responsible for the death became a debt forfeit, in theory, to God, and, in practice, to the crown's High Almoner. That is, the value of a life wrongfully taken was remedied according a logic of Christian charity in which the state, as God's earthly representative, turned evil into good by confiscating the money value of an object that had become accursed by causing a death and using this money as alms to benefit society as a whole.

After 1846, this traditional coroner's inquest was replaced by an autopsy of the corpse by a licensed medical examiner, who determined the physical cause of death, while determination of moral liability became the matter of a private lawsuit for wrongful death; if the complainant prevails, the civil remedy is a monetary quantity figured in a class-weighted manner suitable for a capitalist society. One might compare both these methods to one described by Paul Bohannan in his study of the Tiv (Bohannan 1957:196–203). A public divination was performed at which the body of the deceased was opened and the heart examined for evidence of the life substance *tsav*. If present, its physical condition showed the moral state of the deceased, which decided the most important question: whether the person would become a true ancestor working for the good of the surviving kin or, if the *tsav* was evil, a ghost wandering in the wilderness and endangering the living. If this visible spiritual substance was not found upon inspection of the heart, then it had been consumed by another through witchcraft and the agent of this wrongful death would be sought. The forensic reasoning entailed in traditional English, traditional Tiv, and modern capitalist inquiries into suspicious deaths are fundamental cultural institutions for doing justice when what is at stake is the debt-value of a human life.

In his book *Sacrifice in Africa*, Luc de Heusch argues that sacrifice is itself best understood in terms of debt. What he calls "the sacrificial debt" is the debt people owe for their own lives. In its most general character, he argues, sacrifice is payment for "a debt of life" (Heusch 1985:215). The sacrificial victim or object is, in his view, always a symbolic substitute for the

The Fetish of Civilization

only true payment, one's own living existence: "the most perfect sacrificial debt is that which a man must pay with his own blood in order to continue to exist" (202). The notion of sacrifice as the payment of a sort of existential debt, so famously mocked by Nietzsche (1967:91–92) in reference to Christianity, becomes more plausible if one relates it to the different modes of material valuation found in different cultures. In this age of global capitalism, the sacred value of human life is recognized in what some might dismiss as the esoteric technicalities of tort law. But, as the recent lawsuit in Nigeria brought by the Movement for the Survival of the Ogoni People against Shell Oil for deaths unintentionally caused by industrial pollution suggests, this may be the only salvation available in a thoroughly civilized society.

REFERENCES

Anonymous [Charles de Brosses]. 1760. *Du culte des dieux fétiches, ou Parallèle de l'ancienne religion de l'Egypte avec la religion actuelle de Nigritie*. Geneva.
Bacon, R. H. S. 1897. *Benin, City of Blood*. London: Allen and Unwin.
Bascom, William. 1969. *The Yoruba of Southwestern Nigeria*. New York: Holt, Rinehart and Winston.
Bastholm. 1818. *Historische Nachrichten zur Kenntniss der Menschen* (1805), trans. H. E. Wolf. Altona.
Beecham, John. 1968. *Ashantee and the Gold Coast* (1841). London: Dawsons of Pall Mall.
Bell, John. 1790. *New Pantheon; or Historical Dictionary of the Gods, Demi-Gods, Heroes, and Fabulous Personages of Antiquity*. Vol. 1. London: Bell.
Blackburn, Robin. 1988. *The Overthrow of Colonial Slavery, 1776–1848*. New York: Verso.
Bohannan, Paul. 1957. *Justice and Judgment among the Tiv*. London: Oxford University Press.
Boisragon, Captain A. 1898. *The Benin Massacre*. London.
Bosman, Willem. 1967. *A New and Accurate Description of the Coast of Guinea* (1705), ed. J. D. Fage and R. E. Bradbury. London: Cass. Translated from a Dutch text of 1704.
Böttiger, Karl August. 1808. *Ideen zur Kunst-Mythologie*. Leipzig.
Bowditch, Thomas Edward. 1966. *Mission from Cape Coast Castle to Ashantee* (1819). London: Cass.
Buckley, Thomas, and Alma Gottlieb, eds. 1988. *Blood Magic: The Anthropology of Menstruation*. Berkeley: University of California Press.
Burns, Sir Alan. 1929. *History of Nigeria*. London: Allen and Unwin.
Burton, Richard. 1966. *A Mission to Gelele, King of Dahome* (1864). New York: Praeger.
Buxton, Thomas Fowell. 1967. *The African Slave Trade and its Remedy* (1839, 1840). London: Cass.
Chanock, Martin. 1985. *Law, Custom and Social Order: The Colonial Experience in Malawi and Zambia*. Cambridge: Cambridge University Press.

Chatelain, Heli. 1894. "African Fetishism." *Journal of American Folk-Lore* 7 (October–December): 303–4.
Cruickshank, Brodie. 1960. *Eighteen Years on the Gold Coast of Africa* (1853). Vol. 2. London: Cass.
Curtin, Philip D. 1964. *The Image of Africa: British Ideas and Action, 1780–1850.* Madison: University of Wisconsin Press.
Curtin, Philip, Steven Feierman, Leonard Thompson, and Jan Vansina. 1987. *African History.* New York: Longman.
Dalzel, Archibald. 1979. *History of Dahomey: An Inland Kingdom of Africa* (1793). London: Cass.
Di Cardi, Count. 1901. "Ju-Ju Laws and Customs of the Niger Delta." *Journal of the African Institute* 29:166–70.
Douglas, Mary. 1992. *Risk and Blame: Essays in Cultural Theory* London: Routledge.
Drewal, Henry John, and Margaret Thompson Drewal. 1990. *Gelede: Art and Female Power among the Yoruba.* Bloomington: Indiana University Press.
Dumett, Raymond, and Marion Johnson. 1988. "Britain and the Suppression of Slavery in the Gold Coast Colony, Asante, and the Northern Territories." In *The End of Slavery in Africa,* ed. Suzanne Miers and Richard Roberts, 71–116. Madison: University of Wisconsin Press.
Dupuis, Joseph. 1966. *Journal of a Residence in Ashantee* (1824). London: Cass.
Elias, T. Olawale. 1954. *The Nigerian Legal System.* London: Routledge and Kegan Paul.
———. 1956. *The Nature of African Customary Law.* Manchester: Manchester University Press.
Fortes, Meyer. 1950. "Kinship and Marriage among the Ashanti." In *African Systems of Kinship and Marriage,* ed. A. R. Radcliffe-Brown and Daryll Forde, 264. London: Oxford University Press.
Fyfe, Christopher. 1962. *A History of Sierra Leone.* London: Oxford University Press.
George, Claude. 1968. *The Rise of British West Africa* (1904). London: Cass.
Gluckman, Max. 1965. *The Ideas in Barotse Jurisprudence.* New Haven: Yale University Press.
Gruppe, Otto. 1921. *Geschichte der Klassischen Mythologie und Religionsgeschichte.* Leipzig: Teubner.
Hall, Catherine. 1994. Rethinking Imperial Histories: The Reform Act of 1867. *New Left Review* 208 (November/December): 3–29.
Headrick, Daniel R. 1981. *The Tools of Empire: Technology and European Imperialism in the Nineteenth Century.* Oxford: Oxford University Press.
Heusch, Luc de. 1985. *Sacrifice in Africa: A Structuralist Approach.* Bloomington: Indiana University Press.
Home, Robert. 1982. *City of Blood Revisited: A New Look at the Benin Expedition of 1897.* London: Rex Collings.
Isichei, Elizabeth. 1973. *The Ibo People and the Europeans: The Genesis of a Relationship—to 1906.* New York: St. Martin's.
Jay, Nancy. 1992. *Throughout Your Generations Forever: Sacrifice, Religion, and Paternity.* Chicago: University of Chicago Press.
Kimble, David. 1963. *A Political History of Ghana: The Rise of Gold Coast Nationalism, 1830–1928.* Oxford: Clarendon Press.
Knight, Chris. 1991. *Blood Relations: Menstruation and the Origins of Culture.* New Haven: Yale University Press.

Lander, Richard. 1967. *Records of Captain Clapperton's Last Expedition in Africa* (1830). 2 vols. London: Cass.
Lander, Richard and John. 1832. *Journal of an Expedition to Explore the Course and Termination of the Niger.* 3 vols. London: Murray.
Lang, Andrew. 1897. "Mr. Max Müller and Fetishism." *Mind* 16 (October): 453–69.
Law, Robin. 1985. "Human Sacrifice in Pre-Colonial West Africa." *African Affairs* 84, 334 (January): 53–87.
Leonard, Arthur Glyn. 1968. *The Lower Niger and Its Tribes* (1906). London: Cass.
Lubbock, John. 1898. *Pre-Historic Times.* 5th ed. New York: Appleton.
Maine, Henry Sumner. 1963. *Ancient Law: Its Connection with the Early History of Society and Its Relation to Modern Ideas.* 10th ed. (1861). Boston: Beacon Press.
Minkus, Helaine K. 1975. *The Philosophy of the Akwapim Akan of Southern Ghana.* Ph.D. dissertation, Northwestern University.
Müller, Max. 1882. *Lectures on the Origin and Growth of Religion,* new edition. London: Longmans, Green.
Newbury, C. W. 1961. *The Western Slave Coast and Its Rulers.* Oxford: Clarendon Press.
Nietzsche, Friedrich. 1967. *On the Genealogy of Morals* (1887), trans. Walter Kaufman and R. J. Hollingdale. In *On the Genealogy of Morals and Ecce Homo,* ed. Walter Kaufman, 15–163. New York: Random House.
Orr, Charles. 1911. *The Making of Modern Nigeria.* London: MacMillan.
Pakenham, Thomas. 1991. *The Scramble for Africa.* New York: Avon.
Pietz, William. 1993. "Fetishism and Materialism: The Limits of Theory in Marx." In *Fetishism as Cultural Discourse,* ed. Emily Apter and William Pietz, 119–51. Ithaca: Cornell University Press.
Rattray, R. S. 1956. *Religion and Art in Ashanti* (1927). London: Oxford University Press.
———. 1969. *Ashanti Proverbs* (1914). Oxford: Clarendon Press.
Roth, H. Ling. 1903. *Great Benin: Its Customs, Art, and Horrors.* London: Routledge and Kegan Paul.
Schuyler, Robert Livingston. 1945. *The Fall of the Old Colonial System: A Study in British Free Trade, 1770–1870.* New York: Oxford University Press.
Snelgrave, William. 1754. *A New Account of Guinea, and the Slave-Trade.* London.
Stocking, George W., Jr. 1995. *After Tylor: British Social Anthropology, 1888–1951.* Madison: University of Wisconsin Press.
Thompson, Robert Farris. 1983. *Flash of the Spirit: African and Afro-American Art and Philosophy.* New York: Random House.
Tourneux, Maurice, ed. 1878. *Correspondance littéraire, philosophique et critique par Grimm, Diderot, Raynal, Meister, etc.* Vol. 4. Paris: Garnier.
Wallis, Captain. 1910. "A Tour in the Liberian Hinterland." *Geographical Journal* (March).
Wilson, Louis E. 1990. "The "Bloodless Conquest" in Southeastern Ghana: The Huza and Territorial Expansion of the Krobo in the Nineteenth Century." *International Journal of African Historical Studies* 23 (2): 269–97.

The Rise and Fall of the Indian Aborigines

Orientalism, Anglicism, and the Emergence of an Ethnology of India, 1833–1869

Peter Pels

On March 9, 1869, Thomas Henry Huxley, president of the Ethnological Society of London, opened a special meeting on the ethnology and archaeology of India at the Museum of Practical Geology. Before giving the floor to distinguished veterans of the British Indian administration like Sir Walter Elliot and George Campbell, Huxley gave a brief geographical outline of India. He peopled the Deccan with "thorough savages" closely resembling the Australians, identified a "mongoloid physical and linguistic presence" in the north and east, and left the rest of the continent to "pale-faced Aryans." He emphasized, however, that the bulk of the two meetings on India would be devoted to the "savage hill tribes" (Huxley 1869:91–94). And indeed, the largest part of the Indian veterans' lectures concentrated on these so-called aborigines of India.

Huxley's deference toward the expertise of the lecturers—"I precede my Indian friends simply as a sort of clearer of jungle, in advance of their elephants" (1869:90)—exemplifies the extent to which London ethnology relied on the colonial practice of ethnography until well into the twentieth century (Pels and Salemink 1994; Pels n.d.). This deference, however, obscures that Huxley's emphasis on the Indian "aborigines" betrayed his reliance on an ethnographic tradition that, in the

---

The research that went into this paper was made possible by the International Institute for Asian Studies, Leiden, and the Wellcome Trust. It is an extensively revised, much enlarged and, I hope, more mature version of an earlier publication (Pels 1995). Parts of the paper were presented before audiences at the Centre for Asian Studies Amsterdam, the Department of Anthropology of the University of Minnesota and the Center for South and Southeast Asian Studies of the University of Michigan; I thank the seminar participants for their comments. Special thanks should go to Susan Bayly, Nicholas Dirks, Dirk Kolff, Prabhu Mohapatra, Chris Pinney, Gloria Goodwin Raheja, Oscar Salemink, and Peter van der Veer for their useful comments and advice, and encouragement of the project in general.

colonial practice from which it emerged, had already been superseded by new developments. Indeed, one of his lecturers, George Campbell, had been instrumental in shifting the emphasis of the ethnology of India from the topos of aboriginality to a more pan-Indian perspective (but see also W. Elliot 1869:94–95). In this essay, I hope to show how Indian ethnology emerged on the basis of the imperially marginal ethnographic tradition of Indian aboriginality, to discard it again when ethnology became a central mode of production of colonial intelligence.

This development modifies our understanding of orientalism and the way in which it shaped European perceptions of India.[1] Early Indian ethnology was, like its London counterpart, synonymous with the attribution of aboriginality, the classification of human beings according to the primordial "seat" of their race.[2] But finding "aboriginal races" in India implied that orientalist notions became less central to colonial intelligence than they were around 1800. Rather than turning around "caste" and "Hinduism" throughout the nineteenth century (Inden 1986:402), British discourse on India was increasingly dominated by the notion of "race" (Bayly 1997; Leopold 1974). The vogue of studies on Indian aborigines between 1830 and 1860 introduced an ethnological discourse that, by the end of this phase, came to racialize caste, a reinvention of caste that would inform the production of pan-Indian surveys of "tribes and castes" from the late 1860s onward (cf. Dirks 1992).

This transformation of orientalism into ethnology occurred less at the level of the British imagination of India than at the level of its methodical engagement with it. The orientalist articulation of knowledge on foundational *texts* gave way to the ethnological articulation of knowledge on *bodies*. The suggestion that there was a part of the Indian population that was both "originally" different from, and much older than, Hindu civilization reduced the importance of both the texts of this civilization and the pandits on whom the British relied for their translation (cf. Ludden 1993). At the same time, the emergence and consolidation of novel relationships between colonizer and colonized in the first half of the nineteenth century—statistical and scientific supervision, military and labor recruitment, and missionary activity in the forms of both Christian conversion and secular education—made the bodies of the colonized more important to the colonizer than their utterances in writing. The emergence of an eth-

---

1. This is the notion of orientalism criticized by Said (1978). Even when critical of his work, recent publications about India share his assumption that orientalism is the discourse that governs enunciations about it (Breckenridge and van der Veer 1993; Dirks 1992; Inden 1986, 1990; Mani and Frankenberg 1985).

2. Kaushik Ghosh is, as far as I know, the only one to have used *aboriginality* in much the same way (n.d.; see also Thomas 1994:177). I thank Prabhu Mohapatra for directing my attention to this essay.

nology of India marks the coming of age of colonial practices that tried to mediate between the "politics of difference" of orientalism (van der Veer 1993:23) and the practice of "anglicizing" Indians to become Christians and citizens. Poised between orientalism and anglicism, Indian ethnology emerged as an ambivalent mediator of Indian nationality and imperial citizenship. Until recently, this development escaped the attention of critics of orientalism, who usually skipped the crucial period of transformation from the 1830s to the late 1860s in which it occurred (but see Dirks 1995; Ludden 1993; Viswanathan 1989).

I shall discuss these developments by giving glimpses of two Anglo-Indian careers: first, that of Brian Houghton Hodgson, whom Max Müller called, in 1854, "[o]ur highest living authority and best informant on the ethnology and phonology of the native races of India" (Müller 1854:342); and second, that of (Sir) George Campbell, who in 1865–66 was the leading ethnologist of the Asiatic Society of Bengal and, in 1869, one of the veterans for whom Huxley "cleared the jungle." These career sketches, punctuated by excursions into the careers and thought of comparable Anglo-Indian intellectuals, will allow me to map the changing political contents of the idea of aboriginality in India, and consequently, of Indian ethnology, by showing how it fed upon, and back into, strategies of colonial intelligence. However, I shall first have to unpack the opposition of orientalism and anglicism and the resultant methodical shift from text to bodies in Indian colonial intelligence. In conclusion, I shall consider the relationship between Indian and metropolitan ethnology, guided by the question to what extent one can generalize from the politics of aboriginality in India to the politics of anthropology in general.

From Texts to Bodies, or: Anglicizing Orientalism in Early-Nineteenth-Century India

Twentieth-century Indian anthropologists trace the origins of their discipline to a point long before ethnology was established in Britain: to the orientalist William Jones and his founding of the Asiatic Society of Bengal in Calcutta in 1784 (Vidyarthi 1977:68). It is the more remarkable that the relationship between orientalism and ethnology has seldom been historically researched. Edward Said's influential critique of orientalism has usually been interpreted as a discussion of the Western representation of otherness in general—including ethnology and anthropology (Clifford 1980; Fabian 1983:xiii; Mitchell 1992:289). But it would be wrong to identify the "politics of difference" of orientalist discourse (van der Veer 1993:23) with a *single* "corporate institution for dealing with the Orient" or "systematic discipline" of domination (Said 1978:2–3): such a fusion of "discourse" with "institution" or "discipline" makes the first concept identical to a functionalist notion of "ideology."[3] I want to argue that the orientalist imagery of the eighteenth century was reinvented by the altogether new discipline of ethnology, a discipline that itself owed much to the colonial institutionalization of science and statistics. Whereas classical orientalism—based on the translation of and commentary on foundational texts—was central to the development of colonial intelligence under the aegis of the Asiatic Society of Bengal in the decades before 1800, its locus of development increasingly shifted to Europe afterward. From about 1830 onward, the practical development of such colonial intelligence more and more relied on the ethnographic typification of contemporary statistics and its scientific inscription as ethnology.

James Mill's *History of British India* (1858; first published 1818), as it was edited by the orientalist Horace Wilson in 1844, serves well to outline the basic features of this shift, and to show that it was not so much the *content* of orientalist statements as the *methods* of the orientalists that took a beating in the early decades of the nineteenth century. Mill did away with the ethnographic authority of the members of the Asiatic Society of Bengal—and with the argument that he himself had no Indian experience or language competence—by taking a firmly antiempiricist line and denying that "observing, and . . . acquisition of languages" were necessary for the correct judgment of Indian history (1858, I:xx, xxiii).[4] By arguing that "rude nations seem to derive a peculiar gratification from pretensions to a remote antiquity" (1858, I:107), he damned the "particular respect" with which orientalists such as William Jones regarded the "legendary tales of the Hindus" (1858, I:108). "Hindu fictions" are "marks of a rude age" and the Hindus themselves "perfectly destitute of historical records" (1858, I:115–16). The true history of this "rude age," therefore, can only be written from an English point of view, by a "critical" or "*judging* history" that discriminates between real and false causes and effects (1858, I:xviii; cf. Chakrabarty 1992).

---

3. The absence of such a distinction in his work begins to explain why Said has so often been taken to task for his lack of historical specificity (Appadurai 1993:314; Dirks 1992; Mani and Frankenberg 1985:176; Pels 1994). Said can be accused of misinterpreting Foucault, since it was precisely the advantage of Foucault's conception of discourse that it does not require the unification by an external "system" or "institution" and therefore escapes functionalism. In the classic text on the subject, Foucault argues that a discourse gains its consistency (not: unity or systematicity) from the way it marks its boundaries (1972).

4. This shows why David Ludden's otherwise inspiring argument—that "empiricism" transformed orientalism from the early nineteenth century onward—shows only one side of this process of transformation (Ludden 1993).

In 1844, Mill's editor, the orientalist Horace Hayman Wilson,[5] defended his work and that of his colleagues against Mill's "disdain of the early records of nations," which "may sometimes be suspected to veil a distaste for dry, laborious and antiquarian research" (Mill 1858, I:109). Remarkably enough, Wilson's empiricist critique does not lead him to denounce the authority of Mill's text: on the contrary, his scathing comments on Mill's historical incompetences are relegated to a preface and an avalanche of footnotes, often attached to Mill's footnotes. Against Mill's "critical history," Wilson puts *textual commentary*—a genre to which orientalists were habituated. Mill's scientific critique sought to go beyond orientalist representations by "judging and profaning" the language and texts in which they were formulated, whereas Wilson's edition of *The History of British India*, despite his critical comments, worked rather to further "sacralize" Mill's text (cf. Foucault 1973:81). Foucault's distinction between the "profaning" and "sacralizing" of texts allows for a specification of orientalist method as one predominantly tied to "language," "literature" and "chronicle" (Wilson 1858:x–xi). Orientalism implied collecting, translating and commenting upon the Orientals' *ouvrages fondamentaux*, as Anquetil-Duperron called them (quoted in Halbfass 1988:66). This search for foundational *texts*, rooted in the European classicist tradition, received its major impetus from specific problems of colonial administration, and in particular from the necessity to record Hindu and Muslim law in India—which was what mostly occupied the three leading scholars of the Asiatic Society in Calcutta, William Jones, Henry Colebrooke and Charles Wilkins (Schwab 1984:38). Methodically speaking, Calcutta orientalism and the legal administration of India occupied common ground: by translation and commentary, they set up Sanskrit texts as *sources* of (legal, religious, literary) knowledge and tradition, much as, in an earlier renaissance, Greek and Roman texts were uncovered and revered.

This "sacralization" of tradition as exemplified by a foundational text was allied to a political program that was partly a reaction to the French revolution: the conservative and paternalist cultural relativism of Edmund Burke and his followers in the Indian administration (Majeed 1990:209–11; Stokes 1959:9–16). It was opposed by both Utilitarianism and Evangelicalism, creeds that had little tolerance for any textual authority except the single moral code that they sought to establish as standard (cf. Viswanathan 1989:73). Although Utilitarians and Evangelicals might disagree about the extent to which this single moral code was biblical, they

---

5. H. H. Wilson had been the secretary of the Asiatic Society in Calcutta when he was in the East India Company's employ. He later became the librarian of the East India Company in London and professor of Sanskrit at Oxford and Haileybury. When he edited Mill's text in 1844, he was the foremost orientalist in England.

agreed on two points: that the source of authority was single, and that it was English. When, therefore, the authority of the Bible could not be upheld in India, the anglicizing mission increasingly turned secular, effecting an epistemological break with Indian tradition as it had been codified in its texts, and reinforcing the articulation of colonial intelligence on science and statistics, that is, on immobilizing, labeling, and enumerating *bodies*. The remainder of this section traces the practical developments that carried this shift.

The first of these was the emerging debate on education in India. Gauri Viswanathan has outlined how anglicization, which started as a plea for reform of British morals in the Indian administration under Cornwallis, had by the 1820s turned into a concern with Indian "character," while the initiative of paternalist and orientalist administrators was taken over by Utilitarians and Evangelicals in the 1830s (Viswanathan 1989:36, 38–40). Parliament's allocation of £20,000 to the education of Indians in 1833 divided the Supreme Council of India in a five against five deadlock. The orientalist party, led by Horace Wilson, Henry Prinsep and J. R. Colvin, wanted to safeguard the study of the classical oriental languages like Sanskrit, Persian, and Arabic, while their anglicist opponents, led by Thomas Babington Macaulay and Charles Trevelyan, argued that the only appropriate way to teach Indians the benefits of civilization, and science in particular, was through the medium of English. Viswanathan shows how the decision to institute English literature as the vehicle of Indian education was a compromise between the missionary desire to Christianize and the administrative commitment to religious neutrality. More important, it was the opposition to the idea that oriental literature could be a *source* of intellectual and moral values that welded secular and Christian anglicists into a party (Viswanathan 1989:113). Because the Indian administration had undertaken not to teach the Bible in Indian schools, the anglicizing mission had to secularize: "Christianity in India had of necessity to build into itself the activity of ratiocination . . . validating belief by the techniques of modern knowledge" (1989:98). As Macaulay showed in his famous Minute of 1835, the rhetoric of science—of Francis Bacon—was sufficient to authorize all the changes that both secular and Christian anglicists contended for (1952:720; cf. Viswanathan 1989:138).

As James Mill's fulminations against orientalist history already indicated, the mission of science implied a critical, "judging" epistemology that broke with the representations of oriental texts. Dominated by the model of natural history, science sought to reach behind everyday phenomena by comparing specimens of species, languages, or forms of civilization and establishing their basic units and the relations between them. Botany, zoology, and comparative anatomy dissected everyday appearances to get at organs and the structures that made them move; philology reached behind the surface of language and words to their phonemic units and the inflections, prefixes, and suffixes that bound them together; and political economy sought behind the everyday realities of history, property and wealth the legal and administrative structuring of land and labor. By these operations, science tried to come to new classifications, of the origins of genus, species, and varieties, of genealogies of language families, or of "stages" of civilization. Science ruptured the link between classification and naming, by insisting that true classifications should rely on the primordial cause—the "origin"—that determined the development of an object, rather than the superficial names under which it was presently known (Foucault 1973: passim, but esp. 229, 239).

"Origin" pointed to a time "other" than the present, that yet contained the causes, effects, and possibilities of the present. If ever empirical observation and formal definition would become perfect, that is, completely congruent, the origins of everything—of civilization, of language, of species—would be known. For the development of Indian ethnology, this emphasis on "origin" implied that representations used within the sphere of oriental history had to give precedence to terms expressing a rupture with it. True history had to resemble geology, or natural history, but not Indian chronicle. For scientific analysis, the "original" texts of oriental tradition were surface phenomena, mere symptoms of a "rude age." Names like the Laws of Manu, Sanskrit, and Hindu were surface descriptions, to be superseded by scientific analyses of "oriental despotism" and "division of labor," "Indo-European language families," "Aryan races," and a host of others. Moreover, the hegemony of "natural history," of biological models, guaranteed that such a rupture would take the language of physiology—the description of vegetable, animal, or human bodies—rather than that of classical literature for its model.

If the break that scientific rhetoric presumed to make with everyday representations was apparent in the work of Mill, it was probably even more marked in colonial empiricism (cf. Ludden 1993), where questionnaires and handbooks (like Cuvier's) increasingly replaced the reliance of naturalists and explorers on indigenous knowledge and classifications. Take Francis Buchanan, who wanted to become a botanist but turned into a pioneer of nineteenth-century colonial intelligence instead (Vicziany 1986). As a good scientist, Buchanan emphasized in all of his work that the *personal* observation of specimens should precede their classification. He was therefore always interrogating his informants, questioning their veracity, and manipulating his conversations with them in the attempt to reduce the chance of bias (Emmett 1976:34–35). It is not surprising that he liked to irritate, and was skeptical of, orientalists, who relied heavily on the information of Brahmin informants, a class that Buchanan "hated" (Vicziany 1986:632). Buchanan's survey of Bengal (1806–13), in particular, established a pattern of colonial intelligence that lasted into the twentieth century: the "statistical survey" laid down in the ubiquitous Gazetteers of India (Chaudhury 1965; Emmett 1976). The intimate relationship between the methodology of science and statistics is apparent from the fact that Buchanan was thought to be "in every way well qualified" for statistical research on the basis of his botanical and zoological work (Roxburgh, quoted in Prain 1905:xii).

Here, "statistics" should not be interpreted in its modern, quantified, sense, but in the original German sense of *Statistik* or *Staatenkunde*, "statecraft." It was originally a late-eighteenth-century transformation of the "art of travel" into the format of expeditions, which were sent out to gather knowledge particled into the slots of a questionnaire, and it is no coincidence that the German scholars who invented *Statistik* were also the first to coin the concept of "ethnography" (Stagl 1980:375; 1990:327; Vermeulen 1992:6). "Statistics" was popularized in England by John Sinclair's *Statistical Account of Scotland* of 1788, which revolutionized social research by departing from the model of the "Tour" or travelogue, replacing it by the comparisons made possible by a system of questionnaires (Emmett 1976:15). It had become a vogue word by the 1820s (Cullen 1975:9–10). Just as the census was first developed in colonies like North America and Ireland (Hacking 1990:17), statistics was initially far more popular with the Indian government than with that of Great Britain, as witnessed by the surveys of Francis Buchanan, Colin MacKenzie, and William Henry Sykes, and this may explain why employees of the East India Company played a major role in establishing statistics as a legitimate scientific endeavor in England.[6]

Buchanan embodied, like the late-eighteenth-century German *Statistiker* and John Sinclair, the shift from travelogue to survey—from the temporality of a narrative of fact-gathering to the two-dimensional space of maps and tables—that constituted this early conception of statistics (cf. introduction, section 4). While his first work was still presented as a travelogue (*Journey through Mysore*, 1807), his assignment to the survey of

---

6. See Buckland 1906; Dirks 1992, 1993; Emmett 1976; Farr 1873; Laurie 1887; Vicziany 1986. Four of the founders of the Statistical Society of London (1832) were or would be employees of the East India Company (Malthus, Jones, Drinkwater, Sykes); a former secretary to the Indian Home Department (Mackenzie) was crucial in its revival in the late 1830s (Cullen 1975:79, 101). The quantified conception of statistics emerged in England in the 1840s (Cullen 1975:10–11) and became more important in India in the course of the 1850s and 1860s, although it never displaced the "gazetteer"-type survey. The quantitative notion of "population," the measure of a state's military and economic power, had, of course, been central to state-craft for a much longer period (see introduction, section 4).

Bengal was distinguished by the instruction to include topography and the tabulated enumeration of populations. This mode of abstraction became the model for all subsequent statistics and gazetteers of India (Chaudhury 1965; Emmett 1976; Vicziany 1986). It came to constitute the revenue settlement report: in a model of the genre, the classification and counting of space (topography, administrative divisions, cultivated versus waste land) is followed by the same operation performed on bodies ("population"; Thomason 1839:77–80). The text relies methodologically on "scientific" rhetoric: for the establishment of the "origin" of forms of land tenure, it makes no sense to consult "books of law"; one should rely on personal observation instead (Thomason 1839:89–90). Its association with the Utilitarian rhetoric of James Mill is clear from the fact that, by the time of the annexation of Punjab (1849), the statistical arrangement of colonial knowledge had become a privileged means of supervision and control in India (Stokes 1959:248), a mode of representation complementary to and congruent with Bentham's and Mill's panopticon and pannomium.[7]

Thus, science and statistics shared a methodological vocabulary of "personal" observation, and the redefinition of items observed by means of a classificatory grid, provided by statistical questionnaires or scientific handbooks. This reduced the reliance of the observer on indigenous categories and support, and it subordinated these categories and the informants who provided them to the classificatory activities of the observer. Moreover, the biological paradigm of natural history, and the statistical emphasis on "population," focused the attention of both scientists and statisticians on bodies, their classification and enumeration. And even if this shared methodology did not sufficiently reduce the relevance of textual orientalism to colonial administration, the relationship of both science and statistics to a program of *reform* took care of that. As political economy, science was of course defined by reform, by a scientific revision of law and administration—that was the Utilitarians' brief. Natural history, too, promised reform, especially in the way botany would change agriculture (Vicziany 1986:647). Since Sinclair, statistics had been associated with the "improvement" of society, and this explains why statistics in England was first of all directed at the reform (by education, religion, and medical science) of "others": criminals and lunatics. In India, "otherness" was everywhere; there, statistics was applied to a society that could, as a whole, be perceived as deviant (Appadurai 1993:318). For Utilitarians and Evangelicals, this deviance was, of course, primarily symbolized by the "despotic"

---

7. For the creation of the panopticon (a jail built to supervise every individual convict) and the pannomium (a encompassing scientifically established code of laws) through the influence of Mill in India, see Stokes (1959:70, 247 and passim; Kaplan 1995).

and "superstitious" authority of kings and Brahmins, an authority that was enshrined by oriental texts, the pandits that helped to explain them, and the orientalists who relied on both.

It is no wonder that "oriental" authorities, enshrined by orientalism, could not find a place in the reforms initiated in the 1830s. Even orientalist scholarship had to move away from the content of the texts it analyzed toward a critical redefinition of them that could support arguments for reform. In his orientalist scholarship, the former statistical reporter of Bombay and cofounder of the Statistical Society, William Henry Sykes, argued that Brahmanism was not "unfathomable in its antiquity," that its legends were "invented," and that land belonged not to the king, but to his subjects (Sykes 1841a; 1841b:445, 450). But such redefinitions were makeshift compromises with orientalist methodology. At the time of the publication of Sykes's work, an alternative that was much closer to science and statistics had already been formulated.

Brian Houghton Hodgson: From Colonial Official to Ethnologist

Brian Houghton Hodgson (1800–1894) was the second son of a man of independent means who, after becoming involved in a banking disaster, could no longer support his children's education.[8] Through the connections of his mother, Hodgson was nominated to a writership in Bengal at the age of sixteen and left home to attend Haileybury College, where he was a guest at the house of Thomas Malthus until his entrance examination. Hodgson excelled in political economy and languages, Bengali first of all, and was shaped into a liberal under the influence of Malthus, whose house was the center for Whig intellectuals at the time. He arrived in Calcutta in 1818, to continue his studies at Fort William College (in Persian in particular), but his health broke down, and other good connections were able to get him a (healthy) hill appointment as assistant commissioner of Kumaon, under G. W. Traill.[9]

The Kumaon tour "became the keynote of Hodgson's whole official career" (Hunter 1896:52). Traill taught Hodgson the paternalist mode of rule, the settlement of revenue and its accompanying statistics (to which Hodgson may have been predisposed by Malthus's well-known preoccupation with "population"). Traill's statistical survey of Kumaon was exemplary (Hunter 1896:52–53). It echoes Buchanan's worries about the

---

8. This and the following section summarize a more extensive account published elsewhere (Pels 1995).
9. Biographical data are from Cotton 1901 and Hunter 1896.

reliability of indigenous informants' claims (Traill 1828:151). Topography and population estimates are followed by the attempt to ascertain the "origins" of the inhabitants, and, scorning the "vague traditions and conjectures" of his informants, Traill relied instead on personal observation (of physical appearance, religion, and language), adding some observations on the (nearly extinct) "aborigines" of the region (160). Thus, Traill's statistical survey clearly announced Hodgson's later ethnological activities and shows that statistics provided a perspective on "territories" and "populations" that, by itself, raised questions about Indian "aborigines" and their relation to the dominant Hindu presence, even if the former remained marginal. An encompassing concept of "Indian aborigines," however, would not be formulated on the basis of revenue settlement, but from more marginal sectors of the empire.

Although Hodgson repeatedly showed his ability, health problems cut off a Bengal career, and his highest administrative achievement was the Residentship of Nepal, which he occupied in 1833 after twelve years of accumulated Nepalese experience in subordinate posts. His Nepalese work required him to do research on the country and allowed ample time for it. Since he was not allowed to travel beyond the Kathmandu valley, he had to restrict himself to collecting Buddhist manuscripts and gathering information from local intellectuals for his (never completed) *History of Nepal*, which was drafted on the lines of a statistical survey.[10] After becoming involved with the Asiatic Society in Calcutta, Hodgson quickly made a reputation for himself outside Asia. His work on Northern Buddhism gained him the admiration of French orientalists and procured him the Gold Medal of the Société Asiatique de Paris and the Légion d'Honneur in 1838. He became a corresponding member of the Zoological (1832) and Linnaean Societies (1835) in recognition of his work as a naturalist. He therefore worked as an orientalist, as a statistical reporter, and as a scientist, before he embarked upon strictly ethnological work; and all this without any institutional support apart from shipments of books from Europe (Hooker 1905:xii–xv). To the *Journal of the Asiatic Society of Bengal* alone, he contributed 125 papers, 21 of which were listed as "ethnological," while 13 can be classified as "orientalist"; the others dealt with natural history, zoology in particular (*Centenary Review* 1885:142–44).

We should note the appeal of natural history to an individual researcher on the margins of the empire. In his orientalist work, Hodgson depended on either the knowledge produced by indigenous informants,

---

10. See British Library, Oriental and India Office Collection: MSS Eur D 497.

The Rise and Fall of the Indian Aborigines 93

in both oral and written form (see Hodgson 1830:222–23), or on the commentary of more experienced orientalists (see Hodgson 1828:409–18), to make sense of his findings. In contrast, in his botanical and zoological activities he was master of all he surveyed: he not only observed and collected the "specimens," but also decided how to dispose of them in naturalist classifications (with the help of a handbook, his cherished copy of Cuvier; cf. Hunter 1896:72). The possibilities for protracted personal observation and classification of natural species in a region that was largely unknown scientifically gave Hodgson an intellectual authority that was lacking in his marginal position as Resident, or in his dependent position as collector of oriental manuscripts. The significance of scientific research for Hodgson's career is brought out by the fact that, while his early contributions to the *Journal of the Asiatic Society* are still a mix of statistical, orientalist, and biological reports (excepting 1833 and 1834, discussed later), he hardly published anything but biological papers—including observations on proper zoological classification—between 1835 and 1847, when his first recognizably ethnological papers appear (*Centenary Review* 1885:142–44).

Hodgson's first return to the topic of "aborigines" after his work with Traill was a paper about the military tribes of Nepal in the *Journal of the Asiatic Society of Bengal* (1833). Statistics influenced his tabular representations of the different tribes, while scientific rhetoric gave the paper its title: "Origin and Classification of . . ." Hodgson argued for the incorporation of Nepalese soldiers in the British Indian army (1833:221–23). The "Khas," related to the house of "Ghorka," were originally "creedless barbarians," but were incorporated into the Kshatriya caste by missionizing Brahmins, to become "by far the best soldiers in India" (222–23). However, it was not enough to note that they were successful products of Nepalese military discipline: Hodgson felt he had to classify their ethnic essence by naturalist rhetoric. The opening paragraphs declared the "aboriginal stock" of the "military tribes" to be "Mongol":

> The fact is inscribed, in characters so plain, upon their faces, forms and languages, that we may well dispense with the superfluous and vain attempt to trace it historically in the meagre chronicles of barbarians. (217)

Again, we encounter the suspicion toward indigenous knowledge and the reliance on personal observation. In a second paper (1834) Hodgson promises a classification of Nepalese "aborigines," but in the published version only a legend is given. The absent classification suggests that

Hodgson wanted to move beyond indigenous chronicle to something more "scientific" but did not yet know how to do so.[11]

Mark that Hodgson's first use of the term "aborigines" after his work with Traill was articulated on bodies—providing military labor—and was specific to his personal location on the margin of the empire. The observation that Nepal possessed surplus "military tribes" (one can discern an echo of Malthus in this view of a population exceeding the capacity of the country to employ) led to worries about the stability of British rule in relation to Nepal—the job Hodgson was supposed to do. Hodgson was the first to suggest that this military economy should be systematically coopted by the Indian army, but while Governor-General Dalhousie became interested around 1850 (Hunter 1896:111), consistent British attention for "the Gurkha" as soldier only emerged after the 1857 Mutiny.[12]

A little later, Hodgson involved himself in another practical issue: the dispute between orientalists and anglicists about the languages of Indian education. He argued against the orientalists by saying that Bengali and Hindi, rather than Arabic, Sanskrit, or Persian, ought to be the medium of education, and against the anglicists with the argument that the introduction of English, although admirable as such, would be beyond the budgets of both the Education Department and the Indians seeking education. In a rhetoric akin to Macaulay's suspicion of the "false History, false Astronomy, false Medicine" and other "monstrous superstitions" of Indian religion and its leaders (1952:728), Hodgson granted that the "disenchantment" of the popular mind of India was the first goal, but that English would never "break" the "spell" that guaranteed the "power and wealth and honour unbounded" of the Indian "magicians"—the Brahmins. Instead, that mission should be fulfilled by the vernaculars (letter in *Friend of India*, 1835, in Hodgson 1880:291–92). This middle position was favored

---

11. It is interesting to compare this to a nearly contemporary essay on the Bhils—who were later to be included among the Indian "aborigines" by Hodgson and others—by the orientalist administrator John Malcolm. It wholly lacks naturalist rhetoric and the desire to solve questions of classification by origin; the paper deals with a critique of Hindu and Bhil, written and oral, sources. The emphasis on Indian texts as sources of knowledge is clear from a note to the title that says that this "name of a tribe of barbarians" was first noticed in Hémachandra's *Sanskrit Vocabulary* (Malcolm 1827:65).

12. The first "Gurkhas"—defeated portions of the Western Nepalese army—were enlisted in the Indian army in 1815, but had to serve sub rosa for their families were open to persecution in Nepal (Morris 1936:31). Systematic recruiting seems to have begun only after 1857, when Jang Bahadur (whose grandson was educated by Hodgson in 1848; Morris 1936:30) led his regiments against the mutinous sepoys. It is tempting to speculate on the extent to which Jang Bahadur was acquainted with Hodgson's ideas on the subject. Gurkha recruiting by the Indian army was only formalized in 1886 (Morris 1936:31, 130–31).

by a number of missionaries, but the government ignored it in favor of the anglicists. However, Hodgson kept insisting on it until, around 1854, his ideas were put into practice (Hunter 1896:252, 322). Significantly, this is the context in which Hodgson first published his belief that the "immutability of language" promised language analysis to be a secure guide to ethnic affiliation, a certainty that not even physiological confirmation could give (1880:272). Thus, Hodgson's training in oriental languages and texts, in biology, and in statistics, were fused in ethnological argument.

Making the Indian Aborigines

In 1840–41, Hodgson's successful manipulation of Nepalese politics embroiled him in a dispute with Governor-General Ellenborough. Hodgson resigned in anger and, after a dismal stay in England in 1844, settled in Sikkim. There, he concentrated on the study of the "aborigines of India," on the philological lines set out in the context of the education controversy. Especially his essay on the Kocch, Bodo, and Dhimal tribes (1847) became known as a model of ethnological research among both ethnologists and orientalists.[13] Both groups identified with Hodgson's philological approach. But comparative philology itself had already moved away from indigenous Indian and orientalist expertise in Sanskrit by advocating the dissection of Sanskrit down to its component parts and putting them together again by means of comparisons with Latin and Greek, to create an "Indo-European" language family. Hodgson now increased this distance by concentrating on vernaculars that had rarely been recorded before. This emphasis on the vernaculars implied doing away with oriental literature, which was undeveloped in these languages. The "attempt to separate language from literature . . . established language rather than belief and tradition as a source of value and culture" (Viswanathan 1989:114).

As in the education controversy, the new "source of value and culture" was provided by English science: after the dissociation of language from literature and chronicle, it could be reconnected with a new, "natural" history through the concept of "origin." Language, being historically constant, was supposed to be the prime indicator of "race," and "large and careful induction" told Hodgson that "all the Tamulians of India have a common fountain and origin, like all the Arians"

---

13. Hodgson's admirers included Christian Bunsen, John Barnard Davis, Christian Lassen, Robert Latham, Friedrich Max Müller, and Richard Owen. James Colvile, president of the Asiatic Society of Bengal in 1847, referred to him as the "eminent ethnologist."

(1848:551–52).¹⁴ Thus, the physiological discourse of "race," "specimens," and "stocks," derived from the study of vegetable, animal, or human bodies, was now also applied to grammars and vocabularies. Max Müller warned, in the same essay in which he praised Hodgson's "Tamulian" expertise, against treating ethnological (he meant physiological) and phonological race as commensurate, but he paradoxically illustrated this by examples of Sanskrit dialects spoken by "Tamulian physical types" and Tamulian-speaking peoples "of Arian extraction" (Müller 1854: 349–50), thus showing how far the metaphors of physiology and phonology were allowed to mix. In fact, he argued that "[e]thnological race and phonological race are not commensurate, *except in ante-historical times, or perhaps at the very dawn of history*" (1854:349; emphasis added). In other words, *ab origine*, linguistic and physiological race were one, and aboriginality became the common denominator of both physiological and philological programs of research.

To further test his supposition that all "Tamulians" were originally one, Hodgson tried to organize a group of experienced administrative ethnographers, who were to gather linguistic knowledge from all over India on the lines of his comparative vocabulary. His inclination toward "natural history" rather than oriental chronicle is clear from his introduction to the essay on the Kocch, Bodo and Dhimal tribes.

> All those who are conversant with ethnology are aware that the pagan population [mark the Christian/statistical term—PP] of India is divided into two great classes, viz., the Arian or immigrant, and the Tamulian or aboriginal, and also, that the unity of the Arian family, from Wales to Assam, has been demonstrated in our own times by a noble series of lingual researches—researches which have done for the history of Man a service analogous to that done for the history of the globe by the fossil investigations of Cuvier. (1847:i)

In this context Hodgson first formulated explicitly the politics of aboriginality of his ethnological work, linking the latter to the advocacy of the rights of aboriginal races. Instead of poring over a mere sketch of the past, he argued, the student should address himself to "preparing full and faithful portraits of what is before his eyes," and the statesman should profit by it, "for these primitive races are the ancient inheritors of the whole soil, from which they were wrongfully expelled by the usurping

---

14. *Tamulian* had long been in use for Tamil speakers (OED, s.v.), but Hodgson seems the first to employ *Tamulian* for a single aboriginal "race" other than the immigrant Aryans. Prichard's use of the concept in 1843 excluded "hill tribes" like Bhils and Konds (1843:240–51).

Hindus." One of the objects of this ethnology should be the scientific one, to ascertain when and how the dispersion took place and to bring the fragments together again. "It is *another* object, not less interesting, to exhibit the positive condition, moral and material, of each of these societies at once so improveable and so needful of improvement, and whose archaic status, polity and ideas offer such instructive pictures of the course of human progression" (1847:ii). The use of the term *improvement* marked the practical value of this ethnology: by getting to know the Indian aborigines' moral and material condition, the administration could learn how to make them progress—and thus undo the "usurpation" of the Hindus. As in Hodgson's plea to incorporate the Nepalese "military tribes," the ethnologist acts as both the definer, and the advocate of the people he has defined as his object. Here, however, the politics of aboriginality identifies the colonizer as the impartial arbiter defending "aboriginal" rights rather than as an employer of military labor.

In this context, personal observation, recording "what is before one's eyes," again distanced Hodgson's approach from indigenous information, lending his methodology an additional political weight.

> [T]he rudiments of grammar are to be had only with extreme toil, as creations of your own, from the crude elements of very corrupt sentences supplied by the unlettered children of nature; and, in proportion as all such grammars are likely to be deficient, in the same proportion do copious vocabularies become more and more desirable.[15]

Hodgson's vocabularies were not only meant to provide "true history" through the comparison of linguistic roots (the work of comparative philology), but also by classifying words in what we would now call "semantic fields," which could be analyzed on the presence or absence of meanings. Their presence or absence was a clue to the level of advancement of the society under consideration. Thus, one can infer something about the Bodo and Dhimal, because their language lacks words for God, soul, future state, Heaven, Hell, piety, sin, prayer, repentance, pardon, and so forth (1847:iii)—implying they only communicate with the supernatural through flattery and bribery, in short, through magic. In this way, Hodgson returned to the assessment of Indian thought—"magic" as opposed to "science"—that he and Macaulay employed during the education controversy.

Thus, all elements of Hodgson's official career were brought together in his ethnology of India: first, the speculations about aboriginality,

---

15. Added, in Hodgson's handwriting, to the copy of 1847 in the Oriental and India Office Collection, British Library (T 7039).

encountered in his statistical work with Traill, that were relevant for determining who were "the ancient inheritors of the whole soil"; second, the knowledge of oriental languages, sufficiently important to turn language into the main indicator of race (clearly contextualizing Hodgson's additional work on anthropometry: cf. 1847:193–95); and third, the modification of orientalist expertise by the emphasis of naturalist science on the personal observation of bodies. James Logan, the Malay Settlements administrator and editor of the *Journal of the Indian Archipelago*, expressed the result of this victory of scientific empiricism and the paradigm of physiology in 1854, by writing that Hodgson had shown that "in India, history must be the slight superstructure and ethnology the solid basis" (quoted in Hunter 1896:295). The Indian history that relied on texts and their interpretation by oriental(ist) scholars had been contextualized by the biological racism of ethnology.

This was the pinnacle of Hodgson's intellectual career. From 1849 to 1851, Joseph Hooker, the famous botanist and intimate friend of Charles Darwin and Thomas Huxley, was his guest in Sikkim, where the two built up a strong friendship under endless disputations of Hodgson's theories (Hooker 1905:xiii). He spent much time on his ideas on education when the government of India finally became interested in them. He married in 1853, to spend another happy five years in Sikkim with his wife, until her illness, his father's, and perhaps his dissatisfaction with the increasing racism of Anglo-Indian society after the Mutiny (Leopold 1974:584, n.4) drove him back to England in 1858. There, he soon made over his manuscripts to the India House Library (in 1864) and retired to the life of a country gentleman. However, he continued to entertain his former colleagues and acquired new ones (such as the young William Hunter), and, after remarrying (1870), being elected vice president of the Royal Asiatic Society (1876) and Fellow of the Royal Society (1877), and receiving an Honorary D.C.L. from Oxford (1889), he died in 1894, as old as the century into which he was born.

Of course, Hodgson was not the only pioneer of the idea of Indian "aborigines": one can add the Madras infantryman John Briggs and the missionary Robert Caldwell (Leopold 1974:594).[16] Briggs (1785–1875) was the first to introduce the aborigines of India to the members of the Ethnological Society of London (Briggs 1851). Like Hodgson, he had been a British Resident at a nominally independent court, and, also like Hodg-

---

16. I thank Tom Trautmann for pointing out that there is another candidate, the missionary John Stevenson. Stevenson (1798–1858) discerned a "language of aboriginal Hindus" in the early 1840s. However, he seems to have restricted himself to the linguistic field, writing as if the "aborigines" were a race of the past that has merged with the invading Aryans (Stevenson 1841–44).

son, he had been busy with the possibilities for "pacifying" unruly tribes at the frontier (in his case, the "internal" frontier with the Bhils). Yet, in India Briggs predominantly worked as an orientalist; he seems to have ignored the aborigines until he joined the Ethnological Society in 1845, ten years after his return to England, nor was he ever as concerned with the rights of aborigines as Hodgson was. Briggs seems to have hit upon the idea of a separate aboriginal race in India under the influence of the Ethnological Society (Pels 1995:160–61). (I shall return to the role of aboriginality in the Ethnological Society in the conclusion.) In contrast, Caldwell's notion of the "Dravidian Languages" was a product of India.

Robert Caldwell (1814–91) published his *Comparative Grammar of the Dravidian Languages* (1856) to juxtapose a group of non-Aryan aborigines of India to the superstitious despotism of the Aryans. The Dravidian race embodied his hopes for a Christian future in India: for Dravidians, Brahmanism was not *aboriginally* part of their way of life, and they were therefore, unlike the Aryans, open to conversion. "[T]he chief obstacle to their evangelization is the density of their ignorance," as Caldwell wrote about a group later included among the Dravidians (quoted in Dirks 1995:127). Nicholas Dirks put it this way: "[I]n claiming the independence of the Tamils [from the Aryans, Caldwell] seemed also to claim their souls for Christian conversion" (1995:128). Similarly, Hodgson's declaration of the ethnic independence of Nepalese "military tribes," or Indian aborigines in general, claimed them for conversion into soldiers of the Indian army or into colonial citizens equal to the Aryans. Moreover, both scholars had a need for a politics of aboriginality within the context of these missionary projects: the "improvement" of a specific, non-Aryan part of the Indian population. The fact that both formulated that politics by means of the comparison of language shows how central—better: necessary—linguistic strategies were to any mission, whether religious or secular. Although Caldwell's terminology was to play a more important role in later ethnological thinking about India and in Madras politics today than the one devised by Hodgson (Dirks 1995:132–33), the work of both was crucial in the next phase, when the formerly divisive conception of Indian aboriginality was turned into a pan-Indian classification.

George Campbell, Caste, and the Village Community

Thus far, the formulation of a concept of Indian aboriginality derived from a specific combination of orientalist and anglicist strategies—*specific* because emerging from practical problems arising at the margins of empire. Hodgson exemplifies this development because he embodies both the political preoccupation with military labor at a frontier and the missionary preoccupation with the conversion of savages into responsible citizens in the future. His involvement in Nepalese military affairs and in the education controversy combine the diverse practical concerns of John Briggs and Robert Caldwell, respectively. All three were professionally situated at the empire's boundaries and occupied with the possible conversion of those beyond these boundaries into useful soldiers, citizens, or Christians. Neither of the three, therefore, was at the center of the existing establishment of colonial rule, where the main goal was not conversion, but revenue, law, and order. The administrative establishment was less occupied with the possibility of a transgressive mobility across imperial boundaries by either attack or conversion than with the management of land, property, population, and produce within these boundaries.

The spatial arrangement of statistics was of course admirably suited as a representation of the concern with the management of land, property, and produce. George Traill's "Statistical Sketch of Kumaon" is a good example of how revenue settlement statistics could both provoke speculations about aboriginality and make them marginal to the general administrative project. However, for "improvement" to become pan-Indian (for which "the first and most necessary step" was "correctly to estimate the facts": Campbell 1852:vi), this discrepancy between a marginal ethnology of Indian aborigines and the central statistics of revenue had to be resolved. The solution, embodied, from the 1870s onward, in the pan-Indian statistical and ethnographic surveys of William Hunter and Herbert Risley, was to fuse the discourse on caste—the institution that, since the work of the orientalists, was thought to be characteristic of Indian civilization—with the naturalist rhetoric of ethnology. This racialization of caste can be traced through the career of (Sir) George Campbell.

George Campbell (1824–92) was a remote descendant of the Dukes of Argyll, and his upbringing wavered between his father's Radical politics and the more moderate aristocratic surroundings of the family, all buoyed up by Scotch pride.[17] He was sent through a number of schools before enrolling at Haileybury in 1840, and in his autobiography he records his dislike of classics and his inclination toward "useful science," Benthamite political economy, and "rational" history ("not kings and queens and battles, but the history of nations and peoples," 1893, I:7). Arriving in Calcutta in 1842, he was posted to Robert M. Bird's and James Thomason's "model administration" of the Northwestern Provinces in 1843. There, he

---

17. This preoccupation with his own nationality is clear from Campbell's statement that Scotch is philologically speaking the "purest English spoken" (1893, I:9). Biographical data is from the *Dictionary of National Biography* and Campbell (1893).

gained steady promotion and a coveted transfer to the exciting Punjab service in 1846, where he served until his first furlough in 1851.

The major ethnographic concept of the revenue establishment at the time was the "village community." The Thomasonian settlement school had strong Evangelical and Utilitarian strands, but their "anglicism" was compromised by a respect for indigenous tradition that derived from paternalist predecessors like Thomas Munro and Charles Metcalfe. In fact, the latter were the originators of the concept of "village community." In their work, the idea of the village as an eternal "little republic" that survived each and every change of dynasty was often used conservatively, to argue against radical attempts toward agricultural improvement by the legal imposition of personal property and the alienation of land (Dewey 1972:295; see also Dumont 1966). The Thomasonians, however, although they retained the paternalists' glorification of personal contact with "natives" and their concept of the "village community," transformed the village from a conservative defense against anglicist modernization into the major site of "improvement."

Thus, occupying much the same middle ground between orientalism and anglicism as Hodgson, James Thomason followed up on the latter's advice by instituting vernacular education, urging that it should complement the land settlement by teaching people "their rights in the land" and how to conduct their "agricultural concerns," while at the same time increasing the reliability of the agricultural statistics on which British officers based their assessments of the revenue (Penner 1986:150–52). He therefore differed from Hodgson in employing a concept of "origin" that derived from political economy and was articulated on land rather than bodies, property rather than race. As Thomason wrote in his model settlement report, the origin of land tenure was only clear "where the village communities have flourished for centuries" (1839:97), thus making the "village community" into the origin of revenue. This view was taken up by George Campbell in his *Modern India*—written during his first furlough from 1851 to 1853—where he makes clear that all other forms of land proprietorship, "Zemeendars" in particular, were later derived from or imposed upon the original village arrangements (1852:92). This advocacy of the corporate village was congenial to the Thomasonians' progressive paternalism, because it enabled them to bypass the Indian elite (and the orientalist learning that gave it much of its legitimacy in the Indian administration) to deal with the peasants directly (Ludden 1993:266–68).

The paternalism of the Thomasonians was to give way, by their own "improving" activities, to far more rigid schemes of classification, embodied in the Census. In Campbell's time in the Punjab, the taking of the cen-

sus was still the duty of the Settlement Agency, which had thereby taken up the genre of the statistical survey inaugurated by Buchanan.[18] But the drive toward statistical registration by the Thomasonians produced an increasingly specified and impersonal attribution of status (of "tribe" or community of proprietors and "caste" or diversity of occupation) on the village and district level, decreasing the relevance of former, more contractual, relationships between the paternalist administrator and the representatives of a whole village (Smith 1985:163). Moreover, the focus on land tenure also multiplied the number of types of village communities (see Campbell 1852:82–92). The concept of "village community," therefore, lost its some of its relevance as a generalization about Indian society (on the level of what Smith calls the "rule-by-reports" that guided policy). Although the language of political economy continued to dominate supradistrict surveys in the 1840s and 1850s, classifications in terms of "caste" became increasingly prominent (cf. Smith 1985). The same happened with "race": whereas Henry Elliot still thought he had to apologize for using "ethnology" in 1844 (H. Elliot 1869:xvi), George Campbell advocated an ethnological and philological survey of India in *Modern India* (1852:7), and Richard Temple urged, in 1856, for the inclusion of ethnological categories in the next Census (Smith 1985:156). The latter two are, as far as I know, the first to argue for a pan-Indian ethnology, that is, one that does not only concentrate on "aborigines."

In the early 1850s, George Campbell's ideas about the classification of Indian peoples were still predominantly based on political and economic criteria. The attribution of status through concepts of "caste" and "race" did not appear in Punjab village and district records and settlement reports until the new settlement of 1881 (Smith 1985:156). In Campbell's *Modern India*, the divisions of the Indian population are less important than the fact that India is "one great nation" and "one common civilization" due to the government of the Mughal conquerors (1852:25, 37). This emphasis on a unified "Hindu" or "Indian" nation was common to political economists from Mill to Henry Maine. According to Campbell, these conquerors ruled a country where "corporate villages" were "universal" (5), and tribal divisions within the "nation" of "Hindostanees" could be classified according to the differences in the constitution of these corporate villages, more aristocratic among the earlier "pure" Hindoos and democratic among successive waves of Rajpoots and Jats (4, 9, 82–92). "Hindoo civilization" is stagnant and permanent because of its hereditary division of labor (6–7), and it is only much later in the book that one dis-

---

18. Smith 1985:157; it will be clear that I disagree with Smith's statement that Buchanan's journals were "marginal" to the genre of the settlement statistics that emerged around 1840 (1985:158).

covers that this division of labor is, in fact, "caste" (68). Campbell's first attempt to formulate the parameters of a pan-Indian survey, therefore, defines the nation by political and economic criteria—by Mughal government, corporate village, and hereditary division of labor—that also summarized his own experiences with the natives of India in the revenue establishment, and his training in political economy.

There is, however, one exception to this unified picture of India: the existence of an "aboriginal race" in the interior hills (1852:37). Campbell's essentialization of India as a state based on the extraction of revenue from village communities of settled agriculturalists also defines an "internal frontier" with savage aboriginal tribes and by implication defines these "aborigines" negatively, as *unsettled* hunters and shifting cultivators in the hills, or predatory raiders of the plains. This obscures a history of far more reciprocal balances of power between the military power of hill tribes and the plains settlements, in which the "interior frontier" is better seen as a locus of the production of power rather than as a marginal threat to it (Skaria 1989:5–6), and that is in fact one of the relationships with which both Hodgson and Briggs were concerned before they defined their Indian aborigines. Before he could overcome this dichotomy of center and frontier and create a concept of "aborigines" that was not marginal to a conception of a pan-Indian civilization, Campbell's relationship with both the natives of India and its British government underwent an important change.

Labor, Language, and the Racialization of Caste:
Campbell in Calcutta, 1861–67

On his return from furlough, Campbell served another three years in the Northwestern Provinces and was, after the Mutiny, appointed second Civil Commissioner of Oudh, where he remained until 1861. For unknown reasons, he fell out of favor with the Government and was appointed High Court Judge in Calcutta. Because, in contrast to his work in the Northwest, he now had far more leisure, he could indulge in extraofficial pursuits and protracted tours through the country during vacations. Moreover, he was now at the center of intellectual activity in India, and becoming a member of the Asiatic Society in 1863, he began to take an active part in it, especially in promoting ethnology. The 1860s saw much intellectual ferment both in Calcutta and in other centers of British Indian society, which was still trying to assimilate the shock of the Indian Mutiny of 1857, and this involved much speculation about the role of caste in the revolt (see, for example, Taylor 1989:338). Calcutta intellectual life was excited by Samuel Laing's lecture on the Aryan theory (Leopold

1974:590) and the presence of Henry Maine, whose friend Campbell became.[19] In both the Punjab and the Central Provinces, Evangelical Thomasonians had risen to prominence and, teaming up with educators and missionaries, founded auxiliaries of the Calcutta Society with a marked inclination toward ethnological research.[20] Campbell met its members on his tours during 1864 and 1865. In between these trips, he became the main proponent of the Asiatic Society's new initiatives in ethnology.

The ethnological movement within the Society was started by some of its medical members, who sent out a circular to Indian administrators requesting a series of craniums of the races and tribes of British India. In his first speech to the Society in August 1865, Campbell wanted to know what had become of this initiative and broadened it to the wider field of ethnology general. He argued (like Indian anthropologists a century later) that ethnology was started by William Jones and his fellows of the Asiatic Society (*Proceedings* 1865:142). He noted that one great advantage for the Society had passed away, now that Anglo-Indians no longer controlled access to the source of Sanskrit manuscripts. But

> taking Ethnology in its broad sense, there is at our very doors, another and perhaps an equally rich gold field almost wholly unexplored . . . at this moment [we] have in constant and immediate contact with us—working around us daily—men of a race and of languages wholly different from our own,—a race certainly among the most interesting—perhaps the very oldest in the world . . . (143)

The last sentence shows that Campbell thought he had made a new discovery in Indian ethnology, one even more "aboriginal" than those claimed by his predecessors.

Campbell had read a paper by Edward Dalton, the Commissioner of Chotanagpur, who wrote about the Jushpore Oraons that they were "the ugliest of the race . . . utterly destitute of all ambition to rise into respectability of appearance . . . they approach the Negro in physiognomy." Campbell used it to argue against the "slight philological grounds" on which Hodgson and Max Müller had classified the Indian

---

19. I cannot go into the highly intriguing relationships between Campbell and Maine, except by noting that Campbell anticipated Maine in comparing the German *mark* with the Indian village community (1852:52), and both Dumont (1966:78) and Kuper (1988:33) insist Maine must have known Campbell's book but did not cite it in *Ancient Law* (1861).

20. The auxiliary societies were formed by Central Province Governor Richard Temple teaming up with the Rev. S. Hislop in Nagpur, and Punjab Governor Donald McLeod with the linguist, ethnologist, and educator Gottlieb Leitner in Lahore (*Proceedings* 1865:2). Temple and McLeod were Campbell's colleagues in the NWP and Punjab services.

aborigines as "Tamulians" or "Turanians" descending from a northeastern, Mongolian stock. Enlisting Caldwell as an ally, he pronounced the Indian aborigines (excepting those in the eastern hills) to descend from "the great Negrito race," affiliated to the Australian, and primarily recognizable to the "casual observer" by their "thick lip." He emphasized the novelty of his discovery by saying that, when searching the publications of the Asiatic and the Ethnological Societies for this link between India and Negritos, he found nothing (*Proceedings* 1865:145–46). He then called for a collection of live specimens

> as pure as possible, in fact to get the true type it would be well to seek for, as it were, *exaggerated* specimens—the most aboriginal among the aborigines—the most ugly among the ugly, such as Colonel Dalton found among the more remote hills, and such as I can find any day by a judicious selection of the most ill-favoured Coolees on the Maidan. (148)

This shows that statistics—in which Campbell was sufficiently advanced to be elected on the Statistical Committee of the Asiatic Society in 1865—had not yet embraced the idea of variation and random sampling, but still relied a discourse of ethnographic typification.[21]

This first speech suggests that, in classifying these types, Campbell had switched from his former dependence on political economy (cf. Bayly 1997) to a physiological criterion. However, in listing "divisions of inquiry," language still came first, before "appearance," manners and customs, and "osteology" (*Proceedings* 1865:148). In his pan-Indian manual of ethnology, he listed "physical appearance," "language," "religion," "laws," and manners and customs, in that order, but was not very clear whether this was also an order of preference (Campbell 1866:8–11). Moreover, his reference to the "Coolees on the Maidan" shows that another, more implicit, *economical* criterion of defining aboriginality was also operative: indentured or wage labor. Coolies were the "wholly different race" that Campbell referred to as being "in constant and immediate contact with us—working around us daily," the gold mine Calcutta ethnologists were supposed to exploit.

In fact, wage labor relationships had contributed to the definition of Indian aboriginality ever since the pacification of forest polities. The gradual imposition of either alien land tenures, rapacious trading, or forest

---

21. Essentialist typification still dominated Quetelet's notion of "average man." This would change under the influence of Francis Galton's eugenist anthropology. The divorce between statistical and ethnographic languages only took place in the twentieth century (Asad 1993; Cowan 1972; Hacking 1990).

management policies on hill tribes "led to the creation of an enormous population that had to move out of the region in search of a means to survival" (Ghosh n.d.:6; see also Skaria 1989, n.d.). Aboriginality became a useful concept within these relationships because it signified people without caste, who could therefore be employed in all kinds of occupations and be sailed off to Mauritius and Trinidad with impunity (Ghosh n.d.:12). Again, mobility across ethnic and territorial boundaries was associated with an "aboriginal" race that by default defined Hindu civilization, but this time, it was not Bhil or Nepalese raiding that defined a land of settled agriculturalists, but coolie labor that (like Dravidian conversion) defined a land of "caste." Campbell thought the "Kols" of Chotanagpur were related to the Bombay "Coles," and he claimed to have invented the term for a subdivision of the group of Dravidian languages, the "Kolarian"—derived from "Kols" and "Cooly" (1893, II:129). While in 1852 he could only suggest that in South India, the aborigines had become the coolies and were similar to Alexander the Great's *Calantiae* and the Kols (1852:56), he could now identify them as being linguistically, physically, and economically the most aboriginal race of India. Putting these ideas in immediate practice, he suggested that for a racially representative Ethnological Exhibition planned by the Asiatic Society they didn't have to look farther than "our bazaars and labouring coolies," and "as they are such excellent labourers, they might be utilised as Coolies to put in order the Exhibition grounds at certain times, while at others they take their seats for the instruction of the Public" (*Proceedings* 1866:89)—a practical ethnology, indeed.

This part of Campbell's ethnology reproduced the emphasis on aboriginal human bodies of Hodgson and Caldwell (whose work he cited extensively). But his involvement in the 1866 plans for the Ethnological Exhibition in Calcutta and his manual of Indian ethnology (1866) show how thoroughly he innovated Indian ethnology by making the aborigines into the evolutionary zero point of a pan-Indian classification. Riding on the waves of a more widespread enthusiasm about panoptic surveys of India, he not only invented the aboriginal "Kolarians," but also made them into the bottom layer of a structure that went up all the way to the top of the caste hierarchy.[22] In his handbook of ethnology, he listed the diverse aborigines of India, juggling with Negritos, Dravidians, and

---

22. Similar projects arose from Governor-General Canning's request for a pan-Indian collection of photographs of Indian types as souvenir of his career, a collection that was appropriated, after the Mutiny, by the Secret Department, and, later again, accompanied the survey of the people of India that the Calcutta Society initiated (Pinney 1990:281); and from the appointment of William Hunter as Director of Statistics in 1869, which produced the Statistical Survey of Bengal, the Imperial Gazetteer, and led to Risley's 1901 Ethnographic Survey of India.

Kolarians, but he also included the immigrant "Modern Indians," divided among themselves by the successive waves of Brahmin ("pure Hindu"), Rajpoot, and Jat invaders that he had learned to distinguish during his settlement work in the Northwestern Provinces and the Punjab (1866:56ff.).

Such an all-India perspective required, as we have seen, a weighing of criteria of ethnological classification, and Campbell was never completely clear about the hierarchy pertaining between physiological, linguistic, political, or economic criteria. But two things stand out: one, that his was the first all-India classification of "the various tribes and castes of India" (1866:8), announcing the host of "tribes and castes" volumes that were to appear in subsequent years; and second, that whereas, in his 1852 treatise, he had taken "caste" as a division of labor later modified by the cooptation of other immigrant tribes, he became convinced that "caste" was an "*Aryan* institution," that is, a *sign* of a racial division (1866:10; emphasis added). To be sure, "caste" remained a *legal* institution—showing the roots of the idea of an "Indian" civilization in the legal practices of the Calcutta orientalists—but it now became a surface phenomenon indicating a deeper reality of racial divisions. When this racialization of caste had become commonplace in the Indian administration, culminating in Herbert Risley attributing caste by "nasal index" (Risley 1915), Campbell could claim that he had "always maintained that the great caste divisions are really race divisions," only "modified" by occupational divisions (1893, II:131–32)—a complete reversal of his 1852 position.

This was Campbell's highest achievement in ethnology, although, like Brian Hodgson, he would still have a long life and career after it. He was appointed Chief Commissioner of the Central Provinces in 1867 and went on furlough in 1869, to be a prominent guest at the Ethnological Society's special meeting on India described in this essay's introduction (Campbell 1869a). He reached the peak of his Indian career by becoming Lieutenant-Governor of Bengal in 1871, and, though the work seems to have left him little time to pursue ethnology, he managed to compile a comparative vocabulary on the model of Hodgson's and Caldwell's that was regarded as a predecessor of Grierson's massive *Linguistic Survey of India* (Campbell 1874; Thomas and Turner 1942). After his final return to England in 1874, he dabbled among ethnologists for a while, becoming a member of the Council of the Anthropological Institute in 1876. His new parliamentary duties, however, which involved a spirited defense of Irish land tenure against English rapacity, on the lines of his Indian experience (see Campbell 1869b, 1871), were probably too absorbing to continue this. He died in 1892, remembered as an administrator, but, despite the fact that he pioneered the ethnographic survey of India, forgotten as an ethnologist.

Conclusion: London Ethnology and the Politics of Indian Aboriginality

On the surface, the meeting of the Ethnological Society of London with which I started this essay looks like a coming together, not only of Indian and London ethnology, but also of the different generations of Indian ethnologists sketched previously: George Campbell, who was the foremost theorist of Indian ethnology at the time, was preceded during the meetings by Sir Walter Elliot, who was Brian Hodgson's Madras contact in the project of collecting "aboriginal" vocabularies, and succeeded as speaker by Dr. Archibald Campbell, who was Hodgson's assistant in Nepal and his host in Sikkim where the former produced his ethnology.[23] It was, in fact, Archibald Campbell (1805–74) who seems to have been the major force behind the Ethnological Society's preoccupation with Indian ethnology in these years, especially when acting as departmental secretary for India and vice president of the Society in 1869–70.

Yet this apparent harmony covers a number of sutures, and not only those that, as we have seen, separate the Hodgson and Campbell generations of Indian ethnologists. The devout Christian Walter Elliot used religion as a primary criterion of classifying Indians, and, more importantly, foregrounded Hodgson's politics of aboriginality by stressing the defense, conversion, and political representation of the aboriginal hill tribes, something that hardly occupied Huxley and George Campbell (W. Elliot 1869:128).[24] Archibald Campbell even stressed that a previous paper he presented did not aim "to meet any scientific system" but referred "to the most important considerations which affect a British officer's intercourse with the wild tribes of India while living amongst and governing them" (A. Campbell 1869:143). Another speaker made a plea for the use of archaeological remains as the major criterion of classifying people, while a fourth stressed the advantage that "personal acquaintance with the natives" gave administrators over London's armchair ethnologists. This last stance was elaborated by George Campbell, when he argued that comparative anatomy would give a doubtful criterion of classification (since it would classify himself and his brother as belonging to "widely different races"). The best ethnological tests are those of language and

---

23. Of the others giving papers at the meetings, Philip Meadows Taylor (1869, 1878) was a famous outsider in the field of prehistory, but not a member of the Ethnological Society; the others, Fosberry and Denison, played no role of significance in either Indian or London ethnology.

24. Walter Elliot (1803–87) had a distinguished official career, finishing it as governor of Madras in 1858. In the meantime, he had distinguished himself as archaeologist and antiquarian, zoologist, botanist, linguist, and orientalist, and cofounded the Madras Society of Literature and Science in the 1830s (see Sewell 1896).

"those easily distinguished by the eye—the features, hair, etc." (1893, II:126). This distinguished the administrators, with their "field science" approach of personal observation, from Huxley and his fellow scientific aristocrats, who relied on criteria produced by the clinical method of comparative anatomy (cf. Pels n.d.; Schumaker, this vol.).[25]

The sutures remind us that London ethnology arose from very different *préterrains* and ethnographic occasions than Indian ethnology did. Its genealogy goes back to the Quaker roots of the campaign for the abolition of slavery (see Comaroff and Comaroff 1991:119), again showing the link between aboriginality and the question of a mobile labor force. However, its more immediate background was formed by the activities of the Aborigines Protection Society, which primarily focused on the fate of aborigines in British settler colonies (Rainger 1980; Stocking 1971). The APS opposed the excesses of settler colonialism, and much of its rhetoric can be understood as an inversion of the settler doctrine of *terra nullius* (cf. Wolfe, this vol.) and hardly touched on a revenue administration like India (with the significant exception of its export of coolie labor; APS 1839b:17–18).[26] As a consequence, when APS activism turned out to be singularly unsuccessful, and it changed its objective from protecting the defenseless "uncivilized Tribes" to "recording their history" (compare APS 1838:3 to 1842:3), aborigines were treated more in terms of salvage ethnography—as dead or dying (see Prichard, in APS 1839a:99)—than in terms of a live population whose rights, interests, and education were a source of concern. This serves to show that the foremost préterrain of London ethnology was not a specific colonial, military, or missionary interest but the rise of a (before the 1830s largely nonconformist and evangelical) middle class that saw in abolitionism and the protection of aborigines a fitting cause to

---

25. This anatomical background is, despite George Stocking's early warning (1973:xi–xii), still largely ignored by historians of British anthropology. When Huxley declined the invitation to assist in the Asiatic Society's scheme for an Ethnological Exhibition in 1866, he replied, in jest: "The most difficult task of all will be to prevent the assembled Savans [sic] from massacring the 'specimens' at the end of the exhibition for the sake of their skulls and pelves! I am really afraid that my own virtue might yield if so tempted!" (Huxley 1900, I:274). George Campbell had already anticipated that joke, when saying that the Indians' "not unnatural prejudice against parting with their crania" had to be respected, and an exhibition of live "specimens" therefore preferred (*Proceedings* 1866:71). While the two seem to share a specific sense of humor, the comparison reveals that Huxley's comparative anatomy had *dead* bodies for its object, while Campbell's statement shows that most Indian ethnologists found Coolies, Gurkhas, and Dravidians interesting because they were *alive*.

26. The gap between aboriginality and issues of land and revenue was emphasized by the fact that a separate Society had to be founded for activism in relation to the latter, with John Briggs as a treasurer (Briggs 1830, 1839; British India Society 1839). The British Indian Society briefly exchanged information and personnel with the APS (Martin 1838), but seems to have been short-lived, and its concerns were never discussed in the reports of the APS. Briggs only became a member of the Ethnological Society six years after its demise.

continue "forging the British nation," and the fortunes of its middle classes in particular (Colley 1992:350ff.).

In contrast, state and nation had, in India, been brought to a tenuous fusion by the orientalists' legal practice of codifying Indian law and the subsequent development of a sense of the "Indian" village community stretching from the Himalaya to Cape Comorin. The concept of Indian "aborigines" broke up the unitary conception of "Hindu civilization." Whereas among the orientalists language was tied to text, to constitute the unity of a Hindu civilization, for the early ethnology of India, language indicated racialized bodies whose interests were opposed to "usurping Hindus," as Hodgson called them. This racial division of India can partly be interpreted as a particular phase in a much longer process in which a group of Hinduized British traders turned into a colonial administration, which increasingly saw the cultural, political, and economic involvement with an Indian elite as corrupting and compromising. However, it produced a paradoxical advocacy of Indian "aborigines" that lasts into the twentieth century (see Elwin 1964:140). Hodgson and his fellow advocates were in a peculiar position: in order to defend the rights of Indian aborigines, they had to define them first and propagate their existence afterward. But any attempt to go beyond a merely negative definition of future converts (as "pagans") risks defining people in terms of positive traits of difference that the successful mission should abolish. The politics of aboriginality is always enmeshed in the paradox that the definition of the ethnic essence of such people seems impossible without these people moving *ab origine*, away from the primordial "seat" that characterized them.

However, the paradox, and the advocacy of aborigines that caused it, could again be driven to the margins after the 1850s; it is absent from the talks that George Campbell and Thomas Huxley gave in 1869. For them, aboriginality had done its political work and they could well do without it. Unlike their predecessors, Campbell and Huxley had no cause to advocate or injustice to redress. Huxley embodied the confident evolutionist conviction that the "pale-faced Aryans" of Asia were sufficiently remote in time not to threaten their British descendants' superiority (in sharp contrast to the polygenist anxiety about the possible kinship of European and Asian Aryans of Huxley's predecessor as president; cf. Crawfurd 1867, 1868). Campbell was the pioneer of a new vision of Indian unity based on a racialized concept of caste, a vision that would be put in practice in the next decades by reworking folklore in terms of rigid caste hierarchies (Raheja, this vol.) and policing bodies according to their caste label (Dirks, this vol.).[27] Both, therefore, embody a new imperial conservatism, one that

---

27. For the paradoxical successes of colonial control through caste hierarchies, see Carroll 1978.

articulated the description and analysis of Indian society—and of otherness in general—on the character legible from human bodies. In this way, they incorporated the images of orientalism into an ethnology that was more at home in the biopolitical institutions of the Indian colonial state.

REFERENCES

APS. 1838. *First Annual Report of the Aborigines Protection Society.* London: Aborigines Protection Society.

———. 1839a. *Extracts from the Papers and Proceedings of the Aborigines Protection Society* IV. London: William Ball, Arnold and Co.

———. 1839b. *Second Annual Report of the Aborigines Protection Society.* London: Aborigines Protection Society.

———. 1842. *Fifth Annual Report of the Aborigines Protection Society.* London: Aborigines Protection Society.

Appadurai, Arjun. 1993. "Number in the Colonial Imagination." In C. Breckenridge and P. van der Veer, eds., *Orientalism and the Postcolonial Predicament. Perspectives on South Asia,* 314–39. Philadelphia: University of Pennsylvania Press.

Asad, Talal. 1993. "Ethnographic Representation, Statistics and Modern Power." *Social Research* 61:55–88.

Bayly, Susan. 1997. "Caste and Race in the Colonial Ethnography of India." In Peter Robb, ed., *The Concept of Race in South Asia,* 165–219. Delhi: Oxford University Press.

Breckenridge, Carol, and Peter van der Veer, eds. 1993. *Orientalism and the Postcolonial Predicament: Perspectives on South Asia.* Philadelphia: University of Pennsylvania Press.

Briggs, John. 1830. *The Present Land-Tax in India considered as a measure of finance, in order to show its effects on the government and the people of that country, and on the commerce of Great Britain.* London.

———. 1839. *Speeches delivered by Major-General Briggs and George Thompson, Esq. at the annual meeting of the Glasgow Society for promoting the cause of universal emancipation, protecting the aborigines of the British dependencies, and bettering the condition of the natives of India, held August 1, 1839.* Reprinted from the *Glasgow Argus.* Edinburgh: W. Oliphant, Jun and Co.

———. 1851. "On the Aboriginal Tribes of India." *Rep. Brit. Ass.* 20:169–76.

British India Society. 1839. *Speeches delivered at a Public Meeting for the Formation of a British India Society.* London: British India Society.

Buckland, C. E. 1906. *Dictionary of Indian Biography.* London: Swan Sonnenschein.

Caldwell, Rev. Robert. 1856. *Comparative Grammar of the Dravidian or South Indian Family of Languages.* London: Harrison.

Campbell, Dr. Archibald. 1869. "On the Lepchas." *Journal of the Ethnological Society of London,* n.s., 1:143–57.

Campbell, George. 1852. *Modern India. A Sketch of the System of Civil Government, to which is prefixed, some account of the natives and native institutions.* London: John Murray.

———. 1866. "The Ethnology of India." *Journal of the Asiatic Society of Bengal* 35/ii (special number on Indian Ethnology): 1–152.

———. 1869a. "On the Races of India as Traced in Existing Tribes and Castes." *Journal of the Ethnological Society of London,* n.s., I:128–40.

———. 1869b. *The Irish Land.* London: Trübner and Co./Dublin: Hodges, Foster and Co.

———. 1871. "The Tenure of Land in India." In *Systems of Land Tenure.* London: Cobden Club Symposium.

———. 1874. (Ed.) *Specimens of the Languages of India, including those of the aboriginal tribes of Bengal, the Central Provinces and the Eastern Frontier.* Calcutta: Bengal Secretariat Press.

———. 1893. *Memoirs of My Indian Career.* 2 vols. Ed. Sir Charles E. Bernard. London: MacMillan and Co.

Carroll, Lucy. 1978. "Colonial Perceptions of Indian Society and the Emergence of Caste(s) Associations." *Journal of Asian Studies* 37, no. 2:233.

Centenary Review. 1885. *Centenary review of the Asiatic Society of Bengal from 1784 to 1883.* Calcutta: Thacker, Spink and Co.

Chakrabarty, Dipesh. 1992. "Postcoloniality and the Artifice of History: Who Speaks for 'Indian' Pasts?" *Representations* 37:1–26.

Chaudhury, S. B. 1965. *History of the Gazetteers of India.* New Delhi: Government of India, Ministry of Education.

Clifford, James. 1980. Review of Said's *Orientalism, History and Theory* 19:204–23.

Colley, Linda. 1992. *Britons. Forging the Nation 1707–1837.* New Haven: Yale University Press; London: Pimlico, 1994.

Comaroff, Jean, and John Comaroff. 1991. *Of Revelation and Revolution. Christianity, Colonialism, and Consciousness in South Africa.* Vol. 1. Chicago: University of Chicago Press.

Cotton, James Sutherland. 1901. "Hodgson, Brian Houghton." *Dictionary of National Biography,* vol. 22: 854–57. London: Oxford University Press.

Cowan, Ruth Schwarz. 1972. "Francis Galton's Statistical Ideas: The Influence of Eugenics." *Isis* 63:509–28.

Crawfurd, John. 1867. "On the Physical and Mental Characteristics of the European and Asiatic Races of Man." *Transactions of the Ethnological Society of London* 5:58–81.

———. 1868. "On the Supposed Aborigines of India as distinguished from its Civilised Inhabitants." *Transactions of the Ethnological Society of London* 6:59–71.

Cullen, M. J. 1975. *The Statistical Movement in Early Victorian England.* New York: Harvester Press.

Dewey, Clive. 1972. "Images of the Village Community: A Study in Anglo-Indian Ideology." *Modern Asian Studies* 6:291–328.

Dirks, Nicholas B. 1992. "Castes of Mind." *Representations* 37:56–78.

———. 1993. "Colonial Histories and Native Informants: Biography of an Archive." In C. Breckenridge and P. van der Veer, eds., *Orientalism and the Postcolonial Predicament. Perspectives on South Asia,* 279–313. Philadelphia: University of Pennsylvania Press.

———. 1995. "The Conversion of Caste: Location, Translation, and Appropriation." In P. van der Veer, ed., *Conversion to Modernities: The Globalization of Christianity,* 115–36. London: Routledge.

Dumont, Louis. 1966. "The 'Village Community' from Munro to Maine." *Contributions to Indian Sociology* 9:67–89.

Elliot, Henry Miers. 1869. *Memoirs on the History, Folk-Lore and Distribution of the*

Races of the North Western Provinces of Indian, being an amplified edition of the original Supplemental Glossary of Indian Terms. Original 1844, ed. John Beames. London: Trübner and Co. Reprint, Osnabrück: Biblio Verlag, 1976.

Elliot, Sir Walter. 1869. "On the Characteristics of the Population of Central and Southern India." *Journal of the Ethnological Society of London,* n.s., 1:94–128.

Elwin, Verrier. 1988 [1964]. *The Tribal World of Verrier Elwin. An Autobiography.* Delhi: Oxford University Press.

Emmett, R. C. 1976. *The Gazetteers of India: Their Origin and Development During the Nineteenth Century.* M.A. thesis, Graduate Library School, University of Chicago.

Fabian, Johannes. 1983. *Time and the Other: How Anthropology Makes Its Object.* New York: Columbia University Press.

Farr, William. 1873. Obituary Notice of Col. William Henry Sykes. *Journal of the Statistical Society of London* 35:429–30.

Foucault, Michel. 1972. "The Discourse on Language ('L'Ordre du Discours')." In *The Archaeology of Knowledge and the Discourse on Language.* New York: Harper Torchbooks (orig. French, 1971).

———. 1973. *The Order of Things. An Archaeology of the Human Sciences.* New York: Vintage Books (orig. French, 1970).

Ghosh, Kaushik. n.d. "A Market for Aboriginality. Primitivism and Race Classification in the Indentured Labor Market of Colonial India." Paper for seminar "Labor, Migration and Identity," Johns Hopkins University.

Hacking, Ian. 1990. *The Taming of Chance.* Cambridge: Cambridge University Press.

Halbfass, Wilhelm. 1988. *India and Europe. An Essay in Understanding.* New York: SUNY Press (orig. German, 1981).

Hodgson, Brian Houghton. 1828. "Notices of the Languages, Literature and Religion of the Bauddhas of Nepal and Bhot." *Asiatic Researches* 16:409–49.

———. 1830. "Sketch of Buddhism, derived from the Bauddha Scriptures of Nipal. Extract of a letter from Brian Houghton Hodgson to Dr. Nathaniel Wallich, Nipal, 11 August 1827." *Transactions of the Royal Asiatic Society of Great Britain and Ireland* 2:222–57.

———. 1833. "Origin and Classification of the Military Tribes of Nipal." *Journal of the Asiatic Society of Bengal* 2:217.

———. 1834. "Classification of Newars or Aborigines of Nepal proper, preceded by the most authoritative Legend relative to the Origin and Early History of the Race." *Journal of the Asiatic Society of Bengal* 3:215.

———. 1847. *On the Aborigines of India. Essay the First: On the Kocch, Bódo and Dhimál Tribes.* Calcutta: J. Thomas, Baptist Mission Press.

———. 1848. "The Aborigines of Central India." *Journal of the Ascetic Society of Bengal* 17/II:550.

———. 1880. "Pre-eminence of the Vernaculars; or, the Anglicists Answered: Being Four Letters on the Education of the People of India." In *Miscellaneous Essays Relating to Indian Subjects,* vol. 2, 255–348. London: Trübner and Co. Reprint 1992, New Delhi: Asian Educational Services.

Hooker, Joseph. 1905 [1854]. *Himalayan Journals.* London: Ward, Lock and Co.

Hunter, William Wilson. 1896. *Life of Brian Houghton Hodgson.* London: John Murray. Reprint 1991, New Delhi: Asian Educational Services.

Huxley, Thomas Henry. 1869. Opening Address by the President, Special Meeting on the Ethnology and Archaeology of India. *Journal of the Ethnological Society of London,* n.s., 1:89–94.

Huxley, Leonard. 1900. *Life and Letters of Thomas Henry Huxley.* 2 vols. London: Macmillan and Co.
Inden, Ronald. 1986. "Orientalist Constructions of India." *Modern Asian Studies* 20:401–46.
———. 1990. *Imagining India.* Oxford: Blackwell.
Kaplan, Martha. 1995. "Panopticon in Poona." *Cultural Anthropology* 10:85–98.
Kuper, Adam. 1988. *The Invention of Primitive Society. Transformations of an Illusion.* London and New York: Routledge.
Laurie, W. F. B. 1887. "Colonel W.H. Sykes, MP, FRS." In *Sketches of some Distinguished Anglo-Indians,* 104–9. London: W.H. Allen and Co. (rev. and enlarged edition).
Leopold, Joan. 1974. "British Applications of the Aryan Theory of Race to India, 1850–1870." *English Historical Review* 89:578–603.
Ludden, David. 1993. "Orientalist Empiricism." In C. Breckenridge and P. van der Veer, eds., *Orientalism and the Postcolonial Predicament. Perspectives on South Asia,* 250–78. Philadelphia: University of Pennsylvania Press.
Macaulay, Thomas Babington. 1952. "Minute on Education (1835)." In G. M. Young, ed., *Macaulay: Prose and Poetry.* London: Rupert Hart-Davis.
Maine, Henry Sumner. 1861. *Ancient Law: Its Connection with the Early History of Society and its Relation to Modern Ideas.* With Introduction and Notes by Sir Frederick Pollock. New edition, 1930. London: John Murray.
Majeed, Javed. 1990. "James Mill's 'The History of British India' and Utilitarianism as a Rhetoric of Reform." *Modern Asian Studies* 24:209–24.
Malcolm, Sir John. 1827. "Essay on the Bhills." *Journal of the Royal Asiatic Society* 1:65–91.
Mani, Lata, and Ruth Frankenberg. 1985. "The Challenge of *Orientalism.*" *Economy and Society* 14:174–92.
Martin, R. Montgomery. 1838. *The History, Antiquities, Topography and Statistics of Eastern India.* Reprint of Introduction to vol. 3, from original publication by W. H. Allen and Co. (3 vols.). London: Aborigines Protection Society.
Mill, James. 1858. *The History of British India.* 5th ed. with notes and continuation by H. H. Wilson. 5 vols. London: James Madden/Piper, Stephenson and Spence.
Mitchell, Timothy. 1992. "Orientalism and the Exhibitionary Order." In N. Dirks, ed., *Colonialism and Culture,* 289–317. Ann Arbor: University of Michigan Press.
Morris, Major C. J. 1993. *The Gurkhas. An Ethnology.* Reprint of 2d ed. of the "Hand Book for the Indian Army: Gorkhas," 1936. Delhi: Low Price Publications.
Müller, Friedrich Max. 1854. "Letter on the Turanian Languages." In C. Bunsen, *Outlines of the philosophy of universal history, applied to language and religion.* 2 vols. London.
Pels, Peter. 1994. "The Construction of Ethnographic Occasions in Late Colonial Uluguru." *History and Anthropology* 8:321–56.
———. 1995. "The Politics of Aboriginality. Brian Houghton Hodgson and the Making of an Ethnology of India." In *Yearbook of the International Institute for Asian Studies I, 1994:* 147–68.
———. n.d. "Colonial Service. British Anthropologists and Administrators, 1890–1940." Paper for session on History of European Anthropology, EASA conference, Oslo, 1994.

Pels, Peter, and Oscar Salemink. 1994. "Introduction: Five Theses on Ethnography as Colonial Practice." *History and Anthropology* 8:1–34.

Penner, Peter. 1986. *The Patronage Bureaucracy in North India. The Robert M. Bird and James Thomason School, 1820–1870.* Delhi: Chanakya Publications.

Pinney, Christopher. 1990. "Colonial Anthropology in the 'Laboratory of Mankind.'" In C. A. Bayly, ed., *The Raj. India and the British, 1600–1947.* London: National Portrait Gallery Publications.

Prain, David. 1905. "A Sketch of the Life of Francis Hamilton (once Buchanan), sometime Superintendent of the Honourable Company's Botanic Garden, Calcutta." *Annals of the Royal Botanic Garden, Calcutta* 10, part 1: i–lxxv.

Prichard, James Cowles. 1843. *The Natural History of Man, comprising Inquiries into the Modifying Influences of Physical and Moral Agencies on the Different Tribes of the Human Family.* London: H. Baillière.

Proceedings. 1865. *Proceedings of the Asiatic Society of Bengal,* January to December 1865.

———. 1866. *Proceedings of the Asiatic Society of Bengal,* January to December 1866.

Rainger, Ronald. 1980. "Philanthropy and Science in the 1830s: The British and Foreign Aborigines Protection Society." *Man,* n.s., 15:702–17.

Rendall, Jane. 1982. "Scottish Orientalism: From Robertson to James Mill." *Historical Journal* 25:43–69.

Risley, Herbert Hope. 1915. *The People of India.* 2d ed. (orig. 1908). Reprint, Delhi: Oriental Books Reprint Corporation, 1969.

Said, Edward. 1978. *Orientalism.* London: Routledge and Kegan Paul.

Schwab, Raymond. 1984. *The Oriental Renaissance. Europe's Discovery of India and the East, 1680–1880.* New York: Columbia University Press (orig. French, 1950).

Sewell, Robert. 1896. *Sir Walter Elliot of Wolfelee. A Sketch of His Life, and a Few Extracts from his Notes.* Edinburgh: Private printing.

Skaria, Ajay. 1989. *A Forest Polity in Western India. The Dangs: 1800s–1920s.* D.Phil. thesis, Faculty of History, University of Cambridge.

———. n.d. "Orientalism and Globalism: Conceptions of 'Tribes' in Western India, 1800s–1990s." Ms.

Smith, Richard Saumarez. 1985. "Rule-by-Records and Rule-by-Reports: Complementary Aspects of the British Imperial Rule of Law." *Contributions to Indian Sociology* 19:153–76.

Stagl, Justin. 1980. "Der wohl unterwiesene Passagier. Reisekunst und Gesellschafts-beschreibung vom 16. bis zum 18. Jahrhundert." In B. I. Krasnoaev, Gert Nobel, and Herbert Zimmermann, eds., *Reisen und Reisebeschreibungen im 18. und 19. Jahrhundert als Quellen der Kulturbeziehungsforschung,* 353–84. Berlin: U. Camen.

———. 1990. "The Methodizing of Travel in the Sixteenth Century. A Tale of Three Cities." *History and Anthropology* 4:303–38.

Stevenson, Rev. John. 1841–44. "An Essay on the Language of the Aboriginal Hindus." *Journal of the Bombay Branch of the Royal Asiatic Society* 1:103–26.

Stocking, George W. 1971. "What's in a Name? The Origins of the Royal Anthropological Institute (1837–1871)." *Man,* n.s., 6:369–90.

———. 1973. "From Chronology to Ethnology. James Cowles Prichard and British Anthropology, 1800–1850." In J. C. Prichard, *Researches into the Physical History of Man,* ix–cx. Chicago: University of Chicago Press.

Stokes, Eric T. 1959. *The English Utilitarians and India.* Oxford: Clarendon Press.
Sykes, William Henry. 1841a. "On a Passage in an ancient Inscription at Sanchi, near Bhilsa, proving the Proprietary Right in the Soil to be in the Subject, and not in the Prince." *Journal of the Royal Asiatic Society* 6:246–48.
———. 1841b. "Notes on the Religious, Moral, and Political State of India, before the Mohamedan Invasion, &c." *Journal of the Royal Asiatic Society* 6:248–450.
Taylor, Philip Meadows. 1869. "On the Prehistoric Archaeology of India." *Journal of the Ethnological Society of London,* n.s., 1:157–82.
———. 1989. *Story of My Life.* London: William Blackwood and Sons, 1878. Reprint, London: Pluto Press.
Thomas, F. W., and R. L. Turner. 1942. Obituary: George Abraham Grierson, 1851–1941. *Proceedings of the British Academy* 1942:283–306.
Thomas, Nicholas. 1994. *Colonialism's Culture. Anthropology, Travel and Government.* London: Polity Press.
Thomason, James. 1839. "Report of the Settlement of the ceded portion of the District of Azimgurh, commonly called Chuklah Azimgurh (dated December 1837)." *Journal of the Asiatic Society of Bengal* 8:77–136.
Traill, George W. 1828. "Statistical Sketch of Kamaon." *Asiatic Researches* 16:137–234.
Van der Veer, Peter. 1993. "The Foreign Hand. Orientalist Discourse in Sociology and Communalism." In C. Breckenridge and P. van der Veer, eds., *Orientalism and the Postcolonial Predicament. Perspectives on South Asia,* 23–44. Philadelphia: University of Pennsylvania Press.
Vermeulen, Han. 1992. "The Emergence of 'Ethnography' ca. 1770 in Göttingen." *History of Anthropology Newsletter* 19/2:6–9.
Vicziany, Marika. 1986. "Imperialism, Botany and Statistics in Early Nineteenth-Century India: The Surveys of Francis Buchanan (1762–1829)." *Modern Asian Studies* 20 (4): 650.
Vidyarthi, L. P. 1977. "The Rise of Social Anthropology in India (1774–1972): A Historical Appraisal." In K. David, ed., *The New Wind. Changing Identities in South Asia,* 61–83. The Hague: Mouton.
Viswanathan, Gauri. 1989. *Masks of Conquest: Literary Study and British Rule in India.* New York: Columbia University Press.
Wilson, Horace Hayman. 1858. Preface of the Editor (1844). In James Mill, *The History of British India.* 5th ed. London: James Madden/Piper, Stephenson and Spence.

The Illusion of Consent
Language, Caste, and Colonial Rule in India
Gloria Goodwin Raheja

In 1890 R. Maconachie, Deputy Commissioner for the Gurgaon District in the Punjab, published his *Selected Agricultural Proverbs of the Panjab*, a book of Punjabi proverbs with English translations, together with his running commentary on the peasant "knowledge" exhibited in the texts he had collected. The work had been commissioned by Colonel E. G. Wace, the Financial Commissioner of the Punjab, to be utilized by the government as it prepared an "Agricultural Primer" for use in village schools in the province.[1] Maconachie opened the preface by inviting the reader to visually inspect the environs of a Punjabi house.

> [T]he writer, having accomplished . . . his task, ventures to invite the reader to its perusal as a visit to a humble village home. We are standing, as it were, in the crooked village lane, outside the rough mud wall, and rudely carved door of a zemindar's dwelling. Passing over the lintel of the threshold, we enter the porch . . . and obtain some idea of what is to be seen beyond. From the porch we go up on to the flat mud roof and take a general view of the rooms and their inmates; we catch glimpses too over mud walls . . . of neighbours standing about, or lying at ease on their beds and smoking, of industrious housewives surprised in some domestic

---

Research for this paper was made possible by a McKnight-Land Grant Professorship, a McKnight Research Award, and a Graduate School Grant-In-Aid of Research, Artistry, and Scholarship, all from the University of Minnesota, and by a fellowship from the American Philosophical Society. I am indebted to Richard Bauman, Charles Briggs, Bernard Cohn, John Comaroff, C. J. Fuller, Ann Grodzins Gold, Stephen Gudeman, John Harriss, John M. Ingham, McKim Marriott, Michael Moffatt, and James C. Scott for their comments, and to Peter Pels and Oscar Salemink for editorial suggestions. Versions were presented at the University of London School of Oriental and African Studies workshop on "Caste Today," in July 1993 and at the University of Chicago, Leiden University, the University of Minnesota, and the University of Texas at Austin. I thank members of those audiences for their questions.

1. Wace had issued a circular asking various district officials to forward proverbs to the Deputy Commissioner of each district. As a result, twenty-eight officials (including Denzil Ibbetson) submitted such collections.

occupation, who, as they catch sight of us, stop their tongues which have been moving as fast as their hands, and pull their veils over their bosoms. Coming down to the ground we may examine the house in detail, noting the rough tools and implements, the household vessels, cooking pots and pans: the people will occasionally appear in undress, and somewhat untidy, not at all up to the level of our enlightened age in speech, sentiment, or address. . . . But we shall see things as they really are, and obtain valuable information as to the daily life and habits of the peasant at home. (Maconachie 1890:i-ii)

Paradoxically, for a work that consists primarily of 1,089 Indian proverbs, the preface encourages the reader only to visually survey the house and its inhabitants, and not to listen to the words of those who are thus scrutinized. The only speech taken notice of is that of the women, who fall silent though as soon as they come into view. An eerie hush seems to fall over the village as we approach in Maconachie's company. Though we are to read of proverbial speech in the pages that follow, the prefatory prose shifts its sensory register, from ear to eye, and in so doing elides all possibility of particular strategic intention that might be evidenced in the moments in which proverbs are spoken by one Indian interlocutor to another, or to the colonial investigator. By resolutely obscuring the actual production of peasant speech, and by expunging all traces of the moment in which it is written down by the colonial ethnographer, I suggest that Maconachie, like many other colonial officials and ethnographers in nineteenth-century India, attempted to create the administratively useful illusion of the Punjabi peasant's simultaneous capitulation to invariant "custom" and to colonial rule. This essay investigates the rhetorical means through which this attempt was made in colonial writing, as it incorporates Indian speech into administrative documents, and the disciplinary uses to which this mode of ethnographic representation was put in late-nineteenth-century India.

The proverbs in Maconachie's collection are arranged under such headings as "the merits of various soils," "ploughing," "manuring," "harvesting," and among the chapters on these topics is one entitled "on tribal characteristics." This section of the book contains fifty-eight proverbs that supposedly reveal useful peasant "knowledge" of the characteristics of the various castes of the Punjab, the Brahmans, the Jats, the Rajputs, the Gujars, the Ahirs, and so forth. Thus, we are given to understand that these caste characteristics are on a par with and as knowable as the "humble village home," the cooking pots and pans, and the local ploughing techniques that can be visually surveyed.

Maconachie's text provides a starting point for a consideration of a

The Illusion of Consent

double moment of colonial ethnographic inscription. I consider here the moment in which the speech of the colonized, in the form of oral folklore, is written down by colonial administrators and isolated from the situation of its production. And I consider a second moment, in which these utterances are recontextualized in administrative reports and records that have as their purpose the efficient control of the colonized.

In India as elsewhere, colonial domination comprised both coercive force and attempts to control the flow of discourse about the colonized society and about its relation to the colonizing power.[2] In this essay I will show that between 1870 and 1918 such attempts at discursive control—evidenced especially in land revenue documents, census reports, official glossaries, manuals for the Indian Army, and reference works on caste compiled for the use of colonial officers—included the systematic appropriation of the speech of the colonized in the form of oral folklore, especially proverbial speech, to construct a discourse about the supposedly consensual nature of caste ideology, and to create the illusion that the disciplinary control of specific castes and of the Indian population as a whole was carried out with the consent of the colonized.[3] The mastery of language and the quotation of what was deemed "authentic" native speech were seen to confer authority on particular forms of colonial discourse and colonial discipline as they took shape only in the late nineteenth century. As the forms of discipline changed, so too did the process of inscription; these recontextualizations of Indian speech in colonial writing in the latter decades of the nineteenth century were quite different from the recontextualizations found in the proverb collections and administrative documents of earlier decades.

Manufacturing this illusion of consensus and consent was a constant administrative preoccupation in late-nineteenth- and early-twentieth-century India, as overt rebellion and increasing nationalist activity obliged colonial administrators continually to assert that ordinary Indians welcomed their presence and that India was unfit to rule itself.[4] In colonial

---

2. That colonial discourses also functioned to profoundly transform the supposedly "traditional" social forms they textually inscribed is also becoming increasingly clear. See Cohn 1984; Dirks 1987, 1992; and Smith 1985 for some examples of this process insofar as caste is concerned.

3. I survey here only colonial documents for northern India; in the larger project of which this essay is a part, I consider colonial appropriations of many forms of speech. I am interested in translation strategies, and as I am capable of reading only Hindi, I have restricted this study to texts that focus on this and related north India languages. Most of these colonial documents contain transliterated Hindi texts for much of this translated speech. For reasons of space here, I have deleted most of these and included only the English translations.

4. Unfit to rule itself particularly because of its treatment of women (Chatterjee 1989; Mani 1984, 1989) and because of the supposed divisiveness of caste (Dirks 1992).

discourse of the period one therefore finds frequent references to such reifications as "the deepest feelings of real India"[5] and "national manners and opinions." It was continually asserted or implied that when the "native mind" was known, it would be apparent that British rule had been erected on a bedrock of consent, and that colonial representations of Indian society were flawless mirrors of native opinion. Thus did the colonial power seek to justify its domination of the Indian subcontinent, through representations concerning two kinds of consent: a uniform consent to caste ideology and consent to colonial rule. In the crises occasioned by the Rebellion of 1857, other uprisings and protests, and various kinds of "turbulent" noncompliance, particular varieties of proverbial speech were widely regarded as evidence of invariant "custom" and of the "character and ideas of the common people" (Lyall 1874: app. 5), and they were translated, annotated, and inserted into printed texts to shore up the cracks in the colonial discursive edifice.

Such fissures had certainly begun to appear long before 1857, but the Rebellion so impressed itself upon the colonial imagination that dramatic shifts in administrative policy occurred soon thereafter. Colonial administrators began carefully recording caste identities in the decennial censuses, commissioning the publication of region-by-region caste compendiums for the use of colonial administrators, relying more heavily on caste identities in formulating land revenue policy, and more frequently disciplining certain groups as "criminal" castes and tribes or as castes prone to rebellion. All these changes indicated that the colonial imagination had seized upon caste identity as a way of understanding and controlling the Indian population after the blow to administrative complacency in 1857. In this essay I examine the reasons why, concurrently, the quotation of Indian proverbial speech began to occur so frequently in colonial writing.

I describe here the entextualizing practices that operated to incorporate this speech of the colonized into colonial documents, and the profound transformation in these practices, vis-à-vis speech about caste, that occurred in the mid–nineteenth century. I speak here of the process of entextualization as one through which speech is detached from the situation of its utterance and interpreted without regard to the conditions of its production, as a fixed "authentic" cultural text. This process is, as Bauman and Briggs (1990) and Kuipers (1990) point out, an act of control, an instance in which the political economy of cultural discourses comes to

---

5. See Guha 1993:75 for this phrase. Colonial administrators and nationalists, as Guha points out, engaged in constant struggles over the question of who spoke for the "real India." In this paper, I address the question of how exactly representations of this imaginary "real India" were constructed in official documents.

the fore; marking a body of utterances as a text, and inscribing it as part of a decontextualized or ahistorical "tradition," is frequently part of a larger set of strategies for consolidating or seizing power and authority.

Bauman, Briggs, and Kuipers focus primarily on entextualization and discursive control as it operates within specific societies,[6] but colonial documents exhibit the connection between entextualizing processes and power relationships in a larger arena of cultural politics; the entextualization of indigenous speech in colonial documents was accomplished via complicated and always shifting rhetorical means, as specific colonial administrative agendas changed over time. To wrench certain stretches of speech presumed to be about "caste" from the contexts in which they were uttered and to insert them into colonial documents radically stabilized and transformed their meanings, and excluded, marginalized, or otherwise tamed speech that was not congruent with colonial views of Indian society or colonial political interests.

Paradoxically, this colonial view of proverbs as evidence for consensus and the suasive power of "tradition" may in fact match the intent of those who deploy proverbs in their everyday speech; a "native" may use a proverb precisely in order to draw upon the past or upon "convention" to confer authority upon his own words, to confer an illusory fixity upon "tradition": "the proverb is reproduced as an antique at moments in need of ideological closure; its rhetorical form lends itself to didacticism and defined meaning, the sublimation of occasion to rule" (Stewart 1994:83). It is partly for this reason that an investigation of the colonial uses of proverbial speech may allow us to grasp not only the relation of entextualizing strategies to colonial discipline, but also to begin to discern the role of elite Indian participants—acting as munshis, assistants, and informants—in the entextualization process and the processes through which a colonial discourse on Indian society was constructed.

The entextualization of indigenous speech in colonial ethnographic documents of the last three decades of the nineteenth century and the early years of the twentieth and the failure to see the strategic and situated meanings in specific utterances—in ordinary Indian conversations as well as in their own interactions with native assistants—had significant administrative consequences. Ultimately such entextualization decisively

---

6. Bauman (1993) has written however of the broader political implications of the entextualization of native American folklore in the early nineteenth century, speaking specifically of the erasure of the situated communicative practices that shaped the telling of Ojibwe tales. And Briggs has recently discussed the metadiscursive practices through which stretches of speech—"texts"—are located, extracted, edited, interpreted, and inserted into scholarly or literary or political documents, and the relations of power in which such practices figure (1993).

shaped colonial understandings of Indian society, with lasting consequences for the anthropological and historical imagining of India.[7]

In the late nineteenth and early twentieth centuries, colonial administrators expended considerable effort in such entextualizations, in the collection and translation of tales, songs, proverbs, and folk dramas. Some of the most prominent men in the colonial government were engaged in the enterprise and gave special attention to proverbial speech; their work in India propelled them, later, into important positions in anthropological organizations in Britain. H. H. Risley, for example, began his career in India as an assistant collector in Midnapore district in 1873, went on to be appointed as census commissioner in 1899, as director of ethnography for India in 1901, and as secretary to the government of India in the Home Department in 1902. After returning to England, he served as president of the Royal Anthropological Institute from 1910 until his death in 1911. William Crooke was magistrate and collector in four districts of the United Provinces of Agra and Oudh. After leaving India, he served as president of the Folklore Society of London and the editor of its journal, and in 1910 as president of the Anthropological Section of the British Association. Richard Carnac Temple served for many years in the Indian Army, in Afghanistan, the Punjab, Burma, and the Andaman Islands; he was cantonment magistrate in the Punjab when he carried out most his ethnographic inquiries there. In 1913 he was president of the Anthropological Section of the British Association, and he wrote at length on the value of training in the "practical science" of anthropology for candidates for the Indian Civil Service (Temple 1914). He also served as editor of *The Indian Antiquary* from 1892 until his death in 1931.

In the writings of Risley, Crooke, Temple, and others like them, ethnographic investigation and the entextualization of Indian speech were made to serve the purposes of colonial administration. By the latter decades of the nineteenth century, the description and classification of castes came to be a key element in colonial administration and colonial discipline, and the collection and translation of folklore played a critical role in the construction of representations of caste as the foundation of Indian society. The speech of the colonized, represented in folklore, was appropriated at critical junctures to foster the illusion that "native opinion" on caste and caste identities was unambiguously congruent with these colonial representations—in other words, to create the illusion of consent. From approximately 1870 to 1920, proverbs were the only form of indigenous speech to be admitted into many administrative documents concerned with caste, and they appear with astonishing frequency.

---

7. On the legacy of colonial assumptions about caste and Indian society in Louis Dumont's work, for example, see Dirks 1987, 1992; Raheja 1988a, 1988b; van der Veer 1993.

Talk about Proverbs and Talk about "Tradition"

Proverbs, like other forms of verbal folklore, are situated communicative practices that particularly positioned speakers draw upon to define, redefine, reinforce, or critique prevailing social formations.[8] Yet, when a proverb is recorded, translated, and published in various kinds of administrative and scholarly texts, the inscription of the proverb fixes it, decontextualizes it, and removes it from the situation in which it had been uttered, and its communicative and social functions in a speech community are thus obscured.

The entextualized proverb lies in fact at the intersection of the colonial agendas of mastering and codifying Indian languages and of characterizing and classifying castes during the late nineteenth century and the beginning of the twentieth.[9] In specialized linguistic works (e.g., William Crooke's *A Rural and Agricultural Glossary for the N.W. Provinces and Oudh* [1888], Edward O'Brien's *Glossary of the Multani Language Compared with Punjabi and Sindhi* [1881], and J. Wilson's *Grammar and Dictionary of Western Panjabi* [1898]), and in caste compendiums (e.g., Denzil C. J. Ibbetson's *Panjab Castes* [1916] and Crooke's *The Tribes and Castes of the North Western Provinces and Oudh* [1896]), so-called caste proverbs are given in great numbers; apart from a few caste origin myths, these proverbs are the only "native" speech that is ordinarily recorded in these compendiums. Proverbs are regularly quoted in such administrative documents as the district settlement reports and the caste handbooks of the Indian Army, and in 1908 Risley devoted an entire chapter and an appendix in *The People of India* to "Caste in Proverbs and Popular Sayings." Colonial administrators throughout northern India routinely issued instructions to their subordinates, both Indian and European, to record caste proverbs in their ethnographic investigations and in the ordinary round of their official duties (e.g., Ibbetson 1882:3, 14; Luard n.d.:64; Risley 1907:18). Thus, while other varieties of "folklore" (folktales, songs, riddles, and so forth) were of course collected, translated, and published in almost staggering numbers in many kinds of publications, proverbs were the only genre systematically associated with the classification and description of castes, and the

---

8. On the situated pragmatic meaning of proverbs and the strategic use of this speech genre, see Abrahams and Babcock 1977; Briggs 1985; Burke 1973; de Certeau 1984:18–21; Gossen 1973; Raheja 1996; Seitel 1977.

9. Cohn (1985) has brilliantly described the general relationship between the "command of language and the language of command" in late-eighteenth- and nineteenth-century colonial India. For a discussion of colonial representations of African languages, see Fabian 1986 and Irvine 1993. Rafael (1993) analyzes the politics of translation in the Philippines under Spanish rule.

only genre that appears in the more immediately pragmatic settlement reports and army manuals.

Proverbs drew the attention of colonial administrators for a variety of reasons. At the most general level, proverbs elicited interest because they were seen as tokens of the mode of thought characteristic of a particular people. R. C. Temple for example frequently expressed the prevailing view that knowledge about the "folklore" of India, including proverbs, benefited Englishmen and facilitated, at least in some small way, their governance of the country.

> The practices and beliefs included under the general head of Folklore make up the daily life of the natives of our great dependency, control their feelings, and underlie many of their actions. We foreigners cannot hope to understand them rightly unless we deeply study them, and it must be remembered that close acquaintance and a right understanding begets sympathy, and sympathy begets good government. (Temple 1886, quoted in Dorson 1968:347)

To know the people of India thus required a knowledge of folklore, because Indians, unlike Englishmen, were "controlled" by ancient and traditional custom.[10]

Colonial writers claimed to see both proverbial speech and the institution of caste as primary examples of the hold that "custom" exerted on the natives of India. C. E. A. W. Oldham set forth the general view that proverbs are incontrovertibly persuasive to any of the "country folk" who heard them:

> From time to time I made some collections of proverbs current in the local vernaculars, because I have always held that you cannot get into real touch with a people in the stage of culture in which these country folk live and toil, you cannot fully appreciate the working of their minds,—and therefore, the reasons for their actions,—unless you know something of their folklore and proverbs. It is not easy to realize to what extent these terse, pithy sayings, conveying maxims of conduct and practice embodying the experience of past generations, regulate their conservative lives. An apt proverb never goes amiss. When perhaps a clear logical argument may fail to be understood or convince, a simple, familiar proverb may carry instant conviction.

---

10. For discussions of the broader political ramifications of this colonial discourse that speaks of Indians as in thrall to "tradition," see, for example, Chatterjee 1989; Inden 1990; and Mani 1984, 1989.

Their proverbs mirror their lives, and when their application is correctly appreciated, are a guide to their character and their actions. (Oldham 1930:320–21)

In speaking thus of the authority of "custom" and the proverbial utterance, and the "conservatism" of the peasantry, authors like Oldham assume the existence of a homogeneous and uncontested moral terrain in India, and they assume that proverbs provide colonial officers with a map of this otherwise inaccessible and unfamiliar territory.

Many authors were of the opinion that the colonial administrator would find it easier to control Indians they encountered in an official capacity if they themselves were able to wield a proverb or two. In *Anthropology as a Practical Science*, for example, R. C. Temple spoke of the administrator's and the magistrate's use of proverbs as "a mighty lever for gaining a hold on the people" and as "a powerful force working for influence" (1914:67). Edward O'Brien, working in Multan, also wrote of the power to be gained in appropriating Indian discourse for colonial purposes; he advised administrators that quoting an apposite proverb "in kutcherry" (i.e., in the courts) increased one's influence and control and might induce a truculent native to leave the courtroom peaceably instead of being "hustled out by the orderlies" (O'Brien 1881:viii–ix).

Temple and O'Brien here evince widespread colonial assumptions about the susceptibility of the Indian peasant to "tradition" and also evince the administrator's desire to gain the interactional upper hand over an Indian interlocutor, the desire to make interactional power in official settings square with institutional power—in this instance, the kutcherry and its legal apparatus. In such cases the rhetorics of persuasion—to which, as we will see, administrators were blind when proverbs were used by Indians—were used quite deliberately by the colonial officer.

Collecting the Texts

While colonial officers who wrote on caste and spoken genres of folklore did not seriously reflect on the methods they adopted to amass folklore collections, their prefatory prose occasionally provides some insight into the actual collection procedures that may by their very nature have reinforced these assumptions about the homogeneity of tradition and Indians' "submission" to it. William Crooke's preface to *The Tribes and Castes of the North-Western Provinces and Oudh* reveals the nature of his procedures at some length, as he describes the reactions of low-caste people to colonial investigation.

> There are some special causes which make an inquiry of this kind a work of more than usual difficulty. There is, first, the reticence of the lower castes which must be overcome before they can be induced to yield the secrets of their tribal organization and religious life. To the average rustic the advent of a stranger, note-book in hand, who interrogates them on such subjects, suggests a possibility that he may have some ulterior objects in connection with a coming Revenue Settlement or Income Tax assessment. It requires no ordinary amount of tact and temper to overcome this barrier; and there is besides among the lower castes an uneasy suspicion that rites and ritual, which in the eyes of the average Brahman are boorish and a survival of a degraded savagery, are a matter to be ashamed of and concealed. . . . In connection with this there is another sort of difficulty in the movement which has sprung up among many castes towards claiming a higher status than is usually accorded to them. The Shastras and other literature of the Brahmans have in recent years been ransacked by a number of castes whose so-called Aryan origin is more than doubtful to support a claim to kindred with races whose descent is universally admitted. (Crooke 1896, I:v–vi)

In this passage, the contradictions in the colonial view of caste hierarchy as "inviolable" rise close to the surface. While continuing to write that the position of the high castes is "universally admitted," Crooke acknowledges that people of lower ranked castes have made claims that call into question the unchallenged supremacy of the Brahman and the other castes of "Aryan" descent. But the language that Crooke uses to describe these assertions represents them as violent and unjustifiable acts: low castes "ransack" the Brahmanic scriptures, and the very claims themselves pose a "difficulty" to the order imposed by colonial description and classification. Thus are their distinctive perspectives discounted and excised from the "tradition" that the colonizers inscribe, as heterogeneity is repeatedly reduced to homogeneity.

Crooke is careful, in the same preface, to acknowledge the assistance rendered to him by various "native gentlemen" who devoted their "scanty leisure" to his investigations. This acknowledgment is followed immediately by his paragraph about the reluctance of the lower castes to yield their "secrets" to him. Well-educated Brahmans and men of other high castes are thus praised for their cooperation, while low-caste people are held up to scrutiny and censure because of their resistance. Thus is the notion of a supposedly "inviolable" hierarchy inscribed and validated in the colonial archive.

Ram Gharib Chaube, a Brahman man who served for many years as

Crooke's assistant, sometimes reported similar difficulties in extracting ethnographic material from people of low castes, without ever reflecting on the politics of the elicitation context. In a notice of a "sacred song of the sweepers" from Saharanpur district, for example, he writes only that the text was "given after great difficulty by their *guru* or headman" (Chaube 1894:112).

The contradiction between affecting a pose of disinterested "research" while simultaneously asserting that a knowledge of folklore is a "powerful force working for influence" and a tool promoting "good government" also becomes apparent in Crooke's preface. Crooke writes that people of low caste may hesitate "to yield the secrets of their tribal organization and religious life" because they may suspect that their interrogators have some "ulterior objects in connection with a coming Revenue Settlement or Income Tax assessment" in view as the inquiry proceeds. Crooke's tone here suggests that he viewed this suspicion as a foolish brand of native superstition that can be overcome with a sufficient degree of "tact." Crooke is here rather disingenuously portraying his investigations in purely academic terms, and thus the suspicion exhibited by the lower castes is an object almost of ridicule, a token of the unschooled simplicity of the "rustic" mind. The knowledge/power equation is here quite blatantly disavowed.

R. C. Temple also provided some idea of his own collection and interpretive procedures. S. W. Fallon had amassed a large collection of Hindi proverbs between 1870 and 1880, while he was compiling his *New Hindustani Dictionary*. After his death, R. C. Temple took over the task of translating the proverbs and editing *A Dictionary of Hindustani Proverbs* that appeared under Fallon's name in 1886. In his preface to this dictionary, Temple tells us that Fallon had worked with about a dozen Indian assistants, two of whom continued on with Temple as he translated Fallon's collection. He writes of the assistance given him by Lala Faqir Chand (who is listed as an assistant editor), Thakur Das, and Chaina Mall, and he appears to be concerned about the fact that different versions of proverbs are given by these men, and different interpretations of the sense of particular proverbs.

> Faqir Chand and Thakur Das live at Delhi and Chaina Mall at Ambala, as a matter of fact these have worked quite independently, so that I have had the benefit of advice given me from perfectly separate sources.... Proverbs and sayings are often capable of more than one application ... and consequently, in different localities they are used in different senses. Such variations are a great trouble to the translator. My assistants ... not infrequently differed as to the appli-

cation of a proverb and in such cases put down each variant signification. (Temple, in Fallon 1886:i, iii)

In his article "North Indian Proverbs," published the year before his edition of Fallon's collection, Temple makes it clear that he sees his task as one of adjudicating these differences and deciding which is the most valid or most authentic interpretation.

> [I]n editing the *Hindustani Proverbs* I am working with two separate sets of *munshis* (literate natives), living apart in Delhi and Ambala, so that I get renderings which I can test one against the other; and it is astonishing to see how often the *munshis* differ among themselves as to the right sense of a proverb. (Temple 1885:17)

Thus, Temple recognizes the instability of the meanings of proverbial utterances as he works with his assistants, yet he insists on the reduction of heterogeneity to homogeneity, as he "tests" one interpretation against the other, to discover a single authoritative meaning that will be inscribed in his published collection.

These considerations, then, form a backdrop to the nineteenth-century interest in the collection of proverbs in India, but do not indicate the specific uses to which talk about proverbs was put in the construction of a colonial discourse about caste and Indian society. The quotation of proverbs in fact contributed very specifically to two aspects of this project: to the articulation of a set of assumptions about caste ideology as a whole, and to the development of a perspective on the characteristics of particular castes. In both instances, the insertion of proverbs into the colonial text was connected explicitly with the surveillance and disciplining of the Indian population, viewed as a congeries of castes.

The Temporal Dislocation of Recalcitrant Talk as an Entextualizing Strategy: Asserting the Inviolability of Caste

Writers who give special attention to proverbs place no less stress on the rigidity and unquestionability of caste ideology than other colonial ethnographers. H. H. Risley was particularly interested in proverbs "which are concerned with the caste system as a whole and illustrate the extent of its influence" (1908:150). In *The People of India,* a book based on his report on caste in the 1901 decennial Census of the Empire, he exhibits specimens of proverbial speech that appear to give credence to his views on the "inviolability" of caste:

The authority of caste is of course uncompromisingly asserted. 'When plates are interchanged,' that is to say, when members of different castes intermarry, is a proverb of the impossible. . . . 'A low caste man is like a musk-rat, if you smell him you remember it.' 'As the ore is like the mine, so child is like its caste.' 'The speech fits the caste as the peg fits the whole;' the idea being that you can tell a high-caste man by his refined language and accent.

We note that Risley does not comment on how these proverbs might be used by, say, high-caste people as they attempt to discipline or censure people of lower castes, or how they might figure in strategies of persuasion and dispute. And Risley does not describe the situation in which such proverbs were elicited, nor does he describe the ends a high-caste Indian assistant might have had in view as he dictated certain stretches of speech and not others to the proverb collector. For Risley, the proverbs tell us only of invariant custom and "the supremacy of the caste sentiment in India" (1908:130).

Risley notices, however, that for every proverb that seems to ratify the ideology of caste, there are several that undermine it. The entextualizing strategy used to cope with the difficulty this poses for colonial perspectives on the supposed inviolability of caste is remarkably ingenious. The preceding passage from Risley's *The People of India* is followed immediately by these observations.

Along with these sayings affirming the supremacy of the modern doctrine of the necessity and inviolability of caste, we find others which seem to recall an earlier order of ideas when castes were not so rigidly separated, when members of different castes could intermarry, and when, within certain limits, caste itself was regarded as a matter of personal merit rather than of mere heredity. 'Love laughs at caste distinctions.' 'Caste springs from actions not from birth.' 'Castes may differ; virtue is everywhere the same.' (Risley 1908:150)

Thus, when Risley was confronted with voices that challenged the authority of caste and the authority of his own pronouncements, he dismissed them as mere "survivals" of an earlier less rigid caste ideology. He refused to consider the possibility of dissent, the possibility that anyone, but perhaps particularly a person of low caste, might deploy a proverbial utterance to subvert or at least comment ironically upon notions of the hierarchical ordering and the separation of castes. Though the idea of "survivals" from earlier evolutionary periods was of course prominent in nineteenth- and early-twentieth-century social theory in general, it is an idea that is readily deployed at certain junctures in colonial writing on caste, because of its usefulness in abolishing the contemporary salience of recalcitrant talk.

Although William Crooke, for example, was a "confirmed survivalist" (Dorson 1968:343), and though his work is obviously informed by evolutionary thinking more generally (Cohn 1968:16–17), he invoked the notion of survivals to cope specifically with just such multiplicity of perspective. The festival of Holi is a well-known ritual involving, among other things, the temporary ritual reversal of caste hierarchies.[11] In an article analyzing the ritual Crooke points out that in the course of the annual rite, low-caste people may heap abuse on high-caste people, sometimes using poetic or proverbial verses. But even these temporally contained verbal and ritual challenges to caste status must be interpreted as survivals from an earlier age.

As Crooke describes these Holi observances, he cannot envision any contemporary relevance of these ritual challenges to the supposedly rigid ideology of caste. Like Risley, he invokes the notion of survivals precisely when a voice of challenge is heard.

> The rites are purely animistic, or pre-animistic; at any rate, they have no connection with orthodox Hinduism. The otiose legends which profess to explain the rites are figments of a later age invented to bring it in line with Brahmanism. (Crooke 1914: 77)

Ram Gharib Chaube used much the same discursive strategy to dislocate recalcitrant speech when he encountered oral traditions that may have challenged caste hierarchy. In 1894, he published a brief notice of a Dusadh song in which a man of this low caste defeats a Brahman man in hand-to-hand combat and marries the Brahman's sister. The song appears to be at odds with the idea of unchallenged Brahman superiority, and so Chaube, like Risley and like his employer William Crooke, resorts to the notion of "survivals" to cope with this disorderly discourse: he remarks at the outset that "This is a very curious legend, which illustrates the condition of things before caste as we see it came into existence" (Chaube 1894:62).

If Crooke's assistant had himself been a Dusadh rather than a Brahman, he might have seen things rather differently and acknowledged the possibility that Dusadh oral traditions, like the traditions of many low castes, might contain critiques of the ideology of hierarchy, and he might perhaps have communicated this to Crooke himself.[12]

---

11. On this point, see Marriott 1966.

12. On oral traditions as sites of low-caste dissent, see Prakash 1991; Trawick 1986, 1988; and Wadley 1994.

I suggest that what is at issue for Risley, Crooke, and Chaube in these discussions of "survivals" is not simply the nineteenth-century preoccupation with evolutionary theory. As they write about caste, the notion of "survivals" is deployed at the precise point at which a crack in this set of colonial representations widens before them. Thus, while the evolutionary concept of a "survival" is generally prominent in nineteenth-century social theory, the particular disinclination of Risley, Crooke, and Chaube to imagine a contemporary India in which voices of dissent could be heard is more immediately significant. When they hear a proverb or a song that seems to challenge caste hierarchies, they can only conjecture that it is an innocent relic of a bygone age; it cannot be, for them, a particularly positioned and knowingly critical commentary on a living social form. Temporally dislocating this disorderly talk is an entextualizing strategy that allows the colonial commentator to preserve his vision of the authority and homogeneity of "tradition" and the peasant's capitulation to it, and his vision of the uniformly consensual character of caste ideology.

The Uses of Proverbial Speech: The Crisis of Revolt, the Extraction of Land Revenue, and Military Discipline

A second aspect of the appropriation of Indian proverbial speech by colonial administrators as they developed a set of perspectives on Indian society concerns not caste as a system or overall ideology but the purported characteristics of particular castes and their status in local hierarchies.

Colonial writers repeatedly insist that the natives of India speak in their true "authentic" voices when they speak in proverbs. On the very first page of the preface to the first edition of *The People of India*, Risley writes that he has included the chapter "Caste in Proverbs and Popular Sayings" in an effort "to give a much-described people the chance of describing themselves in their own direct and homely fashion" (1908:vii). It is important for these writers to stress the notion that proverbs represent the true sentiments of the Indian people; as they annotate these proverbs that appear to them to be about caste, they appropriate them into the imperial project of defining and characterizing castes, making Indian proverbial speech appear to be congruent with their own judgments and their own disciplinary measures. Thus, though they may imagine that they are letting the colonized finally "describe themselves," the proverbs are in fact selected, decontextualized, and interpreted to create descriptions that are very much the contrivances of colonial administrators (perhaps with the help of local elites), contrivances that create the illusion that colonial pronouncements are entirely congruent with Indian speech about particular castes, with a "native point of view."

Such appropriation of proverbial speech is particularly evident in the caste compendiums authored by Crooke and Ibbetson,[13] and in the district-by-district settlement reports that were written to describe patterns of landholding and to facilitate the collection of land revenue. Two major administrative issues come to the fore in these documents: the problems involved in extracting revenue, and the problem of explaining why some people and not others participated in the rebellion of 1857. Proverbial speech is regularly quoted in these texts, as colonial authors address these separate but related crises of colonial rule.

Such quotation of proverbial speech appears with great frequency in discussions of the specific patterns of rebellious activity in 1857 and of the causes of later revolts. Colonial authors were eager to explain differential degrees of rebellion in terms of the inherent characteristics of particular castes.[14] For castes they perceived as having risen up against the British in the rebellion of 1857 or as generally hostile to British rule, the code word is always *turbulent*. In the case of castes like the Gujar and Meo whose members did tend to actively rebel in 1857, nearly every author cites proverbs that appear to evaluate the caste in an unfavorable light and comments on the veracity of the proverbial utterance. It is in descriptions of the "turbulent" castes that we encounter veritable torrents of proverbial quotation. In describing the Meos, for example, Crooke writes:

> In the Mutiny, they and the Gujars . . . were notorious for their turbulence, and seriously impeded the operations against Delhi. The popular idea of them is quite in unison with their history: *Pahle lat, pichhe bat; Dekhi tori Mewat; pahli gali, pichhe bat* are common proverbs, which mean that, in dealing with a Mewati, you had better kick or abuse him before doing business with him; their niggardliness is recorded by *Meo beti jab dee, jab okhali bhar rupaya rakhvale:* 'the Meo will not give his daughter in marriage till he gets a mortar full of silver;' his bloodthirstiness—*Meo ka put barah baras men badla leta hai:* 'the Meo's brat takes his revenge when he is twelve years old;' his toughness—*Meo*

---

13. Neither Crooke nor Ibbetson agreed with Risley's view of the immutability of caste, and Ibbetson repeatedly stressed the fluidity of caste (Pinney 1990:257). Further, Crooke and Ibbetson differed between themselves as to the assessment of the centrality of the Brahman or the kingly Rajput in caste organization, but they both nonetheless produced torrents of proverb quotations to illustrate what they apparently regarded as essentialized caste characteristics. The developing formation of a colonial discourse on caste and the developing imperial uses of essentializations of caste identity seem to have been so powerful that they eclipsed some of these important theoretical differences among them.

14. Pinney has also pointed out that caste was of vital interest to the colonial state because, as in Risley's *The People of India*, it was seen as the basis of opposition in the rebellion of 1857 (1990:258).

> *mara jab janiye, jab tija ho jae:* 'Never be sure that a Meo is dead till you see the third-day funeral ceremony performed.' (Crooke 1896, III:493)

For Crooke, proverbial speech justifies the harsh retaliation meted out to those who participated in the rebellion; even Indians themselves say that you've got to beat or kick a Meo.[15] Similarly, in his description of the Gujar caste, Crooke quotes from the emperor Babar's memoirs, in which he wrote that Gujars "were the wretches that really inflicted the chief hardships and were guilty of the chief oppression in the country."[16] Crooke continues, again producing proverbial speech to validate his assertions:

> They maintained their old reputation in the Mutiny when they perpetrated numerous outrages and seriously impeded the operations of the British Army before Delhi. According to the current wisdom of the countryside he is an undesirable neighbor—'The dog and the cat, the Gujar and the Ranghar, if these four were out of the world a man might sleep with his doors open' [and] 'When the Dom made friends with the Gujar he was robbed of house and home.' (Crooke 1896, III:448)

Denzil C. J. Ibbetson, the superintendent of Census Operations in the Panjab in 1881 and the lieutenant governor of that province from 1905 to 1908, also appropriated proverbial utterances for similar imperial purposes and integrated them almost seamlessly into his accounts of "turbulence" and insurrection. In the portion of the Census Report that was published under the title *Panjab Castes*, Ibbetson describes for example the Kharrals, a Muslim Rajput community, as "notorious for turbulence" (1916:174), and he quotes at length from Captain Elphinstone's description of the caste in his Gugaira Report.

> Their most celebrated leader, Ahmad Khan, who was killed in September 1857 by a detachment under Captain Black, headed the com-

---

15. Mayaram (1991) describes colonial appropriations of the oral narrative of Darya Khan used to construct a history of Meo "criminality." The paper effectively critiques essentializing characterizations of Meos as predatory and turbulent, but does not discuss the larger dimensions of colonial representations of caste and caste ideology.

16. For some contemporary Gujar views of their actions in 1857, see Raheja 1988a:4–5, 255 n.3. Stokes (1978, 1986) and Bhadra (1985) document the extent of Gujar participation in the rebellion, but Stokes also rejects the view that patterns of rebellion can be accounted for in terms of caste. Thus, although Stokes's approach to the rebellion of 1857 is limited because it resolutely avoids attributing any causal force to political ideology on the part of those who rebelled, he does critique, indirectly, the colonial tendency to "naturalize" revolt by accounting for it in terms of the inherent traits of particular castes.

bined tribes . . . in no less than five insurrections, which to a certain extent all proved successful. . . . This success had spread his renown far and wide, and had given him a great influence over the whole of the [area], as was proved by the outbreak of 1857, which appears to have been mainly planned and organized by him. In stature the Kharrals are generally above the average height. (Elphinstone as quoted in Ibbetson 1916:175.)

Note how the description of a Kharral leader's "turbulence" is situated within Ibbetson's caste compendium, on a par as a caste characteristic with purely physical traits, and note also how after reproducing Elphinstone's comments, Ibbetson fully integrated Indian proverbial speech with imperial assessments:

In Lahore they appear to bear a no better character than in Montgomery; and there is a Persian proverb: 'The Dogar, the Bhatti, the Wattu, and the Kharral are all rebellious and ought to be slain.' Sir Lepel Griffin writes of them: 'Through all historic times the Kharrals have been a turbulent, savage, and thievish tribe, ever impatient of control, and delighting in strife and plunder.'

British administrators were not in the habit of admiring Indians who were "impatient of control," and thus Ibbetson's account of the slaying of a Kharral leader by the British troops concludes with a proverb, deployed here to make the reader envision a world in which even Indians themselves believe that a Kharral should be killed, and believe also that revolt itself is merely a manifestation of innate Kharral violence.

Such examples of proverbial speech were assumed to characterize wandering groups or groups whose members may once have engaged in peripatetic or thieving activities. As such they were particularly singled out by the British, as they defined categories of crime and criminality for colonial India, and as they attempted to naturalize revolt and noncompliance by confining it to certain castes supposedly set apart from the main body of the rural populace. As Bayly (1983:220–22, 318) and Freitag (1991) have shown, peripatetic banditry was, in pre-British India, often seen as an acceptable mode of establishing political authority, for Gujars and other similar groups. During the nineteenth century, however, critical changes in colonial and Indian elite perception of these groups had occurred, partly as a result of the expansion of the land revenue–based colonial state. As Freitag points out, "British administrators used as their informants members of the elite stratum of landed society," and thus the legal institutions and cultural valuations that emerged from this encounter "reflected an amalgam of sedentary South Asian values and British priorities" (1991:229). Legislation concerning the so-called criminal castes and criminal tribes was complementary to colonial efforts to extend the range of settled cultivation and of marginalizing the pastoral nomads and other inhabitants who did not figure in the plans of the Revenue Department (Agnihotri 1996:43). Thus these proverbs about Gujars, Meos, Kharrals, and the like very probably gained heightened significance as a result of the transformation of rural society in the nineteenth century and reflect the particular position of an agrarian elite struggling to safeguard its own political authority. And it is also possible, in some parts of northern India, that members of the landed elite told such proverbs to administrators as a means of deflecting the responsibility for plundering that they themselves coerced some members of the so-called criminal castes to carry out, providing protection and support in exchange for a large share of the booty (Shakespear 1820; Nigam 1990b). Informants' elite identities were no doubt decisive, as British administrators questioned them about rural society and collected proverbs as specimens of the "ideas of the common people." Yet this positionality is thoroughly erased, as the speech of a particularly situated set of informants was entextualized as invariant "custom" and as native "wisdom."

The relation between proverbs and the disciplinary thrust of the colonial government against the "turbulent" castes is nowhere more explicitly set forth than in C. E. A. W. Oldham's essay "The Proverbs of the People in a District (Shahabad) of Northern India," originally read as an address before the Folklore Society in London. He remarks at the outset that his observations are based on materials gathered during twenty years of administrative service in the district of Shahabad in Bihar. He describes the geography of the district in two sentences and then refers immediately to the "warlike" races of the region: "It is part of ancient Karusadesa, the 'country of the Karusas,' referred to in the old Sanskrit texts as a very warlike race" (1930:322). He writes at some length of the "martial races" of the Bhojpuri region, and of the Bhojpuri Ahir caste in particular.

> [T]he Bhojpuri Ahirs (the cowherd caste) are specially noted for their daring and skill as thieves and burglars, the more law-abiding people in other parts regarding them with terror.... During widespread disturbances in 1917, which broke out without previous warning in this district, and threatened to involve the neighbouring districts in grave communal strife, I had to call in a large force of military and armed police (about a thousand in all) to quell promptly and effectively the lawlessness abroad.

Several proverbial sayings might be cited as exemplifying these characteristics. For instance, there are some very popular verses in praise of their favourite weapon, commonly called the 'Song of the *lathi*,' telling of its uses in crossing a stream or ditch, in dealing with enemies human or canine, and how necessary it is to carry one, even if you have a sword hanging by your side.... Then we have a proverb which means 'If hit, hit back, and don't stop to consider whether you are committing a sin or virtue.' And there is a delightfully terse and suggestive saying, specially quoted of the Bhojpuri, as representing his attitude toward others. The words mean simply 'Is the dish thine or mine?' A Bhojpuri is supposed to ask this question. If the person addressed answers, 'Mine,' a blow of the *lathi* at once settles the proprietorship.... 'The clenched fist for an enemy'; 'the powerful man's *lathi* hits the very middle of the forehead'; and so on. So much for the mere joy of fighting. (Oldham 1930:323–24)

The naturalization of rebellion here could not be more direct. In this passage Oldham characterizes the 1917 events in Shahabad only as "disturbances" that might lead to "communal strife." Violence had in fact erupted in Shahabad in 1917 over the issue of "Cow-Protection," but to argue as Oldham implicitly does here, that this was simply a manifestation of age-old Hindu-Muslim conflict exacerbated by the violent nature of the Ahirs, is to erase the specifically political meanings of the events, just as Risley's notion of "survivals" robs subversive proverbs of their political meanings as tokens of resistance. Ahir participation in the riots was, as Gyan Pandey argues (1983), a response to severe dislocation of social and economic relations brought about under colonialism, and a move on the part of this lower ranked caste to assert a Hindu orthodoxy that would secure for them a higher status vis-à-vis the upper-caste *zamindari* communities, in the wake of Risley's attempt to list castes in an unambiguous "order of precedence" in the 1901 census. Oldham does not tell the reader that these disturbances in Shahabad had followed Gandhi's mobilization of peasants in the neighboring district of Champaran against European indigo planters, that Shahabad had for some time been the scene of organized peasant struggle against the colonial government, *zamindar*s, and moneylenders (Nath 1980:228; Roy Choudhury 1966:86), and that the issue of "Cow-Protection" had for some time been intertwined with rumors about the end of British rule (Sarkar 1983:157).

In Oldham's text these "disturbances" that are quelled by a thousand armed military policemen are instead explained by quoting or paraphrasing proverbial speech that purportedly demonstrates the inherent nature of the Ahirs. Since Oldham sees proverbs used by the people of India as exemplifying the "working of their minds" (1930:320), as a "guide to their character and their actions" (321), as "regulat[ing] their conservative lives" (320), and as accurate portrayals of the traits, habits, vices, and propensities of particular castes (335), his citing of these proverbs about the *lathi*s of the Ahirs thus establishes to his satisfaction that the Ahirs are by nature prone to violence. As he recounts these particular proverbs in connection with the mention of his prompt deployment of the police and the military, the reader is thus expected to understand that the exercise of the armed might of the colonial government was necessitated by the violent nature of the Ahirs as a caste, and not by their response to the burdens imposed by the revenue demands of the landowning *zamindar*s and by the colonial government. The reader is also expected to discern that "the country folk" themselves feel exactly the same way about the Ahirs, given that proverbs illustrate the "working of their minds" (320–21). The essentialization of Ahir character accomplished through this embedding of proverbs in the colonial text serves both to naturalize revolt and to legitimate in Oldham's eyes the deployment of the military police as a disciplinary measure. But the proverbs are used not only to naturalize revolt; their deployment in the text, and the erasure of their situated meanings, serves more importantly in the construction of an illusory congruence between "native opinion" and colonial pronouncement.

Proverbs figured conspicuously in discussions of land revenue as well. The district-by-district land settlement reports—which focus on patterns of landholding and the social characteristics of the district expected to affect revenue collection—often contain lengthy quotations of proverbs that allegedly provide an understanding of the character of specific landholding castes and their inclination or disinclination to meet land revenue demands.

The 1880 *Report on the Revised Land Revenue Settlement of the Rohtak District of the Hissar Division in the Punjab* by W. E. Purser and H. C. Fanshawe provides examples of the entextualizing strategies through which a text about caste and compliance with revenue demands was constructed. For castes that were understood to have rebelled in 1857 and also perceived to fail chronically to meet their revenue demands, proverbs again were used to illustrate the justice of British reprisals. Muslim Rajputs, for example, were universally decried in colonial writing, as bearing "the worst possible reputation for turbulence and cattle-stealing," and for giving the British "much trouble in the mutiny" (Ibbetson 1916). Purser and Fanshawe wrote at length of the Muslim Rajputs, the Ranghars.

> The conduct of this tribe [the Ranghars] in the Mutiny . . . bears the worst possible character among the people of the countryside. . . . Their turbulence and lawlessness is [*sic*] commemorated in the fol-

lowing well-known lines—'Though Kanhaur and Niganah are but 35 kos from Delhi, the people eat themselves what they sow, and pay not a grain (of revenue) to anyone.' (1880:556)

In the section of the Rohtak Settlement Report entitled "Social and Administrative," Purser and Fanshawe list the castes of the district and comment on their supposed habits, level of industry in agriculture, conduct in the 1857 rebellion, and cooperation with revenue collection. The deployment of proverbs to construct a discourse on revenue collection is particularly obvious in their text. The castes of the district are divided into two groups: the agriculturalists and the "non-agricultural portions of the population." The former section contains numerous proverbs, utilized especially to comment on the ease or difficulty attendant on the collection of land revenue; but the descriptions in the latter section are far briefer and contain no proverbs at all; the quotation and annotation of proverbial speech here would apparently have served no useful administrative purpose for Purser and Fanshawe.

A similar tendency to quote proverbial speech only in administratively useful characterizations is evident in Ibbetson's *Report on the Settlement of the Panipat Tahsil and Karnal Parganah of the Karnal District, 1872–1880*. In this report, Ibbetson provides no examples of proverbial speech about the Rajputs, whom he praises as "fine, brave men" whose leaders have preserved a commendable degree of "feudal" authority. But for Gujars, who are said to practice cultivation "of the most slovenly description," the reader again encounters a torrential flow of proverbial quotation, ending with *jitte dekhen Gujar, itte deyie mar*, "wherever you see a Gujar, hit him" (1883:83–84). Similarly, Brahmans are described as "vile cultivators, being lazy to a degree; and they carry the grasping and overbearing habits of their caste into their relations as land owners, so that wherever Brahmans hold land, disputes may be expected. The local proverb goes *Brahman se bura bagar se kal*, 'As famine from a desert, so comes evil from a Brahman'" (86–87).[17]

The appropriation of proverbial speech by Crooke, Ibbetson, Oldham, and others occurred principally, as we have seen, in accounts of various castes and their supposed predispositions to engage in revolt or resistance to revenue demands. Such rhetorical moves appeared to serve the

---

17. Unlike many other colonial administrators, Ibbetson saw caste as centered on Rajput political power rather than Brahmanic supremacy, and he viewed Brahmans as "quarrelsome, and overbearing," obtaining their subsistence "without toil" and by preying upon upstanding revenue-paying Punjabi husbandmen like the Jat. His choice of proverbial quotation is thus different from that of men like Crooke who never quote proverbs that cast Brahmans in an unfavorable light.

The Illusion of Consent

project of naturalizing these challenges to the notion that India was governed with the consent of the colonized. In imperial ethnographic accounts, people were seen as rebelling against British rule not for political or ideological reasons, but because they were by nature predisposed to "turbulence."

Military recruitment is a third area in which proverbs were used in the surveillance and disciplining of castes. Before 1857, military units in India were organized into broadly defined regional units. After 1857, however, a major shift occurred, and Indians were recruited into far more homogeneous and narrowly caste-defined units of the Indian Army, in which loyalty to the military enterprise could be putatively secured on the basis of these "primordial" ties and in which use could be made of the traits held to be characteristic of particular castes, especially the so-called martial races. This overall shift in military policy thus parallels the shift in colonial writing on caste and proverbs that occurred at the same time in the mid–nineteenth century.

A. H. Bingley was responsible for writing a series of caste handbooks for the Indian Army published in 1918 by the Superintendent of Government Printing. In *Caste Handbook for the Indian Army: Rajputs*, he wrote that "Fighting capacity depends not only on race but also on hereditary instinct and social status, therefore it is essential that every effort should be made to obtain the very best men of that class which a regiment may enlist" (Bingley 1918:163). This was the purpose for which the caste handbooks were composed.

In both the Rajput and Brahman handbooks, questions to be put to the recruit are listed as inquiries designed to ascertain if the man is really of the caste to which he claims membership. A man who claims to be a Brahman should be asked about his village and his *gotra* (clan) and his *kul* (lineage). Bingley and Nicholls write that "If the above questions are satisfactorily answered according to Brahmanical custom and the 'Bansa-Bali,' a book which gives detailed information about 'Kuls' and 'Gotras,' then his 'Kul' must be one in the list under this heading in the 'Bansa-Bali.'" More detailed instructions follow as to the conduct of this investigation.

> If the recruit states both his 'Kul' and his 'Gotra' correctly ... then in the case of a recruit, who is a Bala-ke-Sukul of the Bharaddwaj 'Gotra,' his sister, daughters, etc., must have been married into families which do not rank below his own 'Kul' ... but, if on enquiry it be found that his daughters are married into families lower than his own, he should not be considered a true Brahman ... The 'Bansa-Bali' should be the guide and this book should be in the hands of all British officers dealing with Brahmans. (Bingley and Nicholls 1918:50–51)

It thus appears that ascertaining caste identity was of the utmost importance to local Indian Army recruiters in the early years of the twentieth century, precisely because of essentialized understandings of the characteristics of particular castes. And in the caste handbooks, these characteristics are at least partly described through the deployment of proverb quotations or general allusions to the "proverbial" habits of specific castes. Of Brahmans, Bingley and Nicholls write for example that their "personal cleanliness is proverbial" (1918:43) and that Bhuinhar Brahmans are too "pugnacious" for military service.

> Though often admirable soldiers individually, Bhuinhars are generally too quarrelsome and fond of intrigue to render their enlistment desirable. Their pugnacious habits are pithily described in the following well-known couplet . . . 'Babhans, dogs, and elephants, are all three ready combatants.' The term Babhan is rather contemptuously applied to Bhuinhars by other classes, and means a *sham* Brahman. (17)

The purposes of Bingley's entextualizations of proverbial speech in these military handbooks thus go beyond the aims of Crooke, Ibbetson, and others writing on issues of revolt and revenue. In the latter case, quotations of proverbial speech function primarily to legitimate the disciplinary action taken by the colonial government against the so-called turbulent castes. In the army manuals, however, the surveillance of those claiming to be of a particular caste is a major focus. Army recruiters are asked not only to judge a possible recruit on the basis of an essentialized caste identity but also to weigh the claim of membership itself and decide whether a man is or is not an authentic Brahman or an authentic Rajput, according to criteria established partly through the entextualized proverbial speech.

The Erasure of Indigenous Commentary as an Entextualizing Strategy: Transformations in Colonial Discourse on Caste and Proverbial Speech, 1820–1918

An understanding of the ways in which the erasure of indigenous contextualization and commentary served colonial purposes requires an understanding of earlier entextualizing practices in which such commentaries were not erased. Such earlier practices can be discerned in work on language carried out by authors in the employ of the East India Company before 1857.

The College of Fort William was founded in Calcutta in 1800 to teach Indian languages and law to functionaries of the East India Company, in the wake of dissatisfaction with the reliance on Indian intermediaries (Cohn 1987:521–25). Scholars at the college began very early on to collect and publish Indian proverbs. In 1820, for example, John Borthwick Gilchrist published his *Hindee-Roman Orthoepigraphical Ultimatum,* a volume intended for use in the teaching of Hindi at the college, where Gilchrist himself taught. The *Ultimatum* is subtitled "a systematic, discriminative view of the oriental and occidental visible sounds, on their fixed and practical principles for speedily acquiring the most accurate pronunciation of many oriental languages; exemplified in one hundred popular anecdotes, tales, jests, maxims, and proverbs of the hindoostanee story teller."

The one hundred specimens of Indian speech that Gilchrist provides in this volume are untranslated. The selections are first set forth according to Gilchrist's system of transliteration, then in the Devanagari, and finally in the Arabic script, as exercises to be used in the mastery of the language. Unlike most other texts of the period, Gilchrist's *Ultimatum* does not contain imaginary dialogues between the sahib and the Indian servant or sepoy that are to be mastered by the student. The selections in the *Utimatum* appear rather to be stories that Gilchrist collected during his work and travels in India. Especially interesting are the frequency with which proverbs—generally labeled here as *masal* ("proverb," "saying")[18]—occur in Gilchrist's texts, the sorts of proverbs that appear, and the manner in which they are reported.

In the examples of native speech that Gilchrist provides, at least thirty-one proverbs appear. However, there are in this collection no proverbs that purport to describe the characteristics of specific castes, though caste names appear in several of the texts. And in each case the proverb appears at the conclusion of a narrative that provides a context in which the proverb might be deployed as a rhetoric of persuasion or situated moral commentary by a native speaker. The following is a typical narrative that I have translated from Gilchrist's text.

> A cowherd [*ahir*] was walking along with his water-buffalo. In a field outside the city, a bastard landlord [*zamindar haramzada*] was standing with a cudgel in his hand. Seeing that the cowherd was all alone, he intimidated him with the cudgel, seized the water-buffalo, and set off on the road to his house. He had only gone a little way when someone asked him: 'Where have you gotten that water-buffalo that a traveler was taking along?' The landlord replied: 'Haven't you

---

18. This is the only colonial text that I can recall in which a Hindi term is given to characterize a proverbial genre.

heard the proverb 'Whoever has the cudgel [*lathi*] has the water-buffalo'?' (Gilchrist 1820:46–47, from Devanagari text section)

We could, if we wished only to quarrel with Oldham's particular characterization of Ahirs, note that in this proverb-narrative the Ahir is portrayed as a victim of violence rather than a perpetrator.[19] But clearly the story and the proverb are not about castes, but about propensities and situations that are potentially attributable to people of many different social categories; the Ahir's caste identity appears not to be particularly relevant. More significantly, however, the proverb-narrative provides a striking instance of the local metapragmatic understanding of proverbs as instruments of coercive power. In its recognition of the positioned use of this proverb, the contextualizing narrative also enables us to discern here an ironic recognition of the contestability of the proverb as well. Although Gilchrist does not attempt an explication of this awareness of the pragmatic functioning of proverbs, neither does he excise it from his text, as later writers would do.

In any case, the social world that emerges in Gilchrist's narratives is not inhabited primarily by people characterized by caste; the actors populating the stories are far more frequently "old men" (*buddha*), "servants" (*gulam*), "kings" (*raja*), "good men" (*bhala admi*), "thieves" (*chor*), "big men" (*bare admi*) "poor starvelings" (*garib bhukha*), "soldiers" (*sipahi*), "landlords" (*zamindar*), or simply "persons" (*shakhs*). And in these narratives, the situated pragmatic function of proverbs is made far clearer than in any of the colonial compilations of the late nineteenth and early twentieth centuries, in which proverbs are interpreted only in terms of their presumed referential functions, as abstract and uncontextualized *descriptions* of the inherent characteristics of particular castes. In Gilchrist's text, we can see that this proverb about the *lathi* has little to do with caste, and everything to do with power and the ironically critical apperception of it.

This proverb-narrative of the *lathi* appears in Monier Williams's 1858 language text as well, in almost identical form (1858:140), again without translation. In later administrative documents and language and folklore compilations, however, such narratives are erased. For example, this same proverb, *jiski lathi uski bhains*, translated as "Who has the cudgel has the buffalo," appears without the embedding narrative and without any men-

---

19. Many of Gilchrist's stories, like this one, tend to be critical of wealthy landlords and rich merchants, and tend to represent the point of view of those who suffer from their actions. Gilchrist provides little information on his methods of collecting the stories, or the tellers of the tales, although he did frequently don Indian garb and wander through the countryside collecting linguistic materials (Lelyveld 1993:194–96).

tion of the Ahir as victim in Fallon's proverb compilation (1886:119). R. C. Temple, the editor and translator of Fallon's text, notes that the proverb illustrates the idea that "might is right" and the "honoured plan" that "he should take who has the power and he should keep who can." Thus, the critique that is evident in the contextualizing story and the reference to the "landlord bastard" drops out in Temple's later rendering, and the proverb, rather than the critique, comes to be viewed as an example of the "thoughts and mode of life" of the "natives of India" (Temple, in Fallon 1886:ii). Temple occasionally provides brief vestiges of proverb-narratives, but they are seldom given in connection with proverbs mentioning castes, and these proverb-narratives never find their way into administrative documents like settlement reports and the caste compendiums that have as their object the essentialization of caste identities. The narratives undermine the notion that the primary function of such proverbs is the referential one of defining caste identities. Their erasure from colonial accounts thus permits the reader to imagine that proverbs provide a means of knowing and mastering castes.

In 1824, the Hindoostanee Press in Calcutta published Captain Thomas Roebuck's *A Collection of Proverbs and Proverbial Phrases in the Persian and Hindoostanee Languages.* The original plan for the book, laid out by William Hunter, the Secretary to the Council of the College of Fort William, had been to include proverbs in Arabic, Sanskrit, and Punjabi, as well as Persian and Hindustani. Hunter was transferred to Java, however, and he delegated the work to Roebuck, who had learned Hindi from Gilchrist and perhaps acquired an interest in proverbs from him. The book itself, an enormous publication amounting to 803 pages, was edited by H. H. Wilson, as Roebuck died in 1819 before the work could be completed. The task of translating the 397 page section of Hindi proverbs also fell to Wilson.

It is at first glance surprising that the late-nineteenth- and early-twentieth-century colonial documents—otherwise replete with citations of proverbial speech from earlier printed works—*never* mention Roebuck's massive proverb compilation. Gilchrist's text is similarly excised from colonial memory. These omissions are particularly significant because in many of the land settlement reports, glossaries, census reports, and tribes and castes compendiums I have surveyed here, the authors detail long lists of earlier publications that they relied upon in preparing their own; they often quote from earlier administrative documents and invoke the authority of their predecessors' reports. And despite the obsessiveness of proverb collection exhibited by later colonial administrators like Crooke who, asserting that the "published materials are very scanty," claimed to have consulted every available source from the Sanskrit dictionary of Sir Monier Williams to the "native collections of proverbs" published in the vernacular press (1888:iv–v), the books that represented the labor of four important scholars of Fort William College never figure in this archaeology of colonial knowledge. Why did the *Collection,* like the proverb stories in Gilchrist's *Ultimatum,* fall into such total oblivion?[20]

It is not the case that H. H. Wilson was uninterested in the administrative uses of linguistic surveillance. In the 1840s he argued that a comprehensive Imperial Glossary of terms from vernacular languages was of the highest importance to the efficient administration of the East India Company's affairs. Moreover, when he delegated the collection of such terms to Indians employed by the Company, he complained when they did not discern the administrative purposes of such work: "Several of the native officers . . . misapprehended the object of the collection, and admitted a copious collection of words which had no peculiarly official significance" (Wilson 1855:iii).[21]

Why then did later colonial officers see fit to ignore Wilson's translation of Roebuck's compilation, when Wilson himself was so aware of the utility of linguistic compilations and had labored to make his work serve colonial purposes? I suggest that between 1824 and the last few decades of the nineteenth century, colonial discursive practices had shifted dramatically; a process of reifying and essentializing caste identities was under way in imperial documents. In 1824, and, indeed, until the 1855 *Glossary of Judicial and Revenue Terms and of Useful Words Occurring in Official Documents Relating to the Government of British India* was published, a mastery of language was linked in Wilson's mind to the mastery of India. In the last three decades of the century, however, this mastery of India was coupled decisively, by later writers, to the mastery of castes as well, and earlier colonial discourses that did not see caste identities as fundamental in Indian society were marginalized and forgotten. Wilson's translations, like Gilchrist's contextualizing narratives, would have undermined the later colonial project by suggesting that the so-called caste proverbs do not in fact provide capsule descriptions of caste character that could be used to comprehensively classify and survey the Indian population. Consequently, in 1905, James Cassidy could speak only of "an interesting old book" unearthed in the India Office Library, an arcane collection useful, in the late colonialism of the twentieth century, only perhaps as an "original and delightful nursery book were the skill of the artist requisitioned to set them forth" (Cassidy 1905:445). What rhetorical and administrative shift

---

20. The only reference to the *Collection* that I have come across is in a five-page description published in the *Westminster Review* by James Cassidy in 1905.

21. Amin (1989:xxiii) has also taken notice of Wilson's complaint.

rendered Wilson's translations useless and invisible to men like Crooke and Temple, and fit only to be served up in a picture book for English children?[22]

Wilson's translations and explications of what would later come to be viewed as "caste proverbs" are dramatically different from those of colonial authors who wrote so extensively of these proverbs sixty to eighty years later, although the collection he is translating contains some of the same proverbs that appear in these later texts.

Roebuck's text does not provide the proverb stories that Gilchrist's *Ultimatum* includes, but in nearly every case Wilson provided an explication of the actual use of proverbs that makes it clear that he did not regard a proverb that mentions a caste as necessarily descriptive of the character and propensities of people of that caste. We can compare Wilson's treatment of these proverbs with that of administrators like Crooke and Oldham who were interested in just such essentializing characterizations or assertions about the unanimity of opinion about a particular caste group.

Wilson, for example, translated one Hindi proverb as follows: "The Domnee (a female singer) has let the time slip, and sings out of tune" (Roebuck 1824:18). He then adds the note "spoken of one who commits blunders from agitation of mind." We are thus not made to understand that such blunders typify women of the Dom caste; rather, the pragmatic utilization of the statement as a comment on "one who commits blunders" is what is highlighted in the 1824 text. Wilson also translates another proverb that mentions a Domnee: "The Domnee (or songstress) having become familiar, has brought her whole family" (Roebuck 1824:174), and he notes that the proverb is "applied to one, who having been encouraged to expect patronage and protection, presumes to recommend several others. (Eng.) Give him an inch and he'll take an ell" (Roebuck 1824:174).

The change in colonial uses of indigenous speech in the project of constructing a discourse on caste becomes very clear if we compare Wilson's explication of the Domnee proverb with Crooke's treatment of it in his 1896 *Tribes and Castes of the North-Western Provinces and Oudh*, in the entry for "Mirasi, Dom Mirasi, Dum Mirasi." Crooke introduces his discussion of several proverbs by commenting that "The current proverbs illustrate the unfavourable view of the Dom Mirasi." He gives as one example the following: "Encourage the singing woman and she will come

---

22. Apart from the earlier colonial proverb collections of Roebuck and Gilchrist, there were also contemporary Indian vernacular proverb collections that could have provided models for the analysis of proverbial speech as strategic and purposive. See, for example, the nineteenth-century Urdu manuscript described as "A collection of proverbs, with illustrative tales, compiled by Faiz Ali Khan, Nawab of Jhajhar," which contains 2,979 proverbs as well as accompanying narratives that specify the application of proverbs in everyday talk (IOL Mss. Or. 3224-26).

with all her brats" (Crooke 1896, III:497). The proverb that was seen in 1824 as being a commentary on presumption as a general trait has now become a negative assessment of a Dom.

We can see in one colonial manuscript collection the processes of sifting and classification through which administrators attempted to read such proverbs as "native opinion" about supposedly fixed caste characteristics, and we can see something of the arbitrariness of their judgments, and the hesitancy with which they were made. Charles Eckford Luard served in the late nineteenth and early twentieth centuries as the Superintendent of the Gazetteer in the Central Provinces. In that capacity, he asked the Indian Gazetteer officers serving beneath him to provide him with "proverbs regarding castes, with their literal translation in English."[23] Luard seemed to have some trouble in deciding whether or not such proverbs could be read as supplying information about particular castes or not. In the pages of the 1897 report from Narsingarh State, for example, in an apparent effort to create order when faced with some speech that seems to defy such classification, Luard has used red and blue pencils and marked the proverbs with the notation "caste" or "not caste," depending upon his assessment of whether the proverbs in question actually "relate to caste" or not (Luard n.d.:149). Only nineteen of the one hundred and seven proverbs are marked "not caste." But because a number of Luard's translations are identical to those found in Roebuck's collection, I suspect that he had a copy of that earlier collection with him as he worked. And I suspect that it gave him pause, as he sat with his pencils in hand; the markings seem to be arbitrary, and it would appear that Luard had some difficulty in deciding on whether to write in blue or in red, and whether the proverbs could be useful to the colonial project of classifying and characterizing castes. The comments that some of his Indian assistants supplied, though they appear infrequently in the manuscripts, may have had the same effect; Durga Sahai, for example, had commented, like Wilson had before him, on a proverb that may seem at first glance to cast the Potters in an unfavorable light: "this may be generally applicable in the case of any obstinate person." Luard published a number of reports on material gathered in his Gazetteer operations, particularly in the *Indian Antiquary*, but I have been unable to locate a published report that includes such proverbs, or the typifying classificatory schemes in which they were so often entextualized. Perhaps he had become aware somehow of the inadequacies of colonial categorizations and the inevitable incommensurability between the complex knowledge that his Indian officers had nec-

---

23. This task is referred to in letters and reports sent to Luard by officers working in the princely states of Bhopal, Narsingarh, Rutlam, Khilchipur, Maihar, and Sitamau.

essarily to omit from the accounts they supplied to him and his own hesitant markings in blue and in red. Perhaps he had, like his friend E. M. Forster (Forster 1965:13), become at least dimly aware of the limits of imperial ethnographic classification (Forster 1952; Suleri 1992:135).

Conclusion

From Gilchrist's work through Bingley's caste handbooks for the Indian Army, we are able to trace a transformation in colonial representations of caste, and a transformation in the entextualization of proverbial speech. Beginning only in the second half of the nineteenth century, proverbs were repeatedly wrenched from the social practices in which they figured and interpreted not as situated commentaries but as abstract and literal renderings of caste proclivities. These renderings were then quoted or paraphrased and deployed in colonial writing, principally in connection with the "naturalization" of revolt and of revenue noncompliance, and also as guides to military discipline. The discursive reifications of caste, intimately tied at their genesis to the politics of colonial rule, became later the foundation of much anthropological and historical writing on Indian society.

The discursive practices through which proverbial speech was embedded in colonial texts of the late nineteenth century rendered invisible two moments of entextualization. First, officials occlude their own links to proverbial speech by not recognizing the fact that proverbs may be told to them selectively by "informants" (especially members of local elites) who thus position themselves in relation to members of other local groups as they present themselves to the colonial state. Second, by speaking of proverbs as indexes of consensus and of invariant "custom," they conceal the everyday rhetorical and discursive strategies in which proverbs, by their very nature, figure as situated communicative practices, as modes of persuasion and contestation rather than agreement. We see, at least obliquely, evidence of such discursive contexts and of indigenous commentary on them in colonial texts written prior to 1860; but as the crises of colonialism deepened and administrative agendas changed, these contexts and commentaries were erased.

Richard Saumarez Smith has documented a concurrent shift in colonial representations of north Indian society. He shows that before 1853, in both academic discourse and colonial records, Indian society had been spoken about as a federation of thousands of village "republics," with little significant internal differentiation. In the latter decades of the nineteenth century, however, Indian society came increasingly to be viewed in terms of a congeries of castes. In the 1853 land settlement in the Ludhiana

District, for example, proprietors of land, as well as those persons liable for forced labor (*begar*), were specified only in terms of those statuses, but in the 1882 revision, specification was by caste alone (Smith 1985:165–66). Nicholas Dirks has moreover discerned a similar shift in colonial documentation from south India (1992:63–68, 1993). These changes occurred at the same time that proverbs came to be decontextualized and inserted into colonial writing on caste.

As a discourse about caste came to predominate in colonial representations of Indian society there was, I suggest, a corresponding shift in the way that proverbial speech figured in imperial documents; strategies of entextualization were altered, and a form of textual ventriloquism (Haraway 1992; Stewart 1994) became essential to the colonial project in the last three decades of the nineteenth century, as a means of creating the illusion of consensus and consent. It was for this reason that Wilson's translations of Roebuck's proverbs, as well as Gilchrist's proverb-narratives, came to be ignored by all later administrators and folklore collectors. As castes became reified and objectified, and as caste itself became the organizing trope for late-nineteenth- and early-twentieth-century colonial policy and associated writing about Indian society, the earlier translations and contextualizations made no epistemic or administrative sense.

REFERENCES

Abrahams, Roger D., and Barbara A. Babcock. 1977. "The Literary Use of Proverbs." *Journal of American Folklore* 98:85–94.

Agnihotri, Indu. 1996. "Ecology, Land Use and Colonisation: The Canal Colonies of the Punjab." *Indian Economic and Social History Review* 33 (1): 37–58.

Amin, Shahid. 1989. "Introduction." In W. Crooke, *A Glossary of North Indian Peasant Life*, xviii–xlii. Delhi: Oxford University Press.

Bauman, Richard. 1993. "The Nationalization and Internationalization of Folklore: The Case of Schoolcraft's 'Gitshee Gauzinee.'" *Western Folklore* 52:247–69.

Bauman, Richard, and Charles L. Briggs. 1990. "Poetics and Performance as Critical Perspectives on Language and Social Life." *Annual Review of Anthropology* 19:59–88.

Bayly, C. A. 1983. *Rulers, Townsmen and Bazaars: North Indian Society in the Age of British Expansion, 1770–1870*. Cambridge: Cambridge University Press.

Bhadra, Gautam. 1985. "Four Rebels of Eighteen-Fifty-Seven." *Subaltern Studies IV: Writings on South Asian History and Society*, ed. Ranajit Guha, 229–75. Delhi: Oxford University Press.

Bingley, A. H. 1918. *Caste Handbooks for the Indian Army: Rajputs*. Calcutta: Superintendent of Government Printing.

Bingley, A. H., and A. Nicholls. 1918. *Caste Handbooks for the Indian Army: Brahmans*. Calcutta: Superintendent of Government Printing.

Briggs, Charles. 1985. "The Pragmatics of Proverb Performance in New Mexican Spanish." *American Anthropologist* 87:793–810.

———. 1993. "Metadiscursive Practices and Scholarly Authority in Folkloristics." *Journal of American Folklore* 106:387–434.

Burke, Kenneth. 1973. *A Philosophy of Literary Form*. Berkeley: University of California Press.

Cassidy, James. 1905. "A Chapter on Indian Proverbs." *Westminster Review* 164:445–49.

Chatterjee, Partha. 1989. "Colonialism, Nationalism, and Colonialized Women: The Contest in India." *American Ethnologist* 16:622–33.

Chaube, Ram Gharib. 1894. "Pachara Song—Chuhar Mal the Dusadh Hero Marrying a Brahman Girl." *North Indian Notes and Queries* 4:62–63.

Cohn, Bernard S. 1968. "Notes on the Study of Indian Society and Culture." In *Structure and Change in Indian Society*, ed. Milton Singer and B. S. Cohn, 3–28. Chicago: Aldine.

———. 1984. "The Census, Social Structure and Objectification in South Asia." *Folk* 26:25–49.

———. 1985. "The Command of Language and the Language of Command." *Subaltern Studies IV: Writings on South Asian History and Society*, ed. Ranajit Guha, 276–329. Delhi: Oxford University Press.

———. 1987. "The Recruitment and Training of British Civil Servants in India." In *An Anthropologist among the Historians and other Essays*, B. S. Cohn, ed., 500–53. Delhi: Oxford University Press.

Crooke, William. 1888. *A Rural and Agricultural Glossary for the N.-W. Provinces and Oudh*. Calcutta: Superintendent of Government Printing.

———. 1896. *The Tribes and Castes of the North Western Provinces and Oudh*. Calcutta: Superintendent of Government Printing.

———. 1911. "Songs of the Mutiny." *Indian Antiquary* 40:123–24, 165–69.

———. 1914. "The Holi: A Vernal Festival of the Hindus." *Folk-Lore* 25:55–83.

———. 1979. *A Glossary of North Indian Peasant Life*. Shahid Amin, ed. Delhi: Oxford University Press.

De Certeau, Michel. 1984. *The Practice of Everyday Life*. Berkeley: University of California Press.

Dirks, Nicholas B. 1987. *The Hollow Crown: Ethnohistory of an Indian Kingdom*. Cambridge: Cambridge University Press.

———. 1992. "Castes of Mind." *Representations* 37:56–78.

———. 1993. "Colonial Histories and Native Informants: Biography of an Archive." In *Orientalism and the Postcolonial Predicament: Perspectives on South Asia*, Carol A. Breckenridge and Peter van der Veer, eds., 279–313. Philadelphia: University of Pennsylvania Press.

Dorson, Richard M. 1968. *The British Folklorists: A History*. Chicago: University of Chicago Press.

Fabian, Johannes. 1986. *Language and Colonial Power*. Berkeley: University of California Press.

Fallon, S. W. 1886. *A Dictionary of Hindustani Proverbs*. R. C. Temple, ed. Banaras: Medical Hall Press.

Forster, E. M. 1952 [1924]. *A Passage to India*. New York: Harcourt, Brace and World.

———. 1965 [1953]. *The Hill of Devi*. London: Penguin Books.

Freitag, Sandria. 1991. "Crime in the Social Order of Colonial North India." *Modern Asian Studies* 25:227–62.
Gilchrist, John Borthwick. 1820. *The Hindee-Roman Orthoepigraphical Ultimatum.* London: Black, Kingsbury, Parbury, and Allen.
Gossen, Gary. 1973. "Chamula Tzotzil Proverbs." In *Meaning in Mayan Languages,* M. S. Edmonson, ed., 205–33. The Hague: Mouton.
Grierson, George A. 1927. *Linguistic Survey of India.* Calcutta: Superintendent of Government Printing.
Guha, Ranajit. 1993. "Discipline and Mobilize." *Subaltern Studies VII: Writings on South Asian History and Society,* Ranajit Guha, ed., 69–120. Delhi: Oxford University Press.
Haraway, Donna. 1992. "The Promises of Monsters: A Regenerative Politics for Inappropriate/d Others." *Cultural Studies,* 295–337. Lawrence Grossberg, Cary Nelson, and Paula Treichler, eds. London and New York: Routledge.
Ibbetson, Denzil C. J. 1882. *Memorandum on Ethnological Inquiry in the Panjab.* 2d ed. Pamphlet P/V 188: India Office Library.
———. 1883. *Report on the Settlement of the Panipat Tahsil and Karnal Parganah of the Karnal District, 1872–1880.* Allahabad: Pioneer Press.
———. 1916. "Panjab Castes: Being a Reprint of the Chapter on 'The Races, Castes, and Tribes of the People' in the *Report on the Census of the Panjab."* Published in 1883. Lahore: Superintendent of Government Printing.
Inden, Ronald. 1990. *Imagining India.* Oxford: Basil Blackwell.
Irvine, Judith. 1993. "Mastering African Languages: The Politics of Linguistics in Nineteenth-Century Senegal." *Social Analysis* 33:27–43.
Kuipers, Joel. 1990. *Power in Performance: The Creation of Textual Authority in Weyewa Ritual Speech.* Philadelphia: University of Pennsylvania Press.
Lelyveld, David. 1993. "The Fate of Hindustani: Colonial Knowledge and the Project of a National Language." In *Orientalism and the Postcolonial Predicament: Perspectives on South Asia,* Carol A. Breckenridge and Peter van der Veer, eds., 189–214. Philadelphia: University of Pennsylvania Press.
Luard, C. E. n.d. *Central Indian Proverbs.* MSS.Eur.E.139: India Office Library.
Lyall, J. B. 1874. *Report of the Land Revenue Settlement of the Kangra District, Panjab.* Lahore: Central Jail Press.
Maconachie, R. 1890. *Selected Agricultural Proverbs of the Panjab.* Delhi: Imperial Medical Hall Press.
Mani, Lata. 1984. "The Production of an Official Discourse on Sati in Early Nineteenth-Century Bengal." In *Europe and Its Others,* Francis Barker, ed., 89–127. Colchester: University of Essex.
———. 1989. "Contentious Traditions: The Debate on Sati in Colonial India." In *Recasting Women: Essays in Colonial History.* Kumkum Sangari and Sudesh Vaid, eds., 88–126. New Delhi: Kali for Women.
Marriott, McKim. 1966. "The Feast of Love." In *Krishna: Myths, Rites, and Attitudes.* Milton Singer, ed., 200–212. Chicago: University of Chicago Press.
Mayaram, Shail. 1991. "Criminality or Community? Alternative Constructions of the Mev Narrative of *Darya Khan."* *Contributions to Indian Sociology* 25:57–84.
Nath, Shaileswar. 1980. *Terrorism in India.* New Delhi: National Publishers.
Nigam, Sanjay. 1990a. "Disciplining and Policing the Criminals by Birth, Part 1: The Making of a Colonial Stereotype—The Criminal Tribes and Castes of North India." *Indian Economic and Social History Review* 27 (2): 131–64.

———. 1990b. "Disciplining and Policing the Criminals by Birth, Part 2: The Development of a Disciplinary System, 1871–1900." *Indian Economic and Social History Review* 27 (3): 257–87.

O'Brien, Edward. 1881. *Glossary of the Multani Language Compared with Punjabi and Sindhi.* Lahore: Punjab Government Civil Secretariat Press.

———. 1882. *Report of the Land Revenue Settlement of the Muzaffargarh District of the Punjab, 1873–1880.* Lahore: Central Jail Press.

Oldham, C. E. A. W. 1930. "The Proverbs of the People in a District (Shahabad) of Northern India." *Folklore* 41:320–44.

Pandey, Gyan. 1983. "Rallying Round the Cow: Sectarian Strife in the Bhojpuri Region, c.1888–1917." In *Subaltern Studies II: Writings on South Asian History and Society,* Ranajit Guha, ed., 60–129. Delhi: Oxford University Press.

Pinney, Christopher. 1990. "Colonial Anthropology in the 'Laboratory of Mankind.'" *The Raj: India and the British, 1600–1947,* C. A. Bayly, ed., 252–63. London: National Portrait Gallery.

Prakash, Gyan. 1991. "Becoming a Bhuinya: Oral Traditions and Contested Domination in Eastern India." In *Contesting Power: Resistance and Everyday Social Relations in South Asia,* Douglas Haynes and Gyan Prakash, eds., 145–74. Berkeley: University of California Press.

Purser, W. E., and H. C. Fanshawe. 1880. *Report of the Revised Land Revenue Settlement of the Rohtak District of the Hissar Division in the Panjab.* Lahore: W. Ball.

Rafael, Vicente L. 1993. *Contracting Colonialism: Translation and Christian Conversion in Tagalog Society under Early Spanish Rule.* Durham and London: Duke University Press.

Raheja, Gloria Goodwin. 1988a. *The Poison in the Gift: Ritual, Prestation, and the Dominant Caste in a North Indian Village.* Chicago: University of Chicago Press.

———. 1988b. "India: Caste, Kingship, and Dominance Reconsidered." *Annual Review of Anthropology* 17:497–522.

———. 1989. "Centrality, Mutuality, and Hierarchy: Shifting Aspects of Intercaste Relationships in North India." *Contributions to Indian Sociology* 23:79–101.

———. 1996. "The Limits of Patriliny: Kinship, Gender, and Women's Speech Practices in Rural North India." In *Gender, Kinship, Power: A Comparative and Interdisciplinary History.* Mary Jo Maynes, Ann Waltner, Birgitte Soland, and Ulrike Strasser, eds., 149–74. London and New York: Routledge.

Risley, H. H. 1891. *The Tribes and Castes of Bengal.* Calcutta: Bengal Secretariat Press.

———. 1907. *Manual of Ethnography for India: General Instructions, Definitions, and Ethnographic Questions.* Calcutta: Bengal Secretariat Press.

———. 1908. *The People of India.* Calcutta and London: Thacker, Spink.

Roebuck, Thomas. 1824. *A Collection of Proverbs and Proverbial Phrases in the Persian and Hindoostanee Languages,* H. H. Wilson, ed. Calcutta: Hindoostanee Press.

Roy Choudhary, P.C. 1966. *Bihar District Gazetteer/Shahabad.* Patna: Secretariat Press.

Sarkar, Sumit. 1983. *Modern India: 1885–1947.* New Delhi: Macmillan India.

Seitel, Peter. 1977. "Saying Haya Sayings: Two Categories of Proverb Use." In *The Social Use of Metaphor: Essays in the Anthropology of Rhetoric,* J. David Sapir and J. Christopher Crocker, eds., 75–99. Philadelphia: University of Pennsylvania Press.

Shakespear, John. 1820. Observations regarding Badheks and Thugs, Extracted from an Official Report by Mr. John Shakespear, Acting Superintendent of Police for the Western Provinces, dated the 30th April, 1816. *Asiatick Researches* 13:282–92.

Smith, Richard Saumarez. 1985. "Rule-by-Records and Rule-by-Reports: Complementary Aspects of the British Imperial Rule of Law." *Contributions to Indian Sociology* 19:153–76.
Stewart, Susan. 1994. *Crimes of Writing*. Durham and London: Duke University Press.
Stokes, Eric. 1978. *The Peasant and the Raj: Studies in Agrarian Society and Peasant Rebellion in Colonial India*. Cambridge: Cambridge University Press.
———. 1986. *The Peasant Armed: The Indian Rebellion of 1857*. Oxford: Clarendon Press.
Suleri, Sara. 1992. *The Rhetoric of English India*. Chicago: University of Chicago Press.
Temple, R. C. 1885. "North Indian Proverbs." *Folklore* 3:16–44
———. 1914. *Anthropology as a Practical Science*. London: G. Bell and Sons.
Trawick, Margaret [Egnor]. 1986. "Internal Harmony in Paraiyar Crying Songs." In *Another Harmony: New Essays on the Folklore of India,* Stuart Blackburn and A.K. Ramanujan, eds., 294–344. Berkeley: University of California Press.
———. 1988. "Spirits and Voices in Tamil Songs." *American Ethnologist* 15:193–215.
Van der Veer, Peter. 1993. "The Foreign Hand: Orientalist Discourse in Sociology and Communalism." In *Orientalism and the Postcolonial Predicament: Perspectives on South Asia,* Carol A. Breckenridge and Peter van der Veer, eds., 23–44. Philadelphia: University of Pennsylvania Press.
Wadley, Susan S. 1994. *Struggling with Destiny in Karimpur, 1925–1984.* Berkeley: University of California Press.
Williams, Monier. 1858. *An Easy Introduction to the Study of Hindustani*. London: Longman, Brown, Green, Longmans, and Roberts.
Wilson, H. H. 1855. "A Glossary of Judicial and Revenue Terms and of Useful Words Occurring in Official Documents Relating to the Government of British India." London: W.A. Allen.
Wilson, J. 1898. *Grammar and Dictionary of Western Panjabi, As Spoken in the Shahpur District, With Proverbs, Sayings, and Verses.* Lahore: Punjab Government Press.

The Crimes of Colonialism
Anthropology and the Textualization of India
Nicholas B. Dirks

> *For since we are the outcome of earlier generations, we are also the outcome of their aberrations, passions and errors, and indeed of their crimes; it is not possible wholly to free oneself from this chain. If we condemn these aberrations and regard ourselves as free of them, this does not alter the fact that we originate in them.*
>
> Friedrich Nietzsche, *Untimely Meditations*

For all of anthropology's emphasis on its originary encounters, ethnographic presents/presence, and fieldwork, anthropological knowledge has always been heavily dependent on texts. The textual field that is the pretext for fieldwork has been erased for some obvious and other less obvious reasons, but the erasure has further fetishized the anthropological field in relation not only to an earlier disinterest in ethnographic writing (until recently; see Clifford 1983; Clifford and Marcus 1986; Geertz 1988), but also to a systematic inattention to ethnographic reading. The resistance of anthropologists to footnotes is more than a stylistic conceit, for it still conceals a lack of serious concern for the reading behind (before and after) the writing of culture.

Recent interest in the writing of culture has focused some attention on the way earlier anthropologists have inscribed stylistic aspirations and professional investments in the anthropological canon we have inherited as "the literature" of ethnography. For the most part, the invocation of the new commitment to "textuality" has been used to argue for the literary "reading" of the great texts of anthropology, or to focus attention on the anthropologist's keyboard, our own writing of culture. While this has led to an extraordinarily important recognition

---

This paper has been revised and changed in significant ways since an earlier version was published in Daniel and Peck, eds., *Culture/Contexture* (Berkeley: University of California Press, 1985). For help with the most recent version, I would like to thank both the editors of the present volume, as well as Janaki Bakhle and Val Daniel.

of the power of writing and the extent to which textual virtuosity conceals the specific conditions of possibility of anthropological knowledge, much of anthropology has been plunged into positivist despair. The backlash to the recent emphasis on authorial invention has led to a debate that has rehearsed the tired question of whether anthropology is a science, and if so (or for that matter if not) whether it is about "us" or "them," all leading to desperate deliberation about whether anthropology is any longer possible. If anthropology is just a text, can it claim anymore to be real, or true? Ironically, the debate has worked in a peculiar way to make fieldwork (for all the interlocutors) all the more an originary moment. Arguments about textuality thus frequently serve once again to displace anthropological desire into the past, before writing, before encounter.

The focus on writing works to emphasize the individual in the text; as Geertz made clear in his analysis of anthropological writing (Geertz 1988), anthropology, now more than ever, can not concede the death of the author. And the critiques of the author in *Writing Culture* (Clifford and Marcus 1986) resurrect the modernist moment in anthropology even despite the incongruous musings of Stephen Tyler's avowed poststructuralism. My argument here is not that culture is not constituted by writing, for indeed I focus on historical examples of anthropological writing—on moments and processes through which culture is inscribed textually, but rather that we would do well to focus on the textual and contextual field that produces culture, on the reading practices and historical conditions that make writing possible. Although individuals do the reading, reading (not to mention writing) is self-evidently a social and historical practice, and works to focus attention on how certain texts are created and made available as knowledge, on the production and circulation of the assumption, data, and knowledge necessary for fieldwork itself, on the inchoate accumulation of the preconditions for anthropological writing and interpretation, as well of course as subsequent reading. And this focus on reading should remind us that there is really very little difference between what we call text and what we call context: there seems as little good reason today to think of contexts as outside texts as there is to think of texts solely within the discrete covers of autonomous textual fields.

Michael Taussig has recently questioned the conceit of context that drives much of history and anthropology: "I believe that for a long time now the notion of contextualization has been mystified, turned into some sort of talisman such that by 'contextualizing' social relationships and history, as the common appeal would have it, significant mastery over society and history is guaranteed—as if our understandings of social relations and history, understandings which constitute the fabric of such context, were not themselves fragile intellectual contructs posing as robust realities obvious to our contextualizing gaze" (1991:44–45). Taussig's distrust of context reflects his own disquiet about the uses of materiality in social science discourses by Marxists and non-Marxists alike, his insistence on the "flip-flop from spirit to thing and back again—the decided undecidability that could so clearly, so mistily, be seen in Marx's statement regarding the fetish quality of commodities" (5). The commodity form exceeds its materiality by concealing itself through the effects of desire and displacement. The boundary between text and context secures itself by the same logic of reification that Marx so powerfully attacks in his thinking about commodity fetishism. It is imperative to read contexts as texts, even as we set out to read texts in terms of contexts.

When the influential and much debated volume of essays *Writing Culture* was published in 1986, it focused the attention of anthropologists on the textual character of their practice in ways that many found disconcerting, even shocking. Anthropology was portrayed neither as unproblematic science nor as unmediated experience, but rather as the product of textual strategies and moments. Much useful debate was stimulated by these essays, in addition to the kind of backlash that mistook textual discussion for the denial of anthropology's truth. Wherever anthropologists have stood in the debate, it is fair to say that few of them any longer think of "writing up" as the kind of neutral, incidental activity it used to be when it was seen as the straightforward transcription of "analysis." Nevertheless, despite all the penetrating analyses of Conrad's literary influence on Malinowski, or of Geertz's stylistic invocation of his authorial/authoritative presence in his classic essay on the cockfight, the ensuing debate has remained limited to textual analyses of specific texts, balancing textual preoccupations with inchoate calls to recontextualize from within the anthropological field rather than from a much wider, heterogeneous, and troubling historical one. Anthropologists have also not come to terms with the fact that much of the new reflexivity works to re-fetishize fieldwork, once again fashioning the ethnographic encounter as the true originary moment for anthropology's specific disciplinary contribution to social science method and practice. Put differently, the debate neither took history into sufficient account nor worked to historicize anthropology to any meaningful extent.

In invoking a historicist approach, I do not mean to suggest that texts can be inserted into, or simply read in terms of, historical contexts that themselves are no more readily "readable" than the texts that recent critics have placed under such relentless hermeneutic suspicion. Writers as various as Greenblatt (1988) and White (1983), de Certeau (1986) and Žižek (1991), have shown how heterological history itself is, how the past dissolves into its textual mediations at the same time that our discourses about the past secure their rhetorical power by reference to the unknowable. Not only does history have multiple narratives, it is itself a function of historicity, of culturally (and historically) distinctive ways of marking, remembering, realizing, and retelling the "past." Anthropology has introduced the concept of culture to contemporary historians (see Sahlins 1985), and philosophers of history have begun a systematic, and comparative, philosophical interrogation of the forms and categories of historicity itself (e.g., Koselleck 1985; White 1983). But despite these moves toward the anthropologization of history, anthropologists themselves have only very rarely, and nervously, incorporated history as a fundamental component of anthropology; nor have they used it as the basis for reflexive critique within the discipline (see Dirks 1996).

If part of the hesitation here is not just disciplinary shyness, but also a recognition on the part of recent and progressive critics of anthropology that the historicizing move seems usually to refer ultimately to the unproblematized domain of the real, it is also the case that the real is frequently coded by unspoken certainties about the material conditions that constitute the real. Indeed, when material conditions are ascribed to a domain of context that can be taken uncritically to situate and condition the texts at hand, we reproduce the conventional dichotomies between the real and the representational, the contextual and the textual, and for present disciplinary purposes, the ethnographic and the historical. In rethinking anthropological history through an examination of texts, I would not strive to dissolve the usual antinomies through a critical resort to history itself as the deus ex machina of anthropological redemption. History does not, in other words, transcend its own historicity any more than anthropology (or any other modern discipline in the human sciences) can do so. However, history can serve as a reminder of the materiality of all texts (McGann 1991), as well as the institutions that make texts possible, comprehensible, and serviceable. If our modern sense of history, for example, was born at the same time (and not incidentally) as the modern state, we should be prepared to see colonial anthropology as the history of the colonial state. But history in this sense is not just a call to study the past, for I follow Foucault's (and Nietzsche's) injunction that history must ultimately be genealogical, that we do history best when we engage in a history of the present. I would further insist that it also entails a critical sense of the figuration of history as a particular form of normalizing narrative. The implications here are multiple, and provisional. We may debunk origins but seek, with theoretical justification, to discover them. We may use anthropological history to undermine the possibilities of anthropological knowledge at the same time we persevere anthropologically (and ethnographically). And we may use forms of historical rationality that themselves dissolve in the colonial darkness of unambiguously tragic historical pasts. But the history of the present entails the recognition that anthropological knowledge was not long ago constituted in terms that were deeply implicated in the historicity of the colonial state itself, at a time when anthropology was the history of the colonized.

In broad terms, I propose that we think of context as pretext, that is to say as the texts that are read before, the conditions of the production, circulation, and consumption of these texts, as well as the categorical disposition of historical thought and intendment more generally. By the same token, the term *pretext* operates with its double meaning intact: it signifies both what comes before the text, and what makes it possible, its history and its alibi. Texts and contexts both have their pretexts, even as pretexts can be either (or both) textual and contextual. Additionally, I take texts and contexts as at best supplements to each other, those Derridean destabilizing additives that mark the original referent as always already inadequate. By extension, the same is true for history, which is not located outside of texts but rather within an intertextual field, constructed out of the genealogical relations between histories of prior texts and the reflexive conditions that construct, and are constructed by, successive readings of these texts. I will try to show what happens to culture when we focus on reading rather than writing, and what happens to fieldwork when we locate it in larger historical fields than can be encompassed by reference to our own ethnography.

Anthropology and Colonialism

All the same, I begin with a (pre-)fieldwork story. Before I went to the field, I had decided to do an historical anthropological study of a small south Indian kingdom, concentrating on the relationship between political authority and social relations at the local level. In order to gain some preliminary sense of the structure and meaning of caste in areas where these kingdoms had survived well into the colonial period, I turned to a seven-volume work entitled *The Castes and Tribes of Southern India*, by Edgar Thurston (1907). The volumes were thick and authoritative, arranged like an encyclopedia, with entries for more than three hundred caste groups listed in alphabetical order. The entries on each caste ranged in length from one sentence to seventy-five pages, and they included such salient ethnographic facts as origin stories, occupational profiles, descriptions of kinship structure, marriage and funerary rituals, manner of dress and decoration, as well as assorted stories, observations, and accounts about each group. The text was designed as an easy reference work for colonial administrators, for the police as well as revenue agents, district magistrates, and army recruiters. But years later the text still seemed useful, and it has provided the ethnographic baseline for most anthropologists who have worked in southern India. If the information was inevitably flawed by the colonial character of its compilation, it still provided fundamental ethnographic data and provided a rough sense of the hierarchical position and geographical distribution of the core components of south Indian society, organized appropriately by caste.

I looked up the caste entries for those warrior castes that had spawned the most long-lived chiefly families in the early modern period of south India's past and was pleased to find extensive ethnographic detail for these Kallars, Maravars, and Tottiyars. I was somewhat surprised, however, to discover that the very castes that attained the reputation of kingship had also, by the late nineteenth century, been most consistently branded as criminal castes: tribes habitually given over to feckless lives of plunder, disorder, and violence. As my studies proceeded, it became clear that it was precisely the kingly virtues of these castes in the eighteenth century that had been transformed into the incriminating signs of imperial ethnography, the military prowess of royal retinues and armies now disaffiliated from the structures of power, unemployed martial clans cast out into the delegitimated spaces of resistance and disruption under the new colonial regime. Colonial ethnography seemed suspicious; but it has only been years later that I have been able to track the whiff of suspicion through the historical genealogies of these colonial texts, texts that still populate the footnotes of contemporary ethnography, texts that are still important among the pretexts for most anthropological practice that is conducted even today. This essay is about the implication of colonial ethnography in the criminalizing not just of these once royal caste groups, but of the study of Indian society itself.

Slavoj Žižek writes, "At the beginning of the law, there is a certain 'outlaw,' a certain Real of violence which coincides with the act itself of the establishment of the reign of law: the ultimate truth about the reign of law is that of an usurpation, and all classical politico-philosophical thought rests on the disavowal of this violent act of foundation" (1991:204). Žižek is examining here not only the problem of origins, but the fact that this search for origins leads to a recognition of the horror that lies just below the surface of civility, the realization that the law, indeed lawfulness itself, is predicated on its originary establishment in violence. The horror never disappears entirely; paraphrasing Kant, Žižek writes: "From the standpoint of Nature, 'Spirit' itself is a 'crime which can never be effaced'" (209). As anthropologists, we should perhaps read *culture* here instead of *spirit*. Culture as a category originated in some sense out of the colonial experience; and culture was a violent imposition before it became the sine qua non of anthropology, though the histories of colonialism and anthropology are inseparable. When we think about the origins of anthropology in colonialism, it is not difficult to see that the originary/absolute crime has folded into ethnology in a way that confirms Žižek's suggestion about the relationship between violence and the law. Žižek writes: "The absolute, self-relating crime is thus 'uncanny' (*unheimlich*) in the strict Freudian sense: what is so horrifying about it is not its strangeness but rather its absolute *proximity* to the reign of law" (204). Here too we can recognize that we can not efface the original crime and still do anthropology; although I seek here to show the perversity of colonial anthropology, I seek also to suggest that this perversity is familiar, that however much we invoke the tropes of irony or parody we can never totally rupture the colonial genealogy of our enterprise. Indeed, I would suggest that we need to hold onto the uncanny character of the relationship, for fear that we might forget the crime, and then repeat it all over again.

Anthropology and the Police

Crime and anthropology are related in more than Žižek's metaphorical sense. In 1893 Frederick S. Mullaly, a senior official in the Madras police, was appointed the first honorary superintendent of ethnography for Madras Presidency.[1] Mullaly's principal qualification for the job was his publication the year before of a book entitled *Notes on Criminal Classes of the Madras Presidency*. This book, which borrowed heavily from standard mid-nineteenth-century texts on such subjects as caste in India, as also from various district manuals that were being compiled from the 1860s on, was written first and foremost for his fellow policemen. As he states in the preface: "These notes on the habits and customs of some of the criminal classes of the Madras Presidency have been collected at the suggestion of Colonel Porteous, Inspector-General of Police, and put in the present form in the hope that they may prove of some value to Police Officers who are continually brought in contact with the Predatory classes, and of some slight interest to such of the public who may wish to know something of their less favoured brethren." Mullaly went on to suggest his personal authority in terms that sound highly anthropological: "the facts given here have, for the most part, been verified by personal association with the people themselves."

The construction of entire castes by the British in colonial India as "criminal castes" was part of a larger discourse in which caste determined

---

1. G.O. No. 6/6A/Public/10-1-93, Tamil Nadu Archives (TNA), Madras.

the occupational and social character of all its constituent members, though criminal castes were seen simultaneously as typical and deviant (Yang 1985). The colonial notion of caste was that each group had an essential quality that was expressed in its occupational profile, its position in the social hierarchy, as well as in a whole set of moral and cultural characteristics that adhered to each group qua group. The British labeled some castes as martial and recruited them for the army (under the Raj the appellation *martial* implied both physical prowess and political loyalty). Some castes were seen as specifically agricultural, and others as merchant, and the British government attempted to keep these categories from getting mixed up when merchants began assuming land that had been mortgaged for loans in large quantities in the nineteenth century. Although the designation of particular qualities in relation to caste changed over time, often in response to the political evaluation of such factors as loyalty, the notion that each caste had an essence was predicated on a belief in the changelessness of caste. The theories about criminal castes also partook of a set of late-nineteenth-century notions about the genetic and racial character of criminality, characteristics in the Indian case that were always seen to apply to entire caste groups and not, as was often the case in the West, to particular individuals.

Mullaly's book consists of a series of chapters on different criminal castes, each chapter including a large range of ethnographic detail with special attention to the kinds of crimes the group committed. Two of the most conspicuous criminal castes in his book—castes that were subsequently included in the Criminal Tribes Act when it was extended to Madras Presidency in 1911—were Kallars and Maravars. The very word *Kallar* has generally been translated as "thief," and there is little debate that many Kallars and Maravars had engaged in forms of predation (as well as of protection) that were part of a highly volatile political system in eighteenth-century southern India (see Dirks 1987). Mullaly begins his remarks by being reasonably descriptive. He writes about Maravars, that they "furnish nearly the whole of the village police (kavilgars, watchmen), and are at the same time the principal burglars, robbers and thieves of the Tinnevelly District. Very often the thief and the watchman are one and the same individual." About Kallars, he notes, "The word 'kallan' means thief or robber in many of the languages of Southern India, and is supposed to have applied to them as indicative of their peculiar mode of earning a livelihood—their violent and lawless habits. Their profession is that of stealing with or without violence as opportunities offer." Agency here is completely subordinated to the normative principles—the traditions and customs—of Indian society. In the essentialist language of the colonizer, Mullaly refers to the "profession" of these caste groups as lawlessness.

The Crimes of Colonialism

Mullaly, however, does not stop with these fairly perfunctory statements about the historical basis of the criminal castes. He uses ethnographic material not just to exemplify certain assertions but to condemn an entire caste group. For example, he writes as follows:

> The savage disposition of the Kallars appears from the following description of a custom which exceeds in atrocity almost every crime of violence of which history affords an example. The Survey Account states that—The women have all the ill qualities and evil dispositions of the men; in most of their actions they are inflexibly vindictive and furious on the least injury, even on suspicion, which prompts the most violent revenge without any regard to consequences. A horrible custom exists among the females of the class; when a quarrel or dissension arises between them, the insulted woman brings her child to the house of the aggressor and kills it at her door to avenge herself, although her vengeance is attended with the most cruel barbarity.

He goes on to note that if the crime is shown to be true, then the offending husband must kill his child in public in return. "Such is the inhuman barbarity in avenging outrage which proves the innate cruelty of the people and the unrestrained barbarity of their manners and morals." Mullaly concludes this gripping atrocity story by noting casually that these customs are unknown in the present day, and he does nothing to evaluate the evidence or context of the report.

The report serves its purpose, by naturalizing the assertion that criminality and cruelty are innate to Kallars as a whole and by providing irrefutable evidence for their inclusion in the general provisions of police surveillance that consigned certain subcastes to periodic long-term imprisonment (well before the Criminal Tribes Act was officially used). Mullaly also includes within his consideration of these two "criminal" castes the royal genealogies of the ruling families of Pudukkottai and Ramanathapuram, the first the only "princely state" in the Tamil area of Madras Presidency, the other the largest *zamindari* in the same area. Although it seems rather extraordinary to come across a royal genealogy in a book on criminal castes, Mullaly admits neither embarrassment nor contradiction. At best Mullaly is trivializing the kingship of these groups, implying that local kings in India ruled principally by force, though he goes further and charges that the kings themselves were brigands and thieves who ruled by terror and extortion. Here colonial anthropology has displaced Indian history with a vengeance!

The post of honorary superintendent of ethnography had been instituted at the request of H. H. Risley, who in the early 1890s was the secretary to the government of Bengal and the acknowledged expert in matters concerning Indian ethnology. In 1890 he had addressed the government of Bengal advocating the extension throughout India of the ethnographic project he had begun in Bengal.[2] He wrote at the time that anthropological research is conducted by two methods: first, by inquiry into customs; second, by examination and record of physical characteristics. His first concern in Madras was that the appropriate castes and tribes for this kind of study be selected, and thus he was pleased with Mullaly's appointment. However, Risley still felt that the government had not allocated enough importance, and money, for a comprehensive scheme to collect ethnographic information throughout India. In 1901 the government of India resolved its support for a scheme to carry out an ethnographical survey of India. At that time Risley was appointed Director of Ethnography for India; and Edgar Thurston, superintendent of the Madras Museum between 1885 and 1908, was appointed as the superintendent of ethnography for Madras presidency.[3] The replacement of Mullaly by Thurston signified the grander scale and scientific status of the ethnographic project in Madras; ethnography was now to be a general science rather than an applied form of colonial knowledge.

Thurston was the obvious and ideal choice for this position. A medical man by training, Thurston lectured in anatomy at the Medical College in Madras in addition to directing the activities of the Madras Museum. He began his extensive Indian research with work in numismatics and on geology, and began his anthropological research in 1894.[4] His first ethnographic writings were on the Todas, which though superseding in "scientific importance" the earlier writings of missionaries, was itself superseded by W. H. R. Rivers's publication of *The Todas* in 1901. But by that year his "ethnographic researches in the South of India" were already "well known," and Risley in particular was delighted with Thurston's availability because of their common enthusiasm about anthropometry as the principal means for collecting physical data about the castes and tribes of India. Thurston's obsession with anthropometry was so marked that before he delivered a lecture to the Royal Society of the Arts in London in 1909, Lord Ampthill introduced him with the following story: "A visit to the Government Museum at Madras was always a very pleasant experience, although at first alarming. Such was the author's zeal for anthropometry, that he seized every man, woman, or child in order to measure them."

In the proposal for the ethnographical survey of India, the secretary

---

2. G.O. 86/25-1-93/Financial (TNA).
3. G.O. 647/26 June 1901/Public (TNA).
4. Madras Museum Centennial Bulletin; also see preface to Thurston 1907.

to the government of India wrote, "It has often been observed that anthropometry yields peculiarly good results in India by reason of the caste system which prevails among Hindus, and of the divisions, often closely resembling castes, which are recognized by Muhammadans. Marriage takes place only within a limited circle; the disturbing element of crossing is to a great extent excluded; and the differences of physical type, which measurement is intended to establish, are more marked and more persistent than anywhere else in the world."[5] Thus the government justified its project, and its choice of Risley and Thurston, for a survey that was specifically directed "to collect the physical measurements of selected castes and tribes." Risley's advocacy of anthropometry, and his theories about the relation of race and caste, were clearly fundamental to the definition of the ethnographic project in turn-of-the-century colonial India. The scientific claim about caste reflects Risley's justification for the ethnographic survey in terms that make India into an imperial laboratory, for Risley was confident that he could actually test in India the various theories about race and the human species that had been merely proposed on speculative grounds in Europe. Risley scripted the observation that was recorded in the official inauguration of the ethnographical survey of India: "India is a vast storehouse of social and physical data which only need to be recorded in order to contribute to the solution of the problems which are being approached in Europe with the aid of materials much of which is inferior in quality to the facts readily accessible in India, and rests upon less trustworthy evidence."[6] Risley added that reference to Dr. Ripley's *Races of Europe*, and Professor Haddon's *Study of Man*, would amply demonstrate "the extensive use that has been made by European students of the data collected in India." In advocating government expenditure even during a time of famine in India, Risley argued that "the scientific advantages [of such a scheme] are indisputable."[7]

During the 1890s Thurston lectured on the methods and claims of "practical anthropology" to Madras University students, as well as on occasion to members of the Madras Police. In the 1899 issue of the *Madras Museum Bulletin*, Thurston published the syllabus of his course in practi-

---

5. *Man*, I, 1901.
6. See the letter from Risley enclosed in Home Department, Public Records, August 1900, Nos. 6/8, regarding proposals of the British Association regarding ethnography in connection with the census of 1901. This language is reproduced in No. 647, Public Department, 26th June 1901, which allocated initial funds and gave government support to the ethnographical survey and announced government's intention to name Risley as the "Director of Ethnography for India."
7. At the same time, these claims concealed the continuities between the assumptions that castes were biologically discrete and earlier statements, made for example in the context of explaining the difference between phrenology in Europe and India, that consistently treated caste groups in India as equivalent to individuals in Europe (Marshall 1873).

cal anthropology, in which he stated that anthropology, which he saw as a "branch of natural history," was divided into two main divisions. First, ethnography deals with "man as a social and intellectual being, his manners and customs, knowledge of arts and industries, tradition, language, religion, etc." Second, anthropography deals with "[m]an and the varieties or species of the human family from an animal point of view, his structure and the functions of his body." According to Thurston, the most important division of anthropography was anthropometry, which he defined as the "measurement and estimation of physical data relating to people belonging to different races, castes and tribes." Indeed, Thurston felt that his best results came from his anthropographic labors, for example, in scientifically demonstrating that the nasal index was lowest in Aryans and highest in jungle tribes, and that the index increased as body height diminished.[8] But here the underside of Thurston's scientific anthropology was revealed when he noted that one of the by-products of his research was his discovery that "intelligence is in inverse proportion to the breadth of the nose." As he wrote in one of his many "witty" asides, "when I am investigating the claims of applicants for a clerkship in my office, I am in the habit of scrutinising the nose as well as the hand-writing, though I do not advertise the fact, in the local papers or gazette, that 'no one with a nasal index exceeding 78 need apply.'"[9]

Anthropometry included the determination of everything from average height and weight (and average weight relative to stature) to detailed measurements of the shape and size of the skull, the face and the nasal index (breadth × 100/height), the relation of head size to body size, and the relative sizes of different body parts. For example, Thurston measured the relative length of the upper extremities, the arm span and the distance between middle finger and kneecap, for English, Brahmans, Pariahs, Paniyans, and Negroes. As part of his lecture he compared the skeleton of a Negro with that of an orangutan, "in which hands reach far below knees." He complained about the difficulty in measuring the heads of Todas, "whose dense locks offer [an] obstacle to [the] shifting of callipers in search for [the] right spot." Elsewhere he had noted that "the measuring appliances sometimes frighten the subjects, especially [the] goniometer for determining facial angle, which is mistaken for an instrument of torture." He encouraged the offering of a two-anna piece for conciliation, "supplemented by cheroots for men, cigarettes for children, and, as a last

---

8. See Gould 1981 for an insightful analysis of the relation between statistics and prejudice in this kind of research.

9. Edgar Thurston, "The Madras Government Museum as an Aid to General and Technical Education," Nos. 454, 455, Educational Department, 1st August 1896, India Office Records, London (app. E.).

resource, alcohol." He discussed the relative merits of gunshot or seed when measuring skull capacities. He also noted, displaying his perverse sense of humor once again, that "European inhabitants of a hill station objected to my weighing local tribesmen in [the] meat scales of [the] butcher's shop." This perversity took on even more sinister implications for the scientific aspirations of his anthropometric endeavors when he wrote, "The Paniyan women of the Wynaad, when I appeared in their midst, ran away, believing that I was going to have the finest specimens among them stuffed for the museum. Oh, that this were possible! The difficult problem of obtaining models from the living subject would then be disposed of."[10] His long association with the Madras Museum was betrayed in his sense that his anthropometric research would be best conducted by taxidermic methods; indeed, he was only partly joking.

Thurston also noted the importance of anthropometry for criminal identification, which had been the reason for his lectures to the police. In the early 1890s the Bertillon system of using anthropometric measurements had been adopted first in Bengal and then in Madras. The idea was to identify habitual criminals who moved from place to place and shifted their identities. In India, the Bertillon system was applied according to conventions set out by the colonial sociology of criminal castes. The basic operational principle was that "only members of criminal tribes and persons convicted of certain definite crimes" should be so measured.[11] Since most crime was committed by circumscribed groups of people, anthropometry seemed to be the perfect means to apprehend the principal suspects. As E. R. Henry, the Inspector-General of Police in Bengal put it, "With anthropometry on a sound basis professional criminals of this type will cease to flourish, as under the rules all persons not identified must be measured, and reference concerning them made to the Central Bureau."[12]

In the early years of the 1890s the police in both Bengal and Madras became increasingly confident that they were accumulating a central file of measurements that would help them apprehend criminals in a systematic and scientific manner. The major problem was that the measurement process turned out to be rather subjective and required extensive training and great care. In 1893 it was announced that "no officers fit for court duties will be promoted until they hold certificates of proficiency as measurers."[13] Col. C. A. Porteous, Inspector-General of Police in Madras, wrote in 1894 that he had earlier "expressed the opinion that the anthro-

---

10. Thurston, "Anthropology in Madras," Nos. 454, 455, Educational Department, 1st August 1896, India Office Records, London (app. F).
11. G.O. No. 1838, 9/ 9/1893, Judicial Department Records, TNA.
12. Ibid.
13. Ibid.

pometrical system for the identification of habitual offenders was too Scientific and too dependent on extreme nicety of measurement and mathematical accuracy to be suited for universal adoption in this country; a more practical acquaintance with this subject has led me to modify my views."[14] Thus experts such as Thurston were called in to train police throughout the Presidency, and to devise means to make the measurements as standard as possible. By 1895 police officers regularly underwent courses of training in anthropometry. And by 1897 Henry could write that the experience of the previous three years had "shown that success achieved has been progressive, and that the figures compare favorably with those submitted for Provincial France by Mons. A. Bertillon, to the Fourth International Congress of Criminal Anthropology held at Geneva in August 1896." Henry went on to note that "this outturn justifies the opinion that the anthropometric system is being worked on sound lines and effectively since, by means of it, four out of every possible ten cases were identified."[15]

Nevertheless, there was residual concern that measurements varied not only from measurer to measurer but from measurement to measurement. The instruments were costly, the course of instruction was lengthy, the statistics were hard to classify, and the measurement process itself was time consuming. In the last years of the decade anthropometry began to yield to fingerprinting, which in fact was initially developed in Bengal, as a means of criminal identification that had all the advantages of anthropometry, with none of its difficulties. Fingerprinting was considered error-free, cheap, quick, and simple, and the results were more easily classified. By 1898, Henry wrote, "It may now be claimed that the great value of finger impressions as a means of fixing identity has been fully established."[16] Fingerprinting quickly established itself as the universal system of criminal identification (see Ginzburg 1989). In the technologies of policing, as in many other areas, empire served as an important laboratory for the metropole.

The replacement of anthropometry by fingerprinting did not lessen Thurston's commitment to the physical measuring of Indian subjects. During the first decade of the twentieth century Thurston worked systematically on his ethnographic survey along the lines set down by Risley, collecting myriad ethnographic details and extensive archives of measurements, all arranged according to the different castes and tribes in the Presidency. As suggested throughout this essay, Indian subjects were not only organized by but contained in their castes or tribes, which deter-

---

14. G.O. 2454/Judicial/9-10-94 (TNA).
15. G.O. 1472/Judicial/9-10-97 (TNA).
16. G.O. 1014/Judicial/1-7-98 (TNA).

mined the cultural, economic, social, and moral characteristics of their constituent members. Individuals only existed as empirical objects and exemplary subjects. The ethnographic survey ended in Madras with the completion of Thurston's seven-volume work *The Castes and Tribes of Southern India* (1907). Thurston was assisted by K. Rangachari, a lecturer in botany at Presidency College in Madras,[17] and together they solicited the comments and observations of fellow officers and scholars throughout the Presidency. Naturally, Thurston also included the results of his anthropometric researches, which he said were "all the result of measurements taken by myself, in order to eliminate the varying error resulting from the employment of a plurality of observers."

Within the caste entries, the material is mostly made up of quotations from a wide variety of sources. The citations are reported cumulatively and used comparatively, but there is no critical evaluation of the sources, even at the level of noting the particularity of each report. Quotation marks are meant solely for attribution and do not in any way set anything within them off from the authorial narration, at the same time that they accumulate an encyclopedic sense of authority through the citation of so many authorities. For the Kallars, as indeed for the other "criminal castes," we find both citations from Mullaly's work as well as some of the same citations used by him. For example, Thurston reports without comment the remarks of one T. Turnbull, who in 1817 wrote that the Kallars "still possess one common character, and in general are such thieves that the name is very justly applied to them." Turnbull goes on: "The women are inflexibly vindictive and furious on the least injury, even on suspicion, which prompts them to the most violent revenge without any regard to consequences" (III, 54). And then follow the same stories of revenge told by Mullaly, the same generalized indictment of Kallar character, through these reports of the viciousness of their women and the remorselessness of their revenge. One citation leads to the next, the writing of Mr. Nelson, a noted jurist and onetime Collector of Madura District, promiscuously mixed in with articles from the "Illustrated Criminal Investigation and Law Digest" (69). Curiously, Mullaly's disclaimer that the most horrifying of practices had not actually been known to have taken place in living memory is absent here, despite the enhanced scientific status of the account. The ultimate confirmation of Kallar criminality is the statistic that 40 percent of the people jailed in Madura were Kallars, which overlooks the simple fact that whenever there was a crime a Kallar would be accused and arrested. But again, as with Mullaly's text, the ultimate charge was that the Kallars had traditionally been thieves: "The Kallars had until

---

17. G.O. 792/Public/5-9-03 (TNA).

recently a regular system of blackmail, called kudikaval, under which each village paid certain fees to be exempt from theft" (64). In fact, this criminal system had been, through the eighteenth century, a form of local rule articulated through the institution of protection, a local politics that had proved particularly resistant to British colonization at the turn of the century. A precolonial system of authority in which political power was exercised through the provision of protection was taken to be the primordial sign of colonial criminality (see Dirks 1987).

If one turns to the rest of Thurston's ethnographic writing, we see that the relationship of colonial anthropology to criminality is significant in other respects as well. Criminality under colonialism was about both classification and control; thus criminal castes occasioned some of the first ethnological monographs, and thus anthropology collaborated with policing to provide a scientific means to measure—and by measurement to contain the subjectivity of—persons whose identities were otherwise fluid within caste boundaries. Science worked on society at the level of the body; caste was defined as the genetic boundary of the Indian body, which was measured and explained in relation to a displaced Victorian enthusiasm for the colonized body. It is perhaps no accident that Sir Francis Galton purportedly invented regression analysis when surveying—for the greater glory of science—the naked bodies of Hottentot women in southern Africa (Kevles 1985:7–19).

The Colonial Body as Ethnographic Text

In 1906 Thurston published a long ethnographic work while he was in the middle of his labors for the ethnographic survey. This work, entitled *Ethnographic Notes in Southern India,* consisted of a series of essays, some previously published in the *Government Museum Bulletin,* on a variety of ethnographic subjects that Thurston thought held intrinsic interest. Perhaps Thurston also thought that these essays could not be readily contained by the format of the ethnographic survey.

The book begins with two long essays, the first on marriage customs, the second on death ceremonies, that look like compilations of material that had been collected on a caste-by-caste basis. Caste seems slightly less important in the third essay, on "omens, evil eye, charms, animal superstititons, sorcery, etc.," since the ethnographic material is presented as instances of a general set of beliefs and practices. But in subsequent chapters the organizing principle is no longer the conventional frame of caste, and the subjects seem no longer to be standard anthropological fare. The fourth chapter is entitled "Deformity and Mutilation," the next "Torture in Bygone Days," followed by such other chapters as "Slavery," "Fire-walking," "Hookswinging," "Infanticide," and "Meriah Sacrifice." If the caste-by-caste entries of Thurston's ethnographic survey volumes focus on the social (which in India for the British was caste), these essays instead focus on the body.

Thurston's *Ethnographic Notes* can be seen as the critical link in the genealogy connecting official anthropology and the kinds of investigative inquiries and reports that the British collected in their routine administration of Indian society. These chapters are in large parts encyclopedic collections of official material that was generated by the colonial interest in suppressing such practices as hookswinging, slavery, and torture. In Thurston's introduction to his *Castes and Tribes*, he had written that he had followed the scheme for the ethnographic survey that had recommended that he "supplement the information obtained from representative men and by their own enquiries by 'researches into the considerable mass of information which lies buried in official reports, in the journals of learned Societies, and in various books.' Of this injunction full advantage has been taken, as will be evident from the abundant crop of references in footnotes." But it is in the *Ethnographic Notes* that we can see the extraordinary extent of the connection between official colonial reports and official colonial ethnography.

Hookswinging, for example, exercised considerable official concern both in the 1850s and the 1890s, in large part in response to missionary pressure on the government to abolish the rite (see Dirks 1997). Hookswinging was a practice associated with local, mostly goddess temples, where devotees, for various reasons and in different contexts, would attach themselves to hooks and swing from poles. Thurston's ethnographic essay on hookswinging is in fact little more than a compilation of the kinds of writings on the custom that were used to recommend the abolition of what was seen by the British, and at the end of the century by many upper caste/class Indian officials as well, as a barbaric rite. The essay begins (487–501) by quoting a government report of 1854 and notes that in 1852 two men had been killed during the celebration of the festival in Salem district because the pole from which they were suspended had snapped. The unstated motivation for this observation was that the only provision under colonial law that could be used to suppress this rite was one that necessitated the documentation of actual physical harm. Thurston does not always moderate his language, for like earlier missionary and colonial reports he refers to the ritual as a "barbarous ceremony" and quotes indiscriminately from commentators as various (and as contemptuous of Indian customs) as Abbe Dubois and Sonnerat. Aside from the general narrative style, and the lack of any specific argument about suppression, there is little to distinguish this ethnographic chapter from the accounts produced by governmental officials themselves. What is different, of course, is that although there is no moral or legal argument about the suppression of hookswinging, virtually all of the material had in fact been generated out of this concern and was initially narrativized as part of an argument in the context of governmental debate. The absence of argument in Thurston's account has the effect of representing the account as scientific (as do all of Thurston's credentials, and the entire framework of the book), when it can be seen that this representation works to conceal the nature of the genealogical connection between the work and its sources. In ethnography, the once compelling stakes of official debate seem to disappear altogether.

I am not arguing that Thurston attempts to conceal his sources; he is far better than many colonial authors in providing footnotes and references. Furthermore, he is in total agreement with Risley that one of the tasks of the ethnographer is to digest the massive accumulation of material in governmental reports and then to present it in clear and systematic form. Thurston was himself a government servant and saw no contradiction between science and government in the task of accumulating anthropological knowledge about India. The relation of knowledge and rule is not simply a colonial fact; it is a fact that was actively celebrated in such colonial projects as the ethnographic survey. But it is easy in retrospect to lose sight of the genealogies of the relations between knowledge and rule, and readers of Thurston's treatise on hookswinging need never know the historical context in which his footnotes were produced. The same observation applied to Thurston's essay "Meriah sacrifice," where he made a great deal of missionary and colonial reports that the Meriah "tribe" of central India practiced human sacrifice. As is true of most such reports, they are always invariably secondhand, and they become enlivened by the sheer horror of the story in ways that exercised particular forms of attention and misrepresentation, in general travel and missionary literature, in colonial documents, as well as in official anthropological writing. And it is worth noting that Thurston's chapter became a primary footnote for James Frazer in his discussion of human sacrifice in the canonical text of early British anthropology, *The Golden Bough*.

Thurston's essay on torture (407–32)—an odd focus of ethnographic scrutiny in retrospect, but of considerable interest to nineteenth-century ethnographers—was similarly based almost entirely on the report of a commission that was appointed by the government of Madras in 1854 to investigate various forms of torture employed in the Madras Presidency. Thurston notes that the commission used a broad definition of torture, construing it as "pain by which guilt is punished, or confession (and we may add money) extorted." Although Thurston is clear about his use of this source, he tells us nothing about the nature of the commission's task or the historical provenance of the many examples of torture. The inclusion of a series of graphic descriptions of torture under the general title "Torture in Bygone Days" suggests that torture had been a constant feature of southern Indian life, and Thurston shares with the members of the commission the belief that the examples of torture they uncovered were the traditional practices of native revenue and police officers—as the commission's report states, "knowing, as we do, the historical fact, that under the Governments immediately preceding our own, torture was a recognized method of obtaining both revenue and confessions" (4). The report also asserts that "there are many circumstances in the peculiar condition of this country which may well account for the prevalence of even a systematic and general practice of personal violence, used for the purpose of extortion among the native population" and notes the "whole of this mass of testimony emanates from parties intimately acquainted with the country, its administration, the people and their character. It cannot but afford a deep and clear insight into the actual position of matters" (15). But the report also admits that, "In point of fact our investigation starts from a recent definite point" (4–5) and provides no evidence other than assertion and assumption that torture, like caste and custom, is an essential component of Indian society.

In other contexts I have been misread as making the reductive argument that custom and caste were invented ex nihilo by colonialism. It may therefore be necessary for me to point out that I am not suggesting along the same lines here that torture only arrived on Indian soil with the British. Here as elsewhere I mean to identify the complex relationship(s) between knowledge (in this case ethnographic categories), power (colonial governmentality), and history (as a sign of the modern). The torture report is silent about the fact that the revenue demand in the Indian countryside escalated exponentially under British rule. If torture in revenue and police matters was prevalent in the middle of the nineteenth century, as the report convincingly argues, there were other factors at work, principally the new level of revenue demand. Suddenly, dire consequences of noncompliance (loss of jobs and land) and a colonial legal structure that bestowed new powers on policemen (see Arnold 1986) were deeply implicated in the social fact of torture. But these were not part of the commission's brief, and were absent in the commission's explanations, which depended upon a multitude of expert understandings of the Indian "country, its administration, its people and their character." Even more significantly, they were left out of Thurston's ethnographic account, which gave even less contextual information than the actual report about the nature of the material it provided.

It is in this sense that I literally assert that Indian anthropological writing was born directly out of the colonial project of ruling India. On the basis of the writings of Mullaly and Thurston, we can see the key texts of early colonial anthropology as not simply being produced in the context of colonial projects but as culminating what had been a long series of colonial projects (and colonial texts written) to rule and reform India. It is worth reemphasizing that the pretextual field of anthropological writing includes not just the colonial reports and official documents that provide the citational basis for early colonial anthropology (and, through writers such as Thurston, canonical anthropologists such as Frazer and Rivers), but also the crimes of colonialism itself: for example, the pacification campaigns against the Kallar kings, the intensity of revenue collection from the countryside to finance the colonial government, the moral reforms that highlighted and denounced the so-called barbarous practices that always were used to justify the presence of enlightened British government.

One final note: Thurston's *Ethnographic Notes* attracted considerable attention, within official and scholarly circles, as well as from general readers. G. H. Forbes, the secretary to the Madras government, noted that "It is evident that the book, from its title and contents, is being bought up by the tourist, male and female; and there is certainly some matter which, though quite unobjectionable for scientific readers, is scarcely what we should put in the hands of young people who read merely from curiosity or to acquire a general knowledge of out of the way tribes."[18] Forbes did not object to the book as a scientific work, but he was deeply concerned about the ready availability of scientific detail particularly in matters sexual. He recommended that a "bowdlerized edition . . . would be of value and use to the general public and priced low" and that a new edition of the complete work "with full scientific detail" be released at a higher price. In recommending bowdlerization, Forbes highlighted such explicit phrases as "pendulous testes" and "protuberant breasts," as also many of the most graphic examples of torture. Although most concerned about the sexual detail in the chapter on marriage, he also noted that "the subjects of hookswinging, infanticide, and meriah sacrifice are revolting though not prurient." Thus the distillation of ethnography out of government reports led not only to the advance of science, but the production of what outside of its proper domain was seen as pornography. There was little danger that either scientists or ordinary citizens were going to sift through the mass of material that had been accumulated during British rule. This, of course, is my point; and it is important to realize that Thurston's work was

---

18. G.O. 787/Public/2 Nov 1906 (TNA).

generally read without any sense of the multiple readings I have provided. Instead, Thurston was read in decontextualized reference to other ethnographic notes for other areas and to other compendiums on castes and tribes, sometimes even as travel literature. Although I have provided a set of genealogical readings to make my case, my argument also depends on the fact that these connections were obscured by the very project of ethnographic writing engaged in by the new generation of official anthropologists at the turn of the century.

For colonial ethnography, the colonized subject was first and foremost a body, to be known and controlled through the measurement and interpretation of physical subjects organized in caste and gender categories. In all this attention to the body, there was little interest in the subjectivity, will, or agency of colonial subjects. When colonial officials debated the nature or presence of colonized agency, the debate was focused on the denial or suppression of this agency, in contexts where the colonial state sought to regulate or abolish such practices as sati, child marriage, hookswinging, and so on. Agency was an absence, only there when it could be seen as precisely not there. On all other occasions, agency was neither relevant nor significant, expressed as it was in the social body of custom and tradition. Even crime was performed without agency; crime was a function of habit, a social occupation, an effect of caste rather than an act of will. And with the prevalence of anthropometry and ethnographic interest in bodily practices, the materiality of the text of custom, for colonial ethnographers, was the colonized body itself.

The Colonial Archive

This essay is part of a more general effort to historicize anthropology by looking carefully at the history of the discipline, exploring the multiple contexts within and from which anthropological writing has emerged.[19] Ever since Bernard Cohn argued persuasively that the colonial sociology of India left important legacies for postcolonial social science, and Talal Asad brought together a classic group of essays demonstrating the close links between colonial rule and anthropology, it has been widely accepted that such work sheds important light on the conceptual and political history of significant areas of anthropological practice. Until recently, however, the historical scrutiny of anthropology has been seen as largely incidental to the kind of anthropology done today, and historical investigations within anthropology have stopped far short of engaging in thorough, and wide ranging, historical inquiry into the relations between

    19. As is shown by the contributions of this volume, and the coherent and important argument it makes about the relationship between anthropology and colonial history.

foundational categories and historical processes. Anthropology grew out of modern history, becoming the history of those without history as well as the prehistory of those now mired in history. By the late nineteenth century, anthropology became quite literally the history of the colonized.

But even as anthropology is implicated in the same epistemological and institutional histories as the modern discipline of history itself, it can also be situated within a larger set of metahistorical questions that might help move us beyond the present impasse. Modern history could only develop on the ruins of eschatological conventions that were anchored in theological temporalities and religious institutions. But with the eighteenth-century recognition that history had an open future came the steady appropriation of this enlightenment sensibility by the apparatus of the state. Even as historians could evaluate the successes and failures of revolutions and other historical transformations in terms of new humanist eschatologies, the state became the measure for nascent temporalities as surely as it provided the boundaries for nationally conceived social spaces (Koselleck 1985). History served as a principal form of governmentality at the same time that governmentality expressed itself through the categories of historical thought and writing. In more prosaic terms, history was organized theoretically in narratives that made the state (and the nation) into the subject and the object of temporal consequence; it also became primarily located within the formal ambits and agencies of state power. History was written by the state to educate and justify political policies and practices, and it was produced and preserved by the state for future historical reference in the archive. The archive, that primary site of state monumentality, was the very institution that canonized, crystallized, and classified the knowledge required by the state even as it made this knowledge available for subsequent generations in the cultural form of a neutral repository of the past.

For at least two centuries, knowledge about India was largely produced by or in terms of the logics of colonial rule, the imperatives and institutions of the colonial state. As I have argued elsewhere, colonial forms of knowledge progressively de-privileged historical knowledge and replaced it with anthropological knowledge (Dirks 1992, 1997). For example, caste recapitulated the legacies of tradition, and history was perceived as absent from Indian sensibilities. Colonial historiography appropriated to itself the responsibility for antiquarian history, while conceding to anthropology the study of historical subjects who had not yet entered modernity. In this division of disciplinary labor, anthropology, whether of a physical body or a body politic, was less a complement than an extension of modern history, spatialized by the logic of colonial conquest and rule, linked directly to the interests and forms of the state. History was to the modern metropolitan state what anthropology was to the colonial state, reflecting both the similarities and the differences between state systems at home and in the colonies. History constructed a glorious version of the nation in which the present was the inevitable teleological frame; anthropology assumed a history that necessitated colonial rule. History told the story of the nation; anthropology explained why a nation had not yet emerged (as, for example, in Risley's understanding of caste as an impediment to national mobilization; see Dirks 1992; Risley 1908).

If the British failed to see history as a fundamental attribute of Indian culture, it is no coincidence that they established their rule on the ruins of a political order they had aggressively conquered, destroyed, and replaced. It is thus of special importance that anthropologists engaged in the study of their own history approach the colonial archive both as the repository of sources for their research and in terms of larger historical contexts that expose the archive as the primary site for the deployment and articulation of colonial governmentality. And yet it is not without ironic intent that I would also suggest the need for anthropological historians to engage in an ethnography of the archive, for the archive itself reflects the forms and formations of colonial epistemology in ways that have been misrecognized by historians and anthropologists alike.

To do an ethnography of the archive entails going well beyond seeing it as an assemblage of texts, a depository of and for history. The archive is a discursive formation in the totalizing sense that it reflects the categories and operations of the state itself, in this case of the colonial state. The state produces, adjudicates, organizes, and maintains the discourses that become available as the "primary" texts of history. When I did the research for this essay I consulted the records of the "Public" department, the "Political" department, the "Home" department, among many others. I paged through indexes of documents that reflected the quotidian procedures of government, files that considered and then ruled on issues ranging from the appointment of a particular individual to a position (such as superintendent of ethnography) to his salary and his official duties, both of which were scaled in relation to the other positions, financial needs, and political requirements of government. When I found materials about the practice of hookswinging, I read through files that responded to widespread pressure from missionaries and others regarding the suppression of an activity that brought no grievous bodily harm and little in the way of significant social unrest, bringing this practice to the attention of district administrators, who nevertheless had to worry about the representation of governmental activities both within India and back in Britain itself. When I began to correlate the interest of official ethnography in "native" bodily practices with the Torture Commission Report of 1855, I had to rely on my own long archival experience of working with land and settlement records as early as the late eighteenth century in order to dismantle the congealed character of official self-congratulation in relation to the deployment of horror stories around brutality and violence in the south Indian countryside. Each record in the archive references previous records, both as precedent and as paper trail; archival research itself invariably proceeds genealogically—record by record, decision by decision, trace by trace. Although documents are frequently scripted with posterity in mind, history in one sense is an afterthought, only incidentally related to the sources that are fetishized as so fundamental to the craft of history itself. And yet history is encoded on the surfaces of the very files—the numbering systems, the departmental structures, and classificatory rubrics—as well as in the reports, letters, decisions, and scribbles within that make up the archive. The archive contains primary sources, at the same time that it is always already a secondary trace of historical discourse.

The archive encodes a great many levels, genres, and expressions of governmentality. I am only remarking this here in connection with the need for anthropological historians to delve further into archives at the same time that they stand back and survey the monument as an artifact of history and a document of historicity. Commissions of Inquiry have very different histories from routine papers that surface in the government orders of everyday official practice, government manuals and gazetteers very different uses from occasional notes or office correspondence that move in haphazard circuits of official (and demiofficial) exchange. Historical research can reveal connections that become effaced by the effects of history itself: for example, between the rise of the revenue demand in the early nineteenth century (fueled by the needs of the East India Company) and the ethnographic writings of Thurston in the early twentieth century, between the dynamics of early colonial conquest and the social classifications that become hardened into late colonial views of caste, between the concerns of the police to apprehend "habitual" criminals and the early development of anthropometry (and by implication what is now called "physical" or "biological" anthropology in many disciplinary circles). Even as the connections never completely come full circle—never foreclosing the possibilities of other connections and frequently displacing other kinds of possible outcomes or correlations—they move us well away from the certainties of a linear and autonomous textual history of anthropology, dissolving texts into contexts even as contexts constantly become reabsorbed by other texts and historical traces. While the archive has no transparency of its own—its facts can be construed in any number of ways, and the historical record alone can by no means explain why I took the particular path I did in this essay, or made the specific connections previously charted—it is nevertheless the field within which I conducted my research, pushing me by its recurrent recalcitrance, limiting me by its aggravating absences, fascinating me by its own patterns of intertextuality, seducing me by its appearance of the real.

Anthropological Genealogies

Only when we begin to unravel the genealogies of colonial encyclopedias of ethnographic knowledge does it become fully clear how problematic is the knowledge we perforce take, as it were, to the anthropological field with us. Now that colonial texts have been put under ironic question, it is perhaps too easy to think that we have charted a clear postcolonial passage for anthropology, but colonial epistemologies fade most slowly in the categories and frames we still use when we refurbish our anthropological practice. We must remember that the refurbishing has been done before; in the twentieth century the study of caste shifted the site of its inquiry from the body to the mind (see Dirks 1992), from British anthropometry to French and American culturalism,[20] writing caste on the mind of India itself rather than on its corporate bodies. At the same time, the biological basis of caste, and the importance of the bodily frame for cultural hermeneutics, continue to dominate contemporary anthropologies of India, both academic and political. And writing caste on the mind rather than the body still has the effect of removing social formations from historical processes, re-essentializing the body politic of India through the reiteration of this key metaphor of social difference.

By establishing the colonial context for the production of the first official ethnographies of southern India, particularly in Thurston's work, we are led back to a succession of other texts that could be produced and cited only because of a complex colonial history in which certain texts secured the status of context itself. The history of the nineteenth century in India is the history of desperate attempts to fix an inchoate and uncolonizable place in textual form: texts of proprietary title, legal procedure, customary tradition, ultimately of claims to political sovereignty itself. Ethnographic citation produced colonial conviction, the reality effect of context. It is through reading the texts that constitute the pretexts of fieldwork that we learn how the conditions of anthropological knowledge really were con-

---

20. I refer here to the American school of ethnosociology (see Marriott 1990), which, as Dennis McGilvray (1982) has pointed out, mistook medical for social knowledge; and to the work of Louis Dumont in his important writing on caste in *Homo Hierarchicus* (1980).

stituted historically; our exploration of the quotidian features of this history takes us to the heart of darkness, the crime at the beginning of anthropology, the horror that undermines but also undergirds the heterological task of reading culture.

REFERENCES

Arnold, David. 1986. *Police Power and Colonial Ruse in Madras.* Delhi: Oxford University Press.

De Certeau, Michel. 1986. *Heterologies: Discourse on the Other.* Minneapolis: University of Minnesota Press.

Clifford, James. 1983. "On Ethnographic Authority." *Representations* 1:118–46.

Clifford, James, and George Marcus, eds. 1986. *Writing Culture: The Poetics and Politics of Ethnography.* Berkeley, Los Angeles, and London: University of California Press.

De Man, Paul. 1983. "The Rhetoric of Blindness." In *Blindness and Insight: Essays on the Rhetoric of Contemporary Criticism.* Minneapolis: University of Minnesota Press.

Dirks, Nicholas B. 1987. *The Hollow Crown: Ethnohistory of an Indian Kingdom.* Cambridge: University Press. Reprinted 1993, Ann Arbor: University of Michigan Press.

———. 1992. "Castes of Mind." *Representations* 37 (winter): 56–78.

———. 1996. "Is Vice Versa? Historical Anthropologies and Anthropological Histories." In *The Historic Turn in the Human Sciences,* ed. T. McDonald, 17–51. Ann Arbor: University of Michigan Press.

———. 1997. "The Policing of Tradition." *Comparative Studies in Society and History* 39 (1): 182–212.

Dumont, Louis. 1980. *Homo Hierarchicus: An Essay on the Caste System and Its Implications.* Originally published 1966. Chicago: University of Chicago Press.

Geertz, Clifford. 1988. *Works and Lives: The Anthropologist as Author.* Stanford: Stanford University Press.

Ginzburg, Carlo. 1989. *Clues, Myth, and the Historical Method.* Baltimore: Johns Hopkins University Press.

Gould, Stephen J. 1981. *The Mismeasure of Man.* New York: W. W. Norton.

Greenblatt, Stephen. 1988. *Shakespearean Negotiations.* Berkeley, Los Angeles, and London: University of California Press.

Kevles, Daniel J. 1985. *In the Name of Eugenics: Genetics and the Uses of Human Heredity.* New York: Knopf.

Koselleck, Reinhart. 1985. *Futures Past.* Cambridge: MIT Press.

Levinson, Majorie. 1992. "After the New Historicism: Posthumous Critique." Unpublished manuscript.

Marriott, McKim, ed. 1990. *India through Hindu Categories.* New Delhi: Sage Publications.

Marshall, William E. *A Phrenologist amongst the Todas.* Longmans, Green, and Co.

McGann, Jerome J. 1991. *The Textual Condition.* Princeton: Princeton University Press.

McGilvray, Dennis. 1982. "Mukkuvar Vannimai: Tamil Case and Matrician Ideology in Batticaloa, Sri Lanka." In D. McGilvray, ed., *Caste, Ideology and Interaction*, 22–41. Cambridge: Cambridge University Press.

Mullaly, Frederick S. 1982. *Notes on Criminal Classes of the Madras Presidency. Report of the Commissioners for the Investigation of Alleged Cases of Torture in the Madras Presidency.* 1855. Madras: Government Press.

Risley, Herbert H. 1908. *The People of India.* Calcutta and London: Thacher, Spink.

Sahlins, Marshall. 1985. *Islands of History.* Chicago: University of Chicago Press.

Said, Edward. 1983. *The World, the Text, and the Critic.* London: Faber and Faber.

Taussig, Michael. 1991. *The Nervous System.* New York: Routledge.

Thurston, Edgar. 1906. *Ethnographic Notes in Southern India.* Madras: Government Press.

———. 1907. *The Castes and Tribes of Southern India.* 7 vols. Madras: Government Press.

White, Hayden. 1983. *Metahistory.* Baltimore: Johns Hopkins University Press.

Yang, Anand, ed. 1985. *Crime and Criminality in British India.* Tucson: University of Arizona Press.

Žižek, Slavoj. 1991. *For They Know Not What They Do: Enjoyment as a Political Factor.* London: Verso.

Hopi Snakes, Zuñi Corn

Early Ethnography in the American Southwest

Curtis M. Hinsley

Several years ago Jacques Revel made the suggestive observation that from the moment a nation can be associated with a specific spatial area, it can also be "called to mind like a garden of perfection"—a homeland worthy of self-identity, loyalty, even self-sacrifice (Revel 1991:133). The second half of the nineteenth century saw the culmination of Revel's "discontinuous, partly cumulative" process whereby the United States reached that point of development: coast to coast, "from sea to shining sea," the visual representations reflected and determined a sense of completion that immediately found imaginative resonance. The southwestern territories of Arizona and New Mexico, the last contiguous internal colonies of the nation, became states in 1912, thereby filling the continental expanse; in the same period, and not coincidentally, the United States emerged as a global imperium.

The dominant geopolitical characteristic of the American national history has been constant areal expansion of borders and demographic movement within and across them, endlessly occurring within a controlling ideology of "manifest destiny." The American nation has been remarkably stable in imagination—a long-standing "garden of perfection"—but fluid in demographic actuality. Accordingly, at any historical moment the discrete statuses of states, regions, territories, and protectorates seemed to be merely temporary stages in a teleological projection of continental completeness. That is, the *idea* of America always existed beyond the boundaries of the moment. The imaginative effect of this condition was that successive incorporation of new territories seemed repeatedly to re-enact the drama of national destiny, individual acts of a generation confirming the general mission. The processes by which formerly alien, "wild" territories were gradually domesticated into the national polity and imaginatively reconfigured as part of the national identity have varied: outright military power projection; development of trade or migration routes (e.g., the Oregon

Trail, the Santa Fe Trail); landscape naming and renaming; and collection and removal of territorial resources to metropolitan centers as material signs of conquest and incorporation (Stewart 1984). In the case of the American Southwest, this process of regional identity-formation and imaginative domestication was deeply influenced by the ethnographic writings of missionaries, military men, political administrators, and land speculators who settled in, or merely passed through, this "undeveloped" region of the nineteenth century. For such observers, the deserts and mesas of Arizona and New Mexico presented challenge, escape, or opportunity; the aboriginal peoples of the region, no less than the land itself, invited acts of personal and cultural projection. Through these acts of internal colonial discourse, such men (and some women) related individual experience even as they shaped cultural expectations for others.

Fredric Jameson, reflecting on the emergence of modernist literature in the context of western imperialism, has observed that, from the perspective of the imperial center, the consciousness of colonial possessions creates a "spatial disjunction" enforcing the recognition that a "significant structural segment of the economic system as a whole" lies somewhere beyond the metropolis. How to know this component—how to take account of and cognitively map this missing dimension of the national/imperial community—becomes, Jameson argues, a vexing cultural problem of the imperial age, seen not only in literary texts but also in such public arenas as museums and world's fairs. In these venues, Indians and alternative "Others" are exhibited, seemingly happily at work or play, as part of an attempt to re-create and restabilize a social totality; they offer "a utopian glimpse of achieved community" (Jameson 1990:63–64) that appears otherwise at risk or even already lost. Arguing along similar lines, Edward Said demonstrated in *Culture and Imperialism* (1993) that the realms of art and imperial politics have always been deeply intertwined: "At some very basic level imperialism means thinking about, settling on, controlling land that you do not possess, that is distant, that is lived on and owned by others" (7). Ethnography has been predominant among those ideological formations and the allied knowledge forms that have functioned to "mak[e] preparations for" the idea of maintaining imperial dominion and/or colonial possession as ongoing enterprise (11).

John G. Bourke and the Hopi Snake Dance (1881–84)

In the light of postcolonial theory, it is instructive to reconsider early representations of the Indian peoples of the American Southwest. At the end of the American Civil War in 1865, most of the territory west of the 100th meridian was culturally ambiguous: contiguous land, it remained politically and imaginatively unincorporated space. While seemingly embraced in the Manifest Destiny of the nation, it was still largely unexplored, undefined, and unoccupied by settlers. In other words, it stood significantly unmeasured and "uncontrolled" (cf. Revel 1991:134–37). As Kevin Starr's studies (1973, 1985) of the dreaming and inventing of nineteenth-century California have demonstrated, this period saw two closely related developments: the incorporation of the western regions into the national imaginative domain and, simultaneously, their definition as distinct entities based on landscapes, natural resources, and aboriginal inhabitants. With the completion of the transcontinental railroads through northern New Mexico and Arizona in the early 1880s, the public definition of these territories for touristic, economic, and political "development" became a matter of some urgency. The accelerating impact of the railroads on the flow of people, goods, and influence in and out of pueblo country was immediate and powerful, creating a hunger and a market for images, descriptions, and artifacts of the desert region. Thus began the domestication of the Southwest—a process of consumption on many levels. Metropolitan Americans consumed, first and foremost, certain images of the peoples of the region. Among those who provided such images were John Gregory Bourke and Frank Hamilton Cushing.

Between the end of the American Civil War and the Spanish-American War of 1898, the American military establishment had a special role and interest in the trans-Mississippi West, and specifically in the Indian peoples of these regions. Because the "Indian wars" presented, in these three decades of a resurgent domestic militarism, the sole opportunities for fighting experience, career advancement, and military fame, the investment in the existence of "hostiles" as worthy opponents against which to test personal and cultural mettle was heavy; in retrospect, the persistent and popular images of "wily savages" and "bloodthirsty renegades" (the starving, decimated, and desperate Apache bands of the 1870s and 1880s provided the most common examples of such "resistance") now seem little more than the culturally necessary resistance to strenuously attained national destiny. America had to be earned.

Still, the Southwest was not an attractive military assignment (Wooster 1986), and its aboriginal peoples provided a mix of binary images derived from pre–Civil War first impressions: peaceful/warlike, defensive/aggressive, agricultural/nomadic, city-builders/raiders. Perhaps they were merely the projections of metropolitan self-doubts, but these oppositions readily found their way into the writings of the military men who had direct contact with southwestern tribes. The resulting stance appears as ambivalence—a measure of the difficult fit between received categories and immediate experience. In Lieutenant John

Bourke's case, ambivalence and discomfort brought forth shifts in narrative position and ethnographic voice.

Bourke's *Snake Dance of the Moquis*, published in 1884, is widely considered the earliest and classic description of the Hopi snake ritual. It recounts Bourke's adventures in the late summer of 1881, a year in which he was freed by General Philip Sheridan from military duties and provided with assistants and supplies for undertaking full-time study of various Indian tribes of the West (Hutton 1985:341–42). Bourke had joined the army at age sixteen and campaigned, as aide-de-camp to General George S. Crook, in wars against the Cheyenne, Sioux, and Apache peoples during the 1870s. Among the nomadic, horse-riding tribes of the Plains and Southwest Bourke saw a remarkable bravery and stoic nobility in the face of what he recognized as desperate political and economic deprivation. At the same time, he never seriously questioned the accepted wisdom of his society: that the Native American peoples were hopelessly inferior and destined either for physical extinction or for cultural annihilation through education and acculturation. In the thousands of pages of his diary, and in the hundreds of published pages of his ethnographic description of the Sun Dance, the Snake Dance, and Apache medical practices, Bourke consciously engaged in salvage ethnology. He was trying to preserve for posterity life-styles that, he was certain, would—and should—soon disappear from the face of the earth.

Bourke, who died at fifty in 1896, earnestly wanted to be recognized and accepted as an ethnologist, especially in the last decade of his life. It was an ambition that always eluded him. He suffered perennially from the distractions of a military career and the deficiencies of military camp life. His sense of intellectual inferiority was constant. In the preface to *Snake Dance* he apologized and excused himself in advance:

> Only those who have assumed the burden of authorship can appreciate the fatigue and labour of research demanded, when exactness of statement is aimed at. This fatigue and this labour increase tenfold at outlying military stations where libraries are of insignificant proportions, and where books bearing upon special topics are not to be had for love or money. (xix)

Military personnel in colonial situations have often been valued ethnographic observers. Both the Smithsonian Institution and its brief predecessor, the National Institute, relied upon soldiers, explorers, and missionaries to fill out questionnaires and vocabulary lists in their early efforts to comprehend the aboriginal world of North America (Hinsley 1994:48; Fowler 1976). After the Civil War John Wesley Powell argued for ethnographic knowledge as the basis for efficient military and political control of defeated tribes; a similar logic impelled General Philip Sheridan to support Bourke's curiosity. Powell took into his new Bureau of Ethnology in 1879 military men who had campaigned in the Civil War and the post–Civil War western territories: Garrick Mallery, Washington Matthews, Henry C. Yarrow, among others (Hinsley 1994:145–89). Bourke himself considered for years the option of joining Powell's Bureau; he also made plans with Cushing for securing either government or private financing (for instance, that of the aging Francis Parkman and Parkman's close friend, Secretary of War William C. Endicott) for his fieldwork and scholarship (Jacobs 1960: II, 180–81). In the end these plans failed to yield support, and Bourke struggled until his death to find the leisure to write up his years of field observations. He always considered himself marginal to the anthropological community being formed in the United States in the closing decades of the century. Sadly, Bourke's diary entry on his last birthday characterized his life as a "general failure": he described himself as "The author of a few writings, which altho' true and exact, will not long survive me" (Porter 1986:307).

The full title of Bourke's *Snake Dance* indicates his multiple intentions: *The Snake-Dance of the Moquis of Arizona: Being a Narrative of a Journey from Santa Fe, New Mexico, to the Villages of the Moqui Indians of Arizona, with a Description of the Manners and Customs of this Peculiar People, and especially of the revolting religious rite, The Snake-Dance; to which is added a Brief Dissertation upon Serpent-Worship in General with an Account of the Tablet Dance of the Pueblo of Santo Domingo, New Mexico, etc.* As the title suggests, Bourke combines several genres: journey travelogue; description of "manners and customs"; comparative "dissertation" on serpent-worship; and an account of a summer dance at a Rio Grande pueblo. The central narrative structure is a journey—a "summer's ramble," as Bourke called it (1984:57)—westward from Santa Fe to the Hopi mesas in the high desert of Arizona. His account of the Tablet Dance precedes the Snake Dance description because the Bourke party passed through the Rio Grande pueblo of Santo Domingo on the way to Hopi, sojourning only long enough to observe the ceremony. At Santo Domingo both Bourke and his artist-companion, Peter Moran, were thrown bodily out of a kiva, which they had had the effrontery to attempt to enter. Like his behavior, Bourke's observations have the superficial, anecdotal quality of one passing through, but they also occasionally show serious effort to describe ritual and material culture. The literary result is a feeling of uncertain purpose and a wavering voice, as Bourke first approaches, then retreats from his subject people. For example, having described Indian food offerings to Santo Domingo in the church, he adds:

> The amount of offerings was considerable; the quality was not very good. It looked to me as if this part of the proceedings was more complimentary than otherwise, since no man in his sound senses would think of eating the immature melons and plums unless he had his life at a high figure. (45)

Following this passage Bourke notes that the "monotonous" drumming and nasal singing of the Indians in the plaza soon grew "wearisome," so he took a "leisurely saunter" through the village, encountering two lovers along the way (45). The effect of such narration is first to draw the reader toward the experience (religious offerings in the church), but then to retreat by referring back humorously to the safeguards and familiar conditions of civilized life (such as a large life insurance policy). Bourke's strategy was common in contemporary southwestern writing: it is the nervous humor of the traveler, making an effort to find psychic balance in the search for safe excitement.

Bourke creates safe distance, too, at those moments when he expresses disgust and revulsion. An individual of apparently keen olfactory sensibilities, Bourke remarks frequently on filth, foul odors, and noxious food. "[T]he sight of a neatly-arranged supper or dinner" seemed to him "a gratifying demonstration of the rapid approach of railroad connections, of increasing wealth and commerce, and consequent refinement of manners and sentiment"—indeed, Bourke rated a well-laid table and well-stocked larder as "the best index" of civilized progress (89). He severely criticized the culinary habits and hygiene of the pueblo peoples. His recorded occasions of revulsion—again, a widely shared descriptive element—served as ethnographic boundary-markers, just as military clothing or certain tools (pencil, notepad, camera) demarcated civilized status. All functioned to establish and maintain the comfort of distance. Later, they also came to serve as behavioral signs for future tourists.

On August 11, 1881, Bourke's party, totaling fifteen men, arrived in the village of Walpi, on the easternmost mesa ("First Mesa") of the Hopi reservation. Bourke's actual account of the Snake Dance of the next several days comprises only a fraction of his monograph. As we have seen, the preceding chapters tell of adventures en route; the latter half of the book culls passages from ethnological authorities (Fergusson, Tylor, et al.) on serpent-worship in general, with an impressionistic account of Hopi kinship and "manners and customs." He concludes with more adventures of travel, including brief visits to Oraibi and other Hopi villages.

In describing the Snake Dance itself, Bourke vacillates between close, claustrophobic kiva-watching, which he likens to standing in Dante's inferno, and lyrical, romantic scene-painting. Because he was one of the first Anglo-Americans to directly observe snake-handling in the kivas, Bourke's descriptions enjoyed considerable notoriety—more for his own courage and nausea than for ethnographic details. Here he describes the snakes on the kiva floor:

> They sinuously writhed along the foot of the wall, slimily crawling along the floor, and climbing up along the rough surface of the adobes and rocks until their tails alone seemed to rest upon the ground, and then falling down again upon the foetid, stinking mass of their comrades. The lazier coiled and knotted themselves in venomous clusters, suggesting the head of Medusa; those that were more ambitious, or more energetic, would languidly thrust out their flattened heads and peer at us with leaden, lack-lustre eyes, in which scintillated a faint glitter that a moment's excitement would fan into flame.
>
> The air was heavy with a stench like that of a rotten cesspool: only a stern sense of responsibility kept me at my post. Moran remained with me for some time, sketching as fast as time, bad light, and foul air would permit; the other members of our party came down and departed at once; some of them could not stand it at all. (137–38)

A short while later he resumes the account:

> The stench had now become positively loathsome; the pungent effluvia emanating from the reptiles, and now probably more completely diffused throughout the Estufa [kiva] by handling and carrying them about, were added to somewhat by the rotten smell of the paint, compounded, as we remember, of fermented corn in the milk, mixed with saliva! I felt sick to death, and great drops of perspiration were rolling down forehead and cheeks, but I had come to stay, and was resolved that nothing should drive me away. (150)

Yet a few pages (and minutes) later, Bourke and Moran come out into the fresh air and ascend to a viewpoint overlooking the village and mesa country. With this important positional shift, the vista becomes breathtaking, and Bourke grows rhapsodic as he verbally paints the scene.

> Not a sign of animation breaks the placidity of the scene, since yonder sedate donkey, trudging solemnly down to the springs for a drink, that great herd of goats and sheep browsing in the middle distance, or this half-dozen old women toiling so slowly up the almost vertical

Hopi Snakes, Zuñi Corn 187

> face of the precipice with five gallon ollas of water wrapped in their old and faded blue blankets, can scarcely be called animate.
>
> They have rather the appearance of vague, dim, hazy recollections, dreams of things which have been alive, than of things which are. (155)

Thus Bourke draws strong contrast between the darkness of the horrid, secret ritual, with its subterranean preparations, and the hazy placidity of southwestern dream-life. The recurrent theme of Bourke's Snake Dance narrative is nightmare, as the army lieutenant employs such terms as *horrified, ghastly,* and *lurid*. It is as if the spirits of the dead have arisen to life, and Bourke struggles with the reality: "I stuck a pin in my leg. Could this be the nineteenth century? Could this be the Christian land of America?" (128).

The exposure of primitive survivals—the savage underside of the industrial, rational, daylight America—within the national boundaries of the United States lent strong resonance to Bourke's account; it subsequently became a central element in the imaginative construction of the American Southwest. Bourke reveled in his own mediating and informative position in such high drama: he was announcing to the American people the savage evolutionary depth of this new region of their nation, defining a place of dream and nightmare, surface placidity and secret primitivism.

> The south-western part of our own country has been penetrated by the railroad and the telegraph since the years when Mr. [Hubert H.] Bancroft completed his then monumental collection of data. Not a day passes that some new discovery is not made by the ubiquitous newspaper correspondents, untiring mining prospectors, tourists, or government scouts, who are poking about in all the bends and angles of what less than a decade ago was more of a *terra incognita* than Central Africa. (224–25)
>
> This was the Snake-Dance of the Moquis, a tribe of people living within our own boundaries, less than seventy miles from the Atlantic and Pacific Railroad in the year of our Lord 1881. (169)

The revelation of hellish depths of savagery, and their presumed survival within the emergent national borders, rather than ethnographic discovery per se, propelled Bourke to a brief fame and the Snake Dance into immediate cultural popularity. Within a decade the Hopi mesas were overrun by camera-wielding tourists from the East Coast and from Europe, seekers after the safely exotic.

Frank H. Cushing and *Zuñi Breadstuff* (1884–85)

"America offers no suitable field for you," wrote Bourke to his good friend Frank Cushing in September 1884. "Very few of our people care for the Indians and nearly all of them manifest a suspicion of a man who presumes to consider their manners, customs, and ideas worthy of note and preservation" (Hinsley 1994:200). Cushing certainly so presumed. At the time of his friend's advice, Cushing had only recently been forced to return to Washington, after nearly five years at Zuñi pueblo, as a result of political pressures exerted on Powell's Bureau of Ethnology. Bourke's *Snake Dance* had just appeared, and Cushing was beginning publication of a remarkable series of articles on Zuñi life, entitled *Zuñi Breadstuff*. The "breadstuff" of the title referred to the heart of Zuñi cultural and material life: corn.

Unlike Bourke, Cushing has long been recognized as a central figure in the early years of professional anthropology: Powell called him a genius, and Claude Lévi-Strauss saw in him a brilliant, intuitive precursor of structuralist thought. He was a valued and active member of the Bureau of Ethnology from its founding in 1879 until his death (like Bourke, at a relatively young age, 43) in 1900. Above all, his years at Zuñi, like Franz Boas's sojourn in Baffinland, have provided a classic and much-studied model of ethnographic participant-observation. And yet in significant ways Cushing remained an outsider, marginal to the developing late-nineteenth-century profession despite his official connections.

Cushing possessed an unusual tentativeness toward truth, values, and mores. His insistence on creating as well as "discovering"—that is, his free insertion of imagination in his work—placed him on the fringes of the scientific community. He spurned institutional bonds, though he readily used individuals and organizations for his own purposes. Generally speaking, he found little use for the language, channels, and forms of dialogue within established scientific circles. Not that he denied the importance of sound methods in anthropology. He once lamented to Otis T. Mason, curator of ethnology at the Smithsonian's U.S. National Museum, that "America has no *Science* of Ethnology or Archaeology, and (I may add) that every Boer who has correctly or incorrectly described an arrowhead or a simple mound, is at once considered an archaeologist and styles himself, 'Professor.'" Previous literature on Zuñi, he told Spencer F. Baird soon after arrival in the Southwest in 1879, was "nothing," and he predicted that "my method [of participant-observation and etymological study] must succeed." During his years as director of the Hemenway Southwestern Archaeological Expedition (1886–89) he made plans to found a "Pueblo Museum" in Salem, Massachusetts, to teach his methods.

And at one low point in his career, when he thought that he was dying in 1889, Cushing begged Bourke to "let the world know of my hard work and say that my method was the correct one in ethnological investigation" (Hinsley 1994:193). Still, he always remained on the margins, for Cushing was too idiosyncratic to consistently recognize the primacy of a scientific peer audience or to contribute in a major way to its creation. He knew personal friendships and bitter feuds, but—even allowing for the relatively inchoate condition of anthropology as a field of inquiry in his time—it is fair to say that he never developed a strong sense of professional community.

Language was always the center of Cushing's method. He struggled repeatedly to find a scientific poetics and a textual form to express it, unrestricted by the expectations of public or private patrons and the conventions of scientific discourse. He never really found that voice, but he came closest to it in *Zuñi Breadstuff*. The conditions of its writing are, therefore, important.

As Jesse Green has shown in *Cushing at Zuñi* (1990), by 1884 Cushing had become deeply involved in the life of Zuñi pueblo. Not only was he a Bow Priest, but he had moved his wife, sister-in-law, and a family cook into his new adobe home on the edge of the pueblo. Here he entertained a constant stream of Zuñi and non-Zuñi visitors. He had become a celebrity, a spokesperson for Zuñi interests, and a controversial figure. But he had also become embroiled in controversies with powerful Washington politicians and religious groups. Partly as a result of these complications, Cushing delayed producing the studies of pueblo life that Powell had hoped to see for Bureau publication, and he suffered from chronic, serious sickness (among other things, diverticulitis and an undiagnosed tapeworm).

For all of these reasons, in February 1884, Powell ordered Cushing back to the Washington office to write up more than four years of fieldwork. Cushing managed to postpone his departure from the pueblo until the end of April, but he was entering a chaotic period personally. While he published very little in the next two years for Powell's Bureau—his nominal employer—and complained constantly of sickness, *Zuñi Breadstuff* appeared in monthly installments from the spring of 1884 through the summer of 1885 in *The Millstone*, an agricultural and milling trade journal published in Indiana (1883–91). As with his earlier publications in *Atlantic Monthly* and *Century*, Cushing's motivations were chiefly monetary: D. H. Ranck, publisher of *Millstone*, paid him $25.00 per page for the nineteen installments—money Cushing desperately needed to meet expenses incurred in building his Zuñi home. One suspects also, however, that Cushing's poetic style would have received heavier editing in Powell's Washington offices.

Zuñi Breadstuff constituted Cushing's most complete ethnographic statement on Zuñi and the clearest exposition of his methods and style—which makes its publication in an obscure, midwestern trade journal all the more remarkable. What was the essence of the *Breadstuff* style? As early as 1880 Cushing had recognized that language was the key to ethnography: "As gradually their language dawns upon my inquiring mind not the significance of the ceremonials alone but many other dark things are lighted up by its meanings," he had informed his Smithsonian superiors. As the years passed, however, Cushing came to question the possibility of transmitting Zuñi reality to non-Zuñi audiences. In 1882, for example, he wrote to a Boston admirer, Edward Everett Hale:

> The life and language, the religion of the Zuñis, are intensely poetic. With no amount of poetry to which my words or pen may aspire, can I hope to give to the world as I feel it, in listening to the rituals, folklore, or even councils of this innocent people, their imagery and their poetry and their quaintness. I have, thus, inadequately told the truth about my Zuñis; yet I have told the truth so far as my abilities enable me to . . .

Accordingly, while he took corn as the central cultural fact of Zuñi life, he approached the "breadstuff" as food item, ritual object, mythology, aesthetic focus, metaphor and symbol, and much more. His goal in *Zuñi Breadstuff* was to demonstrate the close-knit texture, and the cultural logic, of Zuñi life. His primary means of analysis was linguistic: etymological study provided for him the strands that disclosed the Zuñis' views of causality and connectedness. Every article in the *Breadstuff* series demonstrated both the Zuñis' reasoning and Cushing's method; one example may suffice to demonstrate the point.

In his description of "Zuñi Farming: Starting a New Field" (*Millstone* 9:4 [1884]; reprinted in Green 1979:249–56), Cushing draws a "Plan of a Zuñi Cornfield" (fig. 1) and describes at length not only the dams, barriers, and embankments which the Zuñi farmer builds to trap and guide water flows through the arroyo, but also the Zuñi logic in so "tempting" the water into the desired directions. The field is then "consecrated" in a prescribed ritual, involving the use of feathers of various birds and planting plumed sticks. Cushing's summary description and explanation are powerful and evocative.

> Having taken the cloud-inspiring down of the turkey, the strength-giving plume of the eagle, the water-loving feather of the duck, the path-finding tails of the birds who counsel and guide Summer, hav-

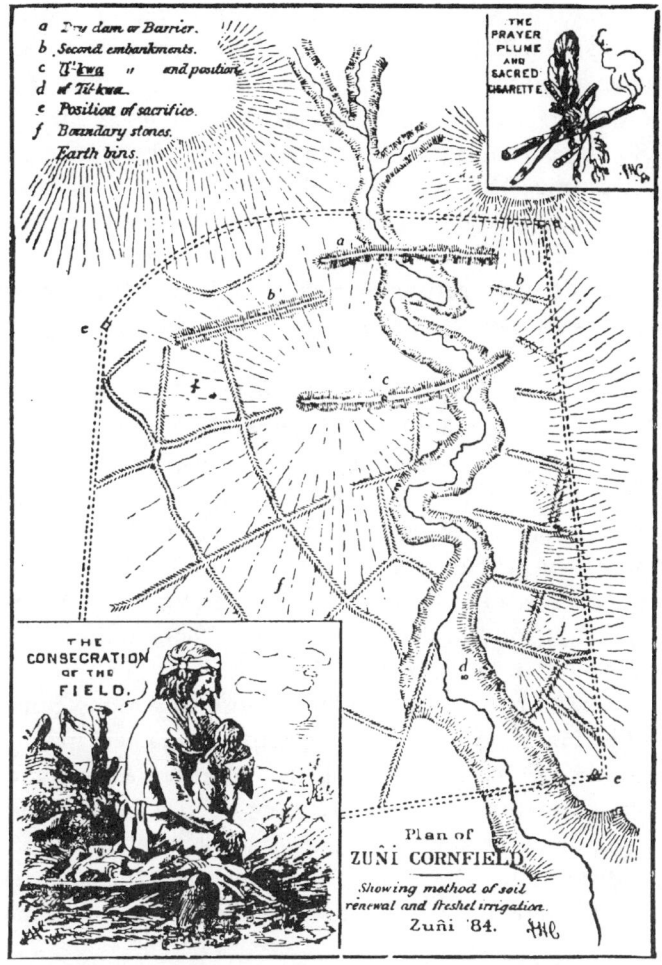

Fig. 1. Plan of a Zuñi Cornfield. (Reproduced from Frank Hamilton Cushing, "Zuñi Farming," *Millstone* 9:4 [1884].)

ing moreover severed and brought hither the flesh of the water-attracting tree, which he has dipped in the god-denizened ocean, beautified with the very cinders of creation, bound with strands from the dress of the sky-born goddess of cotton—he beseeches the god-priests of earth, sky and cavern, the beloved gods whose dwelling places are in the great embracing waters of the world, not to withhold their mist-laden breaths, but to canopy the earth with cloud banners, and let fly their shafts little and mighty of rain, to send forth the fiery spirits of lightning, lift up the voice of thunder whose echoes shall step from mountain to mountain bidding the *mesas* shake down streamlets. The streamlets shall yield torrents; the torrents, foam-capped, soil-laden, shall boil toward the shrine he is making, drop hither and thither the soil they are bearing, leap over his barricades unburdened and stronger, and in place of their lading, bear out toward the ocean as payment and faith-gift the smoke-cane and the prayer-plume. Thus thinking, thus believing, thus yearning, thus beseeching, (in order that the seeds of earth shall not want food for their growing, that from their growth he may not lack food for his living, means for his fortune) he this day plants, standing in the trail of the waters, the smoke-cane and prayer-plume.

The force of this remarkable passage lies in Cushing's rhetorical effort and poetic effects. Cushing attempts, in English syntax, to convey the dynamics of Zuñi cosmology as seen in the acts of corn-planting. Through object-participles ("cloud-inspiring," "strength-giving," "water-attracting," etc.) he gives expression to Zuñi notions of natural causality; through long and complex sentence structures he textually embodies the intricate and inviolable connectedness of all things in the Zuñi world, pulling the reader from one (Zuñi) causal moment to the next. "Thus thinking, thus believing, thus yearning, thus beseeching," Cushing's Zuñi farmer emerges as a figure in prayerful but hardly helpless relationship to the gods and forces of his world. "He this day plants"—a simple human act that in Cushing's hands becomes a richly complex, "thick" cultural phenomenon.

Cushing was ill at ease with his own poetics, because he sensed its heterodox nature. In a revealing, even confessional letter of 1888 to his patroness at the time, Mary Tileston Hemenway, Cushing attempted to express his understanding of the distinction between poesis and science.

> It is characteristic of savage or Primeval thought that it reversed the Nature *we* conceive. It insisted on *Subjectivizing* every object, and objectivizing every Subject and on always personifying [im]personalities. This made a Myth of every Philosophy and a Poem of everything. My[thology], then, constituted the Religion and Philosophy of Primaeval man. Thus, it is only by aid of the imagination, of the sympathies of poetic conception, that we can wholly understand the [in]stitutions, the doings, even the Things of Primitive man! (Cushing 1888)

By the time he wrote these words, however, Cushing had already suspected for some time that what he was attempting to convey was finally, perhaps tragically, unconveyable across the cultural boundaries between Zuñi and American. And so: switching voices, pulling back into scholarly distance, he added the following footnote to the description of the Zuñi cornfield previously cited.

> The kind of philosophy which can give rise to faith in this remarkable reversal of nature's order—making the growth of willows the explanation of the presence of waters, instead of the consequence; making summer birds the *bringers* of summer instead of summer the incentive of their yearly migration—is, strange as it may seem, the teaching of nature by her appearances, for natural philosophy is hidden under natural phenomena. Therefore, wonder not, ridicule not the retrogressive reasoning of savages. Rather, look to this, this one great dissimilarity between child-mind and civilized mind, as the fruitful cause of misunderstanding between the American and the Indian—a misunderstanding which will end, moreover, only with the death of this peculiar philosophy or the doom of its devoted adherents. (256)

Conclusion

Bourke and Cushing wrote at a critical transitional moment for the southwestern landscapes and aboriginal peoples of the United States. "God help my poor doomed Zuñis!" Cushing cried in his diary seven years later, as he saw the traditional authority structures of Zuñi pueblo crumbling from external pressures and internal dissension. By the 1920s professional ethnographers were swarming over a vastly transformed Zuñi social landscape, picking at the scientific shards. In this process the early impacts of Bourke the soldier and Cushing the maverick participant/observer were both instrumental and instructive. Because they did not speak directly or solely to what we would today characterize as "professional" audiences—the public/professional lines were hardly so clearly drawn at the time—they helped to shape public perceptions of a region that had been, as Bourke noted, unknown territory only a few years previously. The essential lesson of their writings was the denial of history to the region and its aboriginal peoples—a denial argued, though, through contradictory logic. On the one hand, they presented secret rituals or farming techniques, like the canyons and deserts of the Southwest, as immutable, unchanged over centuries and immune to human intervention. Thus, Cushing compared Zuñi mythology to Homeric legends, handed down through preliterate generations virtually unaltered. On the other hand, Bourke, Cushing and their generation could not help seeing that the Indian world as they experienced it directly must inevitably (and soon) disappear; thus their strong salvage efforts. Standing in the very vortex of historical change, they wrote as if Native America was inevitably approaching an evolutionary abyss, at the same time ignoring the human struggles going on directly before their eyes—the real, mundane history of war, alcohol, greed, and deprivation with which they were both intimate and implicated. Change, as they chose to understand it, was evolutionarily inexorable, rather than contingent and determined moment by moment.

As elsewhere in the world, blindness to historical agency on the part of metropolitan cultural representatives proved to be immensely costly to the colonized landscapes and peoples of the American Southwest. But it has also proved vital to the growth of tourism. Here, after all, came to be located Aldous Huxley's reservation-reprieve from the horrors of a *Brave New World* of the 1930s—and here American, European, and Asian metropolitans still arrive daily for therapy among pastel scenery and friendly Indians. "See it before it disappears" has been the ubiquitous slogan of the tourist agent for decades—but the marketing of cultural desire insists (and insures) precisely that it *not* disappear. The abyss, forever approaching, must never arrive. Whatever their private agonies ("My poor doomed Zuñis . . ."), Cushing and Bourke publicly denied the changes going on around them in the Indian Southwest. Jameson's spatial disjunction of colonial separateness and incompleteness has been bridged by marketplace imaginings, and the modern Indian Southwest has consequently become a site of projected desires and market-mediated consumption.

REFERENCES

Bourke, John G. 1884. *The Snake-Dance of the Moquis.* New York: Scribner. Reprinted 1984, Falstaff: University of Arizona Press.

Carter, Paul. 1988. *The Road to Botany Bay: An Exploration of Landscape and History.* New York: Alfred A. Knopf.

Cushing, Frank Hamilton. 1884–85. *Zuñi Breadstuff. Millstone* 9, nos. 1–12, and 10, nos. 1–4, 6–8.

———. 1888. Letter to Mary Tileston Hemenway. June 1. Cushing Letterbooks 4:341–49. Huntington Free Library, Bronx, New York. (Brackets in the quoted passage are my additions due to illegibility in the original document.)

Fowler, Don D. 1976. "Notes on Inquiries in Anthropology—a Bibliographic Essay." In *Toward a Science of Man: Essays in the History of Anthropology,* T. H. H. Thoreson, ed. The Hague: Mouton.

Green, Jesse. 1979. *Zuñi: Selected Writings of Frank Hamilton Cushing.* Lincoln and London: University of Nebraska Press.

———. 1990. *Cushing at Zuñi: The Correspondence and Journals of Frank Hamilton Cushing, 1879–1884.* Albuquerque: University of New Mexico Press.

Hinsley, Curtis M. 1990. "Authoring Authenticity." *Journal of the Southwest* 32, no. 4: 462–78.

———. 1994. *The Smithsonian and the American Indian: Making a Moral Anthropology in Victorian America.* Washington: Smithsonian Institution Press.
Hutton, Paul Andrew. 1985. *Phil Sheridan and His Arm.* Lincoln: University of Nebraska Press.
Jacobs, Wilbur R., ed. 1960. *Letters of Francis Parkman.* 2 vols. Norman: University of Oklahoma Press.
Jameson, Fredric. 1990. "Modernism and Imperialism." In *Colonialism and Literature,* Terry Eagleton, Fredric Jameson, and Edward Said, eds., 50–51. Minneapolis: University of Minnesota Press.
Porter, Joseph C. 1986. *Paper Medicine Man: John Gregory Bourke and His American West.* Norman: University of Oklahoma Press.
Revel, Jacques. 1991. "Knowledge of the Territory." *Science in Context* 4 (1): 133–61.
Said, Edward. 1993. *Culture and Imperialism.* New York: Alfred A. Knopf.
Starr, Kevin. 1973. *Americans and the California Dream, 1850–1915.* New York: Oxford University Press.
———. 1985. *Inventing the Dream: California through the Progressive Era.* New York: Oxford University Press.
Stewart, Susan. 1984. *On Longing: Narratives of the Miniature, the Gigantic, the Souvenir, the Collection.* Baltimore and London: Johns Hopkins University Press.
Wooster, Robert. 1986. "'A Difficult and Forlorn Country': The Military Looks at the American Southwest, 1850–1900." *Arizona and the West* 28, no. 4: 339–56.

White Man's Flour
The Politics and Poetics of an Anthropological Discovery
Patrick Wolfe

Late in 1896, amid the lurid grandeur of Central Australia, Spencer and Gillen made an extraordinary discovery. They were observing the last great *Intichiuma* ceremony, a swan song to savagery staged for their benefit[1] by the men of the Arunta tribe.[2] In the course of the proceedings, the two ethnographers came across

> the idea firmly held that the child is not the direct result of intercourse, that it may come without this.... (Spencer and Gillen 1899:265)

At that moment—though not for long afterward—such astounding ignorance was without parallel in the ethnographic record. Bespeaking, as it seemed, the deepest recesses of prehistory, it rounded off the Arunta's

---

This essay originally appeared as " 'White Man's Flour': Doctrines of Virgin Birth in Evolutionist Ethnogenetics and Australian State-Formation," *History and Anthropology* 8, nos. 1–4: 165–205. Reprinted by permission of Harwood Academic Publishers.

1. Gillen, a Justice of the Peace, had had a local mounted constable named W. H. Willshire arraigned for the murder of a number of indigenous people. Though Willshire was acquitted by the Adelaide court, he was not reassigned to the Centre, so Gillen's action had effectively terminated his homicidal reign there. As T. G. H. Strehlow (1969:48–49) takes up the story, "Gillen's courage was never forgotten by the Aranda; and some years later their gratitude found its expression in the ceremonial festival held at Alice Springs in 1896, where the secret totemic cycle of Imanda was revealed for the first time before the eyes of white men—to Gillen and to his friend, Baldwin Spencer."

2. This paper deals with European discourses about indigenous people in Australia rather than such people(s) themselves. Accordingly, "Aborigines," "aborigines," "Arunta," "Aranda," "savage," "native," "Black," "black," "blackfellow," "Australian," etc., are figures of discourse, here reproduced as they appear in the primary textual data. I have generally spelled and capitalized these terms in accordance with the usage of the text or author(s) currently under discussion. To avoid offense, however—and bearing in mind that others can legitimately quote from what follows without reference to this note—I have used a capital "A" for Aborigine/Aboriginal except in the case of direct quotations. Where I intend reference to indigenous people in Australia themselves rather than to others' representations about them, I shall use the name Koori, the indigenous name in use in southeastern Australia, which is my place of writing.

status as the ultimate in living savagery.³ A century later, however, the curious ethnogenetics of Spencer and Gillen's Arunta point more to the history of anthropology than to any credible version of prehistory. Thus it was not only the fruit of a well-organized venture into ethnographic fieldwork, but it inaugurated one of the most resilient controversies in twentieth-century anthropology, one that was to constitute something of a shibboleth for proponents of relativism.⁴ Moreover, as we shall see, both epistemologically and politically, the discovery pointed as much to anthropology's evolutionist past as it did to its relativist future. In Hegelian terms, it represents an ingestion of evolutionist anthropology, a dense summation of the historical determinations that had combined to produce the paradigm. Through a reconstruction of its deeper genealogy, therefore, we can move toward a relativization of relativism.

This is not merely playing with words, doubling up on the relativist's own game. Rather, through recovering the conditions that produced Spencer and Gillen's announcement as an ethnographic event, we can map out key relationships between anthropological theory and colonial power. These relationships are at once both local and global. By stressing the former at the expense of the latter, relativism has disguised the systematicity of colonial domination—in universalizing particularity, it has hidden its own. To counter this effect, we can return relativism to the geopolitical conditions that have nurtured and sustained it. We can begin this by retrieving what relativism suppresses: the homogeneous, the global, the unitary—which is to say, preeminently, the economic.

Relativism has often been criticized for privileging the noneconomic, the ideational, the superstructural.⁵ This is particularly true of those versions of the literary turn that reduce social processes to a set of textual strategies. These two features of relativism—the particularism and the idealism—converge as commonly obscuring the unified economics of global imperialism. In what follows, therefore, I intend to situate one of relativism's most celebrated examples in this wider context.

---

3. As Freud would observe in *Totem and Taboo*, "People who had not yet discovered that conception is the result of sexual intercourse might surely be regarded as the most backward and primitive of living men" (1960 [1913]: 115).

4. Some of the more well-known contributions to this controversy include Lévy-Bruhl 1910; Read 1918; Leach 1969; Ashley-Montagu 1937; Spiro 1968; Kaberry 1936, 1968; R. Tonkinson 1978; Barnes 1973; Scheffler 1976; Yengoyan 1978; Malinowski 1916, 1929; Mountford 1981; and Delaney 1986. It shows little sign of abating; cf. Hodge and Mishra 1991:60; Trigger 1993.

5. The most explicit such critique is probably Maurice Bloch's (1977) "ritual discourse," although W. E. H. Stanner's (1967) critique of Durkheim is analogous. More recent examples include David Lloyd's (1990) "aesthetic culture" and Jeremy Beckett's (1988) "homo religiosus," with which my own "homo superorganicus" (Wolfe 1994:109–18) is clearly cognate.

For convenience, the allegation that Spencer and Gillen's Arunta did not realize that conception was the result of sexual intercourse will be termed *nescience*. This term not only reflects fin de siècle usage.[6] It also has the advantage of emphasizing how diametrically the Arunta were discursively counterposed to the scientific ideals with which their ethnographers identified. This polarity provides an initial convergence of ethnography and imperialism since it replicates the opposing territorial interests at stake in the context of settler colonialism. Thus we can consider whether or not it was merely coincidental that the one bifurcation should obtain in both the scientific and the geopolitical domains. In this regard, the career of Baldwin Spencer is exemplary since, as well as marking a high point in evolutionist ethnography, Spencer was centrally involved in constructing a policy with which Australian governments sought to eliminate the Aboriginal race.

His and Gillen's ethnographies attained such international renown that, in Australia, Spencer acquired a virtually unrivaled authority on Aboriginal matters. In 1911, after Australia's Northern Territory had been placed under the jurisdiction of the federal government, Spencer was appointed Chief Protector of Aborigines, with a brief to report on the Aboriginal situation in the Territory (Mulvaney and Calaby 1985:264–304). In his report, Spencer distinguished between "half-castes" and "quadroons who may be regarded as belonging to the white population." The procedures that he recommended for dealing with "half-castes" were simple but effective:

> No half-caste children should be allowed to remain in any native camp, but they should all be withdrawn and placed on stations. So far as is practicable, this plan is now being adopted. In some cases, when the child is very young, it must of necessity be accompanied by its mother, but in other cases, even though it may seem cruel to separate the mother and child, it is better to do so, when the mother is living, as is usually the case, in a native camp. (Spencer 1913:21)

Spencer made this recommendation at a time when the abduction of Aboriginal children was becoming central to the state-forming strategy of the fledgling Commonwealth of Australia, a national amalgam of previously distinct colonies that had only been constituted in 1901. Such abductions, which were carried out until the late 1960s, were a key element in what

---

6. "The proof of Arunta primitiveness, the only proof, has been their nescience of the facts of generation" (Lang 1905:193).

came to be known as the assimilation policy.⁷ This policy, which, as will be seen, was standardized for all the states of mainland Australia in 1937, sought to eliminate Aborigines through the eugenic expedient of "breeding them white."

As it relates to Baldwin Spencer, therefore, the question of the relationship between ethnography and imperialism becomes the question of whether it was merely by chance that the same man should have come to promulgate both nescience and the assimilation policy. I contend that the coincidence was neither random nor particular to Spencer. Rather, it was symptomatic of a determinate logic that was common to the ostensibly separate projects of ethnography and ethnocide.⁸ To substantiate this, I shall first establish the two genealogies involved—an epistemological series running through evolutionary anthropology and a politico-economic series involving the establishment and consolidation of Australian settler-colonization—and then show that nescience precipitated the cultural logic that bound these two genealogies together. This cultural logic rendered ethnography organic to the settler-colonial project in a manner at once more subtle and more thoroughgoing than can be expressed by "handmaiden of colonialism"-style analyses in which anthropology figures as inertly determined by colonizing imperatives. In the 1990s, there can hardly be any remaining need to demonstrate that evolutionist ethnography, presupposing as it did the extreme inferiority of colonized indigenes, legitimated their oppression. Though undoubtedly true, this is both too obvious and too general to repay proving again. If we remain satisfied with catchall descriptive congruencies such as "epistemic violence" we miss the specific connections whereby hegemony is realized in local practice. This can be appreciated once the relevant contexts have been filled in. Thus we turn first to the epistemological series, situating nescience in the context of evolutionary-anthropological theory.

The Circumstantial and the Cognitive

Nescience conjoined two originary narratives in evolutionary anthropology, a social-organizational one deriving matrilineal kinship systems

---

7. This deeply contentious issue received widespread national publicity in 1997 in the report of a national commission of enquiry established by an earlier (Labor) government (Commonwealth of Australia 1997).

8. I use this term in this context because, as opposed to genocide, which suggests physical extermination, ethnocide is directed against collective identity, which does not preclude leaving individuals alive (cf. Clastres 1988). See also Orlando Patterson's "social death," in particular the element of natal alienation (Patterson 1982:5). For a general discussion of the concept and definition of genocide (which is Raphael Lemkin's term) see Legters 1988.

from primal promiscuity and a cognitive or ideographic one that attributed beliefs in supernatural impregnation to the doctrine of animism. The former, which came to be known as "mother-right," was of considerable cultural depth, dating back at least as far as classical antiquity. For our purposes, however, it is sufficient to locate it in John Millar's (1771) *Observations Concerning the Distinction of Ranks in Society*, which, being published as Cook returned to England after his first landing in Australia (at the time New Holland), made no reference to the land or its inhabitants and shows no sign of being influenced by earlier reports or speculations about them. Thus it is safe to take Millar's narrative as a European—or, at least, wholly non-Koori—invention. Indeed, as might be gathered from his title, Millar's discussion was directed toward his own society, his purpose being a liberal argument for the emancipation of slaves, women, and Scottish miners. Where he could, Millar supplemented his conjectural history of human society with travelers' reports culled from sources ranging from classical antiquity through to his own day. Though contending that society developed out of despotically patriarchal families in which women were chattels without rights, he also noted that Herodotus and other classical writers had suggested an even more barbarous arrangement, which could "in some countries" have preceded any form of marriage whatsoever.

> To a people in this situation it will appear that children have much more connection with their mother than with their father. If a woman has no notion of attachment and fidelity to any particular person, if notwithstanding her occasional intercourse with different individuals she continues to live by herself, or with her own relations, the child which she has born, and which she maintains under her own inspection, is regarded as a member of her own family, and the father, who lives at a distance, has no opportunity of establishing an authority over it. In short, the same ideas which obtain among us, with regards to bastards, will, in those primitive times, be extended to all, or the greater part of the children produced in the country. (Millar 1771:30)

In the next century, as a result of the writings of McLennan and Morgan, this scenario of primitive promiscuity precluding the possibility of nominating fathers came to dominate evolutionary anthropology, constituting the central premise behind the theory of mother-right. Moreover, Australian natives were held to be living embodiments of the theory.

Though predicated upon amorality and confusion, mother-right acquired its name from a book in which the female principle figured as sublimely virtuous. In his famous and convoluted treatise on the subject, Johann Jakob Bachofen took issue with Herodotus' dismissal of the Lycian custom of reckoning descent through the mother as an isolated, non-Hellenic aberration (1969 [1861]). "Closer observation," contended Bachofen (1967:70), "must lead to a deeper view. We find not disorder but system. Not fancy but necessity." *Das Mutterrecht* was devoted to chronicling the historical unfolding of this necessity. The chaste vision that he thus detailed was not, however, reflected in the consensus that came to dominate evolutionary anthropology. Rather, for McLennan, Morgan, Lubbock, Wilken, and others,[9] mother-right consisted in a matrilineality that resulted from a generalized uncertainty of paternity along precisely the lines suggested by Millar (whom no one acknowledged), which situation was held to be the evolutionary precursor to a patrilineal patriarchy more consistently termed *father-right*.

The initial statement of the evolutionary-anthropological version of mother-right came in John Ferguson McLennan's (1865) *Primitive Marriage*. Though McLennan later conceded to Bachofen the distinction of first proposing a stage of descent through women, he maintained that his theory had been conceived independently of Bachofen's, which he deemed a descriptive and inferior account on the grounds that Bachofen had merely seen "the *fact* that kinship was anciently traced through women only but not why it was the fact" (McLennan 1886a:323). McLennan's own theory explicitly focused on kinship (understood as perceptions of consanguinity) to which the scenario that Millar had envisaged was central.

> The connection between these two things—uncertain paternity and kinship through females only, seems so necessary—that of cause and effect—that we may confidently infer the one where we find the other. (McLennan 1865:161)

Citing contemporary Welsh and Bedouin marriage rites in which mock captures of the bride were enacted by men of the groom's party, McLennan's theory of the origins of kinship linked marriage with violence with all the system of that catchphrase of a later anthropology, "we marry our enemies." He invented the terms *endogamy* and *exogamy* to denote, respectively, in-marrying and out-marrying tribes (McLennan 1865:48–49), the latter operating by virtue of a "rule which declares the union of persons of the same blood to be incest." Though according a fundamental role in the origin of society to the avoidance of incest, McLennan's theory is notable

---

9. E.g., Morgan 1866, 1871, 1877; Lubbock 1875, 1885; Wilken 1884, 1921; Tylor 1885, 1889, 1896.

for the lengths to which he went to exclude psychological or instinctual factors from the origins of incest regulations. His developmental engine was a Malthusian one, "the early struggle for food and security," whereby warring hordes engaged in a constant and ruthless battle for survival against other groups and surrounding nature. From this it followed that, whereas men would have been at a premium, the relative weakness of women would have rendered them unwelcome additions to a horde (or "stock"), so that female infanticide would have arisen as a general practice.[10] The ensuing shortage of women meant that they had to be captured from outside and shared around. This ecologically motivated need to obtain women from other groups formed the basis of McLennan's theory of the development of exogamous tribes.

> If it can be shown, firstly, that exogamous tribes exist or have existed; and secondly, that in rude times the relations of separate tribes are uniformly, or almost uniformly, hostile, we have found a set of circumstances in which men could get wives only by capturing them. (McLennan 1865:54)

Citing George Grey's journal of exploration, McLennan could confidently assume that Australian savages would be recognized as fitting the bill.

> That the practice of getting wives by capture de facto prevails among the natives of Australia, is a fact familiar to most readers. . . . The reader may imagine the extent to which, among the myriad hordes of savages, the women are being knocked about, and the men accustomed to associate the acquisition of a wife with acts of violence and rapine. (McLennan 1865:73, 77–78)

Thus evolutionary anthropology had been capitalizing on the possibilities of ignorance of paternity long before Spencer and Gillen were to record nescience in the 1890s. But there are considerable differences between the ignorance entailed in mother-right and the ignorance that Spencer and Gillen were to allege. In particular, McLennan's untraceable paternity did not involve the cognitive deficiency that was to be inherent in the failure to appreciate the principle of insemination as Spencer and Gillen were to report it. In fact, quite the reverse was the case: as Millar's reference to bastards in his own eighteenth-century Scottish society indicates, the whole point of an uncertainty arising from promiscuity was that it was only too

---

10. In *The Descent of Man*, Darwin (1871:i, 132–35) took up McLennan's theory, approvingly citing infanticide as a mechanism for the selection of human varieties that would be favorable enough to secure humanity's break with the lower primates.

consistent with civilized logic. Indeed, the critical bite of McLennan's theory came precisely from its uncomfortable bearing on the sexual double standard that maintained a thriving Victorian underlife of prostitution and "illegitimacy" (it was a wise Victorian who knew his own father).[11] At least insofar as the British evolutionists are concerned, the theory of mother-right had immediate links to domestic sexual politics. Gripped by a post-Malthusian obsession with population growth, the British state, notably by means of a series of Contagious Diseases Acts that were introduced in the 1860s, intervened crudely and repeatedly into the sexuality (ostensibly the fertility) of in the main working-class women (Harrison and Mort 1980; Jeffreys 1985; Lynd 1945; McHugh 1980; Smith 1971; Weeks 1981). So far as more respectable women were concerned, a long-running battle over women's rights (or the lack of them) to hereditary marital property was to result in the landmark Married Women's Property Act of 1882, which curtailed the automatic passing of a daughter's property to her husband upon marriage (Holcombe 1977). In cases of divorce, women did not have rights to their children. All in all, it requires little interpretive license to recognize the distinctive themes of the mother-right narrative—primal promiscuity, uncertain paternity, the subordination of maternal descent, the primacy of patriarchal property, and so on—as refractions of Victorian sexual politics (cf. Coward 1983). In the case of mother-right, the motive for ignorance of paternity was, clearly, circumstantial confusion rather than cognitive deficiency.

Yet we cannot simply say that there were two different kinds of nescience, one of which was circumstantial and merely concerned fathers' identities, the other of which was cognitive and concerned the principle of insemination itself. This is because, as was to be made explicit by Spencer and Gillen among others, the full nescience of the principle of insemination could also result from circumstantial causes. Assuming the kind of sexual chaos that sprang so readily to the repressed Victorian imagination, a chaos in which young girls and old women were alike involved, sexual intercourse would be a constant rather than a variable. As a result, there would be no call to correlate it either with the onset of menstruation or with the menopause—on the basis of the available evidence, sex need have no more to do with conception than had eating or sleeping.

For clarity, therefore, we need to distinguish two kinds of nescience and two kinds of motive, noting that the distinctions are not coterminal. So far as the motives are concerned, the distinction between cognitive and

---

11. As McLennan (1865:167) put it: "Savages are unrestrained by any sense of delicacy from a copartnery in sexual enjoyments; and, indeed, in the civilised state, the sin of great cities shows that there are no natural restraints sufficient to hold back man from grosser copartneries."

circumstantial seems straightforward enough. The two types of nescience can be distinguished as nescience of agent (paternity uncertain) and nescience of principle (insemination unknown).[12] Nescience of agent, the inability to nominate fathers on account of a surfeit of candidates, was exclusively circumstantial. As Shouten, in 1757, seems to have been the first to state in so many words (which later authorities never tired of repeating), "maternity is a matter of fact; paternity one of inference." Since nescience of agent was a discourse on immorality, it was taken for granted that Aborigines would be prime exemplars, an expectation that their ethnographers did not disappoint. Thus, as Lorimer Fison, one of the founding fathers of Australian ethnography, famously put it in relation to the Kamilaroi of New South Wales:

> when a woman is married to a thousand miles of husbands, then paternity must be, to say the least of it, somewhat doubtful. (Fison and Howitt 1880:73)

Though nescience of principle, the failure to link intercourse to impregnation, could spring from the same promiscuous factors as those underlying mother-right, it added a cognitive narrative that was separate from the moral discourse underlying the circumstantial version. This cognitive narrative was Edward Burnett Tylor's theory of animism, which Spencer and Gillen's announcement empirically confirmed.

Tylor, a Quaker and a rationalist, was a prominent advocate of the principle of the psychic unity of mankind. This principle sustained the side of Reform in relation to two recurrent nineteenth-century issues. Despite the 1833 banning of slavery throughout the British empire, the issue of slavery had periodically resurfaced (especially, of course, in the United States) in the controversy between monogenists and polygenists, since different Adams could have generated offspring of an order of difference profound enough to warrant separate standards of moral treatment. In this regard, the psychic unity of mankind represented a comprehensive negation of polygenesis (cf. Stocking 1987:159, 270). Secondly, where the question of progress versus degeneration was concerned, the same principle made it impossible for the whole of mankind to have started out on an equal footing from which an unequal distribution of innate endowment must have caused some races to progress while others fell into decay (Stocking 1987:161).

In keeping with his emphasis on psychic unity, Tylor was an intel-

---

12. Were it not so confusing, the two forms could be more precisely expressed as being nescience of "principal" and of "principle" respectively.

lectualist, seeking cognitive explanations for social phenomena. Hence he attributed a whole range of obsolescent customs to a savage mental propensity that he called "the association of ideas." This distinguished his theories from those of McLennan, who, as noted, went to considerable lengths to avoid resorting to psychological or instinctual explanations for social phenomena. To this extent, therefore, the difference between cognitive and circumstantial expresses the difference between Tylor and McLennan respectively. Thus the two forms of nescience encompassed perhaps the deepest anthropological dichotomy of all—that between the concrete mechanics of social organization (the umbilical binding of matrilineal stocks) and the genesis of abstract ideas (spirit conception). Tylor's theory of animism is an illustration of his intellectualism. In common with other evolutionary anthropologists, Tylor aspired for his new discipline to solve the great human questions, in particular those concerning the origins of religion and abstract thought. It is important to recognize that this goal was common. For, though McLennan and his successors—in particular, William Robertson Smith (1894 [1889]) and Emile Durkheim (1912)—attempted to start their explanations from morphological or social-organizational bases, their *explananda* were no less ideational than Tylor's. This meant that critical moments arose in their theories at points where they tried to switch from social morphology to ideational levels of explanation. By contrast, Tylor's problem was to disguise the fact that, though he was offering an account of the genesis of ideas, there was nothing social about it.

To achieve his end, Tylor simply substituted universal for social, attributing abstract concepts to reflections upon the experience of dreaming that could theoretically occur to anyone (or, at least, to any savage). He coined the term *animism* for a theory that, once elaborated in his epochal (1871) *Primitive Culture,* exercised enormous influence on late-nineteenth-century thought. For evolutionary anthropologists, metaphysics defined humanity, in that the problem of the origins of human consciousness was conceived as a requirement to account for the way in which people had first come to populate the material world with invisible entities residing in or behind concrete objects. Divinities being abstractions par excellence, theology and epistemology coincided around this problem, whose principal props were fetishism and totemism. In this context, Tylor's theory of animism proposed that the idea of a spiritual double connected to bodies or to other physical objects initially arose from the memory of moving about in dreams and trances despite others' reports that one's body had remained still. Herbert Spencer's (1870:537) "ghost theory," which was also influential, displaced the same idea from sleeping bodies to dead ones. Either way, it was the initial duality that mattered: animism having accounted for the attribution of vitality to one inert body, it could readily be generalized to others. Once conceived, abstract vitalities, whether as invisible spirits residing in things or as the ghosts of dead ancestors, were invested with powers. This was the beginning of religion.

In keeping with the conventional evolutionist conflation of phylogeny and ontogeny, or species and individual developments, Tylor (1871:i, 431) dubbed animism a childish doctrine, "the infant philosophy of mankind," which was no different from the nursery belief that sticks or toys were alive. Twenty years later, this was precisely the basis on which the English solicitor and folklorist Edwin Sydney Hartland commenced his series of investigations into "the savage philosophy of things," a faithfully Tylorean concept which he described as

> that infantine state of mind which regards not only our fellow men and women, but all objects animate and inanimate around us, as instinct with a consciousness, a personality akin to our own. (Hartland 1891:25)

The savage philosophy of things proceeded from three premises: animism, transformationism, and witchcraft (understood as the power to cause transformations) (1891:334–37). Hartland's 1891 book ended with the observation that, if there were a human state more primitive than the savagery whose mental echoes were preserved in fairy tales, then work would have to be done to ascertain it. The questions that such work would raise would be avowedly cognitive, taking the investigator "across the border of folklore into pure psychology" (1891:352).

On the basis of the savage philosophy of things, people could enter into transactions with animals and objects in the surrounding world on just the same terms as they could with other humans. This possibility would even extend to marriage, "wherein one party may be human and the other an animal of a different species, or even a tree or plant" (1891:27). Since it was possible to marry such an entity, one could also have one for an ancestor. This was Hartland's explanation for totemism, which he viewed as the worship of mythic ancestors of material or animal form. A direct offshoot of this construction, appearing two years later, was Hartland's notion of "substitution," by which he meant the doctrine that a person's vital principle could be extended to an object, so that action on the object would have a corresponding effect upon the person (he instanced the "learned chirurgeon" of three centuries previously anointing and dressing the weapon rather than the wound that it had caused [1893:466]). This version of action at a distance lent itself to the derived idea that, rather than a person's life merely spreading to an object by sympathy or contagion, it might be transferred in toto for storage or safekeeping in the object. From this, two years later, sprang the theory of external souls, or "life-tokens" (Hartland 1895), which were material entities whose fate was tied to a person's life, as with Dorian Gray's picture or the knife that went rusty when someone died. (There was, of course, an immediate link between these ideas and the bond that, in Frazer's *Golden Bough*, tied the mistletoe in the sacred grove at Nemi to the life of its distractedly vigilant priestly guardian.)

The possibility in animism that interested Hartland was thus the idea of a sharing or exchanging of vitality between people and things. Hence he ascribed the origin of the concept of property to shared identifications (1895:53–54, 442). He was interested in exchange since, if a person transferred the whole of their life to an object, it followed that they would actually become transformed into that object. This account of such a belief was pure animism:

> Starting from his personal consciousness, the savage attributes the like consciousness to everything he sees or feels around him. And holding that outward form is by no means of the essence of existence or of individuality, he looks upon the transformation as an ordinary incident, happening to all men at death, happening to many men and other creatures whensoever they will. (Hartland 1895:441)

The idea that death could furnish a hinge for transformation amplified an equivalence between transformation and transmigration that Hartland had established in a book published the previous year (1894:226–27). Transmigration, understood as a transformation mediated by death, thus derived from the same elaboration of animism as the life-token. For our purposes, the crucial feature of transmigration is that, since it provides for people's preexistence, it only involves a short step to pregnancy without procreation (it constitutes, as it were, precreation). Nevertheless, even if individual lives do not need to be started, there still has to be some conduit whereby they transmigrate or transform themselves into the fetus in the womb. This recalls Hartland's view of totemism. Transactions between women and nonhuman entities would furnish the requisite mechanism. This was precisely the form that Hartland's thinking of the previous year had taken.[13]

Correlating stories of transformations, a collection of magical fertility practices, and a body of myths involving supernatural births (or births

---

13. I have overshot the actual introduction of nescience in order to show how it was integral to the trajectory of Hartland's thinking.

resulting from metaphysical visitations upon women), Hartland had argued (1894:v) that the concept of life that underlay them was a sacramental one (the rhetorical implications for Christianity were overt). Though conceding (180) that magical practices such as the carrying of fertility dolls, as well as the superstitions justifying them, often augmented rather than replaced natural processes, Hartland had asserted that the parthenogenetic explanation preceded the natural one. He had claimed that myths involving supernatural births were to be found universally distributed, and that, rather than survivals of an era in which the bizarre or bestial unions recounted might actually have been practiced, these myths were evidence of an evolutionary stage in which the principle of insemination had not been recognized. In other words, in what must surely count as an ethnographic equivalent of the discovery of Pluto, barely two years before Spencer and Gillen were to announce the Arunta's nescience, Hartland had theorized its prehistoric occurrence in the course of a conjectural reconstruction that led from animism to transmigration. The actual "prophecy" (retrodiction?) came about as follows.

Hartland (1894:1–3) took the legend of Perseus as his key myth. After an oracle pronounced that Acrisius would be killed by the son of his daughter Danae, Acrisius locked her up in a brass tower to ensure her celibacy, a plan that Jupiter frustrated by visiting Danae in a shower of gold, after which she gave birth to Perseus.[14] Hartland's statement of this myth's significance juxtaposes the different themes that it brings together so clearly that one could draw lines through the text to divide them up. Thus our two types of nescience are distinguished, with the first reflecting circumstantial causes and the second implying these as well as an "attitude of mind."[15] Furthermore, though this attitude of mind is suggested by antiquarian evidence, Hartland makes an ethnographic reference to native Australians at the very point where he hypothesizes nescience of

---

14. Needless to state, Acrisius's precaution presupposes physiological awareness on his part. The point is the content, rather than the persuasiveness, of Hartland's theory.

15. As in the case of other implications of his theory, the perspicacious McLennan had anticipated the circumstantial possibility of nescience of principle, only he had not developed it: "blood-ties through fathers could not find a place in a system of kinship, unless circumstances usually allowed of some degree of certainty as to who the father of a child was, or of certainty as to the father's blood. A system of relationship through fathers could only be formed—as we have seen that a system of relationships through mothers would be formed—after a good deal of reflection upon the fact of paternity. And fathers must usually be known before men will think of relationship through fathers—indeed, before the idea of a father could be formed" (1865:158). For all his perspicacity, though, McLennan could not think beyond *men* thinking of relationship through fathers. Indeed, for all the ingenuity—and it was considerable—that two generations of evolutionists devoted to this issue, not one of them ever entertained the prospect of the polyandrous mothers sharing a secret smile across the inexhaustible throng of unwitting suitors.

principle. In this regard, it is, however, noteworthy that mother-right was seen as a surviving trace of a long-superseded nescience, and that he does not suggest that contemporary native Australians might still persist in such ignorance.

> The researches of the last five-and-twenty years have established that among many savage races the father was held to be no relation to his children. Even where he exercised, as among the native Australians, despotic power over his wife and children, the latter were held to be his rather as owner than as begetter; and the ownership of both wife and children passed at his death to his brothers, while at the same time the relationships of the children were reckoned exclusively with their mother's kin. This system of relationships, known scientifically as Mother-right, traces whereof are almost everywhere found, can only have sprung either from a kind of promiscuity wherein the true father could not have been ascertained, or from an imperfect recognition of the great natural fact of fatherhood. Both causes, perhaps, played their part. But at least we may say that the attitude of mind which favours the practices and beliefs we have been discussing is one which would be consistent, and consistent alone, with the imperfect recognition of paternity. And it is unquestionable that the superstitions, once rooted, would be likely to survive long after paternity had become an accepted fact, and tenacious of their existence, would seek new grounds of justification. (1894:180–81)

Such a restrained formulation may not seem much like prophecy. At this stage, however, it is not prophecy. It only becomes so retrospectively, in the light of Spencer and Gillen's Australian ethnography. The clearest symptom of this process is Hartland's tensing. In 1894, the illustrative allusion to Australia notwithstanding, his savagery is empirically a thing of the past ("the father *was* held to be no relation to his children"). In this regard, it contrasts strikingly with the robustly ethnographic presentism (and, it might be noted, increasingly cognitive emphasis) of his remarks once Spencer and Gillen's verification of his hypothesis had been established as the realization of an anthropological prediction.

> Ignorance of the real cause of birth, it might be thought . . . would not long survive the habitual commerce of men and women and the continual reproduction of the species. It would not, in our stage of civilisation and with our social regulations . . . [but] the savage who has not been thus favoured is still by comparison underdeveloped. . . . His attention, not habitually directed to the problems of the universe,

is easily tired. His knowledge is severely limited; his range of ideas is small. Credulous as a child, he is put off from the solution of a merely speculative question by a tale which chimes with his previous ideas, though it may transcend his actual experience. Hence many a deduction, many an induction, to us plain and obvious, has been retarded, or never reached at all; he is still a savage. (Hartland 1909:255, 256)

Between Hartland's two statements, Spencer and Gillen's "discovery" had transformed his genteel literary speculation into a scientific prediction experimentally confirmed in the ethnographic laboratory. That the initial postulate had been framed in the context of a different milieu is suggested by his having perceived it necessary to paraphrase the concept that was "known scientifically as Mother-right." Thus it is revealing to retrace his first steps from letters to science.

Hartland's initial reaction to Spencer and Gillen's confirmation of his suggestion was one of bemusement. In fact, in his review of their 1899 book, which established Arunta nescience as a cause célèbre, he made no mention of *The Legend of Perseus,* confining nescience to a few understated remarks manifestly overshadowed by his preceding discussion of bilateral kinship.

> Besides all this we are given to understand [citing the pages] that paternity is not understood. It is distinctly held not to be the direct result of conjugal relations, but, if I rightly apprehend the author's [*sic*—he clearly meant Spencer's] meaning, because some spirit from the Alcheringa ["dream-times"] seizes an opportunity of reincarnation, or is induced by magical practices to seek such an opportunity. (Hartland 1899:236)

It was not until the following year, in the course of his presidential address to the Folk-Lore Society, that Hartland acknowledged the substantiation of his conjecture. Even here, however, he displayed a distinct hesitance to accept the idea that his suggestion should have met with such a literal confirmation.

> Some years ago I ventured to suggest that certain archaic beliefs and practices found almost all over the world were consistent only with, and must have arisen from, imperfect recognition of fatherhood. I hardly expected, however, that a people would be found still existing in that hypothetical condition of ignorance. Yet, if we may trust the evidence before us, it is precisely the condition of the Arunta. They

hold the cause of birth to be simply the desire of some Arunta of earlier days to be reincarnated. (Hartland 1900:65)

In both passages, Hartland seems unsure of Spencer and Gillen's evidence. This is understandable, since their 1899 testimony fell appreciably short of unambiguous clarity. On the same page (Spencer and Gillen 1899:265) as the statement that children were not the direct result of intercourse, they had suggested that intercourse could prepare the way for spirit children. Hartland even cited this page in relation to a statement by Frazer that the Arunta believed that immaculate conception was the sole cause of human birth, adding the remark, "But it looks as though they 'had their suspicions'" (Hartland 1900:66, n.1).

As we have seen, though, Hartland was to come round. In so doing, however, he only endorsed a construction that others were putting upon the sequence of events. Thus, when Arnold van Gennep chided Andrew Lang for not conceding to Frazer that Arunta nescience was neither isolated nor aberrant, his question was rhetorical: "Doesn't he know Mr. Sydney Hartland's study of the topic of supernatural births?" (1906:LXVII). Van Gennep's question is central to the development of nescience, since it emphasizes the generality implicit in Hartland's hypothesis. As an evolutionary stage through which all must pass, nescience was unlikely to remain an idiosyncrasy of the Arunta, but could be expected to surface wherever there were people whose status was deemed commensurable.

This implication had been anticipated from the very first response that Spencer and Gillen's book had received, from the influential pen of Frazer, who had been in consultation with Spencer through all the stages of its preparation. Unlike Hartland himself, Frazer unhesitatingly proclaimed a direct link between the Arunta and *The Legend of Perseus.* The way in which this link was expressed is illuminating, since it presaged a subsequent chain. For Frazer, the Arunta did not merely exemplify an extraordinary belief; they were "the first"—a term that not only suggested that Spencer and Gillen had won a race, but assumed that others would follow them in.

> Students of folk-lore have long been familiar with notions of this sort occurring in the stories of the birth of miraculous personages [here he cites *The Legend of Perseus*], but this is the first case on record of a tribe who believe in immaculate conception as the sole cause of the birth of every human being who comes into the world. (Frazer 1899:649)

The issue is not the accuracy of Frazer's claim (Spencer and Gillen had merely reported that the Arunta believed themselves to be thus conceived) but the preexistence of a theoretical space that drew Spencer and Gillen's report into its implicational economy. Thus anthropological theory has been discussed before the account of Spencer and Gillen's fieldwork because that is the order that best reflects the empirical chronology. This body of theory was there before Spencer and Gillen. While he was still in England, Spencer had worked with Tylor on the reinstallation of the Pitt Rivers anthropological museum (Mulvaney and Calaby 1985: 59–61). While preparing for his fieldwork, he had been in correspondence with both Tylor and Frazer (Marett and Penniman 1932). In establishing a theoretical context before proceeding to the ethnography, therefore, we are repeating Spencer's own historical experience. More generally, this procedure illuminates the projection onto Aborigines of European fantasies about Europe's own prehistory, fantasies whose origins were demonstrably independent of empirical Koori data.

Walter Baldwin Spencer, who had studied anatomy under Maudsley at Oxford (where Tylor had recruited him for the museological work), had gone to Australia to take up the foundation chair in biology at the University of Melbourne. In 1894, the year of *The Legend of Perseus,* he went to Central Australia as the biologist on a scientific expedition financed and led by an Adelaide businessman, William Horn, the expedition's anthropologist being Edward Charles Stirling, professor of medicine at the University of Adelaide. In Alice Springs, which was the end of the overland telegraph line, Spencer met Frank (Francis James) Gillen, postmaster and Sub-Protector of Aborigines, who had local knowledge and established relations with members of the Arunta tribe. The ethnographic possibilities offered by the combination of Gillen's local knowledge and Spencer's scientific competence appealed to both men, eventually leading to the publication of their two great works (Spencer and Gillen 1899, 1904). The first of these, *The Native Tribes of Central Australia,* sprang from the *Engwura* ceremonial ground, while the second, *The Northern Tribes of Central Australia,* resulted from an expedition that they mounted from Alice Springs up to the Gulf of Carpentaria in 1901–2.[16]

Following nescience through Spencer and Gillen's publications, it is asserted with a steadily growing confidence that strikingly mirrors the development of Hartland's responses to their discovery. The report of the Horn Expedition, edited by Spencer, appeared in 1896. In the course of Stirling's anthropological contribution, nescience of principle was to all intents and purposes asserted, only by means of some negative phrasing which, while unequivocally cognitive, was almost perversely inconclu-

---

16. For compendious details concerning Spencer and his partnership with Gillen, see Mulvaney and Calaby's (1985) biography.

sive. In response to the suggestion that the operation of urethral subincision might be intended as a contraceptive measure, Stirling objected that such an explanation would imply

> a knowledge of physiological processes, which, it appears to me, we are not justified in attributing to people of the mental status of Australians any more than we should attribute circumcision to the knowledge of the hygienic or pathological disadvantage of a long prepuce. (Stirling 1896:34)

After the Horn Expedition, Spencer and Gillen's partnership was consolidated in fieldwork undertaken together from 1896 to 1897, which resulted in their classic 1899 book. In this book, the Arunta's nescience was explicitly asserted in the course of their own denial that subincision was an attempt at contraception.

> Time after time we have questioned them on this point, and always received the reply that the child was not the direct result of intercourse, that it may come without this, which merely, as it were, prepares the mother for the reception and birth also of an already-formed spirit child who inhabits one of the local totem centres. Time after time we have questioned them on this point, and always received the reply that the child was not the direct result of intercourse. (265)

Early in the new century, Spencer and Gillen mounted the expedition from Arunta country up to the shores of the Gulf of Carpentaria from which, in 1904, their second major ethnography resulted. The 1904 version of nescience was stronger than the previous one on two counts. First, the idea that conception could occur without intercourse even taking place was strengthened by the omission of any suggestion that intercourse might constitute some kind of preparation for childbirth. Second, the belief was now alleged of all Aborigines living between Alice Springs and the Gulf of Carpentaria.

> [T]he natives, one and all in these tribes, believe that the child is the direct result of the entrance into the mother of an ancestral spirit individual. They have no idea of procreation as being directly associated with sexual intercourse, and firmly believe that children can be born without this taking place . . . In every one of the tribes dealt with by us there is fundamentally the same belief with regard to conception as we have previously described in connection with the Arunta.

> Every individual is regarded as the reincarnation of an ancestor. (Spencer and Gillen 1904:330, 606)

In view of this level of certainty, it is instructive to observe how, in an article published while their 1899 work was still in preparation, nescience had been alleged with much more circumspection. Indeed, following a year after Stirling's Horn Expedition report, Spencer's prose is only marginally more affirmative.

> When a woman conceives it is supposed that it is one of such a group of spirits who goes inside her and thus it naturally follows, granting the premises firmly believed in by the natives, that the totem of the child is determined solely by the spot at which the mother conceived, or, what is the same thing, believes that she conceived, the child. (Spencer and Gillen 1897:25)

Like Hartland, therefore, Spencer and Gillen grew in confidence. In Hartland's case, there are all sorts of possible reasons. He may just not have been convinced (the ethnography left plenty of room for doubt), he may not have liked Frazer's appropriation of the topic, or he might have resisted the idea that his antiquarian achievement of penetrating further back in time than history or philology could go might still be emulated by ethnography. Such possibilities do not, however, apply to Spencer and Gillen. Indeed, it is hard to see why an open-and-shut question like nescience should be expressed with differing degrees of equivocation. In this regard, it is difficult to ignore the presence, over in Queensland, of Walter Roth, who had been a comember with Spencer of Maudsley's Oxford anatomy group (Mulvaney and Calaby 1985: plate 11). As is well known, in 1903 (a year before Spencer and Gillen's second book), Roth was to allege nescience of principle of the Tully River blacks (Roth 1903; cf. Leach 1969). More intriguingly, however, back in 1897—the year after Stirling's Horn Expedition report and the year in which Spencer's first circumspect formulation appeared—Roth too had made a statement on the relationship between urethral operations and contraception, one whose not-quite-conclusiveness was, if anything, even more tantalizing than Stirling's.

> In this connection it is interesting to note that even the possibility of taking artificial measures to prevent fertilisation, &c. (I am not speaking of abortion), is apparently beyond their comprehension: thus I have reports from station-managers who assure me that only with

great difficulty could their 'boys' be made to understand, if ever they did, the object of spaying cattle. (Roth 1897:179)

All in all, it is as if Spencer and Gillen were engaged with Roth in a race to fulfill Hartland's prophecy. In their 1899 book, Spencer and Gillen noted the correspondence between Roth's 1897 data and theirs (ix, 265). Roth's fifth bulletin of 1903 was then somewhat less equivocal about Tully River beliefs than Spencer and Gillen had been about the Arunta's, whereupon their 1904 book presented the strongest statement of all (cf. Spencer and Gillen 1904:145, n.). It was at this juncture that Hartland himself seems to have given up resisting the prophetic momentum (although in a way that avoided subscription to the Frazer camp), observing of Spencer and Gillen's 1904 book:

> Its special value is that it supplies in great measure the links which unite the beliefs and practices of the Arunta with those described by Mr. Walter Roth. (Hartland 1904:474)

But if there was a race, why did Roth (and, for that matter, Stirling) hold back? Why did they not come out and proclaim their discovery of a people who did not connect copulation to pregnancy? While it is, of course, hard to say, it is worth noting that neither Stirling nor Roth, both physiologists by training, would have had any particular call to be aware of Hartland's book until the reaction to Spencer and Gillen's revelations gave it a wider than folkloric significance.[17] Spencer, on the other hand, was in constant contact with Frazer, who was not only well aware of Hartland's conjecture but, like Hartland, was endeavoring to devise a theory that could account for the data of totemism. Frazer had already pinned his hopes on two separate theories of totemism, neither of which had worked. Nescience of principle was to provide him with a third and final explanation, "conceptional totemism," according to which totemism originated spontaneously as an animistic account of pregnancy. The satisfaction that this explanation afforded Frazer (1905:457–58) was palpable: "after years of sounding, our plummets seem to touch bottom at last."

With Spencer and Gillen's Arunta nescience, the displacement from a Eurocentric antiquarianism to (settler-)colonial ethnography was consum-

---

17. Thus an earlier claim about the Arunta (Aranda) escaped such attention, presumably because it was made outside British scientific discourse—in German, in a relatively obscure periodical, by one of the first of the German Lutheran missionaries to the Aranda at Hermannsburg Mission, who reported the Aranda to believe that God gave them children—"Die Kinder, sagen sie, schenkt Altjira (Gott)" (Kempe 1883:53).

mated in two major respects. Cognitively, it gave animism an empirical foundation (cf. Stocking 1987:236–37) that, being independent of dreaming, did not derive its plausibility from individualist introspection. Thus savage ignorance no longer needed to be something that we all shared. As a result (and secondly), the moral implications could also be categorically externalized in a way that had been precluded by the nescience of agent that had sustained mother-right. As a cognitive condition, nescience need no longer be of a piece with Millar's Scottish bastards or the contradictions of Victorian sexual practice. Though potentially continuous with mother-right so far as the circumstantial narrative was concerned, Spencer and Gillen's Arunta nescience of principle actually effected a thoroughgoing cognitive divorce.

So far as the epistemological series is concerned, then, it is clear that nescience was anticipated to the point of overdetermination by the antecedent context of evolutionary-anthropological theory. Thus it remains to situate Spencer and Gillen's text in the context of Australian settler-colonization. Here, there is no doubt about the empirical complicity whereby ethnography and politics converged—Spencer was chosen to be Protector of Aborigines and commissioned to prepare his report on account of his ethnographic credentials. On its own, however, this convergence does not explain very much. To appreciate its systemic nature, we need to explore the cultural logic whereby Spencer's combination of the two roles symptomatized rather than brought about their commonality.[18] Thus we turn now to the political series, situating Spencer's text in the context of Australian state-formation.

Nation and MiscegeNation

In its broad context, Australian settler- (or creole-) colonization is part of the western European project of global colonization that stems from the fifteenth century. Thus it is consistent that the first fleet of British settler-colonial invaders, made up of convicts and their custodians under the command of Captain Arthur Phillip, should have been commissioned in the wake of the American colonies' attainment of independence from Britain, a development that, among other things, closed off an outlet for convict shipment. When the First Fleet first set foot on Gamaraigal land, on January 26, 1788, their enterprise was already horizoned with prece-

---

18. As Talal Asad (1979:607) put it, in opening his Malinowski Memorial Lecture, the really interesting questions concern "the ideological conditions of anthropology, and the implications of these conditions for its discourse, and not the very occasionally direct but on the whole insignificant practical role that British anthropologists played in support of British imperial structures."

dents, conventions, and expectations. Moreover, the new land was by no means completely new, having already been mapped and named by Cook and Banks, whose reports had suggested New Holland (*Terra Australis*, the Great South Land, or the Antipodes to earlier navigators and speculators) as a suitable place for settlement (Carter 1987; Frost 1990). Though instructed to engage in friendly commerce with the natives, Phillips's party very soon resorted to shooting them (Stanner 1977), establishing a pattern that was to be repeated across the face of the continent over the next century and a half. For, regardless of instructions to the contrary, the invaders entertained few practical doubts as to their entitlement to settle the land, an entitlement whereby native self-defense was itself seen as invasion.

Phillips's instructions (and, for that matter, the Mabo judgment)[19] notwithstanding, Australian settler-colonization was phrased in terms of the doctrine of *terra nullius* rather than of any acknowledgment of native title. As it had been elaborated by eighteenth-century jurists such as Wolff, Vattel, Pufendorf, and Blackstone, land had to become property for rights of ownership to apply to it. Property entailed a twofold criterion, one material or technical and the other political or regulative. In the first instance, the land should have been improved—which is to say, rendered a more efficient provider of human subsistence than the natural state—through labor being mixed with it. Practically, this meant that the land should have been cultivated, irrigated, built on, and enclosed. Second, a system of legitimate sanctions had to operate whereby those who had improved the land should have the right to unfettered enjoyment of the fruits of their labor—or, in other words, to private property in it. Practically, this meant centralized governance, formal laws, policing, and, again, enclosure (or acknowledged boundaries). Unless these two criteria were met, the inhabitants were not a society but legally transparent entities, so that, for ownership purposes, the land was no one's (a bourgeois elaboration of the Roman *vacuum domicilium*). A third, pragmatic criterion, which was generally derived from the first two, reflected the growth of urbanizing Europe's concern over population densities. It held that, if an area was being so inefficiently used that it was only supporting a fraction of the population that it otherwise might, then more efficient societies were entitled to export their surplus population to realize its potential (the convicts being a paradigm case).[20]

---

19. In this judgment, in 1992, the Australian High Court negated the doctrine of terra nullius.

20. For analyses and discussions of the primary formulations of terra nullius (Blackstone 1783; Vattel 1758; Wolff 1764; Grotius 1609; Locke 1690; Pufendorf 1688) see, e.g., Frost 1990; Hulme 1990; Reynolds 1992.

Though ostensibly codifying natives' rights (or lack of them), *terra nullius* was primarily a systematization of the mutual rights and obligations of rival European powers. It specified the conditions under which one such power could lay claim to a foreign territory as against all the others. Its obvious relation to bourgeois society is confirmed by the fact that it only began to take hold from the seventeenth century on, displacing the earlier formula for laying claim to a colony, which (held longest by feudal and Catholic Spain) had been based on the Pope's authority over islands (Frost 1990:65).

As progressively encoded into Australian law,[21] terra nullius was, of course, a rationalization rather than a motive for colonial invasion. The motive was greed—specifically, greed for land. The specification is necessary because it expresses the particular nature of settler-colonialism. In contrast to franchise or dependent colonies, settler (or creole) ones were not primarily established to extract surplus value from native labor. Rather, they are premised upon displacing natives from (or *re*placing them on) the land. The relationship between Native and African Americans provides the clearest illustration: in the main, Native North Americans were cleared from their land rather than exploited for their labor, their place being taken by displaced Africans who provided the labor to be mixed with the expropriated land. In the Australian case, the labor that was imported to add value to the land was primarily that of British and Irish convicts. In such a situation, it is awkward to speak of an articulation between colonizer and colonized, since the determinate articulation is not to a society but directly to the land, a precondition of social organization. Since it is incoherent to talk of an articulation between humans and things, this social relationship can be conceived of as a negative articulation.

The cultural logic that is organic to a negative articulation is one of elimination. In its purest form, as in the case of the Guanches (indigenous Canary Islanders), Tainos, Caribs, and so on, the logic of elimination strives to replace indigenous society with that imported by the colonizers. In local Australian practice, this cultural logic was actualized by virtue of the fact that the economic use to which the colonized land was principally turned was that of pastoral settlement, whose requirement for territory was inherently exclusive. This is because the introduced cattle or sheep

---

21. As the British Privy Council declared in the case of Cooper v. Stuart (1889.14. Appeal Cases, 286), "There is a great difference between the case of a colony acquired by conquest or cession, in which case there is an established system of law, and that of a colony which consisted of a tract of territory practically unoccupied, without settled inhabitants or settled law, at the time it was peacefully annexed to the British dominions. The colony of New South Wales belongs to the latter class."

competed with indigenous fauna for subsistence, consuming the tubers, shoots, and seeds whereby the indigenous flora reproduced itself and rapidly reducing waterholes to mud. In a relatively short time the only subsistence remaining available to indigenous humans was the introduced fauna whose protection was axiomatic to the pastoral project (McGrath 1987:1–23; Reynolds 1981:128–30). Hence pastoral settlement became a zero-sum conflict. Thus the pattern of violence established by the First Fleet was neither gratuitous nor random but systemic to settler-colonization.

Since frontiers moved across Australia from coastal beachheads variously established over the century following the landing of the First Fleet, it is not possible to date the development of Australian settler-colonization as a whole. Thus it is convenient to organize its establishment and consolidation into a typology of phases, a heuristic that is enabled by the consistency of the general pattern.[22] The initial phase, in which the land was first seized, is principally characterized by indigenous mortality, attributable to four main (and mutually supportive) agencies: homicide, sexual abuse, disease, and starvation.[23] Though conditioned by ecological factors, this phase was very short. As the settler, anthropologist, and Victorian government official Edward Curr put it,

> In the first place the meeting of the Aboriginal tribes of Australia and the White pioneer, results as a rule in war, which lasts from six months to ten years, according to the nature of the country, the amount of settlement which takes place in a neighbourhood, and the proclivities of the individuals concerned. When several squatters settle in proximity, and the country they occupy is easy of access and without fastnesses to which the Blacks can retreat, the period of warfare is usually short and the bloodshed not excessive. On the other hand, in districts which are not easily traversed on horseback, in which the Whites are few in number and food is procurable by the Blacks in fastnesses, the term is usually prolonged and the slaughter more considerable. . . .
>
> . . . The tribe, being threatened with war by the White stranger, if it attempts to get food in its own country, and with the same consequences if it intrudes on the lands of a neighbouring tribe, finds itself

---

22. For alternative typologies for this process, see Beckett 1989; Broome 1982; Drakakis-Smith 1984; Read 1988.

23. See, e.g., Butlin 1985; Christie 1979; Critchett 1990; Elder 1988; Green 1984; Jenkin 1979; Loos 1982; Markus 1974; Milliss 1992; Pepper and Araugo 1985; Plomley 1991; Reece 1974; Reid 1982, 1990; Reynolds 1981, 1995; Rowley 1970; Turnbull 1949; et al.

reduced to make choice of certain death from starvation and probable death from the rifle, and naturally chooses the latter. (Curr 1886:100–101, 103–4)

In addition to the differences in firepower, Koori resistance to the settler-colonial invasion, though universally offered (Broome 1982; Lippmann 1981; Miller 1985; Morris 1989; Read 1988; Reynolds 1981), was hampered by a number of factors. Chief among these were the ravages of introduced diseases—smallpox, syphilis, typhoid, whooping cough, diphtheria, tuberculosis, dysentery, influenza, and the rest—against which they had not developed immunities (Butlin 1985; Campbell 1983:198; cf. Crosby 1986), the activities of native police or troopers recruited and armed by settler authorities to put down their tribal enemies (Rosser 1991; cf. Fels 1988), and other intranecine conflicts resulting from refugee crises occasioned by the invasion (Rowley 1970:36–37).[24] As it turns out, the standard pattern was one of decimated but largely pacified survivors improvising a variety of livelihoods in the pores of the now-established settler society, which generally regarded them with distaste. The varied subsistence that tribal territory had previously provided was now replaced by the ubiquitous ration of tea, sugar, and "white man's flour," which thus condensed and potently signified the historical process of expropriation. To this day, flour laced with strychnine still stands for genocide in Australian parlance. In the second phase, the survivors were generally gathered at fixed locations, either by the lure of rations or by coercive measures,[25] a procedure that, while no longer directly homicidal, continued the effect, consistent with the logic of elimination, of vacating Koori country and rendering it available for pastoral settlement. In keeping with both evolutionist premises and the tangible evidence of their decimation, these people's sojourn on the missions, stations, and reservations where they had been gathered was seen as a temporary expedient, since they were a dying race (the evolutionist rationale for this being that, unstiffened by selection as they were, they would be altogether unfit to survive in the presence of

---

24. Insofar as it constitutes an apology for the invasion, the claim that more Aborigines died at the hands of other Aborigines than at the hands of whites (Blainey 1975:108–9; Nance 1981) betrays a depressing paucity of historical reflection. It should surely be unnecessary to point out that the invasion could not but have produced refugee crises in regions where resources were already subjected to unprecedented strain. There are no prima facie grounds for imagining that the consequences should have differed greatly from ones which have characterized comparable situations in Europe. The causal chain required to attribute such consequences to the invasion is hardly too long to tax a normal historical intelligence.

25. See, e.g., Attwood 1989; Brock and Kartinyeri 1989; Brook and Kohen 1991; Christie 1979; Critchett 1980; Gunson 1974; Haebich 1989; McLeod 1982; Rosser 1978, 1985.

their immeasurably distant future). Though couched in philanthropic rhetoric that contrasted strongly with the homicidal sentiments of the first phase (the missionary role was held out as "smoothing the dying pillow"), the premise of the dying race was no less consistent with the logic of elimination.

During both these phases, the colonists exploited native labor. The example of the Native Mounted Police, who were used extensively in the Port Phillip District (later to become Victoria) and the Mareton Bay District (later Queensland), has already been cited. Beyond this, though, settler-colonization relied on Koori labor at every stage and in every site of its development. Kooris guided, interpreted for, and protected explorers. They cut bark, built fences, dug, planted, maintained, shepherded, stock-rode, mined, pearl-dived, sealed, and performed every conceivable settler-colonial task except governance.[26] Above all, they kept house and provided sexual services, whereby pastoralists "bred their own labour" (Bleakley 1961:317; McGrath 1987:68–94; Huggins 1988). Thus it is not the case that, in practice, settler-colonization *only* eliminated the natives. It is rather the case that the exploitation of native labor was subordinate to the primary project of territorial acquisition. Settler-colonists went to stay. In the main, they did not send their children back to British schools or retire "home" before old age could spoil the illusion of their superhumanity. National independence did not entail their departure. Thus even though, being established too late and too far north for convicts to be available, the northern Australian cattle industry relied very heavily indeed on Aboriginal labor, it represents an exception that does not disturb the rule (moreover, no sooner were equal wages introduced in the 1960s and 1970s than Aboriginal labor was dispensed with and relegated to container-settlements at a revealingly rapid rate [Berndt and Berndt 1987; Rowse 1993]).

This notwithstanding, one element in the foregoing stands out as particularly contrary to the logic of elimination. White men's sexual exploitation of Koori women produced offspring who, growing up (as they almost invariably did) with their maternal kin, could be accounted native rather than settler. Moreover, far from dying out, this section of the native population threatened to expand exponentially. Crucially, in other words, the sexual element of the invasion contradicted the logic of elimination (to put it another way, the behavior of individual colonizers was bound to negate the interest of colonization). In other colonial situations, where native (as opposed to imported) labor is at a premium, people with combined ancestry

---

26. See, e.g., Beckett 1977; Christie 1979; Curthoys 1982; Evans 1984; Haebich 1989; May 1983, 1986; McGrath 1978, 1987; Pope 1988; Reynolds 1990; Ryan 1981; M. Tonkinson 1988.

can be accounted settler-become-native (as in the case of Latin American *mestizaje* [Bartra 1992; Canny and Pagden 1987; Mörner 1967, 1970]) or something separate from either native or settler (as in Guillaumin's sharp specification [1988:27] of South African "Coloureds" as a "class formed by people belonging in fact to one *and* the other group [which] is declared to belong to neither one nor the other but to itself"). In Australia, by contrast, as the logic of elimination would indicate, the only category whose expansion was tolerable was the settler one. In other words—and in stark contrast to situations in which a metropolitan society depicts itself as being contaminated from within, as in the case of Nazi Germany—the answer to the problem of "miscegenation" could only be absorption into the settler category.[27]

As the nineteenth century progressed, the romance of the dying race steadily gave way to the specter of "the half-caste menace." Toward the end of the century, a movement for the federation of the separate Australian colonies gathered momentum. As envisaged by its predominantly entrepreneurial promoters, federation would dismantle barriers hindering free trade between the separate Australian colonies, a development that would prepare the ground for separate nationhood (with dominion status). At the turn of the twentieth century, this goal was achieved, with the Commonwealth of Australia being constituted by an act of the British parliament that took effect from January 1, 1901. At this moment, "Australia" became a national as well as a geographic entity. This was not a natural convergence. Despite Australia's insular geography, New Zealand was at one stage to be included in the federation, while, at another, Western Australia was not. Nationalist rhetoric aside, therefore, before 1901, "Australia" was a natural rather than a cultural category. Hence Edward Curr's previously cited book *The Australian Race*, published in 1886, was about Aborigines, who were part of the natural features of the land mass on which the several colonial polities were constituted. Accordingly, at a single stroke (the last one of 1900) settlers became, and Aborigines ceased to be, Australians—an inversion that was formalized by aboriginal natives' exclusion from the terms of the new constitution. As if in anticipation of structuralism, therefore, the "half-caste menace" straddled the boundary between nature and culture, threatening the basis on which the citizenship and geography of the new imperialist nation-state were predicated.

---

27. Here and elsewhere (e.g., Wolfe 1994), I stress the specificity of constructions of "miscegenation" to the structural particularities of the different colonial relationships that produce them. Inclusive discourses (assimilation, etc.) harmonize with the eliminatory character of settler-colonial social formations once they have reached a point at which the natives are multiply outnumbered (which need not take long at all). In this respect, my analysis differs from the general stress on exclusion that is a feature of Ann Stoler's stimulating analyses (Stoler 1989; 1995:50–52, 133).

The official response to the "half-caste menace" was the assimilation policy, whereby people of mixed descent were not to be accounted Aboriginal—which is to say, they were to be accounted settler. As administratively implemented, this meant the separation of people of "mixed race" from their natal kin. This strategy constitutes the third phase of Australian settler-colonization. The first instance of such legislation occurred in Spencer's colony, Victoria, in 1886 (the year of Curr's book), when an act was passed that provided for the expulsion of "half-castes" from Aboriginal reserves (Attwood 1989:81–103; Christie 1979:178–204; Critchett 1980; Wilkinson 1987). As federation approached, other colonies began to follow suit. This process was effectively completed by the outbreak of World War I, the conflict that, in nationalist mythology, constitutes the national baptism.

For Kooris, however, the baptism of blood depended on whether or not their particular portion of it was "full." As the new nation and the twentieth century unfolded, official policy progressively turned from a negative strategy of expelling "half-castes" from reserves (which, so far as it worked at all, only produced "fringe-camps" and a rural landscape punctuated by destitute Kooris shuffling between the margins of more or less hostile country towns) to a positive strategy whereby the products of "miscegenation" were taken from their kin and incorporated into the settler domain.[28] This strategy was applied to children, whose natal links could more readily be obliterated. Assuming continued "miscegenation," the policy of leaving behind a "full-blood" population as the only officially recognized aboriginal category would ensure that this aboriginal category became an ever-dwindling one. In other words, the legislation was intended to reinstate the dying of the dying race—or, as it was put by J. A. Carrodus, secretary of the Australian government Department of the Interior, at the national conference that formulated a version of assimilationism for uniform implementation in all of the states:

> It would be desirable for us to deal first with the people of mixed blood. Ultimately, if history is repeated, the full bloods will become half-castes. (Commonwealth of Australia 1937:21)

Thus the assimilation policy continued the logic of elimination by rendering Aborigines the pure term of a descending opposition whereby "part-aboriginal" meant "non-aboriginal." Hence it was not merely an expression of some unspecified racial prejudice but continued the cul-

---

28. See, e.g., Beckett 1988; Edwards and Read 1989; Hasluck 1988; Jacobs 1990; Mulvaney 1989:199–205; Neville 1947; Read 1983a, 1983b, 1984; Wilkinson 1987.

tural logic subtending Australian settler-colonization in a manner consistent with the homicidal activities of the first phase. That this continuity obtains in cultural logic does not mean it is merely an analytical abstraction. On the contrary, the overlap between frontier homicide and the social death attending "miscegenation" was constant. Indeed, Gillen's nemesis, mounted constable Willshire, did not scruple to publicize his homicidal exploits in the outback. In one passage, for instance, he clarified an account of a massacre that he had directed with the material qualification that "[i]t's no use mincing matters—the Martin-Henry carbines at this critical moment were talking English in the silent majesty of those great eternal rocks" (Willshire 1896:41). Yet Willshire saw no tension between this account and a comparison that he had ventured a few pages earlier, in which the "full-blood" had been unequivocally valorized.

> I do not object to them; they are the pure aborigine, who are gradually going to extinction. But I certainly do object to the mongrel half-caste, who inherits only the vices of civilization. If it is a male he is born for the gallows or to be shot; if a female, she becomes a wanton devoid of shame, and despair she knows not. (Willshire 1896:35)

The context in which Spencer recommended to the Commonwealth government that "half-caste children ... should all be withdrawn and placed on stations" was, in sum, one in which an emergent nation-state was deploying a post-frontier version of a cultural logic that was generic to settler-colonization. The policy that Spencer helped to construct stayed in place until 1967, when a national referendum overwhelmingly authorized the ending of Aborigines' constitutional invisibility. More recently, the Koori community organization Link-Up, established to reunite families that were officially broken up under the policy, estimated the number of people directly affected to remain in excess of 100,000 (Edwards and Read 1989:xvii).

Though assimilation and homicide conduced to a common settler-colonial end, they belong to different phases in the formation of a satellite state. As Benedict Anderson (1983) has influentially argued, nationalism promulgates shared memories whereby historical happenstance becomes converted into collective destiny. In the Australian case, though there is no shortage of appropriate memories (pioneers, gold diggers, bushrangers, etc.), the project of national memorization was above all one of forgetting the criminal legacy of genocidal theft upon which, in the absence of any form of treaty or mutual resolution, the settler-colonial state continued (as it continues) to be established.[29] As nationalist ideology, in other words, the Australian state was proclaiming its own virgin birth. Thus the recalcitrant presence of Aborigines within the pores of the body politic embodied a decisive refutation of the legitimatory narrative whereby the national community (comprising the normative citizenship regulating non-Aborigines) was officially imagined. Throughout the twentieth century, the anxiety produced by this primal flaw in Australian nationhood has rendered Aborigines a legislative preoccupation to an extent entirely disproportionate to the demographic numbers involved.

In contrast to the invasive frontier strategy of outright homicide, assimilation was not simply more "benign." It also consummated the shift from satellite colony to nation-state. Constructing an autochthonous citizenship within finite national boundaries requires an ideological regime altogether different from one appropriate to the process of territorial expansion. Assimilation provided for Aborigines' civic invisibility, an ideological rather than a material elimination. Though the ultimate aim was "breeding them white," the threat that Aborigines posed to the nation-state was not primarily physical (they could no longer materially impede the state's access to the continent's economic possibilities). Rather, Aborigines signified a differently grounded rival memory that contradicted the national narrative on which a homogeneous citizenship was predicated. Hence assimilation sought to detach Aborigines from that memory. So long as they could be grafted onto the new history imagined by the nation-state, their physical characteristics were relatively unproblematic. In taking the children away, therefore, the Australian state sought to remove a primary obstacle to its own legitimation.

It remains, therefore, to characterize the logic of assimilationism in order to correlate it with that of evolutionary anthropology. Now that the respective genealogies of the two series have been shown to be distinct, this will enable us to focus on the cultural priorities that precipitated their mutuality.

As observed, the essential feature of assimilationism, the principle that "part-aboriginal" meant "non-aboriginal," can be described as a descending opposition. This consists of a rigorous identity criterion whereby anything that does not embody all and only all the features of a given category is not merely outside that category but is, rather, positively

---

29. Thus the frankness in relation to the violence visited upon Kooris that characterized many nineteenth-century accounts of settlement was generally suppressed in twentieth-century Australian history-writing (cf. Stanner 1967), resurfacing in the radical tradition of frontier historiography that is conventionally traced back—with some injustice to Bill Beatty (1962:168–84)—to the work of Charles Rowley in the late 1960s (Biskup 1982:12).

categorized in opposition to it. Thus a single homogeneous category collectively denominates the rest of the world. To put it more formally, appropriating Wittgenstein (1955:73), "The propositions 'p' and 'not p' have opposite senses, but to them corresponds one and the same reality."[30] For our purposes, the salient characteristic of such a category is that it has no tolerance of contamination. Rather, contamination means conversion into the other (i.e., from the Australian state's point of view, into self), which is to say, contamination assimilates. To begin to relativize the virgin birth narrative, therefore, we will turn now to the question of how this logical structure of descending opposition also animated evolutionist ethnography. To this end, we can begin by noting that, for evidenciary purposes, "miscegenation," the key term of the assimilation policy, was also central to nescience—if there was any doubt as to whether or not the Arunta really "knew," the surest test would be the grounds on which they accounted for light-skinned babies. Thus we move now to the direct interface between the ethnographic and the political logics.

Textual Symptoms

A key premise of evolutionary anthropology was the collapse of time and space whereby ethnography recapitulated prehistory—to leave Europe was to travel back in time (cf. Fabian 1983:25). Hence the equivalence asserted between contemporary Aborigines and Europeans' primal forebears was not just a projection onto colonized people of European fantasies of self. It was also an evidenciary supplement. The nineteenth century was obsessed with origins. The prehistoric record, restricted as it was to material traces, was necessarily incomplete, a condition that could be alleviated by ethnography. In this, there lies one of the possible motives for Hartland's resistance to Spencer and Gillen's realization of his evolutionary conjecture. Social evolutionists were methodological rivals, competing over whose theoretical vehicle could penetrate furthest back into prehistory. In Bachofen's case, the vehicle had been texts; in McLennan's, marriage rites; in Morgan's, kinship systems; in Tylor's, cultural survivals; and so on. Hartland's vehicle, suggesting a German inspiration, was folklore.

Methodologically, therefore, ethnography could represent a rival as well as a supplement. Hartland's personal motivation aside, this consideration underscores the symmetry between ethnography and prehistory. Both were originary narratives that strove to recover the primal, defined in terms of distance from the modern. For prehistory, this distance was

---

30. Thanks to Graeme Marshall for bringing this formulation to my attention.

constituted temporally within the space of Europe, its ethnographic reflex being cultural distance beyond that space. The problem posed by prehistoric data was that they were materially fragmentary and semantically blunt. Conversely, the problem with ethnographic evidence was that, though theoretically complete, it decayed on contact, which instantaneously condensed all the time it had taken to reduce European prehistory to fragments. Hence all anthropology was salvage anthropology (cf. Clifford 1987; Gruber 1970).[31] Societies were significant not in themselves but for the light that they could shed on Europe's past. This varied to the extent that societies retained their original purity, which meant the extent to which they remained uncontacted. Thus ethnography was inherently contradictory, its data being jeopardized in the gathering. The irony of salvage anthropology is that the anthropologists' mere presence substantiates their sense of urgency. Spencer and Gillen's Arunta were already not there.

This much is, of course, not new. The point, however, is not the contradiction in the logic of evolutionist ethnography but its identity with the logic of assimilationism. As explained, the operative logic of assimilationism was the descending opposition that produced a radically unstable otherness that constantly converted into self. The crucial factor is the extreme instability of otherness, whereby "part-aborigine" automatically meant "non-aborigine." This instability is the point at which the logic of assimilationism fused with that of evolutionist ethnography. For either discourse, contact with Europeans despatialized savagery, displacing it out of the present and into a different time frame.[32] In crossing the frontier (or in being crossed over by the frontier) the native crossed into history. The point is that this was not a spatial progression. It could be done while standing still. As Deborah Bird Rose has pointed out (1991:46), settler-colonization means that, to get in the way, all the native has to do is stay at home. Rather than spatial, the movement into history was a purely discursive progression, one that undid the evolutionist conflation of time and space. Bereft of its spatial dimension, savagery was left as a thing of the past. This spatiotemporal split produced a hypersusceptibility to contact that was asserted by evolutionist ethnography and the Australian state alike. Both specified minimally inclusive, prehistoric criteria for authentic Aboriginality, a coincidence that, given the prestige attaching to scientific

---

31. As Malinowski (1922:xv) was to put it, "Ethnology is in the sadly ludicrous, not to say tragic position, that at the very moment when it begins to put its workshop in order, to forge its proper tools, to start ready for work on its appointed task, the material of its study melts away with hopeless rapidity" (cf. Lévi-Strauss 1973).

32. This aspect of my analysis is, of course, consistent with Fabian's (1983) "denial of coevalness."

validation, powerfully naturalized assimilationism. On this basis, it is not hard to see why evolutionist ethnography was so well adapted for appropriation into Australian state discourse—or, accordingly, why an ethnographer should be entrusted with recommending an appropriate policy on Aborigines.

Put thus, the logical symmetry between the two series is clear, but it lacks historical realization. Just as any number of geometries could construct spatial relations as well as the Euclidean, so can various logical designations be imposed on complex historical phenomena. How can we know that this logical structure, common to ethnography and colonialism, is not simply an analytical imposition of my own making but was active in the minds of historical actors? To know this, we need an example or examples of its entry into practice. In presenting Spencer and Gillen with an evidentiary dilemma that precipitated the logical linkage between their ethnography and settler-colonization, nescience prompted such an example. For, if the Arunta failed to distinguish the paternity of "half-caste" children, then Spencer and Gillen would have proof positive of their extraordinary discovery.[33] But the cost of such proof would be high—if the Arunta were so uncontaminatedly savage, how was it that their women had produced white men's children? Thus Spencer and Gillen's dilemma was that the very "miscegenation" that could have corroborated nescience simultaneously undermined their ethnography in relation to the general project of salvage anthropology, which nescience otherwise preeminently validated (as observed, such astounding ignorance was unparalleledly savage). Thus categorical purity subverted itself—as well it might in a situation where, whatever black men may have said about paternity, white men were definitely denying it.

In response to this dilemma, Spencer adopted a textual strategy that revealingly encodes the threat posed by "miscegenation." Cultural brokership, the fruit of long-term local residence, was Gillen's contribution to the partnership. As a result, to the ethnographic testament of Spencer's peerless photography, they could add the qualification of being accepted as initiated Arunta (though there was no mention of subincision). A further element in their claim to have gained access to an otherwise intact savage world was Gillen's linguistic expertise, their 1899 book being liberally strewn with italicized Arunta words. Having thus established their credentials, it was presumably immaterial that their subsequent expedi-

---

33. "In a society where children are believed to have been reincarnated from totemic ancestors, there are no parents in our sense of the term. The ancestor himself, or something that once belonged to him, has entered the baby of a married woman in order to be reborn as a human being; and there can be no question of illegitimacy even when a half-caste infant is born to a full-blooded aboriginal couple" (Strehlow 1947:21).

White Man's Flour

tion took them outside Gillen's territory and, despite the offices of their Arunta assistants, necessitated an exclusive reliance on pidgin. In any event, in their 1904 book, Aboriginal discourse continued to be rendered in italicized Aboriginal idioms.

Since, by 1911, Gillen was dead, Spencer undertook on his own the expedition from which his recommendations to government resulted (Mulvaney and Calaby 1985:265). In addition to the report, he produced another ethnography, of which italicized Aboriginal words were still a feature. There was, however, a conspicuous exception, when the bastard pidgin was not merely acknowledged but actually reproduced in a manner that, had it appeared in other contexts, could only have undermined ethnographic credibility. The exceptional topic was "miscegenation," addressed in relation to nescience (which Spencer was asserting of a more westerly portion of northern Australia than had been encompassed in his and Gillen's earlier works). The difference between the newly fledged settler-colonial administrator and the descriptive ethnographer of fifteen years earlier is striking. For, where nescience was concerned, not only were "miscegenation" and pidgin now acknowledged but, in a manner reminiscent of Stirling's Horn Expedition report (a model that Spencer had not adopted at the time), genetic hybridity acquired a linguistic correlate. But note how, at the moment of contradiction, Spencer cordons it off by means of the crucial "for some time" that lasts long enough for nescience, "miscegenation," and Spencer to coincide, but surely no longer:

> There is one very interesting and suggestive point in this connection [nescience], and that is the common explanation of the existence of half-castes given universally by their mothers, speaking in pidgin English, viz., "Too much me been eat em white man's flour". The chief difference that they recognised between their life before and after they came into contact with white men was, not the fact that they had intercourse with white men, instead of or side by side with, blacks, but that they ate white flour and that this naturally affected the colour of their offspring. I have seen old natives in Central Australia accept, without question, their wives' half-caste children, making no difference whatever between them and the pure bred ones. On the other hand, it is, of course, naturally, a belief that is one of the first to become modified when the natives have been *for some time* in contact with white men. (Spencer 1914:25–26, emphasis added)

The loaded "for some time" enables an ethnographic corridor to be inserted into history, so that precontact culture might survive for long enough for Spencer to salvage it. After this, despite the physical persistence of some of its erstwhile inhabitants, the lost world only survives in his record, to which subsequent information must conform if it is to be admissible. Thus the salvage paradigm makes Aborigines a textual construct that evaporates on contact.

Spencer's telltale resort to pidgin is a textual symptom of the primary linkage between his ethnography and the politics of assimilation, which consisted in their common production of a time-bound Aboriginality that was thereby maximally "pure." In this regard, the contradictory relationship between nescience and "miscegenation" worked both ways, for, to maintain its purity, the Aboriginal category should have mirrored white society's aversion to "half-castes" (hence the ideological significance of the reports of "half-caste" children being killed at birth [Beckett 1988:198, n.10]). Ignorance of paternity would have frustrated this occurrence. Thus not only could "miscegenation" corroborate nescience but, reciprocally, nescience could sustain "miscegenation." Either way, therefore, both the salvage paradigm and assimilationism would be subverted.

As a symptom, Spencer's pidgin text is intrinsically empty. A form of historical parapraxis, it signifies extrinsically—its content is its context. This does not mean that nescience made Spencer's policy happen or even, more generally, that ethnography produced assimilationism. Clearly, assimilationism was produced by settler-colonization. To specify a positive determination, therefore, it would be necessary to account for the settler-colonizing impulse, an agency that is conventionally derived from Western Christendom's fifteenth-century struggle to break Muslim trade monopolies. But even this could only furnish a *why*, rather than a *how*. To reconstruct the weighted play of unintended consequences whereby global determinations unfold through definite relations that are, as Marx put it, indispensable and independent of people's will, we have to try to decipher the mediations and affinities around and through which prevailing tendencies are socially sustained. To suggest the complexity of the definite relations that brought together ethnography and Australian state-formation, it is important to retain the relative independence or self-containedness of the two series, which is why they have been recounted separately. But complexity is not indeterminacy. Thus, though it is not the case that the salvage paradigm was simply produced in the interests of genocide, it nonetheless is the case that, given the salvage paradigm, a scientific warrant was available for the social elimination of those whose expropriation was prerequisite to settler-colonization. Thus it is necessary to distinguish between determinacy and necessity.

The qualified (or, perhaps, elective) determinacy of Spencer's dual role takes us back to the statement that it was not an individual coincidence. Insofar as he was an anthropologist, Spencer's policy expressed sentiments that had been and would be shared by other anthropologists (e.g., the support for a nationwide implementation of the assimilation policy that was to be voiced half a century later by a subsequent doyen of Australian Aboriginal anthropology, A. P. Elkin [1947; cf. Wise 1985:200, 202]). Nor was Spencer alone so far as the specific link to nescience was concerned. As we have seen, Stirling's contribution to the Horn Expedition's report had contained an offhand remark that seemed to prefigure Spencer and Gillen's discovery. Eighteen years later, the correspondence was no less striking. Two months after Spencer's recommendations to the Australian government, Stirling was suggesting to a South Australian royal commission on Aborigines a plan that, while like Spencer's in acknowledging maternal bonding, was more developed in terms of specific implementation. Stirling was of the opinion that the more "half-caste" children who could be absorbed into white families the better, proposing that the "attractiveness of infancy" rendered it desirable to remove them early, since whites who were "disinclined to take them when they were older" might nonetheless be prepared to take them young. By "young," however, he meant two or three years, since, in the case of absolute infants,

> then you would have the burden of them that all children are at such a young age. When they are a couple of years of age they do not require so much attention and they are young enough to be attractive. (Stirling 1913:125)

Thus the coincidence of nescience and assimilationism was not an individual idiosyncrasy on Spencer's part. On the other hand, neither was it simply a predictable reflex of, say, the doctrine of progress. Rather, as this essay has tried to illustrate, its determinacy lay in a cultural logic that Australian settler-colonization (but not necessarily other forms of imperialism) shared with an ethnography that, as Frazer's distinctive rhetoric was to illustrate, epitomized the salvage paradigm.

> [W]e may conjecture that in many other parts of the world a similar ignorance of physical paternity may have led to the institution of similar totemism, wherever that institution has been found. If that is so, we may say that the secret of the totem has been longest kept by the isolated tribes of Central Australia—till at last they revealed it to Spencer and Gillen, who snatched it from them just before that final decadence of the tribes set in, which otherwise would have rendered the revelation for ever impossible. (Frazer 1938:viii)

But the decadence had already set in, even back on the Horn Expedition. For that matter, so had the use of pidgin as a marker for "miscegenation." So, too, had the special context of white man's flour, densely signifying the expropriation on which Australia was founded. Here again, Stirling's contribution is revealing. For, in the following passage, it is hard not to see a model for his editor Spencer's packaging of ethnographic contradiction. Unlike Stirling, however, Spencer would not have admitted the damaging possibility of an Aboriginal husband being "perfectly satisfied of his own paternity."

> the little accident of the birth of a suspiciously light-coloured offspring of a full blooded lubra was thus explained by the mother in full belief that the statement of cause and effect was perfectly rational, and indeed the legitimate husband, also a full-blooded black, was perfectly satisfied of his own paternity—'sposen lubra eat 'um flour picaninny long a pompey eat 'um too, then him jump up close up whitefellow; flour all day, like it, that make 'um.' Suppose the woman eats flour the child in the belly eats it too, and then the child is born closely resembling a white. (Stirling 1896:129, n.)

As historical parapraxis, this pidgin becomes impossible to contemplate in isolation from the imperialist context in which it is entangled, which it presupposes and reproduces. Though the context is epochal and global, the entanglement is quite particular. Beginning to trace this entanglement is beginning to relativize the text, which is—or should be—to precipitate history.

REFERENCES

Asad, T. 1979. "Anthropology and the Analysis of Ideology." *Man*, n.s., 14:607–27.
Anderson, Benedict. 1983. *Imagined Communities: Reflections on the Origin and Spread of Nationalism.* London: Verso.
Ashley-Montagu, A. M. F. 1937. *Coming Into Being Among the Australian Aborigines—A Study of the Procreative Beliefs of the Native Tribes of Australia.* London: George Routledge and Sons.
Attwood, B. 1989. *The Making of the Aborigines.* Sydney: Allen and Unwin.
Bachofen, J. J. 1967. *Myth, Religion and Mother Right. Selected Writings of J. J. Bachofen,* tr. R. Manheim, ed. R. Marx. Princeton: Princeton University Press.
———. 1969 [1861]. *Das Mutterrecht: Eine Unterschung über die Gynaikokratie der alten Welt nach ihrer religiösen und rechlichen Natur.* Brussels: Culture and Civilisation.
Bartra, R. 1992. *The Cage of Melancholy: Identity and Metamorphosis in the Mexican Character.* New Brunswick: Rutgers University Press.

Beatty, B. 1962. *Early Australia With Shame Remembered*. Melbourne: Cassell.
Beckett, J. 1987. *Torres Strait Islanders: Custom and Colonialism*. Sydney: Cambridge University Press.
———. 1988. "The Past in the Present: the Present in the Past: Constructing a National Aboriginality." In J. Beckett, ed., *Past and Present: The Construction of Aboriginality*, 191–217. Canberra: Aboriginal Studies Press.
———. 1989. "Aboriginality in a Nation-State: The Australian Case." In M. C. Howard, ed., *Ethnicity and Nation-Building in the Pacific*, 118–35. The United Nations University.
Berndt, R. M., and C. H. Berndt. 1987. *End of an Era: Aboriginal Labour in the Northern Territory*. Canberra: Australian Institute of Aboriginal Studies.
Biskup, P. 1982. "Aboriginal History." In G. Osborne and W. F. Mandle, eds., *New History: Studying History Today*,11–31. Sydney: Allen and Unwin.
Blackstone, W. 1978 [1783]. *Commentaries on the Law of England*. 9th ed. (facsimile). New York: Garland Publishing.
Blainey, G. 1975. *Triumph of the Nomads: A History of Ancient Australia*. South Melbourne: Macmillan.
Bleakley, J. W. 1961. *The Aboriginals of Australia. Their History. Their Habits. Their Assimilation*. Brisbane: Jacaranda.
Bloch, M. 1977. "The Past and the Present in the Present." *Man,* n.s., 12:278–92.
Brock, P., and D. Kartinyeri. 1989. *Poonindie. The Rise and Destruction of an Aboriginal Agricultural Community*. Adelaide: Government Printer.
Brook, J., and J. L. Kohen. 1991. *The Parramatta Native Institution and the Black Town: A History*. Kensington: University of New South Wales Press.
Broome, R. 1982. *Aboriginal Australians: Black Responses to White Dominance, 1788–1980*. Sydney: Allen and Unwin.
Butlin, N. G. 1985. "Macassans and Aboriginal Smallpox: The '1788' and '1829' Epidemics." *Historical Studies* (Melbourne), 21, 84: 315–35.
Campbell, J. 1983. "Smallpox in Aboriginal Australia, 1829–31." *Historical Studies* (Melbourne), 20:536–56.
———. 1985. "Smallpox in Aboriginal Australia: The Early 1830s." *Historical Studies* (Melbourne), 21:336–57.
Canny, N. P., and A. Pagden, eds. 1987. *Colonial Identity in the Atlantic World, 1500–1800*. Princeton, N.J.: Institute for Advanced Study.
Carter, P. 1987. *The Road to Botany Bay: An Essay in Spatial History*. London: Faber and Faber.
Christie, M. F. 1979. *Aborigines in Colonial Victoria, 1835–86*. Sydney: Sydney University Press.
Clastres, P. 1988. "On Ethnocide." J. Pefanis and B. Maher, tr. *Art and Text* 28, 1988:50–58.
Clifford, J. 1987. "Of Other Peoples: Beyond the 'Salvage' Paradigm." In M. Foster, ed., *Discussions in Contemporary Culture* (no. 1), 121–30. Seattle: Bay Press.
Commonwealth of Australia. 1937. *Aboriginal Welfare*. Initial Conference of Commonwealth and State Aboriginal Authorities held at Canberra, April 21–23, 1937. Canberra: Government Printer.
———. 1997. *Bringing Them Home* (Report of the National Inquiry into the Separation of Aboriginal and Torres Strait Islander Children from their Families). Canberra: Commonwealth of Australia.

Coward, R. 1983. *Patriarchal Precedents: Sexuality and Social Relations.* London: Routledge and Kegan Paul.

Critchett, J. 1980. *Our Land Till We Die: A History of the Framlingham Aborigines.* Warrnambool: Warrnambool Institute Press.

———. 1990. *A Distant Field of Murder: Western District Frontiers, 1834–1848.* Melbourne: Melbourne University Press.

Crosby, A. W. 1986. *Ecological Imperialism: The Biological Expansion of Europe, 900–1900.* Cambridge: Cambridge University Press.

Curr, E. M. 1886. *The Australian Race.* 4 vols. Melbourne: John Ferres, Government Printer.

Curthoys, A. 1982. "Good Christians and Useful Workers: Aborigines, Church and State in N.S.W., 1870–1883." In Sydney Labour History Group, ed., *What Rough Beast? The State and Social Order in Australian History.* Sydney: Allen and Unwin.

Darwin, C. 1871. *The Descent of Man, and Selection in Relation to Sex.* 2 vols. London: John Murray.

Delaney, C. 1986. "The Meaning of Paternity and the Virgin Birth Debate." *Man,* n.s., vol. 21: 494–513.

Drakakis-Smith, D. 1984. "Advance Australia Fair: Internal Colonialism in the Antipodes." In D. Drakakis-Smith and S. Wyn Williams, eds., *Internal Colonialism: Essays Around a Theme,* 81–103. Institute of British Geographers.

Durkheim, E. 1912. *Les Formes Elémentaires de la Vie Religieuse. Le système totémique en Australie.* Paris: Alcan.

Edwards, C., and P. Read, eds. 1989. *The Lost Children.* Sydney: Doubleday.

Elder, B. 1988. *Blood on the Wattle: Massacres and Maltreatment of Australian Aborigines since 1788.* Sydney: Child and Associates.

Elkin, A. P. 1947. "Introduction." In A. O. Neville, *Australia's Coloured Minority: Its Place in the Community.* Sydney: Currawong Publishing.

Evans, R. 1984. "'Kings in Brass Crescents': Defining Aboriginal Labour Patterns in Colonial Queensland." In K. Saunders, ed., *Indentured Labour in the British Empire,* 183–212. London: Croom Helm.

Fabian, J. 1983. *Time and the Other: How Anthropology Makes Its Object.* New York: Columbia University Press.

Fels, M. 1988. *Good Men and True: The Aboriginal Police of the Port Phillip District, 1837–1853.* Melbourne: Melbourne University Press.

Fison, L., and A. Howitt. 1880. *Kamilaroi and Kurnai. Group-Marriage and Relationship, and Marriage by Elopement, Drawn directly from the Usage of the Australian Aborigines, also the Kurnai Tribe, their Customs in Peace and War.* Melbourne: Geo. Robertson.

Frazer, J. G. 1898. "Observations on Central Australian Totemism." *Journal of the Anthropological Institute* 28:281–86.

———. 1899. "The Origin of Totemism." *The Fortnightly Review,* n.s., 65: 647–65, 835–52.

———. 1905. "The Beginnings of Religion and Totemism among the Australian Aborigines." *The Fortnightly Review,* July to December 1905, n.s., 78; o.s., 84: 162–72, 452–66.

———. 1938. Preface to W. B. Spencer and F. J. Gillen, *The Native Tribes of Central Australia,* vii–x. London: Macmillan. Original edition, 1899.

Freud, Sigmund. 1960 [1913]. *Totem and Taboo. Some Points of Agreement between the Mental Lives of Savages and Neurotics.* J. Strachey, trans. London: Routledge/Ark Paperbacks.

Frost, A. 1990. "New South Wales as *Terra Nullius:* The British Denial of Aboriginal Land Rights." In S. Janson and S. Macintyre, eds., *Through White Eyes,* 65–76. Sydney: Allen and Unwin.
Green, N. 1984. *Broken Spears: Aborigines and Europeans in the Southwest of Australia.* Perth: Focus Education Services.
Grotius, H. 1916 [1609]. *Mare Liberum (The Freedom of the Seas: or, the right which belongs to the Dutch to take part in the East Indian trade).* New York: Oxford University Press.
Gruber, J. 1970. "Ethnographic Salvage and the Shaping of Anthropology." *American Anthropologist* 72:1289–99.
Guillaumin, C. 1988. "Race and Nature: The System of Marks. The Idea of a Natural Group and Social Relationships." *Feminist Issues* 8 (2): 25–43.
Gunson, N., ed. 1974. *The Australian Reminiscences and Papers of L.E. Threlkeld.* Canberra: Australian Institute of Aboriginal Studies.
Haebich, A. 1989. *For Their Own Good. Aborigines and Government in the South West of Western Australia, 1900–1940.* Nedlands: University of Western Australia Press.
Harrison, R., and F. Mort. 1980. "Patriarchal Aspects of Nineteenth Century State Formation: Property Relations, Marriage and Divorce, and Sexuality." In P. Corrigan, ed., *Capitalism, State Formation and Marxist Theory.* London: Quartet.
Hartland, E. S. 1891. *The Science of Fairy Tales. An Inquiry Into Fairy Mythology.* London: Walter Scott (Contemporary Science Series, ed. H. Ellis).
———. 1893. "Pin-wells and rag-bushes." *Folk-Lore* 4:451–70.
———. 1894, 1895, 1896. *The Legend of Perseus. A Study of Tradition in Story, Custom and Belief.* 3 vols. London: David Nutt.
———. 1894. *The Supernatural Birth.* Vol. I of Hartland 1894–96. Grimm Library no. 2.
———. 1895. *The Life-Token.* Vol. II of Hartland 1894–96. Grimm Library no. 3.
———. 1899. Review of Spencer and Gillen 1899. *Folk-Lore* 10:233–39.
———. 1900. Presidential Address [to the Folk-Lore Society]. *Folk-Lore* 11:52–80.
———. 1904. Review of Spencer and Gillen 1904. *Folk-Lore* 15:465–74.
———. 1909. *Primitive Paternity.* 2 vols. London: Folk-Lore Society.
Hasluck, P. 1988. *Shades of Darkness. Aboriginal Affairs, 1925–1965.* Melbourne: Melbourne University Press.
Hodge, B., and V. Mishra. 1991. *Dark Side of the Dream: Australian Literature and the Postcolonial Mind. Sydney:* Allen and Unwin.
Holcombe, L. 1977. "Victorian Wives and Property: Reform of the Married Women's Property Law, 1857–1882." In M. Vicinus, ed., *A Widening Sphere: Changing Roles of Victorian Women,* 3–28. Bloomington: Indiana University Press.
Huggins, J. 1988. "'Firing on in the Mind': Aboriginal Domestic Servants." *Hecate* 13 (2): 5–23.
Hulme, P. 1990. "The Spontaneous Hand of Nature: Savagery, Colonialism and the Enlightenment." In P. Hulme and L. Jordanova, eds., *The Enlightenment and Its Shadows.* London: Routledge.
Jacobs, P. 1990. *Mister Neville: A Biography.* Fremantle: Fremantle Arts Centre Press.
Jeffreys, S. 1985. *The Spinster and Her Enemies: Feminism and Sexuality, 1880–1930.* London: Pandora.
Jenkin, G. 1979. *Conquest of the Ngarrindjeri.* Adelaide: Rigby.

Kaberry, P. 1936. "Spirit-Children and Spirit-Centres of the North Kimberley Division, West Australia." *Oceania* 6:392–400.

———. 1968. "Virgin Birth" (letter). *Man*, n.s., vol. 3: 311–13.

Kempe, H. 1883. "Zur Sittenkunde der Centralaustralischen Schwarzen." *Mitteilungen des Vereins für Erdkunde zu Halle, 1883*, 52–56.

Lang, A. 1905. *The Secret of the Totem*. London: Longman, Green and Co.

Leach, E. R. 1969. "Virgin Birth." In E. R. Leach, *Genesis as Myth and Other Essays*. London: Jonathan Cape.

Legters, L. H. 1988. "The American Genocide." *Policy Studies Journal* 16:768–77.

Lévi-Strauss, C. 1973. *Tristes Tropiques*. London: Jonathan Cape.

Lévy-Bruhl, L. 1910. *Les Fonctions Mentales dans les Sociétés Inferieures*. Paris: Librairie Félix Alcan (Travaux de *l'Année Sociologique*).

Lippmann, L. 1981. *Generations of Resistance: The Aboriginal Struggle for Justice*. Melbourne: Longman Cheshire.

Lloyd, D. 1990. "Analogies of the Aesthetic: The Politics of Culture and the Limits of Materialist Aesthetics." *New Formations* 10 (spring): 109–26.

Locke, J. 1970 [1690]. *Two Treatises of Government*. P. Laslett, ed. Cambridge: Cambridge University Press.

Loos, N. 1982. *Invasion and Resistance: Aboriginal-European Relations on the North Queensland Frontier, 1861–1897*. Canberra: ANU Press.

Lubbock, J. 1875. *The Origin of Civilisation and the Primitive Condition of Man: Mental and Social Condition of Savages*. London: Longman, Green and Co.

———. 1885. "On the Customs of Marriage and Systems of Relationship among the Australians." *Journal of the Anthropological Institute* 14:292–300.

Lynd, H. 1945. *England in the 1880s*. London: Frank Cass.

Malinowski, B. 1916. "Baloma: The Spirits of the Dead in the Trobriand Islands." *Journal of the Royal Anthropological Institute* 46:353–430.

———. 1922. *Argonauts of the Western Pacific: An Account of Native Enterprise and Adventure in the Archipelagoes of Melanesian New Guinea*. London: Routledge and Kegan Paul.

———. 1929. *The Sexual Life of Savages in North-Western Melanesia*. London: Routledge and Kegan Paul.

Marett, R. R., and T. K. Penniman, eds. 1932. *Spencer's Scientific Correspondence with Sir J.G. Frazer and Others*. Oxford: Clarendon.

Markus, A. 1974. *From the Barrel of a Gun: The Oppression of the Aborigines, 1860–1900*. West Melbourne: Victorian Historical Association.

———. 1990. *Governing Savages*. Sydney: Allen and Unwin.

May, D. 1983. "The Articulation of the Aboriginal and Capitalist Modes on the North Queensland Frontier." *Journal of Australian Studies* 12:34–44.

———. 1986. *From Bush to Station: Aboriginal Labour in the North Queensland Pastoral Industry, 1861–1897*. Townsville, Queensland: History Department, James Cook University.

McGrath, A. 1978. "Aboriginal Women Workers in the N.T., 1911–1939." *Hecate* 4 (2): 5–25.

———. 1987. *Born in the Cattle: Aborigines in Cattle Country*. Sydney: Allen and Unwin.

McHugh, P. 1980. *Prostitution and Victorian Social Reform*. London: Croom Helm.

McLennan, J. F. 1865. *Primitive Marriage. An Inquiry into the Origin of the Form of Capture in Marriage Ceremonies*. Edinburgh: Adam and Charles Black.

Merlan, F. 1986. "Australian Aboriginal Conception Beliefs Revisited." *Man*, n.s., 21:474–93.
Millar, J. 1771. *Observations Concerning the Distinction of Ranks in Society*. London: John Murray.
Miller, J. 1985. *Koori: A Will to Win*. Sydney: Angus and Robertson.
Milliss, R. 1992. *Waterloo Creek: The Australia Day Massacre of 1838, George Gipps and the British Conquest of New South Wales*. Ringwood, Victoria: McPhee Gribble/Penguin.
Morgan, L. H. 1866. "A Conjectural Solution of the Origin of the Classificatory System of Relationship." In *Proceedings of the American Academy of Arts and Sciences, Vol. VIII, 11/2/1866*, meeting no. 591: 436–77, reprinted 1868. Cambridge, Mass.: Welch, Bigelow and Co.
———. 1871. *Systems of Consanguinity and Affinity of the Human Family*. Smithsonian Contributions to Knowledge, vol. XVII, no. 218. Washington, D.C.: Smithsonian Institution.
———. 1872. "Paper on Australian Kinship." In *Proceedings of the American Academy of Arts and Sciences, Vol. VIII, 12/3/1872*, meeting no. 642: 412–28.
———. 1877. *Ancient Society—or Researches in the Lines of Human Progress from Savagery through Barbarism to Civilization*. 1963 reprint, E. B. Leacock, ed. New York: Meridian.
Mörner, M. 1967. *Race Mixture in the History of Latin America*. Boston: Little, Brown.
———, ed. 1970. *Race and Class in Latin America*. New York: Columbia University Press.
Morris, B. 1989. *Domesticating Resistance. The Dhan-gadi Aborigines and the Australian State*. New York: Berg.
Mulvaney, D. J. 1989. *Encounters in Place. Outsiders and Aboriginal Australians, 1606–1985*. St. Lucia: University of Queensland Press.
Mulvaney, D. J., and J. H. Calaby. 1985. "So Much That Is New." *Baldwin Spencer, 1860–1929. A Biography*. Melbourne: Melbourne University Press.
Nance, B. 1981. "The Level of Violence: Europeans and Aborigines in Port Phillip, 1835–1850." *Historical Studies* (Melbourne) 19 (77): 532–52.
Neville, A. O. 1947 [n.d.]. *Australia's Coloured Minority: Its Place in the Community*. Sydney: Currawong Publishing.
Patterson, O. 1982. *Slavery and Social Death. A Comparative Study*. Cambridge: Harvard University Press.
Pepper, P., with T. de Araugo. 1985. *The Kurnai of Gippsland: What Did Happen to the Aborigines of Victoria*. Vol. 1. Melbourne: Hyland House.
Plomley, N. J. B., ed. 1991. *Jorgen Jorgensen and the Aborigines of Van Diemen's Land, being a reconstruction of his 'lost' book on their customs and habits and his role in the Roving Parties and the Black Line*. Hobart: Blubber Head Press.
Pope, A. 1988. "Aboriginal Adaptation to Early Colonial Labour Markets: The South Australian Experience." *Labour History* 54:1–15.
Pufendorf, S. 1934 [1688]. *De Jure Naturae Et Gentium*. Facsimile edition. Oxford: Clarendon Press.
Read, C. 1918. "No Paternity." *Journal of the Royal Anthropological Institute* 48:146–54.
Read, P. 1983a. "The Stolen Generations." *NSW Ministry of Aboriginal Affairs Occasional Paper No. 1*. Sydney.
———. 1983b. "'A Rape of the Soul So Profound'. Some Reflections on the Dispersal Policy in NSW." *Aboriginal History* 7 (1): 23–33.

———. 1984. "'Breaking Up These Camps Entirely': The Dispersal Policy in Wiradjuri Country, 1909–1929." *Aboriginal History* 8 (1): 45–62.
———. 1988. *A Hundred Years War: The Wiradjuri People and the State.* Canberra: Australian National University Press.
Reece, R. H. W. 1974. *Aborigines and Colonists: Aborigines in Colonial Society in NSW in the 1830s and 1840s.* Sydney: Sydney University Press.
Reid, G. 1982. *A Nest of Hornets: The Massacre of the Fraser Family at Hornet Bank Station, Central Queensland 1857 and Related Events.* Melbourne: Oxford University Press.
———. 1990. *A Picnic with the Natives: Aboriginal-European Relations in the Northern Territory to 1910.* Melbourne: Melbourne University Press.
Reynolds, H. 1981. *The Other Side of the Frontier: Aboriginal Resistance to the European Invasion of Australia.* Townsville, Queensland: James Cook University History Department.
———. 1990. *With the White People.* Penguin Australia.
———. 1995. *Fate of a Free People.* Penguin Australia.
Rose, D. B. 1991. *Hidden Histories: Black Stories from Victoria River Downs, Humbert River and Wave Hill Stations.* Canberra: Aboriginal Studies Press.
Rosser, B. 1978. *This Is Palm Island.* Canberra: Australian Institute of Aboriginal Studies.
———. 1985. *Dreamtime Nightmares: Biographies of Aborigines under the Queensland Aborigines Act.* Canberra: Australian Institute of Aboriginal Studies.
———. 1991. *Up Rode the Troopers: The Black Police in Queensland.* St. Lucia: University of Queensland Press.
Roth, W. E. 1897. *Ethnological Studies among the North-West-Central Queensland Aborigines.* Brisbane: Government Printer.
———. 1903. "Superstition, Magic and Medicine," *North Queensland Ethnography Bulletin No. 5.* Brisbane: Government Printer (Home Secretary's Department).
Rowley, C. D. 1970. *The Destruction of Aboriginal Society.* Canberra: Australian National University Press.
Rowse, T. 1993. "Aboriginal Resistance: The Example of the Community Employment Development Projects (CDEP) Program." *Oceania* 63:268–86.
Ryan, L. 1981. *The Aboriginal Tasmanians.* St. Lucia: University of Queensland Press.
Smith, F. B. 1971. "Ethics and Disease in the Later Nineteenth Century: The Contagious Diseases Acts." *Historical Studies* (Melbourne) 15 (57): 118–35.
Smith, W. Robertson. 1894 [1st ed. 1889]. *Lectures on the Religion of the Semites, First Series: The Fundamental Institutions* (The Burnett Lectures, 1888–89). London: Adam and Charles Black.
Spencer, H. 1870. "The Origin of Animal Worship, etc." *Fortnightly Review*, n.s., vol. 2; o.s., vol. 13: 535–50.
Spencer, [W.] B., ed. 1896. *Report on the Work of the Horn Scientific Expedition to Central Australia.* London: Dulan and Co.
———. 1913. *Preliminary Report on the Aboriginals of the Northern Territory* (Northern Territory Bulletin, no. 7). Melbourne: Australian Ministry of External Affairs (Mullett, Government Printer).
———. 1914. *The Native Tribes of the Northern Territory of Australia.* London: Macmillan.
———. 1921. Presidential Address to the 15th (Hobart-Melbourne) Meeting of ANZAAS, 10/1/21, Melbourne: Mullett (Government Printer).

Spencer, W. B., and F. J. Gillen. 1897. "An Account of the Engwurra or Fire Ceremony of Certain Central Australian Tribes" (abstract) [read 8/4/1897]. *Proceedings of the Royal Society of Victoria*, n.s., vol. 10, pt. 1: 17–28.

———. 1899. *The Native Tribes of Central Australia*. London: Macmillan.

———. 1904. *The Northern Tribes of Central Australia*. London: Macmillan.

———. 1912. *Across Australia*. Vol. I. London: Macmillan.

Spiro, M. E. 1968. "Virgin Birth, Parthenogenesis and Physiological Paternity: An Essay in Cultural Interpretation." *Man*, n.s., 3:242–61.

Stanner, W. E. H. 1967. "Reflections on Durkheim and Aboriginal Religion." In M. Freedman, ed., *Social Organization: Essays Presented to Raymond Firth*, 217–40. London: Cass.

———. 1977. "The History of Indifference Thus Begins." *Aboriginal History* 1:2–26.

Stirling, E. C. 1896. "Anthropology." in [W.] B. Spencer, ed. *Report on the Work on the Horn Scientific Expedition to Central Australia*, 1–158. London: Dulan and Co.

———. 1913. "Called and Examined." In "Progress Report of the Royal Commission on the Aborigines." *Proceedings of the Parliament of South Australia, 1913*, vol. 2, item no. 26: 123–25.

Stocking, G. W., Jr. 1987. *Victorian Anthropology*. New York: Macmillan Free Press.

———. 1992. "Paradigmatic Traditions in the History of Anthropology." In G. W. Stocking, Jr., *The Ethnographer's Magic and Other Essays in the History of Anthropology*, 342–61. Madison: University of Wisconsin Press.

———, ed. 1984. *Functionalism Historicized: Essays on British Social Anthropology*. Vol. 2 of *History of Anthropology*. Madison: University of Wisconsin Press.

Stoler, A. L. 1989. "Making Empire Respectable: The Politics of Race and Sexual Morality in Twentieth-Century Colonial Cultures." *American Ethnologist* 16 (4): 634–60.

———. 1995. *Race and the Education of Desire: Foucault's History of Sexuality and the Colonial Order of Things*. Durham, N.C.: Duke University Press.

Strehlow, T. G. H. 1947. "Anthropology and the Study of Languages." Presidential Address read before Section F (Anthropology) of ANZAAS, at its Perth Meeting, August 1947.

———. 1969. *Journey to Horseshoe Bend*. Sydney: Angus and Robertson.

Tonkinson, M. 1988. "Sisterhood or Aboriginal Servitude? Black Women and White Women on the Australian Frontier." *Aboriginal History* 12:27–40.

Tonkinson, R. 1978. "Semen versus Spirit-Child in a Western Desert Culture." In L. R. Hiatt, ed., *Australian Aboriginal Concepts*, 81–92. Canberra: Australian Institute of Aboriginal Studies.

Trigger, D. S. 1993. "No Place for Vague Radicalism in Cultural Studies." *The Australian, Higher Education Supplement*, 20/1/93.

Turnbull, C. 1949. *Black War: The Extermination of the Tasmanian Aborigines*. Melbourne: Cheshire.

Tylor, E. B. 1871. *Primitive Culture: Researches into the Development of Mythology, Philosophy, Religion, Art and Custom*. 2 vols. London: John Murray.

———. 1885. "The Patriarchal Theory" (review of McLennan 1885). *The Academy* 28:67–68.

———. 1889. "On a Method of Investigating the Development of Institutions: Applied to Laws of Marriage and Descent," *Journal of the Anthropological Institute* 18:245–72.

———. 1896. "The Matriarchal Family System." *The Nineteenth Century* 40:81–96.

Van Gennep, A. 1906. "Les Idées des Australiens sur la Conception et la Reincarnation." *Mercure de France,* n.s., 61 (May–June): 204–20.

Vattel, E. 1916 [1758]. *The Law of Nations.* Facsimile ed. Washington: Carnegie Institute.

Weeks, J. 1981. *Sex, Politics and Society. The Regulation of Sexuality since 1800.* London: Longman.

Wilken, G. A. 1912 [1884]. "Het matriarchaat bij de oude Arabieren." In *De Verspreide Geschriften van Prof. Dr. G. A. Wilken, Deel II: Geschriften op het gebied van vergelijkende rechtswetenschap* (F. D. E. van Ossenbruggen, ed.), 1–55. Soerabaja, Netherlands Indies: G. C. T. Van Dorp and Co.

———. 1921. *The Sociology of Malayan Peoples, Being Three Essays on Kinship, Marriage and Inheritance in Indonesia* (G. A. Hunt, tr.). Kuala Lumpur: Committee for Malay Studies.

Wilkinson, L. 1987. "Fractured Families, Squatting and Poverty: The Impact of the 1886 'Half-Caste' Act on the Framlingham Aboriginal Community." In D. D. Kirkby, ed., *Law and History in Australia,* vol. 4: 1–25.

Willshire, W. H. 1896. *The Land of the Dawning. Being Facts Cleaned from Cannibals in the Australian Stone Age.* Adelaide: W. K. Thomas and Co.

Wise, T. 1985. *The Self-Made Anthropologist. A Life of A. P. Elkin.* Sydney: Geo. Allen and Unwin.

Wittgenstein, L. 1955 [1st ed. 1922]. *Tractatus Logico-Philosophicus.* London: Routledge and Kegan Paul.

Wolfe, P. 1994. "Nation and MiscegeNation—Discursive Continuity in the Post-Mabo Era," *Social Analysis* 36:93–152.

Yengoyan, A. 1978. "Copulation, Conception and Deception in Aboriginal Australia" (review of 1974 ed. of Ashley-Montagu 1937). *Annual Review of Anthropology* 1978:108–15.

The Making of Traditional Bali
Colonial Ethnography and Bureaucratic Reproduction
Henk Schulte Nordholt

The island of Bali is without doubt one of the most densely studied places in the world. Well over 1,800 books and articles on Bali were published through 1990 (Lekkerkerker 1920; Stuart-Fox 1992). Nowadays a large group of Western academics studying Bali form a "Baliology" community that has its own newsletter, conferences, and internal ranking order. With respect to anthropology, the island has become a kind of laboratory where, except for a down-to-earth political economy approach, many of the current anthropological fashions are practiced. Moreover, thanks to anthropologists like Gregory Bateson, Margaret Mead, Hildred Geertz, Clifford Geertz, Jim Boon, Mark Hobart, and recently Unni Wikan and Fredrik Barth, Bali figures prominently on the map of Anthropologyland.

Well into the 1970s the work by Bateson, Mead, and Jane Belo, who did their fieldwork in Bali during the 1930s, marked the beginning of anthropological research on the island.[1] Consequently, earlier writings by Dutch colonial ethnologists were either ignored or only consulted as far as they were available in translation (Swellengrebel 1960, 1969). However, by focusing exclusively on Mead and her colleagues as the creators of the first anthropological image of Bali, two important things tend to be obscured. First, long before academic anthropologists dis-

---

This essay is a revised version of an earlier and preliminary attempt (Schulte Nordholt 1986) to analyze the impact of Western colonial conceptions on Balinese society and is partly based on chapters 8 and 9 of my monograph on the history of a South Balinese dynasty (Schulte Nordholt 1996). Stimulating comments and criticisms on earlier versions were given by Hildred Geertz, Jean-Francois Guermonprez, Hedi Hinzler, Jeremy Kemp, Peter Pels, Tessel Pollmann, Geoff Robinson, Oscar Salemink, John Stowell, David Stuart-Fox, Heather Sutherland, Adrian Vickers, and Carol Warren, to whom I am very grateful.

1. Essays based on research conducted during the 1930s are collected in Belo 1970a, under the significant title *Traditional Balinese Culture*. For the influence of Bateson on Clifford Geertz, see Geertz 1966. Because the present essay is concentrated on the colonial period I will not discuss the work of C. Geertz on pre- and postcolonial Bali.

covered "traditional" Bali, the place had already been conceptualized by colonial philologists and ethnographers and reorganized by Dutch administrators; second, the findings of these foreign academics fitted very well within the larger colonial conceptualization of Bali.

Although ample attention has been paid to the creation of images of Bali by Boon (1977) with regard to ethnography and by Adrian Vickers (1989) who concentrated on popular images as well, both have insufficiently emphasized the role of the colonial state in these processes. In the following pages I will therefore investigate how the various and often contradictory colonial images of Bali were created, and how these images were related to each other and to administrative practice. The history of these images and their practical implications illustrate that power and knowledge were closely interwoven. It also reveals that the colonial state should not be seen as a monolithic agent, since important tensions between the center of the state and local administrators gave shape to the distinctive character of Bali within the larger colonial context.

Despite the large number of anthropologists working on Bali and their impressive production of knowledge about its society, it is striking that all this seems to have surprisingly little impact on local perceptions, that is, the way Balinese intellectuals conceptualize their own society. Instead, old colonial conceptions about Bali are still being reproduced among modern Balinese intellectuals and especially government officials, either in reports by government institutions and government-sponsored research projects, or in university courses and seminars. Among Balinese bureaucrats and intellectuals interested in their own society the Dutch administrator and ethnographer Victor Korn is better known than Clifford Geertz.[2] This leads to a final theme: the importance of bureaucratic reproduction of knowledge, which has its origin in the colonial period.

Nineteenth-Century Bali:
Hindu Courts and Village Republics

From 1597, when the first Dutch-Balinese encounter took place, till the late nineteenth century the Balinese were in Dutch eyes synonymous with violence. Until the first half of the nineteenth century Bali was in the first place known as one of the biggest slave markets in the archipelago, while continuous internal warfare as well as violent resistance prevented the Dutch from controlling the island (Schulte Nordholt 1996: chaps. 2 and 3). However, despite the violent nature of the Balinese, Bali soon represented something else.

---

2. In this respect see Korn 1983, which is a translation of Korn 1932. To my knowledge there are no Indonesian translations of C. Geertz's publications on Bali.

Philologists at Work: Old Java Recovered

During the first half of the nineteenth century it was T. S. Raffles (1817), followed by J. Crawfurd (1820), who created the Hindu image of Bali. The idea that ancient Hindu Java could be rediscovered in Bali gained ground when in the middle of the nineteenth century, on the insistence of W. R. van Hoëvell (then president of the Batavian Society for the Arts and Sciences), the Sanskrit scholar and orientalist R. T. Friederich was commissioned to do research there. Implicitly, Friederich was given the task of discovering ancient Java in Bali, for there was no doubt in Van Hoëvell's mind that the former still survived on the island: "It is certain that the Balinese are in the same situation as the Javanese at the beginning of the fifteenth century" (Van Hoëvell 1846a:32).

From then on Bali began to represent to orientalists a culture that must have been lost in Java in the fifteenth century with the advent of Islam: the old and "classical" Hindu civilization. In their eyes Islam had destroyed this Hindu culture in Java, after which there could follow only spiritual and moral degeneration. But, fortunately, Bali had been spared (Van Hoëvell 1846a, 1846b).

In Bali Friederich found what he was supposed to find. Being a philologist by training, he had immersed himself in the "old texts" and extracted his material primarily from these. In his work Friederich (1849-50) further developed the Hindu image of Bali, and for that matter the image of Bali as a repository of Old Javanese culture. He had found in Bali a culture of Hindu-Javanese origin embodied in the Balinese nobility, which had supposedly been established there in the fourteenth century by conquerors from the Javanese realm of Majapahit and had since then survived there virtually intact in "the lee of the winds of history." This image has proven itself extremely persistent and is still repeated today (Swellengrebel 1960; Covarrubias 1973; Hanna 1976). Born of nineteenth-century orientalist notions and strong anti-Islamic sentiments, this image was to have a great political impact on Bali in the late colonial period. In 1922, for instance, the Dutch Resident (i.e., the highest colonial authority in Bali) H. T. Damsté stated that the Balinese nobility was something of an aristocratic "canopy" that was extraneous to the rest of the Balinese (Damsté 1922:7-8); and in 1921 his Assistant-Resident thought that Bali had to be preserved from the "damaging" effects of Islam, because "the whole of the history of the Indies has demonstrated that conversion to Islam has caused moral, physical and financial decline."[3] These statements summarize briefly two principles of twentieth-century colonial policy with

---

3. KITLV Leiden, Coll. Korn (Or.435), 284, private letter Assistant Resident Berkhout to V. E. Korn 5-8-1921.

regard to Bali: first, that Hindu Bali should be preserved and hence protected from the outside world, including Islam; second, that the Balinese nobility, as far as descent was concerned, consisted of "foreign conquerors" who in fact had little to do with the "real" Bali.

Administrative Ethnology: Village Bali

About forty years after Van Hoëvell and Friederich had rediscovered ancient Hindu Java in Bali, Dutch colonial control was established in North Bali.[4] And it was there that a young and promising colonial official, F. A. Liefrinck, discovered the "real" Bali. In contrast to his orientalist predecessors, who had created their image mainly from the written word, Liefrinck was an administrator in the field. Not only did his perspective differ from that of the philologists, but his priorities also diverged because he had to solve the practical problem of establishing colonial authority in a foreign environment. As a result he attached the greatest importance not to the nobility but to village Bali. Liefrinck discovered in North Bali local—and in his eyes autonomous and egalitarian—traditional communities, such as the village (*desa*) and irrigation society (*subak*), which represented to him "primeval" Bali (Liefrinck 1886–87; 1890; 1927). He even called the villages *republics* (Liefrinck 1927:281), a term that was to echo for a long time in the pages of colonial ethnography.

At first sight Liefrinck's village model of Bali seemed difficult to reconcile with Friederich's earlier conception of Hindu Bali with its hierarchy of nobles. But one did not need to choose between them since the two models were not mutually exclusive. They could be applied alongside of each other, because noble Bali and village Bali were seen as separate worlds, essentially without interaction. Despite the presence of princely conquerors, originating from Java, "village Bali" had succeeded in protecting itself from the nobility in the isolation of small "republics."

Liefrinck's idea was not altogether new, since it was congruent with the nineteenth-century Western concept of the Asian state in which despotic kings ruled over autonomous village communities. This view was mainly based on British material on India, and it is likely that Liefrinck was also influenced by European images of the Indian state.[5] Like the British view on India, Liefrinck's perspective fitted equally neatly

---

4. Dutch colonial presence in North Bali dated from 1854, and the area was brought under direct colonial rule in 1882.

5. In his description of North Balinese village society Liefrinck (1890) refers for instance to Gustave le Bon, *Les Civilisation de l'Inde* (Paris 1887: Librairie de Firmin-Didot). On India, see P. Anderson 1974:462–95; Cohn 1987; Dewey 1972; and Inden 1986.

into the context of the requirements of colonial administration. The rule of the nobility should, namely, be replaced by colonial government, because the princes were after all no more than usurpers, whereas the Dutch officials would respect, and if necessary "restore," Balinese village society. It was, of course, not altruism that led the Dutch to protect the village. It simply seemed far more efficient and much cheaper to introduce an administration of villages rather than control of individuals (for Java, see Breman 1980).

Through his work on North Bali Liefrinck has enjoyed the reputation of being one of the founding fathers of the so-called Adat Law School established at the University of Leiden at the beginning of the twentieth century (Van Vollenhoven 1928). The adat law approach was committed to the recording of local customs and institutions according to Western juridical concepts and was characterized by two principles. First there was the belief in a gradual evolution that led closed communal villages slowly toward more individual freedom, but still within the boundaries of the local community. Second, it had a strictly legalistic approach. Formal rules and institutions, not actual, changing and conflicting social relationships, formed the object of research. Consequently, the only change that was perceived was seen in terms of "decay" and "destruction" of local communities as a result of royal "despotism."

The extent to which these principles influenced Liefrinck's perception becomes apparent from other, unpublished material that cast serious doubts on his rather simple village model of Bali. From archival reports emerges a North Bali—contemporaneous with the period in which Liefrinck was active there—that was much more complex, in which many tensions existed and swift transitions occurred. No doubt Liefrinck must have been aware of this but he probably did not consider these changes relevant, for they did not fit into his abstract analytical framework.

Liefrinck was not the only administrator who wrote on North Bali, but his conclusions won the day during the process of establishing colonial rule. Moreover, his model became the authoritative blueprint for the rest of Bali as well. Three reasons can be given for this. First, the model was a simple one that proved to be applicable in administrative practice.[6] Second, Liefrinck's writings received academic legitimation from Profes-

---

6. In contrast to South Bali (discussed later), Liefrinck's model fitted probably fairly well within the North Balinese context. North Balinese villages were more isolated and had experienced less penetration by the ruling dynasty whose power base was to a large extent seaborne. Moreover, in contrast to South Bali where large-scale irrigation dominated, irrigation in the north was generally a local affair.

sor C. van Vollenhoven, the undisputed authority on adat law at Leiden University. Finally, Liefrinck's ideas gained authority within the Dutch colonial bureaucracy as he progressed in his career: between 1896 and 1900 he was Resident of Bali and Lombok, and he gained even more prestige when he became a member of the Council of the Indies (1904–9), the highest echelon of officialdom in the colonial hierarchy. Any subordinate official would have thought twice before disputing Liefrinck's model. A process of bureaucratic reproduction was now set in motion through which the model was not only to persist until the end of the colonial period, but till the present day in many government reports and textbooks as well.

The Reorganization of South Bali 1906–20: "Traditional" Institutions and Administrative Functions

With the dawn of the twentieth century a whole new era began in South Bali. Three of the six royal courts in the south faced a dramatic defeat, and, in the aftermath, the area was swept into the political and ideological system of the late colonial state. During the term of Governor General J. B. van Heutsz (1904–9) the formation of the Dutch East Indies empire was completed, and the last territories outside Java were brought under Western control under the banner of the Ethical Policy, which consisted of a mixture of benevolent development programs and military expeditions.

In 1915 a former Resident of Bali and Lombok related how he had an audience with Van Heutsz in 1905, just before taking up his appointment in Bali. It was the Governor General who

> upon my request for some instructions led me to a map of Bali and pushing his hand across the provinces of South Bali said no more than "all this has to be changed." (de Bruyn Kops 1915:466)

And change it did. After the military expedition to South Sulawesi in 1905, it was Bali's turn during the years 1906 through 1908. Not all South Balinese kingdoms were captured by force. Three of the six rulers had perceived in time that it was better not to offer any open resistance but to accommodate the Dutch to such a degree that, for the time being, they could preserve a reasonable degree of autonomy. These were the kingdoms of Karangasem, Gianyar, and Bangli, which were granted a kind of indirect rule due to the influence of F. A. Liefrinck in his capacity as Resident of Bali and Lombok and later as a member of the Council of the Indies. Liefrinck wanted to leave Balinese society as "untouched" as possible, and in this respect he was an opponent of Governor General Van Heutsz, who wanted to sweep Bali quickly and forcibly into the "modern" era. In the end, both had their way, because the remaining three kingdoms, Badung, Tabanan, and Klungkung, were subjugated by force of arms.

It was above all the unexpected violence that occurred in Badung on September 20, 1906, that was to cause quite a sensation. The ruler, together with his family and retainers, had decided on a mass death, the *puputan,* or "ending." Although the Dutch did everything to cover up the precise number of killed Balinese, it may be assumed that on that day more than 1,100 people lost their lives. This outburst of violence has never been seriously investigated. At most it is written off as a cultural curiosity of Bali, a thing of the past connected with the then-defeated rulers. Moreover, the bloodbath had to be forgotten quickly because, for the Dutch, it was a nightmare that did not fit in their Ethical Policy. It was soon forgotten because for the next thirty-four years (1906–42) Bali was to enjoy the *Pax Neerlandica,* an imposed peace that was soon considered to be an essential characteristic of Balinese culture.

Having imposed peace, the Dutch were by no means out of the woods, because South Bali still had to be governed. The administrative apparatus of the colonial state, which became increasingly bureaucratic, could only function with a great degree of uniformity. Consequently, a uniform administration was introduced in South Bali, although the area was almost entirely composed of local differences. These differences never presented a dilemma to the Dutch, because, since they were in power, they were in a position to reformulate Balinese reality. South Bali did not even become a new area to be researched; rather, it was seen as a region badly in need of a restoration project along the lines set out in the authoritative writings of Friederich and Liefrinck. After 1906 the first Dutch administrators used their models as a matter of course. The prevalent notion was that "national feeling, a bond between villages holding together a kingdom—that sort of thing did not exist; every village is a small republic" (*Gegevens* 1906:9), and that "the institutions of the people—village and *subak*—make no caste distinctions" (Van Roon 1916:262). In short, the Dutch were convinced that in South Bali, too, they would be able to find the "original Bali," covered with an "aristocratic dome" that was essentially "alien" to the population (Damsté 1922:7–8).

The result of this severance of the nobility and the people was that the Dutch left no room for the dynamics of vertical relationships between lords and followers that had characterized precolonial Bali (cf. Schulte Nordholt 1996). Instead, a compartmentalized and static image of Bali arose, in which nobles and commoners lived their separate lives in a world of their own. Moreover, it conferred on the colonial government a guiding and corrective role. The Dutch took it upon themselves to repair the "damage" to "original Bali" caused by royal rule. In 1909 the Resident wrote with confidence:

> Many excesses have come to cling to the adat like parasites, due to utter arbitrariness on the part of the powerful, and this, of course, ... can be done away with.

He had to admit, however, that at times it might be difficult to distinguish "genuine adat" and "royal parasites":

> ... the colonial official will find it far from easy to know whether he is dealing with an exaggerated display based on some old institution, or with an unjustified distortion of adat. He will find it almost impossible if the native judges and headmen prove to be incompetent or unreliable informants.[7]

Eventually these problems were solved by applying the models constructed by Friederich and Liefrinck. This was believed to be a legitimate way of operating since the Balinese themselves were obviously at a loss as to how their society was actually meant to be. Colonial power and knowledge formed the twins that reorganized South Balinese society. The knowledge and the perceptions that issued from it did not exclusively belong to the realm of ideas alone, because eventually pragmatic considerations dominated the desire to restore South Bali to its "original state."

The Caste System

In the "new order" that followed upon the chaos created by the colonial conquest the Dutch attitude toward the South Balinese nobility was ambiguous. On the one hand they wanted to get rid of the ruling dynasties, but on the other hand they were most unwilling to upset the (lower) nobility as such. Consequently, notwithstanding the fact that, according to Liefrinck's model, Bali consisted basically of egalitarian village communities, the very opposite became true, for the Dutch created a new caste system to the benefit of the nobility. In precolonial days the hierarchical order had been flexible and typically displayed a good many regional variants. It had known a degree of openness and vertical mobility, but the

---

7. The Hague, Algemeen Rijksarchief (ARA), Ministerie van Koloniën (MvK) Memorie van Overgave (MvO) Resident G.de Bruyn Kops 1909.

colonial bureaucracy could not attune to this dynamic sort of framework, which is why the Dutch felt it "best to conform as much as possible to the theoretical four-caste system" (Korn 1932:174–75). This happened in September 1910 when it was decided "to uphold the caste system, being the principal foundation of Balinese society."[8]

And so the old order was transformed into a uniform and rigid system of three closed castes. These were the *Brahmana, Satria,* and *Wesya*— jointly known as the *triwangsa*—to which some 6 to 8 percent of the population belonged. Below the triwangsa and separate from them were the "rest" of the Balinese, collectively given the name of *Sudra*.

In addition to an awareness that the nobility represented a unique Hindu culture, it was especially the colonial need for law and order and the desire to render the hierarchical structure perspicuous that gave rise to this decision. Political control of Bali would be assured as long as the nobility was not made to lose face too much. This was explicitly stated by the Dutch administrator J. Fraser (1910). He acknowledged the primacy of the egalitarian nature of Balinese society as formulated by Liefrinck, but, referring to the lessons taught by the Mutiny of 1857 in India, he felt that it was politically more opportune not to go too far in alienating the nobility. As a result a large number of the new native district officials were recruited from among the nobility. In order to legitimize the colonial caste system the Dutch fell back on Friederich's hierarchical model of Bali and two Old Javanese codes of law.[9] Though rife with inconsistency and far from exhaustive, these lawbooks henceforth counted as absolute standard.

The colonial caste system served another practical purpose as well. This happened when the Dutch administration penetrated South Bali by constructing an extensive road system. Forced labor was imposed on the Balinese, though not everyone was subjected to it. Those who belonged to the nobility, or triwangsa, were exempted from heavy physical labor and had to perform only light duties like courier services. The Sudras on the other hand were put to work on the roads without pay for thirty-six days per year (Schulte Nordholt 1996: chap.8). Corvee labor was from then on tangible proof of the rift between nobles and commoners. Obviously

---

8. KITLV, Coll. Korn (Or 435) no.166, Minutes of an administrative conference, September 15–17, 1910. This meeting was attended by all members of the Dutch administration on Bali while some Balinese nobles acted as advisers. To be sure, the four-caste model had long been known in Bali, but not until Dutch rule was it subjected to a uniform and stringent classification.

9. These were the *Adi-gama* and *Agama*, published in 1909 by the Dutch. They consisted of a compilation of Old Javanese texts, augmented and mixed with royal decrees written in Balinese. Probably the codes had functioned as normative source of law with room for interpretation and, in many cases, subject to the ruler's fiat.

many intermediate groups, such as those commoners who belonged to local notable families and members of the lower nobility, felt especially threatened and sought to avoid conscription. The point was not so much that they objected to the heaviness of the work; what bothered them was the fact that their "being fully obligated to perform corvee led to the conclusion that they were Sudra" (Korn 1932:176). For this reason they made every effort to retain their traditional status. A run on noble titles was the result. Many families of the lesser nobility did their best to have dormant claims to titles officially recognized as quickly as possible, because the demarcation between nobility and nonnobility was no longer fluid but became rigid. Those who missed the boat were to be excluded for a very long time. Protest came as well from a number of commoner groups that had enjoyed special privileges under royal rule. Now they had suddenly been lumped together with all the other commoners, once a new Sudra caste had been created. Especially in the mountain areas of Central and East Bali, repeated armed intervention and heavy sentences were needed in order to teach obstinate commoner groups that they were just ordinary Sudras.

The newly invented tradition of a rigid caste system rapidly took root in Bali. Already in 1917 a colonial report unhesitatingly concluded that

> ... the selfsame laws that were being observed in Java about the time of the fall of Majapahit [ca. A.D. 1500] are being observed in full force at this very moment in Bali.[10]

The creation of the new castes was not only influenced by a few Balinese of high noble birth who functioned as key informants for the Dutch, but the system as such was also supported by colonial courts of justice (the so-called *Raden Kerta*) that were heavily dominated by members of the nobility. These courts consisted of Balinese judges and were chaired by a Dutch official. In 1932 there were twenty-three judges in Bali, only one of whom was a commoner (Korn 1932:416). As a result, Bali was endowed with an administration of justice that primarily reinforced the colonial caste hierarchy. At the same time, however, many rules of law were far from clear. In a burst of frankness Fraser had already expressed his doubts on this subject in 1910.

> ... when such an old, venerable pedanda [Brahman priest/judge] with his imperturbably friendly and benign countenance—but from

---

10. ARA MvK Verbaal (V) 18-6-1918-39, report by the Head of the Archeological Service of the Netherlands Indies 13-2-1917.

> whom one, in urgent matters, has such a difficulty in obtaining certain information about a particular subject—when such a pedanda, after the close of a court session or meeting, wraps his old and yellowed lawbook in the same dirty cloth and takes up his staff, the symbol of his dignity, in order to return home, then a mystery walks away from me. (Fraser 1910:908)

The colonial administration had indeed sought refuge in a mystery and continued to believe in a uniform caste system so that well into the 1930s there was gross overestimation of the supposedly Hindu-Javanese legal principles. This continuation of misinterpretation should be explained in terms of bureaucratic reproduction. Victor Korn was probably one of the very few Dutch officials who understood this mechanism.

> Every civil servant who arrives to take up duty on Bali knows that he has been transferred to the island of Hinduism. He goes in search of that Hinduism and he finds it: on his desk, in the court, in the titles and temples. . . . All of which makes for the same administrative errors over and over, without end. (Korn 1932:57)

Legal matters especially generated such an amount of paperwork that the Dutch administrators were for most of the time confined to their offices. Moreover, because of the fact that these administrators were rapidly transferred to other regions, they scarcely had the opportunity to gather a sufficient amount of local knowledge. Many administrators relied on so-called standard descriptions of their region that had been made by one of their predecessors. These reports often survived for decades and facilitated the reproduction of standardized knowledge.[11] It was the nature of the colonial administration that prevented readjustments of an image once it had been firmly rooted in bureaucratic routine.

Village Restoration

While the reorganization of the nobility fitted in the hierarchical model of Friederich, the creation of an undifferentiated caste of commoners was legitimized by Liefrinck's model of egalitarian Bali. In this respect the vast majority of the Balinese carried a double identity. On the one hand they

---

11. Examples are the reports written by the Assistant Residents of South Bali H. Schwartz (1909) and W. Kroon (1912). Unfortunately these reports are lost, but their importance can be deduced from the fact that well into the 1920s their successors refer to them as the authoritative descriptions of South Bali.

were labeled by the caste system as "Sudras," but on the other hand they also represented "original" Bali.[12]

Liefrinck's model of village Bali contained three elements that were useful to the Dutch in controlling the South Balinese population. First, every village was a "micro-republic"; second, relationships within a village were "entirely democratic"; third, the village was religious in character (Liefrinck 1927:281, 285). As indicated above, the Dutch used the myth of the democratic village republic as a pretext to strengthen the caste system. Abuse of power on the part of the nobility was inconceivable, since the closed egalitarian village community was strong enough to keep the nobility at bay.

With respect to the supposed religious character of the village a dichotomy emerged, since "religion" was to be kept separate from administration. Religion was equated with traditional order, or adat, whereas administration belonged to the external domain of the colonial state. By restricting themselves to administrative control, the Dutch wanted to leave the religious—or adat—domain of the village "untouched." Consequently, the Dutch pretended to govern Bali without violating its religious "essence." They even prided themselves on their ability to respect and protect the traditional integrity of the Balinese village. In order to effect this, though, a thorough reorganization was needed, because the situation as encountered in 1906 by the newly arrived Dutch officials bore little similarity to Liefrinck's model. In comparison with North Bali, villages in the south were less isolated due to different ecological conditions, while the ruling nobility exercised more influence. Nevertheless, in-depth research into the socio-political relationships in South Bali was considered superfluous because Liefrinck's ideas served as a blueprint for the village restoration project. The Dutch completed this project with considerable speed within three years (1907–10). Dutch administrators started to "purge village administration of royal impositions and intrusions" in order to "simplify the village administration and return it to its original state."[13] As early as 1909 the Resident of Bali concluded that the whole operation had been successful and that "no actual change was made in the essence of the village administration, except that there will be more regularity and order."[14]

---

12. There are indications that the colonial Census of 1920 reinforced the "Sudra identity" of commoner groups. Several informants told me that their (grand)fathers went in search for their ancestors in order to establish their identity because the Dutch wanted to know to which caste they belonged. See on the impact of the colonial census Anderson 1991: chap. 10.

13. ARA MvK MvO Assistant Resident H. Schwartz 1909, quoted in MvO Assistant Resident A. Couvreur 1920.

14. ARA MvK V28-10-1910-1, monthly report, January 1909.

Such was the official colonial ideology. If we now turn to colonial practice a different picture emerges, for it turned out that the myth of the democratic village republic was a pretext that facilitated efficient colonial control. In the first place a new type of administrative village was created, usually consisting of several smaller villages grouped together under a new name. Sometimes existing villages were split arbitrarily and grouped with different administrative villages. The reason was that the Dutch wanted to create local administrative units of more or less equal size. Apparently, an important criterion was that these territorial units should consist of groups of 200 able-bodied men who could be recruited for colonial corvee labor (cf. Korn 1932:129).

A further change concerned the power relationships at the local level. Since the complex and competing networks of lords and followers with their many intermediaries were, at least formally, abolished, many lesser nobles had lost their local power positions. The Dutch were afraid that these nobles might prove a threat to the colonial order and therefore recruited most of the new village heads from among the former noble intermediaries. Whereas the Dutch pretended to have reinstated the villages in their traditional character, new colonial chains of command had replaced the old vertical relationships from the days of royal rule.

The most remarkable feature of the village restoration project was that in the end the nobility exercised an unprecedented power at the village level, since the new village head was backed by the power monopoly of the colonial state. This meant that former village leaders were shorn of their power. In many cases these former leaders even lost their position. The Dutch maintained, nevertheless, that actually nothing had changed. They based their argument on the new distinction between secular, or administrative authority and religious, or adat authority. The new colonial village head represented secular authority, while the former village leaders—most of whom were local notables of commoner descent—were seen as the authorities concerning adat or religion. As the Dutch wanted to see it, administration and adat formed separate worlds, hence logic would have it that local adat remained untouched by colonial interference.

Local adat as embodied in the traditional village was forbidden territory for the colonial government. Nevertheless the Dutch penetrated it by studying adat law in order to classify, codify, institutionalize—in short to control—the "traditional situation." Basing their power ascendancy on the authority of Dutch adat law studies the colonial administrators could eventually decide what should be considered as "genuine" adat and what should be dismissed as being not truly Balinese. Finally the Dutch officials in Bali created their own village in which the distinctions between administration and adat, or secular and religious affairs, were believed to be a "natural" characteristic of Bali. And so the ancestor of the present-day Balinese village was created.[15]

Irrigation: The Birth of the Traditional Subak

A second colonial myth flanked that of the village republic and referred to the local irrigation collectives in South Bali, the *subak*. The image was that, separate from the village and independent of higher bodies, the subak was an autonomous and harmonious cooperative, efficiently distributing the water over the plots of its members, who were all treated equally, whether wealthy or poor, meek or mighty.[16] Village and subak formed the democratic pillars on which "original" Bali rested.

As in the case of the village model, Dutch administrators had not gained their knowledge about the irrigation in South Bali through research of their own. Instead, they relied, again, on the authoritative writings of Liefrinck (1886–87, 1927) on North Bali when they started their subak restoration project. There were, however, significant ecological differences between North and South Bali. The north of Bali featured small-scale irrigation systems, whereas the south had large, dam-controlled regions. Second, an important aspect of South Bali was the interaction between the regional nobility and the local irrigation networks. Finally, organization of the irrigation in South Bali varied according to locality, and the boundaries between village and subak were often fluid (Schulte Nordholt 1996 chaps. 2, 4). Liefrinck, however, had presented a uniform model in which consideration was given neither to local variants nor to the role of the regional nobility. As he saw it, royal rule originally was in essence unrelated to the subak; rather, it had penetrated into the local irrigation networks, appropriating taxes as self-appointed arbiter.

Wielding Liefrinck's model, the first Dutch administrators observed that in South Bali little was left of the "original" subak. Assistant Resident J. Schwartz accordingly concluded that irrigation in this area was "sorely neglected." Immediately he embarked upon an ambitious restoration program. Already after eight months he announced its first successes. For at

---

15. In the course of the 1930s colonial influence extended still further into the local level to reach the wards (*banjar*) of the village. Just like the village, the ward was split up into an administrative sphere, called *dinas* (from the Dutch word *dienst*, service/task) and an adat domain. From then on the Balinese were confronted with two kinds of leadership, and boundaries were drawn between entities that were in practice not easily kept asunder. For government policy with regard to the village in present-day Bali, and the way in which local adat can be turned into a weapon against unwanted state penetration, see Schulte Nordholt 1991:22–32 and Warren 1990.

16. See for a standard description of this subak Grader 1960.

that time he reported that the subak in the former South Balinese kingdom of Badung had been "restored" in conformity to the North Balinese model.[17] Two years later, the leaving Resident noted with satisfaction that "in Badung the subak system . . . is now regulated on all the more important matters."[18]

The "restoration" of the subak to its supposed original state, like the village, fitted the needs of the colonial administration. The idea of restoration was no more than a flimsy facade behind which lurked administrative pragmatism. Here too, smaller units were joined together to form fewer irrigation networks, all of them organized along the same lines. In this way the basis was laid for a new colonial system of taxation, the Landrent. Just as the village had become the recruitment unit for corvee labor, the subak became the lowest unit for taxation. A memorandum concerning the former kingdom Klungkung is a telling instance of this.

> The irrigation system, too, ought to be overhauled drastically. In the days of the kings the hogs were many and the wash poor. All the nobles and prominent had their own tax collector who made sure that his own land was watered aplenty. Urgently needed is a separation between irrigation officials and administrative personnel; a division of irrigation areas . . . must be designed; the subak have to be assigned in groups to avoid too large a number of subak heads which would impede administrative control.[19]

Within a few years time the Dutch replaced the plurality of relations from the royal days with a far smaller bureaucracy managing irrigation in South Bali.[20] While the Dutch looked upon the reorganization as providing well-defined and controllable entities, many Balinese thought differently. For them the colonial "restoration" project bred disintegration and confusion. Countless small irrigation cooperatives were amalgamated into large subaks. Due to this scaling-up many of the newly formed subak lacked internal cohesion. Moreover, the new subaks were joined together into overarching irrigation areas often coinciding with the boundaries of administrative districts. As a result the new irrigation districts were hardly coherent ecological wholes, so that a proper distribution of water was seriously hampered. On the regional level coordination was now in the hands of new Balinese officials who were often not familiar with irri-

---

17. KITLV Coll. Korn (Or 435) nr. 97, monthly reports on January and August 1907.
18. ARA MvK MvO Resident G. de Bruyn Kops 1909.
19. ARA MvK V15-9-1909-30, report Resident of Bali 8-9-1908.
20. See for a detailed description of the transformation of the irrigation systems in South Bali under colonial rule, Schulte Nordholt 1996: chap. 8.

gation. In the selection of these officials the Dutch preferred candidates from among the nobility with bureaucratic skills, whose principal task it was to collect taxes.

Because the Dutch replaced many of the old earthen—and vulnerable—dams with concrete—and permanent—constructions, the former connections between local irrigation and central water supply, involving labor and ritual, fell into disuse. This was reinforced when a special colonial service, the Public Utilities Department, began to concern itself with irrigation control on the supra-local level (cf. Van Doorn 1982). It was only because of these new conditions that the South Balinese subak was made into a strictly local affair. Liefrinck's model had been forced upon South Bali, the credibility of which was reinforced when later generations of Dutch administrators not only found it in reports but in practice as well.

The Restoration of Kingship

The Great Shock

On the morning of January 21, 1917, South Bali was hit by a powerful earthquake. More than 1,350 people died and countless houses and temples were destroyed. Dams and conduits also collapsed, and destructive streams of mud crippled agriculture. That year almost nothing was left to harvest. Disaster took a dramatic turn when in 1918 the worldwide influenza epidemic swept over Bali and an estimated 22,300 people succumbed to this "Spanish flu." Old informants recall that every few days the death toll rose. The atmosphere was one of fear; death stalked the yards and refused to go away.[21] On top of that in 1919 South Bali was visited by a plague of mice causing yet another crop failure. As all these calamities transpired, life in South Bali lost every vestige of orderliness. Many were convinced that the anger of the gods had descended on the land. Under colonial rule Bali had become ritually "unclean" and was now being punished. However, the Dutch did not consider ritual purifications as their responsibility, since they conceived of themselves as in charge of "secular" order and left "religion" to itself. But in so doing the Dutch administration had saddled the Balinese with an enormous problem. Colonial rule had created a ritual vacuum that the old dismantled dynasties were no longer able to fill. Although the Dutch were powerful it became clear that they could not ward off evil and in fact felt not called to do so. Great disquiet was arising concerning the fearful disorder brought about by a decade of Dutch rule.

---

21. Schulte Nordholt 1996: chap. 8.

"Popular Chiefs"

At about the same time a degree of uneasiness arose among the Dutch regarding the way colonial rule had taken shape in Bali. Gradually it became evident that the Dutch administrators hardly knew what was actually happening in their districts. Ensconced in their offices, swamped by growing mountains of paperwork, they were far removed from the Balinese. In this respect the Assistant Resident of South Bali observed in 1920 that "our administrators have long since lost touch with the population and have lost their essential function as antennae; one never gets into the real village."[22] They also found their subordinate Balinese officials less reliable. Although many of them were still from noble descent, a new type of indigenous administrator had emerged, that of the young Western-educated official who was repeatedly transferred to new posts and other districts. According to Korn (1932:647), the Dutch no longer appreciated those "who were familiar with their own arts and literature," but preferred "someone who could write a letter in the least broken Dutch."

Based on their experience in Java, where a large-scale political mobilization had occurred, the Dutch feared that they would lose control over the Balinese population as well.[23] In response to what was seen as a dangerous undermining of the colonial system, the Dutch invented the so-called popular chief. This was a leader to whom "traditional authority" was ascribed and who was expected to act as a native official within his own environment. At the same time this chief would be part of the colonial bureaucracy, though in practice he would have little to say. There could be no misunderstanding regarding the role to be played by these chiefs on Bali.

> An intellectually well-developed official is useful for administrative purposes. But to rule the country, hence to keep in touch with the population, it is better to fall back on less talented persons, as long as they are natives and possess prestige.[24]

But this choice in favor of a noble popular chief was not without its problems. The question was whether this sort of support for the nobility would

---

22. ARA MvK MvO A. J. L. Couvreur 1920.

23. See Onghokham 1978 for the widening gap between colonial administration and the population on Java at the beginning of the twentieth century; Sartono Kardodirdjo 1973:142–85 on local protest movements in Java inspired by the Sarekat Islam between 1912–14; Takashi Shiraishi 1990 on the popular movements in Central Java in the beginning of this century.

24. ARA MvK MvO Assistant Resident A. J. L. Couvreur 1920. On the popular chief in Java, see Sutherland 1979: chap. 10.

not detract from "original" and "egalitarian" Bali. Resident H. T. Damsté (1919–23) was particularly aware of this dilemma. On the one hand he was very much opposed to popular chiefs because he did not want to see Bali dominated by a "non-indigenous" nobility, "essentially foreign" to the island, who would seriously threaten the "ancient democratic girders" of Balinese society (Damsté 1922, 1923). On the other hand, however, if the noble centers were to be dismantled further still, the unique Hindu religion of Bali would certainly collapse, which eventually would spell the end of Balinese culture. And this, of course, should be prevented, whatever the cost. Willy-nilly, then, Damsté had to choose in favor of the nobility, not only in order to reinforce colonial control in Bali, but also to fend off evil influences from outside in the shape of Islam and nationalism. His Assistant Resident concurred with him: "We must, in the very first place, uphold the caste system, otherwise the religion is done for and the Muslims will take their chance."[25] The need to keep Bali separate from Java was, again, emphasized by Damsté's successor who lamented: "Can we not widen and deepen the Strait of Bali? At any rate, let us not build a bridge across those troubled waters to still more troubled regions."[26]

Royal Administrators

The introduction of the popular chief, who would provide colonial rule in Bali with a "traditional" face, resulted in the restoration of royal rule. In 1929 eight representatives of former dynasties were appointed as "royal administrators." The reinstatement of the old dynasties within the framework of the colonial administrative bureaucracy had a quasi-apolitical character. The Dutch treated the royal chiefs as powerless puppets, without much room to maneuver on the administrative level. They were thought to have a purely religious task, because in the old days

> the king was, first of all, the religious leader; his administrative task was a means rather than a goal; he maintained peace and order so that the people could serve the gods in peace.[27]

From then on this was the new standard definition of traditional kingship in Bali. It was probably based on a speech delivered by the administrative

---

25. Private letter Assistant Resident Berkhout to V. Korn 5–8–1921, KITLV Coll. Korn (Or.435) 284. Elsewhere Korn added another argument in favor of the popular chief: "Should the recognition of traditional authority disappear and should we wish to keep in check a people as courageous as the Balinese, we shall need to take vastly different measures" (KITLV Coll. Korn (Or.435) 147, report 22–12–1925).

26. ARA MvK MvO Resident P. Moolenburgh 1926.

27. ARA MvK Report on Tabanan by H. J. Hoekstra 1938, and Report on Klungkung by W. F. van der Kaaden 1938.

The Making of Traditional Bali

ruler of Karangasem, Gusti Bagus Djelantik, in 1929, which was quoted in the authoritative adat law study on Bali by V. Korn.[28] In his speech Djelantik had used the colonial distinction between politics and religion and emphasized his "religious" responsibility. However, both the Dutch and the Balinese were well aware that a lot of politics was involved. The Dutch needed the rulers and their religious authority as "pillars of Dutch authority and a bulwark against nationalism";[29] the Balinese rulers used their freedom in the field of religion to increase their informal power base.

Restored Kings

Characteristic of the late-colonial state were its conservatism and its faith in the traditions it had itself created. Both came to expression when a more comprehensive reinstatement of the former kingdoms finally took place in 1938 (Schulte Nordholt 1996: chap. 9). Emphasis was laid on "a policy of reinforcing existing old-indigenous organizations and the authority of chiefs rooted therein."[30]

Viewed from the center of the colonial state the reinstatement of kingship was part of a larger political scheme, but in the eyes of the Balinese it was a unique event. In 1932 and again in 1935 the royal administrators had requested the Governor General that they be fully reinstated as kings. This time they not only stressed their "religious" task but also openly mentioned political advantages.

> Fortunately, Bali has not been infected as yet with evil as other regions are; but the danger exists that evil may infiltrate from without; introduction of self-rule may counteract this.[31]

---

28. "Surely, the Dutch Indies Government is an equitable government, but it looks to our material interests alone. The [former] Balinese kings were less concerned with these matters, but they taught the people to respect the gods and they provided the means of customary ritual so that the people could send the souls of the dead on their appointed way" (Korn 1932:341). To what extent parts of this speech were written by Dutch ghostwriters remains open to speculation.

29. ARA MvK Mailreport (Mr) 1934:1095x.

30. KITLV Coll. Korn (Or.35) 110, government memorandum presented to the *Volksraad*, an assembly of representatives from the Netherlands East Indies, Batavia, 1937–38. In tandem with the "restoration" of royal rule an extensive administrative reform took place. In the regions outside Java three large administrative territories were created, where "restored" royal rule was to be operative. Bali belonged to the new territory, the Great East, which had its administrative center in Makassar. The other territories were Sumatra and Borneo. The position of these chiefs was anchored in a kind of "adat state law" meant as theoretical underpinning of the link between the old indigenous systems and the colonial state (cf. Haga 1924).

31. ARA MvK V15-7-1938-14, report by the Director of the Department of Interior Administration 3-5-1935.

The "evil" referred to was nationalism; the candidate kings, then, presented themselves as guardians of colonial order. Finally in 1937 their request was granted. The Dutch were convinced that both colonial control and traditional Balinese culture were best preserved by the reinstatement of the former kingdoms. There was yet another very important argument: in the end restoration of royal rule proved to be the cheapest form of colonial administration.

Still, despite the consensus, some uneasiness was felt on the Dutch side. Could one really be sure that the Balinese people were best served with royal rule? Had the situation of the younger generation Balinese, those with Western schooling, been taken into account sufficiently? In Batavia the director of the Department of Interior Administration anticipated no problems. During a brief visit to Bali he had heard no complaints, and he assumed therefore that the desire for royal rule was shared by the people at large. Moreover, there was no reason to think that the kings would make misuse of their position. After all, he opined, "if one takes into account the democratic nature of Balinese society, it is not likely that restoration of self-rule on Bali would mean introduction of autocratic self-rule."[32] The myth of the autonomous and egalitarian village community proved to be very much alive.

The younger generation of Western-educated Balinese was marginalized from the outset. The fear expressed by this group that royal rule would encourage conservatism and fossilization was not taken seriously. On the contrary, according to the director, "Young Bali demonstrates enormous overestimation of Western forms of democracy, alongside of utter under-estimation and denial of Oriental institutions and customs." In a telling addition to this statement he wrote:

> Happily, the time is past that Western democracy finds general acclaim and is held up as an example. The recognition has dawned that administration is served better if the state structure adapts to Oriental relationships, and structures proper to the East are increasingly meeting with approval.[33]

---

32. KITLV Coll. Korn (Or.435) 110, proceedings *Volksraad* 16-2 and 29-3-1938. The Resident of Bali supported him by arguing that "the people generally have no need of a council [i.e., a kind of regional assembly]. . . . they have their voice in their own adat communities, the desa and the subak. There true democracy prevails. The masses are happy to leave representation of interests on a higher level to more elevated chiefs" (ARA MvK V15-7-1938-14, report Resident of Bali 20-7-1936).

33. ARA MvK V15-7-1938-14, report, Director of the Department of Interior Administration 13-10-1936.

The Making of Traditional Bali

Freely interpreted one can read into this that the Dutch had begun to appreciate what they had created themselves: a traditional Eastern society that became increasingly "traditional" as Western dominance grew. It also illustrates that ethnographic knowledge about Bali, in combination with comparable knowledge on other Indonesian societies, had now been fully internalized by the colonial bureaucracy. One could therefore safely conclude that it was not the kings but the younger generation who were not in tune with the times.[34]

On both the central and the local levels the Dutch authorities certainly did not intend for the "self-rulers" to actually rule their kingdoms. They were considered entirely unfit for this. Rather, the Dutch would keep administrative matters firmly under control. In fact, the bureaucratization and centralization of the colonial state continued apace, and within this process there was no place for autonomous rulers who governed themselves. It was the Dutch administrators who smoothed over the rough patches and covered up the absurdity from the eyes of the world. It did not matter whether a ruler did not understand a word of the documents he had to sign. One ruler had his desk in an open gallery and right in front of him he had a full-length mirror placed. Sometimes he used to go and sit at his desk to gaze at himself a while. And if there were really troublesome documents to deal with he rang up the Dutch administrator and asked his help. Actually, the self-rulers did not meet with much sympathy from the Dutch. According to a former local Dutch administrator, one high-ranking Dutch official entrusted with the introduction of self-rule was said to have lamented: "Oh wouldn't I love to kick these natives [i.e., rulers-to-be] back to where they belong!"[35] Nevertheless the play had begun and had to be played out. If the term *theatre state* is to be applied to Bali (C. Geertz 1980), then the restored kings of the 1930s fit the bill.

If the position of the kings relative to the Dutch was one of powerlessness, within their restored kingdoms their personal power reached a peak. They lost no time capitalizing on their renewed royal status to look after their own interests first. They appointed, for instance, many relatives to lower administrative positions and expanded their landed property in

---

34. Eventually each of the "restored" rulers was advised by a council, but membership was generally restricted to relatives and close associates of the ruler. Before establishing these councils, the Dutch administration had asked the philologist R. Goris, who served as a language expert in Bali, for advice in this matter. Goris produced a report—based on data from the ninth through the thirteenth centuries—in which he demonstrated that such a council was an original Balinese institution, whereas the position of a *patih*, or second in command, was only a "recent phenomenon," which had existed since the sixteenth century. Hence, the advisory council of the ruler was reinvented, the *patih* not.

35. Interview with C. J. Grader, 1982.

various ways. The Dutch knew that some of these practices could not be tolerated officially, but, on the other hand, did not want the fiction of "self-rule" eroded either. Reminiscing, a former Dutch administrator formulated the quandary as follows.

> Look, we just put those kings back in. Surely we couldn't drag them into court the next day, bring them before a judge because they had stepped out of line, could we?

To which another former administrator added:

> We were aware of the goings on around a certain ruler that weren't cricket; things like palace murders and such, but . . . we were not supposed to know that sort of thing.[36]

The colonial intervention at the end of the 1930s completed a process in which a fixed hierarchical system was created. In spite of the fact that they played but a minor role within the colonial state, the restored rulers were more powerful than ever before within their own realms, and resistance had virtually no chance of success.

Order and Harmony in the Colonial House

When in 1929 the old dynasties were restored, the Dutch Resident L. Caron used an interesting metaphor. He pictured Balinese society as a house. Important rooms in this house were the village and the subak, while royal rule was to provide a "protective roofing."[37] As he saw it, Balinese society was a fully integrated whole worthy of assiduous conservation. One of the main architects of this "Balinese house" was the Dutch administrator V. E. Korn.[38] Together with Liefrinck, Korn was not only the

---

36. Interviews with respectively Professor J. van Baal and Dr. F. W. T. Hunger, 1981.
37. ARA MvK MvO Resident L. Caron 1929.
38. Victor Emanuel Korn (1892–1969) had between 1917 and 1931 a variety of positions in Bali. He was district administrator in South Bali (1917–21); during a sickness leave (1921–24) he wrote his doctoral dissertation on Balinese adat law (1924); in 1925 he returned to Bali and served as adat specialist (1925–27), then as secretary of the Resident of Bali (1927–28), and became Assistant Resident of South Bali (1929–31); in 1932 he published a revised version of his thesis. After his career in Bali he went to Sumatra where he became Resident of Tapanuli (1936–39). In 1939 he retired from the colonial administration and accepted a position as professor of adat law at the University of Leiden; in 1958 he retired (cf. Prins 1970). He was never married, because, as one of his former colleagues said, he suffered from a venereal disease that he had picked up during the very early years of his colonial career. During his years in Bali he had a Balinese housekeeper or *nyai*, who was the sister of his clerk. This intimate relationship is perhaps a good example of an "ethnographic occasion" realized on the pillow.

most important colonial ethnographer on Bali but also one of the most influential administrators. Based on his ethnographic knowledge he formulated several administrative paradigms that were to be reproduced by the government bureaucracy.

"Bali Is Unique..."

Korn was among the important colonial opinion makers who argued that Bali should be closed off from the outside world to keep harmful influences at bay. According to him Bali was not only threatened by nationalism and Islam but by Christianity as well. In 1925 he wrote an article titled "Bali is unique ... more finely grained than any other part of the Indies," in which he opposed missionary activities by the Roman Catholic church on Bali, which would have a devastating effect on Balinese culture. His protest was successful but in 1932 great alarm was sounded again when it appeared that Protestant evangelizing activities were in progress in Bali. Established Bali experts opposed this "Christian action" en bloc. Language official and adviser to the Dutch administration in Bali Dr. R. Goris warned that "unrest of state-endangering proportions" would be the result if Christianity were to infiltrate Bali, because unemployed Brahman priests would pose a political threat and "Calvinism" would be an agent of "cultural destruction."[39] Goris's arguments won the day and the Governor General forbade "Christian action" in Bali.[40] During the debate on the missionary issue the Balinese themselves had not been consulted. Although some Balinese could not understand why the Dutch did not introduce their own religion—the rulers from Majapahit had done this in the past, so why not the new masters?—the colonial administrators were of the opinion that Balinese culture was so fragile and in fact incapable of standing on its own feet that they should speak and decide on behalf of Bali.

In the field of education the same sort of thing applied. Initially there had been much demand for Western-educated young people to fill up the lower ranks of the Balinese administrative corps. But around 1920, when "popular chiefs" gained ground, the tide turned. "What are we to do with all those Dutch-speaking Balinese?" Korn asked. Later he added that higher colonial education groomed a kind of "half-baked intellectuals ... making for a fateful element in a still primitive society."[41] As a result,

---

39. Private Coll. Prof. C. Hooykaas, letter Goris to the Resident of Bali 4-8-1932. See also Lekkerkerker 1933 and Kraemer 1933.

40. Ibid. Decision Governor General 2-2-1935-23. In the event, however, missionaries were tolerated as long as no active conversion activities were undertaken. In 1940 some 1,600 Balinese were Protestant.

41. ARA MvK MvO Administrator Badung, V. Korn, 1921l; KITLV Coll. Korn (Or 435) 147, report 22-12-1925.

access to higher education was purposely blocked. Instead, more attention was given to the three-year elementary education in village schools. Moreover, to prevent young people from being exposed to undesirable influences the curriculum was adapted to the "indigenous atmosphere," through a process called "Balinization."[42] Neither the restricted access to secondary education nor the Balinization of the curriculum could prevent young Balinese from coming into contact with new ideas. This happened especially in the informal schools established on Bali by Javanese representatives of the nationalist movement. These schools attracted many students who were denied entry to the government schools and spread the seed of nationalism over Bali.[43]

In conjunction with the pursued educational policy, the caste system, too, was meticulously maintained. Primacy of the caste hierarchy was underscored by the restoration of the old dynasties and guarded with zeal by the courts of justice. Even so, there was some commotion when during the 1920s an association of commoners was established that opposed the increasing caste barriers within the indigenous administrative corps. Its members pleaded for assessment in terms of achievement rather than birth, but due to colonial interference the association was short-lived, and caste hierarchy took precedence.[44]

Architecture and Art

A truckload of books, catalogs, and articles have been written on modern Balinese art, which has become one of the major export commodities of the island. Most writings focus on the work of individual artists or groups of artists, and although ample attention has been paid to the influential role played by Western artists, next to nothing is written about the colonial context in which this modern art was born. The political economy of Balinese art still needs to be analyzed.

After the great earthquake of 1917 the burning question was to what extent the Dutch administration should be actively involved in the reconstruction of the many ruined temples and noble houses. Financial support was not handed out heedlessly because the Dutch wanted to supervise the rebuilding activities. In this respect an important role was played by the Dutch architect and president of the Batavian Society of the Arts, P.

---

42. Cf. Pollmann 1990. The showpiece of this kind of education was the private elite school Siladarma in Klungkung, which was opened in 1928 and led by Dutch teachers (Te Flierhaar 1941).

43. In 1940 there were fifteen of such schools; ARA MvK MvO Resident H. Moll 1941.

44. Korn 1932:124–25; Vickers 1989:150–55. The commoner association was mainly based in North Bali, where, due to external influences and a lack of dynastic conservatism, a more liberal intellectual climate existed.

Moojen. He had a close relationship with Governor General J. van Limburg Stirum (1916–21), who appointed him as supervisor of a restoration program in Bali. Moojen immediately beat the alarm, speaking of an emergency situation because repairs done by the Balinese were totally inappropriate. Rather than rebuilding the structures in the old style the Balinese introduced all kind of novelties aped from the Europeans, which, of course, could not be tolerated. In particular, "erratic whims," such as funny statues of European soldiers as temple guards or temple shrines with carved clocks—*the* symbols of colonial rule—were fiercely rejected by him. Moojen had no appreciation of the great talent for improvisation of some of the Balinese artists. Rather, restoration had to follow strictly traditional lines that were determined by Moojen himself.

This colonial interference did not occur without discussion, for at least some Dutch officials recognized that there was something amiss: "It is better to admit honestly that only Western interests profit from keeping Balinese culture pure."[45] However, this critical view was counteracted by the dominant opinion that

> [a]mong our people a consciousness is dawning of the duties that we owe to the people under our government, that excludes a contrast between the interests of the Balinese on the one hand and those of the Europeans on the other; quite the contrary, our positive duty imposes protection for the benefit of the Balinese educated posterity.[46]

This set the tone. Balinese culture had to be trussed up in a sort of symbiotic harmony with traditional bonds. In practice this could not succeed. In 1922 Moojen lost his privileged position and the financial support from the colonial government.[47] Although individual Dutch administrators certainly used their authority to keep architecture as traditional as possible, it turned out that the Dutch administrative bureaucracy was not the proper apparatus to pursue an effective policy regarding the arts.

However, Balinese art remained under Western supervision. Toward the end of the 1920s a small but influential group of Western artists settled in Bali and took it upon themselves to protect indigenous culture against

---

45. ARA MvK V18-6-1918-39, report advisory committee 18-9-1917; see also KITLV Coll. Moojen (H.1169).

46. Ibid., report, acting Resident Bali 26-11-1917.

47. In 1922 Moojen was no longer protected by Governor General Van Limburg Stirum, while in Bali, Resident Damsté strongly opposed the subsidizing of noble houses and temples. Damsté not only resented the fact that Moojen's activities were beyond the control of the local colonial administration, he also believed that Balinese religion was in a process of decay due to the weakness of the nobility. In his eyes Roman Catholicism, with its emphasis on rituals, was the best candidate to replace Hinduism in Bali.

"decadence" and "degeneration." Prominent in this group were Walter Spies and Rudolph Bonnet who gave the village of Ubud its international fame (cf. Vickers 1989:105–14). On first impression both Spies and Bonnet had gone very native and were, in comparison with Dutch administrators, in close contact with the Balinese population. On the other hand, however, they still belonged to the "caste" of Western powerholders and displayed a benign but coercive paternalism. A telling instance of this attitude is the following statement by Spies.

> Upon us—a race that would contribute to culture, and in possession of a certain degree of knowledge of the development and demise of other, widely diverse races and their native art—devolves the task to point to the harm which neglect of indigenous, original elements can do in terms of dulling and decay of native art, to warn of the dire consequences when modern affectations are short-sightedly adopted, to counteract especially the blind, superficial aping of foreign expressions of art taken over from strange races and with complete lack of understanding.[48]

Bonnet was also worried about the harmful effects of Western influences on Balinese culture. Architecture and dress served as examples to show the degree of degeneration that had already occurred, and, by way of illustration, he printed photographs with the captions "good" (i.e., traditional) and "wrong" (i.e., Western) (Philokalos 1936).

Ironically, the same Western artists who warned against decadence and decay effected the most important innovations in South Balinese painting in terms of colors, size, themes, and marketing. The majority of the new Balinese paintings pictured idyllic scenes from village life against an impressive green decor of nature. Balinese arcadia, primarily representing the dreams of Western artists living in Bali, was born. This image of Bali was sold worldwide through mediation of, among others, Spies and Bonnet, who also stimulated the making of small-sized paintings that fitted into the suitcases of tourists.[49]

---

48. KITLV Coll. Korn (Or.435) MvO District Administrator of Gianyar, H. Jacobs 1934, in which Spies wrote a paragraph on art. See for rather uncritical studies on Spies Rhodius 1965 and Rhodius and Darling 1980. An earlier painter and image maker of Bali was W. O. J. Nieuwenkamp. His work (1922) shows traditional Bali in a Jugendstil decor.

49. Because most attention has been paid to South Balinese art and in particular the small community of Western artists in and around Ubud, interesting developments in North Bali have by and large been neglected. There the influence of the cinema and a kind of popular opera (the *Stamboel*) was most apparent, and many new forms of dances and music were created without Western interference. Although Spies acknowledged the innovative spirit in

The Making of Traditional Bali

It seemed as if only under Western guidance could true Balinese art survive. The Dutch looked at the expatriate community of Western artists in Bali with mixed feelings. On the one hand Spies and his friends were good at advertising Bali as a fancy tourist resort. On the other hand, however, there was also the image of Bali as a sexual permissive society, a paradise for homosexuals (Vickers 1989: 119–22). And that was not tolerated by the Dutch. Suddenly in 1938 a witch-hunt was started against homosexuals all over the Netherlands Indies. In Bali, Spies was arrested, others left the island, and the expatriate community was decimated (Rhodius and Darling 1980:43–45). Colonial conservatism and modern artists were not made for each other.

Adat, Structure, and Personality

The policy of the late colonial state toward Bali was characterized by a major contradiction. On the one hand, the Dutch wanted to protect the island from evil influences like nationalism, Islam, Christianity, and Western "decadence" by keeping it as traditional as possible. At the same time, however, Bali had been absorbed into the colonial state, which unleashed on the island an ever-expanding number of administrative rules and services. Gradually it became clear that one of the most dangerous forces was the central state itself. To an increasing extent local administrators protested against the uniform approach of the centralized bureaucracy in Batavia, which in their eyes threatened the traditional integrity of Bali. As one Resident put it:

> What struck me in particular is that only by hard and persistent struggle it is sometimes possible to convince [central] government offices of the particular demands of Bali. These . . . offices . . . used to rubber-stamp work, do not want to take this into account, or lack the goodwill or the capacity to cut their uniform service to fit the special Balinese body.[50]

North Bali his opinion was a negative one. According to him North Balinese were a rough kind of people and their culture was more vulgar: "they have taken very quickly to white material culture, and under the impetus of the contact new ideas emerge which are brought finally to South Bali, mainly by the taxi drivers, who are all good gamelan players and very manly with a different girl every night; they act as chief diffusers [sic!]. The new form is then taken over in South Bali, polished and refined and elaborated almost out of recognition and made into an art form" (quoted by Margaret Mead, Library of Congress, Washington, Coll. Bateson and Mead; I owe this reference to Yayasuki Nagafuchi to whom I am very grateful).

50. ARA MvK MvO Resident P. Moolenburgh 1926. Korn was probably the author of this paragraph.

In this tension between central bureaucracy and local administration, the study of adat law became an important tool in the hands of local administrators, not only to control local society but also to prevent unwanted penetration by the central state. In order to resist this penetration Resident Damsté (1919–23) had put in a plea for the encouragement of adat-law research (Damsté 1923; Korn 1955). He succeeded, and it was the administrator Korn who was allowed to conduct such research. The results were published in 1924 and, in a revised edition, in 1932. Traditional systems of local administration and law regarding village and subak, rules of marriage and inheritance, and the caste system were all brought together in this authoritative standard work on Balinese adat law. The bulk of Korn's material consisted of earlier Dutch writings on Bali, administrative reports, Balinese texts, questionnaires that were distributed among Balinese officials, and data derived from a few Balinese key informants who were also part of the colonial administration. Interestingly, Korn did very little actual fieldwork. In contrast to his predecessor Liefrinck he remained first and foremost an administrator who stayed in his office.[51]

Korn not only emphasized the uniqueness of Bali but also pointed at countless local variations within Balinese adat. He was, moreover, very well aware of the rapid changes that took place as a consequence of Dutch colonial rule in Bali. Adat, as a set of written and unwritten rules for daily affairs and collective conduct, had always been a flexible and normative system primarily aimed at reconciliation rather than rigid verdicts. But when these rules were laid down in monographs and used in colonial courts, flexibility disappeared and the character of adat was transmuted into judicial prescriptions framed in timeless tradition and approved by colonial authorities. This happened in Bali as well. Korn's magnum opus (1932) represented Bali according to Dutch academic categories, and any further research was thought to be superfluous. As one former administrator put it: "Korn's book became our bible."[52]

Referring to Korn's work local Dutch administrators were not only able to represent the interests of Bali vis à vis the central state, but to operate within Bali as social engineers as well. In this respect Korn, too, believed that the study of adat law was the only possible way

> to perceive the meaning of legal institutions and rules, since only then can be judged what should be preserved without useless material being preserved along with it. (1932:676)

---

51. Even Korn's monograph on the "village republic" of Tnganan (1933) was mainly based on "indirect research" that he had conducted from his office. By telephone he had instructed local Balinese officials what to investigate and they reported their findings along bureaucratic lines to him.

52. Interview with Dr. W. F. T. Hunger 1981.

The Dutch version of structural functionalism implied that knowledge of "legal" institutions would explain the mechanism of society; that, if necessary, one could repair that mechanism; and that it was the task of Western adat experts to give guidance to this process. Consequently, knowledge of adat—emanating from a power ascendancy—was not only essential to the preservation of Balinese society, it simultaneously legitimized a protracted Dutch control of the island. It was unthinkable that the restored self-rulers and the "fragile" society would be able to stand on their own feet in the foreseeable future.[53]

As Dutch knowledge accumulated and no political disturbances threatened colonial rule, Dutch images of Bali tended to become more and more static and abstract. Instead of recognizable individuals and everyday life, constantly recurring models and types were described: the village, the subak, traditional leadership. Moreover, during the 1930s Bali excellently suited analyses and speculations in the field of the symbolic structure of society. The two-, four-, five-, eight-, nine-, and elevenfold divisions of the cosmos, the belief that the cosmic order determined social structure, and the bipartition of the "Old Balinese" village attracted the spotlight of attention. Influenced by the so-called Leiden School of Ethnology of that time, a search for the "primeval Bali" started. Inspired by scholars such as F. D. E. van Ossenbruggen and H. W. Rassers, local administrators like Korn and C. J. Grader were convinced that under the "recent layers" of colonialism and Hinduism there still was an original, genuine Indonesian "prime" structure in Balinese society. This "primeval" Bali with its supposed dualism had to be found in the so-called Old-Balinese mountain villages where Hinduism had not taken root and where Western influences were thought to be absent. This explains why during the 1930s several monographs were written about the symbolic structure of these mountain villages, whereas no research was conducted on lowland villages.[54] Finally, toward the end of the colonial period, the Dutch had discovered and understood the "real" Bali by removing the Balinese from the scene.

The construction of the "traditional Balinese house" by Dutch colonial administrators was as good as completed when foreign anthropologists like Margaret Mead, Gregory Bateson, and Jane Belo arrived there in the 1930s. Whereas Dutch writings tended toward impersonal structural-

---

53. For a general overview of the politics of Dutch adat law studies in the Netherlands East-Indies in relation to Islam and nationalism, see Benda 1958:61–99 and Ellen 1976:313–21.

54. See, for instance, Swellengrebel 1960: Introduction; Korn 1933; Grader 1937a, 1937b, n.d.; Boekian 1936; for the echo of these notions in administrative reports, ARA MvK MvO Resident G. de Haze Winkelman 1937 and C. J. Grader, *Nota van Toelichting Buleleng* 1938. See for the Leiden School of Ethnology Koentjaraningrat 1975: chap. 8, and for an early critique Geertz 1961.

ism, Mead and her entourage concentrated on the relationship between culture and personality in order to identify the collective Balinese character.[55] Roughly summarized, they saw Bali as a society characterized by stasis and equilibrium, while nature and culture were finely attuned to each other. Jane Belo, for instance, concluded her article "The Balinese Temper" as follows.

> If we see in the equilibrated, delicately adjusted and essentially unstrained behaviour of the people the clue to their happy temper, we must conclude that a static, traditional society as theirs, solving all problems, prescribing every act, does form a desirable background against which well-balanced personalities may be reared. (Belo 1970b:110)

On another level Bateson analyzed in an influential article the nature of Balinese society as a "Steady State." Such a "Steady State"—a condition of the Balinese mind—was characterized by a balanced, "non-progressive" change (1970a:400). Although they were of course aware of the Dutch colonial presence in Bali, Mead and her colleagues thought that they could "factor out" Western elements in order to find traditional Bali. Ironically, however, it was Walter Spies who introduced them to Balinese culture and seduced them to a belief in a harmonious Bali. Despite her initial interest in schizophrenia and fear as dominant elements of Balinese culture, Mead, too, accepted this romantic image in which stasis and balance were the key notions (Pollmann 1990). In this respect they were also influenced by the Dutch colonial officials Goris and Grader who had a friendly relationship with Spies.

Although at first sight the legalistic adat law school, with its structural functionalist flavor, the Dutch version of symbolic structuralism, and the Culture and Personality approach had very little in common, they did not exclude each other. On the contrary, together they structured the traditional "Balinese house." While Dutch administrators had built this house, Mead, Bateson, and Belo provided its inhabitants with a fitting cultural identity.

The Hidden Crisis in Paradise Bali

As the 1930s progressed the image of Bali that emerged was one of a splendid place for romantic foreigners looking for an eastern paradise. The image

---

55. I will not discuss here in detail the findings of Mead, Bateson, and Belo (cf. Belo 1970a). See Vickers 1989:118–24 and especially Pollmann 1990 for an in-depth analysis of Mead's research in Bali.

The Making of Traditional Bali 271

of savage Bali was forgotten. Instead Bali was now synonymous with beauty and sensuality (bare-breasted women), artistic talent (every Balinese was by nature an artist), mixed with glimpses of exotic anger (trance) (cf. Vickers 1989:78). This romantic image of Bali was made known to the world by the photobooks by Gregor Krause (1920) and *Island of Bali* by Miguel Covarrubias (1973). Covarrubias's book was published in 1937 and became the standard description of Bali read by an increasing number of tourists who visited the island (cf. Vickers 1989:114–17). Like Mead, Covarrubias was also influenced by Walter Spies when he wrote his popular representation of the "happy and peaceful island of Bali" (1973:405). Moreover, Covarrubias summarized the images that had by now been established and brought them together in a well-rounded synthesis: the image of the noble elite from foreign Hindu-Javanese descent, the village and subak as age-old traditional communities, the balance and equilibrium of the Balinese character, combined with descriptions advertising the arts and exotic rituals.

During the 1930s Bali represented an escape for those who no longer felt at home in the Western world that was threatened by the Depression and political turmoil. In the words of Margaret Mead:

> Many Americans in the 1920s sought for an escape as single individuals from a society which denied them self-expression. Many in the 1930s sought a formula by which we could build our society into a form which would make possible, on a firm economic basis, both simple happiness and complexity of spiritual expression. Of such a dream, Bali was a fitting symbol. (1970:340)

The island had become "the dream of a summer's afternoon" (Kraemer 1933:19). Although not everyone believed in the images that had been created, and dissident voices were raised, these were drowned by the great chorus of administrators, ethnologists, artists, travelers, and journalists who continuously reinforced the images that constituted traditional Bali. These images gained credibility every time they were reiterated; when travelers left for Bali they saw what they wanted to see. At the same time more and more Western Bali experts filtered in to keep watch over "their" culture, and little by little Balinese had to acquiesce in those strange but powerful images of themselves.

There emerged what Taufik Abdullah has called a *schakel*-society, by which he refers to a relationship between colonial powerholders and the population that was only partly connected. For it was also

> a world of pretence that created its own realities of both ruler and ruled. . . . It was an artificial world, a theatre, where both ruler and

ruled played their roles while maintaining their separate sense of reality. (Taufik Abdullah 1976:144, 148)

The places where Balinese and foreigners met were the abstract terrains of village structure, general adat rules, cosmic classifications, literature, art, and ritual. There, both Westerners and Balinese could meet and communicate interminably with each other without trespassing too much on each other's territory. The Westerners determined of course the agenda of this discourse, and the Balinese had learned to behave themselves: they knew too well that they should not offend the upper caste of white powerholders. As long as politics were not discussed both sides could leave each other in a state of reciprocal delusion (cf. Pollmann 1990). In order to preserve the stereotypes of the *schakel*-society, seemingly timeless Bali had to be locked and barred. How illusory this idea was becomes clear when we turn to Balinese experiences of the 1930s and realize to what extent Bali had become part of the world market.

"Suffering" was not a concept frequently associated with Bali in the 1930s. Few Westerners were aware of the fact that most of the reinstated self-rulers, and other powerful noble families as well, besides enjoying colonial protection, commanded a regional power base that grew very quickly. Increasing ownership of large tracks of rice fields and, as a result of that, control of large numbers of sharecroppers was one sign of this. If in former times peasants were dissatisfied with their lord they could take themselves off to a rival lord who might offer them marginally better conditions. Under colonial rule, however, few outlets for expressing dissatisfaction existed for the peasants, since the regional nobility exercised an unprecedented power. Moreover, within the colonial structure ordinary Balinese had no direct access to the anonymous Dutch administrators, who were generally ignorant of what went on the village level. In this way the image of the equable, friendly Balinese peasant without problems came into being. According to W. Hanna, "[t]he ordinary people had on the whole plenty of rice and relatively few complaints" (1976:107), and Bateson even remarked that the Balinese were "not hungry or poverty stricken. They are wasteful of food" (1970:391). These observations proved unreliable barometers. A second look shows that the economic World Crisis of the 1930s caused widespread poverty and despair among Balinese peasants, which were aggravated by the unchecked power of the higher nobility. Korn was one of the very few people who paid attention to the impoverishment among the ordinary people at an early stage.

> Those who get to know more intimately the living conditions of the common people on Bali discover just how gray and poverty-stricken

The Making of Traditional Bali

is the mass populating this beautiful island. . . . In Gianyar, Badung and Karangasem the majority of the people live in abject poverty . . . conditions deteriorating steadily.[56]

However, the beautiful appearance of Bali and the well-established image of a carefully isolated traditional society did it a disservice. Luxuriant nature and colorful rituals created the impression that life in Bali was one long feast. And, for that matter, this was indeed the case with the various Western travelers who could live there for next to nothing.[57] For Balinese peasants (the majority of whom owned about 0.5 ha.) and sharecroppers (approximately 40 percent of the households), life was quite different.

In the 1920s a new colonial land revenue system had been introduced. The new system was no longer controlled by the local Dutch administration but by an autonomous state agency, the Landrent Bureau. This Bureau operated with considerable success because Bali became by far the most heavily taxed area in the Netherlands Indies.[58] It was also new for peasants to have to pay with Dutch Indies money instead of Balinese currency (the *kèpèng*) or in kind. Although under the new system noble large landowners were taxed as well, they managed to have their sharecroppers do most of the paying.[59]

Up to 1930 paying the new land revenue was still possible. As a result of an increased export of pigs, copra, and rice by individual households, a large flow of Dutch Indies money entered Bali. With that money, earned from trade, one could pay the tax. However, in 1931 exports almost collapsed as a result of the World Crisis, and the bottom dropped from under export prices.[60] Consequently, far less Dutch Indies money flowed in whereas Balinese peasants still had to pay the land revenue, which remained unchanged halfway through the crisis. By 1933–34 reserves in Bali were exhausted, but the end of the crisis was not yet in sight. To add

---

56. Korn 1932:336–37. During the following years Korn's voice was no longer heard because he was transferred to Sumatra. See for a detailed analysis of the effects of the World Crisis in Bali Schulte Nordholt 1996: chap. 9.

57. See in this respect a revealing letter by Spies from 1939 in which he called his life in Bali "my eternal birthday" (Rhodius 1965:392, quoted in Pollmann 1990:6).

58. *Verslag Belastingdruk* 1929. In 1927 Bali yielded close to two-thirds (i.e., Dfl.2 million) of the total land revenue collected from the islands outside Java. Alongside the introduction of the new land revenue, the Landrent Bureau reorganized in Bali the irrigation system again whereby countless subak were amalgamated into larger taxation units. Eventually there was little left of the local irrigation bonds from the precolonial days.

59. This meant that a sharecropper generally had to take care of the entire Landrent sum, as well as deliver the regular share of the crop—half to three-quarters—to the landowner and provide periodic labor for his lord.

60. In 1928 export amounted more than Dfl. 8 million, but in 1935 it had declined to a level of Dfl. 1.9 million.

to the calamity the rice crop failed twice in succession (1935–36) in large parts of South Bali.

Colonial measures for dealing with the crisis came late and were far from sufficient. Actually, Dutch administrators evaluated the situation with qualified optimism. Despite Korn's warnings in 1932 the Resident opined that same year that on Bali there was no poverty, merely "austerity." To his mind the Balinese could easily fall back on traditional barter trade. "In this way, then, equilibrium is reached," he concluded reassuringly.[61]

By 1934 the situation proved hopeless. In South Bali arrears in revenue payments were roughly 50 percent. Only when demand notes and official forced executions failed to yield the required cash did the Dutch decide to decree a general exemption varying from 25 to 40 percent. When shortly afterward the tax was further reduced it looked as if the greatest troubles were over. But this was a false impression because the land revenue still had to be paid in Dutch Indies money, which continued to be in short supply. In fact Dutch Indies money had become much more expensive in comparison with the local currency![62] The tax reduction was, in other words, for the Balinese far less sizable than the Dutch thought it was.

Neither the Dutch administrators nor the Landrent Bureau had a clear notion of how the revenue was collected in practice since this was delegated to lower Balinese officials. The Dutch were also not involved in actions leading to confiscation. While official records mention a very moderate number of confiscations, interviews during my fieldwork tell a very different story. Beyond Dutch control numerous rice fields changed hands without entering the ledgers, and all over South Bali countless indebted peasants lost their land. Powerful landowners, on the other hand, who had access to Dutch Indies money, expanded their landed property with considerable speed. Large landownership and landlessness were only mentioned in passing in Dutch sources. It never became an important issue because the image of "village Bali" implied that landed possessions were distributed in an egalitarian way.[63]

---

61. ARA MvK MvO Resident H. Beeuwkes 1932. When in 1932 some prominent Balinese had pleaded for a reduction of the land revenue the Assistant Resident declared that this was not to be considered. Instead, he said, the Balinese should follow the example set by Britain and the Netherlands where the people were asked to sacrifice for their country (ibid.).

62. In 1931 one paid from Kèpèng 1,375 to 1,875 for one rix-dollar, but by 1934 the price had gone up to K. 2,025 or even 2,300. In 1937 the exchange rate dropped to about K. 1,750; ARA Coll. M. Boon, MvO Administrator Karangasem, M. Boon 1934.

63. On average each Balinese household was thought to hold some 0.48 ha. of sawah (Bakker 1937); Hunger 1933 and Peddemors 1933 took exception in this respect. There were no clear data available on landownership since each piece of land was registered separately.

While Dutch administrators remained faithful to the myth of Bali's splendid isolation and naive Western anthropologists and travelers thought of Bali as a well-balanced artistic culture or an exotic paradise, to the greater part of the Balinese the 1930s were dark and dismal years. People like Spies and Mead advocated the view that every Balinese was an artist, be it painter, dancer, or musician, but they overlooked the fact that during the misery of the 1930s many Balinese were very eager to enter this field for which the relatively wealthy Westerners were willing to pay in hard currency. During the closing years of colonial rule the Western images of Bali had turned themselves against the Balinese. Adrian Vickers (1989:144–45) points in this respect to other genres of Balinese paintings and drawings current in the 1930s in which anger, fear, and exorcism are the dominant themes. These images evoke a Balinese world to which Westerners had no access and that was fundamentally unstable.

Bureaucratic Reproduction

The crisis that had started in the early 1930s lasted till the late 1960s, a period as long as the colonial era. Besides economic hardship, the Balinese also experienced several political upheavals during these years, culminating in the terrible bloodbath that took place between November 1965 and February 1966, when a coup in Jakarta was followed by unprecedented massacres of (alleged) members of the Communist Party in Indonesia. Until very recently these violent conflicts have not been studied seriously (Robinson 1992, 1995). Instead, the old and powerful images of Bali were reproduced by reprints of publications by Dutch scholars (Swellengrebel 1960, 1969), Mead, Bateson, and so on (Belo 1970a; Covarrubias 1973), as if nothing had happened in between. The reproduction of the colonial images of Bali served of course the interests of the tourist industry, which was revived under the New Order regime of President Suharto. Listening to modern Balinese tourist guides one can hear statements about their own culture that stem directly from those images. They know very well what tourists want to believe, and many tourists conclude that Bali has remained remarkably authentic. In this respect the *schakel*-society still functions (cf. Picard 1990).

In the preceding pages I have shown how a coherent set of Western conceptions of Bali was created by only a handful of powerful image makers. Among them Korn became the most outstanding Bali expert of the late colonial period. He was a complex figure who wrestled with the main dilemma posed by the late colonial state. On the one hand he was the exponent of paternalistic authority and powerful colonial knowledge urging the isolation of Bali in order to protect its fragile culture, but on the other hand he knew Bali too well to believe in the dominant images he himself had helped to create. Eventually he realized that time could not be stopped to freeze Balinese society. As an administrator he wanted to control developments in Bali, but as a scholar he realized how illusory this was. Therefore he concluded his book on Balinese adat law as follows.

> Knowing what something is or was, and to understand whither the new era is leading an old people, can alone prevent the present transitional period with its many and sudden changes from becoming a period of unspeakable suffering for the Balinese people. (Korn 1932:677)

These were, as we know now, prophetic words, which were not understood by his contemporaries. Instead of recognizing the dramatic changes that occurred during the 1930s other colonial ethnographers went into the mountains in search for timeless symbolic structures while Mead and Bateson uncovered the "Balinese character" that remained "unchanged" (1942:263).

I have argued that the making of these Western images should be understood within the context of the colonial state. Behind the ideological rhetoric, which proclaimed the restoration of the original society as the prime task of Dutch colonial rule, there was a hidden agenda consisting of practical administrative purposes. Once the images proved to be effective they entered the administrative bureaucracy and were repeated time and again in official documents, varying from routine reports to particular policy decisions. It is in this respect important to realize that most of the Dutch who have served in Bali were either career bureaucrats or anonymous officials populating the lower echelons of the administrative apparatus. They came from various places in the archipelago and were soon transferred to yet another place. They knew very little about Bali and had no ambition to invest much energy in learning about Balinese culture and society during their relatively short stay in the island. For them true Bali was to be found in the reports and documents of their predecessors that were part of a larger bureaucratic memory. The nucleus of this bureaucratic memory was formed by a few standard reports—the so-called *Memorie van Overgave*[64]—and a handful of publications like Korn's study on adat law, the resonance of which can be found in countless other documents.

Where do Balinese fit into this story? They are by and large absent and were not allowed to participate in Western discourses about them-

---

64. Memorandum of transfer. Note that *Memorie* also means memory.

selves. Only one or two members of the elite wrote short articles on very traditional and harmless subjects like traditional rice growing, or the way Balinese are dressed (Sukawati 1924, 1926). When, however, politics were discussed colonial censorship immediately came into action.[65] Even Margaret Mead supported the taboo on political issues as her Balinese assistant Made Kaler remembered (Pollmann 1990:20). The whole atmosphere of the late colonial period was penetrated by fear of the Dutch.

By and large Balinese were not asked for their opinion. As informants they were not particularly important because the Dutch already had the blueprints of South Balinese society at their disposal when they conquered the area. Consequently, Balinese informants had little room to maneuver. Instead, they had to deliver the material with which the Dutch implemented their own prefabricated models. Obviously, the nobility profited most from the colonial transformation of South Bali. Noble informants eagerly confirmed the Dutch image of their caste system, and many noble houses took the opportunity to increase their local power in the shade of the colonial state.[66]

In South Bali colonial power generated knowledge, and Balinese informants learned very soon what kind of answers the Dutch wanted to hear, and also that it was safer to give information in general and neutral terms. Sometimes, however, things went wrong. When Korn, in his capacity as adat researcher—that is, not as a district administrator—interviewed in 1926 an old Balinese, the man suddenly said that he was fed up with answering all those questions and walked away. Korn's comment on this incident is revealing: "Balinese are wonderful people as long as we are in power. But when, as in my case, you have no direct authority, they snap their fingers at you."[67]

To conclude that the Western images of Bali were wrong would be too simple. Once these images had become part of the bureaucratic memory they started to produce their own realities. The images resembled the world of the Balinese to a certain extent. The information given by the Balinese often represented normative models, which had always been flexible and negotiable within the local contexts of daily practice. When, however, such normative notions were absorbed by the bureaucratic

---

65. When in 1939 the Balinese school teacher G. Nyoman Wiryasutha published a booklet in which he challenged the caste hierarchy, it was immediately blacklisted. Even the writings of children in school did not escape colonial control. An essay by a young Balinese boy about "My future" was reported to the Assistant Resident because it contained dangerous nationalist thoughts; ARA MvK MvO Assistant Resident South Bali, B. Cox 1940.

66. See for a detailed account of one particular noble house Schulte Nordholt 1996: chaps. 7–9. When after 1950 the powerful noble families in Bali lost state protection their prominent positions declined.

67. KITLV Coll. Korn (Or.435) 284, private letter Korn to B. Haga 8-4-1926.

apparatus and implemented in administrative measures their character changed fundamentally. The words were still the same but their content and meaning had been transformed, since they functioned now within the context of powerful external state institutions that were characterized by fixed uniformity and offered less opportunity for negotiation.

In Bali, then, powerful Dutch administrators effectuated a process of "retraditionalization" according to Western concepts by using fixed and authoritative models to which the Balinese tried to accommodate themselves as well as possible.[68] Such implemented and bureaucratized traditions did not, of course, replace existing local customs and rules. Instead, they added another level of reality to the world of the Balinese and are still part of it. This does not mean that "local reality" and "imposed reality" are totally separate things. On the contrary, in practice there is a variety of dynamic articulations between the two levels. If this imposed level of reality and its interaction with local perceptions is ignored, most of the changes, tensions, and conflicts in present-day Bali cannot be understood.

REFERENCES

Abdullah, Taufik. 1976. "The Making of a Schakel Society. The Minangkabau Region in the Late Nineteenth Century." In *Papers of the First Dutch-Indonesian History Conference*, 143–53. Leiden: Bureau of Indonesian Studies.
Anderson, B. 1991. *Imagined Communities*. 2d rev. ed. London: Verso.
Anderson, P. 1974. *Lineages of the Absolutist State*. London: New Left Books.
Bakker, P. 1937. "Belastingheffing van gronden in Zuid-Bali." *Koloniaal Tijdschrift* 26:177–84.
Barth, F. 1993. *Balinese Worlds*. Chicago: University of Chicago Press.
Bateson, G. 1970. "Bali: The Value System of a Steady State." In J. Belo, ed., *Traditional Balinese Culture*, 384–401. New York: Columbia University Press.
Belo, J., ed. 1970a. *Traditional Balinese Culture*. New York: Columbia University Press.
———. 1970b. "The Balinese Temper." In J. Belo, ed., *Traditional Balinese Culture*, 85–110. New York: Columbia University Press.
Benda, H. 1958. *The Crescent and the Rising Sun: Indonesian Islam under Japanese Occupation, 1942–1945*. The Hague/Bandung: Van Hoeve.
Boekian, I Dewa Putu. 1936. "Kajoebii, een oud-Balische bergdesa." *Tijdschrift Bataviasch Genootschap* 76:127–76.
Boon, J. 1977. *The Anthropological Romance of Bali, 1597–1972*. Cambridge: Cambridge University Press.
Breman, J. 1980. "The Village on Java and the Early Colonial State." *Comparative Asian Studies Programme* 1. Rotterdam: Erasmus University.

---

68. The Balinese case shows the opposite results when compared with Sahlins's analysis of the transformation of Hawaiian culture following the death of Captain Cook alias Lono (Sahlins 1981).

Bruyn Kops, G. de. 1915. "Het evolutietijdperk op Bali 1906–1915." *Koloniaal Tijdschrift* 4:459–79.
Cohn, B. 1987. "Notes on the History of the Study of Indian Society and Culture." In B. Cohn, *An Anthropologist among the Historians and Other Essays*, 136–71. Delhi: Oxford University Press.
Covarrubias, M. 1973. *Island of Bali*. New York: Knopf. 1st ed. 1937.
Damsté, H. 1922. *De toekomst van het Binnenlandsch Bestuur*. Buitenzorg.
———. 1923. "Balische bestuursproblemen." *Indisch Genootschap* 111–42.
Dewey, C. 1972. "Images of the Village Community: A Study in Anglo-Indian Ideology." *Modern Asian Studies* 6:291–328.
Ellen, R. 1976. "The Development of Anthropology and Colonial Policy in the Netherlands: 1800–1960." *Journal of the History of the Behavioral Sciences* 12:303–24.
Flierhaar, H. te. 1941. "Aanpassing van het inlandsche onderwijs op Bali aan de eigen sfeer." *Koloniale Studiën* 25:1–24.
Fraser, J. 1910. "De inheemsche rechtspraak op Bali." *Indische Gids* 32:865–910.
Friederich, R. 1849–50. "Voorlopig verslag van het eiland Bali." *Verhandelingen Bataviasch Genootschap* 22–23.
Geertz, C. 1961. Review of Swellengrebel 1960. *Bijdragen Taal-, Land- en Volkenkunde* 117:498–502.
———. 1966. *Person, Time, and Conduct in Bali: An Essay in Cultural Analysis*. New Haven: Southeast Asia Studies, Yale University.
———. 1980. *Negara. The Theatre State in Nineteenth Century Bali*. Princeton: Princeton University Press.
Gegevens. 1906. *Gegevens betreffende de zelfstandige rijkjes op Bali*. Batavia.
Grader, C. 1937a. "Madenan." *Mededeelingen Kirtya Liefrinck-Van der Tuuk* 5:73–122.
———. 1937b. "Tweedeling in het oud-Balische dorp." *Mededeelingen Kirtya Liefrinck-Van der Tuuk* 5:45–71.
———. 1960. "The Irrigation System of Jembrana." In J. Swellengrebel, ed., *Bali. Studies in Life, Thought, and Ritual*, 267–88. Den Haag: Van Hoeve, 1960.
———. n.d. Sociale orde en cosmische orde (ms.).
Haga, B. 1924. *Indonesische en Indische democratie*. Den Haag: De Ster.
Hanna, W. 1976. *Bali Profile. People, Events, Circumstances, 1001–1976*. New York: American Universities Fields staff.
Hunger, W. F. T. 1933. "Balische deelbouwcontracten gewijzigd als gevolg der huidige crisis." *Koloniale Studiën* 17:174–82.
Koentjaraningrat, 1975. *Anthropology in Indonesia*. Den Haag: M. Nijhoff.
Inden, R. 1986. "Orientalist Constructions of India." *Modern Asian Studies* 20:401–46.
Korn, V. 1924. *Het adatrecht van Bali*. Den Haag: De Ster.
———. 1925. "Bali is apart. . . . is fijner bezenuwd dan eenig ander deel van Indië." *Koloniaal Tijdschrift* 14:44–53.
———. 1932. *Het adatrecht van Bali*. 2d rev. ed. Den Haag: G. Naeff.
———. 1933. *De dorpsrepubliek Tnganan Pagringsingan*. Santpoort: Mees.
———. 1955. In memoriam H. T. Damsté, *Bijdragen Taal-, Land- en Volkenkunde* 111:113–16.
———. 1983. *Terjemahan hukum adat Bali*, 61–341. Denpasar: Kantor Gubernur Bali. Trans. of 1932.

Kraemer, H. 1933. *De stijd over Bali en de zending.* Amsterdam: Paris.
Krause, G. 1920. *Bali.* 2 vols. Hagen: Folkwang.
Lekkerkerker, C. 1920. *Bali en Lombok. Overzicht der litteratuur omtrent deze eilanden tot einde 1919.* Rijswijk: Blankwaardt & Schoonhoven.
———. 1933. "Drieërlei visie op het Balische zendingsvraagstuk." *Koloniaal Tijdschrift* 22:343–58.
Liefrinck, F. A. 1886–87. "De rijstcultuur op Bali." *Indische Gids* 1886:1033–59, 1213–37, 1557–68; 1887:17–30, 182–89, 364–85, 515–52.
———. 1890. "Bijdrage tot de kennis van het eiland Bali." *Tijdschrift Bataviasch Genootschap* 33:233–427.
———. 1927. *Bali en Lombok. Geschriften.* Amsterdam: De Bussy.
Mead, M. 1970. "The Arts in Bali." In J. Belo, ed., *Traditional Balinese Culture,* 331–40. New York: Columbia University Press.
Mead, M., and G. Bateson. 1942. *Balinese Character.* New York: New York Academy of Sciences.
Nieuwenkamp, W. 1922. *Zwerftochten op Bali.* Amsterdam: Elsevier.
Onghokham. 1978. "The Inscrutable and the Paranoid: An Investigation into the Sources of the Brotodiningrat Affair." In R. McVey, ed., *Southeast Asian Transitions,*112–57. New Haven: Yale University Press.
Peddemors, M. 1933. "Balische deelbouwcontracten gewijzigd als gevolg der huidige crisis." *Koloniale Studiën* 17:689–96.
Philokalos. 1936. "De keerzijde." *Djawa* 16:139.
Picard, M. 1990. "'Cultural Tourism' in Bali: Cultural Performances as Tourist Attraction." *Indonesia* 49:37–74.
Pollmann, T. 1990. "Margaret Mead's Balinese: The Fitting Symbol of the American Dream." *Indonesia* 49:1–36.
Prins, J. 1970. In memoriam Victor Emanual Korn. *Bijdragen Taal-, Land- en Volkenkunde* 126:193–202.
Raffles, T. S. 1817. *The History of Java.* 4 vols. London.
Rhodius, H. 1965. *Schönheit und Reichtum des Lebens Walter Spies,* Den Haag: Boucher.
Rhodius, H., and J. Darling. 1980. *Walter Spies and Balinese Art.* Zutphen: Terra.
Robinson, G. 1992. "The Economic Foundations of Political Conflict in Bali, 1950–1965." *Indonesia* 54:59–93.
———. 1995. *The Dark Side of Paradise: Political Violence in Bali.* Ithaca and London: Cornell University Press.
Sahlins, M. 1981. *Historical Metaphors and Mythical Realities.* Ann Arbor: University of Michigan Press.
Sartono Kartodirdjo. 1973. *Protest Movements in Rural Java.* Singapore: Oxford University Press.
Schulte Nordholt, H. 1986. "Bali: Colonial Conceptions and Political Change, 1700–1940." *Comparative Asian Studies Programme* 15. Rotterdam: Erasmus University.
———. 1991. "State, Village and Ritual in Bali. A Historical Perspective." *Comparative Asian Studies* 9, Amsterdam: CASA/Free University Press.
———. 1996. *The Spell of Power: A History of Balinese Politics, 1650–1940.* Leiden: KITLV Press.
Shiraishi, Takashi. 1990. *An Age in Motion: Popular Radicalism in Java, 1912–1926.* Ithaca: Cornell University Press.

Stuart-Fox, D. 1992. *Bibliography of Bali. Publications from 1920 to 1990.* Leiden: KITLV Press.
Sukawati, Cokorda Gde Raka. 1924. "The Romance of the Rice Grain." *Inter Ocean* 15:787–92.
———. 1926. *Hoe een Baliër zich kleedt.* Weltevreden.
Sutherland, H. 1979. *The Making of a Bureaucratic Elite. The Colonial Transformation of the Javanese Priyayi.* Singapore: Heinemann.
Swellengrebel, J. 1929. *Verslag van het onderzoek naar den belastingdruk op de 1929 inlandsche bevolking in de Buitengewesten.* Weltevreden.
———. 1969. *Bali. Further Studies in Life, Thought, and Ritual.* Den Haag: Van Hoeve.
———, ed. 1960. *Bali. Studies in Life, Thought, and Ritual.* Den Haag: Van Hoeve.
Van Doorn, J. 1982. "The Engineers and the Colonial System. Technocratic Tendencies in the Dutch East Indies." *Comparative Asian Studies Programme* 6. Rotterdam: Erasmus University.
Van Hoëvell, W. R. 1846a. *Nederland en Bali. Eene stem uit Indië tot het Nederlandsche volk.* Groningen.
———. 1846b. "Wetenschappelijke nasporingen op het eiland Bali." *Tijdschrift van Nederlandsch-Indië* 8 (iii): 223–43; (iv): 205–16.
Van Roon, J. 1916. "Enkele aanteekeningen omtrent Bali." *Jaarverslag Topografische Dienst Ned.-Indië* 11:213–87.
Van Vollenhoven, C. 1928. *De ontdekking van het adatrecht.* Leiden: Brill.
Vickers, A. 1989. *Bali: A Paradise Created.* Ringwood (Victoria): Penguin.
Warren, C. 1990. "Adat and Dinas: Village and State in Contemporary Bali." Ph.D. thesis, Dept. of Anthropology, University of Western Australia, Perth.
Wikan, U. 1990. *Managing Turbulent Hearts. A Balinese Formula for Living.* Chicago: University of Chicago Press.
Wiryasutha. 1939. *Tjatoer wangsa di Bali.* N.p.

Ethnography as Martial Art
Ethnicizing Vietnam's Montagnards, 1930–1954
Oscar Salemink

As we argued in the introduction to this volume, war is perhaps one of the most neglected ethnographic occasions in the study of modern colonial discourse. The frequently horizontal nature of military relationships during geographical explorations and wars of colonial conquest makes war into an anomalous ethnographic occasion, because it lacks the stability and finality that the application of a system of panoptic surveillance requires. Between the uncertainties of colonial struggle and an established colonial panopticon we find the military relationship that is perhaps even more characteristic of colonial rule, that of "pacification." This is well brought out in the writing of one of its major theorists in Southeast Asia and Morocco, the French Colonel (later Marshall) Galliéni, "Pacificator of Tonkin" (northern Vietnam) in the late nineteenth century and later defender of Paris during World War I. Galliéni explained the importance of incorporating military and geographical relationships in concepts of territory and ethnic division for the establishment of the space for good government.

> It is the study of the races who inhabit a region which determines the political organization to be imposed and the means to be employed for its pacification. An officer who succeeds in drawing a sufficiently exact, ethnographic map of the territory he commands, has almost reached its complete pacification, soon followed by the organization which suits him best [. . .] If there are habits and customs to respect, there are also rivalries which we have to untangle and utilize to our profit, by opposing the ones to

---

Although the argument in this essay is new, it is partly based on material published before in Salemink 1995. The research for this essay was made possible by grant W52-456 of the Netherlands Foundation for the Advancement of Tropical Science (WOTRO).

the others, and by basing ourselves on the ones in order to defeat the others. (Galliéni 1941:217)

Though this can be read as a classical statement of divide-and-rule, representative of the "pacification" phase of colonial rule, Galliéni's insights heralded and influenced later ethnographic traditions, both of an administrative and of a military nature.

With the eventual achievement of colonial pacification, war as a major ethnographic occasion in colonial discourse would be succeeded by the more vertical relationships of administration, missionization, and settler colonization. However, traces of horizontal relationships can be recognized in ethnographic traditions deriving from a qualitatively different military occasion constructed during a previous colonial period. This is evident in the romantic view of "military tribes" (or "races") that pictured former valiant enemies as respected soldiers of the colonial armies. One such "race" can be found in colonial Indochina, the "Montagnards" in the Central Highlands of Vietnam.[1] This area's population consisted mostly of minority tribal groups that are culturally and linguistically different from lowland Vietnamese and from each other, and that often practiced shifting cultivation rather than wet rice cultivation. In this essay I shall describe how Vietnam's war of independence against French rule constituted a new préterrain (see the introduction), altering the nature of ethnographic occasions in the Central Highlands and resulting, toward the end of French colonial rule in Indochina (1955), in an ethnographic tradition characterized by cultural relativism.

Histories of anthropology are mostly written from a metropolitan perspective, including histories of French ethnology and French ethnographic practices. James Clifford's essays on the ethnographic oeuvre of Maurice Leenhardt (1982) and Marcel Griaule (1983), or the work by Jean Copans on anthropology and imperialism (1975), are cases in point. They show that there is a distinct French ethnographic tradition with different ideals from an Anglo-Saxon tradition that typically defined fieldwork as an immersion of at least one year in the life of a village. In contrast, the prewar French ethnographic tradition maintained a distinction between academic ethnologists producing synthesizing works in the metropole

---

1. The highland population of central Vietnam is often juxtaposed to the lowland population, the Kinh or Viêt (ethnic Vietnamese), or *annamites* in French. Highlanders have been generically called *Moï* (Vietnamese for "savage"), a label that was eventually replaced by the less offensive French term *Montagnard,* but many other labels have been used. These Montagnards were often classified in tribes with separate languages, cultures, and territories. Some of the major "tribes" are the Austronesian Rhadé (Edê) and Jarai, and the Austroasiatic Sedang, Bahnar, Mnong, and Koho. Classifications have changed over time, notably with every new political regime.

and colonial (amateur) ethnographers whose work was taken seriously in the academy. The latter would provide the former with research data, which could then be used for scientific abstraction. This was evident in the relationship between the colonial ethnographer and administrator Léopold Sabatier and the Paris-based ethnologist Lucien Lévy-Bruhl (see next section). There were, of course, ethnologists who did fieldwork themselves, like Maurice Leenhardt who combined missionary, ethnographic, and ethnological endeavors (Clifford 1982), but fieldwork as a scientific method did not receive the attention it got in the Anglo-Saxon part of the world. In retrospect, the French tradition allowed for a greater variety of models for both research and writing, which today often goes under the label of ethnographic experimentation (see, for example, the present-day reevaluation of the work of Marcel Griaule, [Clifford 1983]). Georges Condominas did long-term field research after the Anglo-Saxon model, but experimented with the writing-up in the form of a diary, which also allowed him to describe the impact of colonial rule on the community where he lived (1957; 1965; his work will be analyzed in greater detail later). However, in this paper I do not deal with such ethnographers as members of a specific "national" tradition of anthropology, but as actors in the colonial history of the French empire, and of the Central Highlands of colonial Vietnam in particular. Thus, I shall try to trace an alternative history of anthropology, in which professional anthropology is not the point of departure, but the horizon of the interplay between the préterrain, ethnographic occasions, and ethnographic traditions that were situated in the changing historical circumstances in the Central Highlands of colonial Vietnam.

The theater for this history has known almost fifty years of warfare since it was plunged into World War II in 1940, but this essay limits itself to the period before 1955. In what was then known as French Indochina, the Central Highlands were seen as the strategic key to control of Indochina and were therefore hotly contested between France and the Viêt Minh independence movement from 1945. During the 1930s, when political and military tensions were building up in the region, strategic considerations concerning the Central Highlands began to make important inroads into the ways the Montagnard populations were conceptualized, represented, and governed. The institutionalization and professionalization of post–World War II ethnographic practice were conditioned by politico-military calculations that put greater emphasis on the political attitudes of Montagnards. The allegiance of the Central Highlands' indigenous populations became therefore a major asset in that struggle, making them into an object of struggle themselves. The struggle for control of the highland populations often took the form of a struggle about their ethnic and linguistic classification, as well as about more down-to-earth issues like land rights, the recruitment of soldiers for the colonial army, and plantation labor. While ethnographic discourse itself was conditioned by changing historical circumstances in Vietnam, it also produced its effects on the ground in terms of ethnic classification, ethnic identity and gender relations. In these complex, interlocking processes, ethnographic practice was institutionalized and professionalized as much in response to local colonial governmental concerns as in response to academic changes in the metropole, France.

The composition of this essay will partly be chronological, constructing a periodization of the political history of the Central Highlands. The watershed years for this periodization are 1937, when a millenarian movement in the Central Highlands highlighted their strategic value during times of rising political and military tensions; 1945, when the Japanese army staged a coup against the French colonial regime and created the space for Vietnamese nationalism to assert itself; and 1955, when the French colonial administration in Indochina was dismantled following the major Viêt Minh victory at Diên Biên Phu and the Geneva Agreements in 1954. However, the composition will also reflect the various processes involving ethnographic practice and ethnographic discourse with respect to the Montagnard populations. In the sections that follow I shall describe these changes in terms of tribalization, ethnicization, territorialization and gender transformation. In these complex and interlocking processes, ethnographic practice was institutionalized and professionalized as much in response to local colonial governmental concerns as in response to academic changes in the metropole. While ethnographic discourse itself was conditioned by changing historical circumstance in Vietnam, it also produced its effects on the ground in terms of ethnic classification, ethnic identity, and gender relations. Moreover, there was a gradual shift from evolutionist toward more relativist representations of Montagnard cultures that had to do with war as an ethnographic occasion, and the increasing horizontality of military relationships: While a recruitment officer tried to subject tribal warriors to military discipline in order to better police the colony, his success often depended on his ability to conform to local cultural ideals. I shall elaborate on this in a section on the martial uses of ethnographic discourse.

The Politics of Tribalization and Ethnicization

Through the identification of ethnolinguistic groups and their classification as "tribes," ethnic identities and ethnic boundaries were constantly (re)constructed and rigidified in a process baptized *tribalization* by

Georges Condominas (1966:168). For the Central Highlands, it is impossible to describe the process of tribalization through a collusion of ethnographic classification and administrative practice without mentioning the name of one individual, Léopold Sabatier, and the name of one institution, the *Ecole Française d'Extrême-Orient* (EFEO). Sabatier was one of the first administrators of the Darlac region in Vietnam's Central Highlands, first as *délégué* (1913–23) and then as Resident of Darlac province till 1926. The EFEO was and continues to be France's most prestigious Orientalist institute. Officially established in 1898 in Hanoi, the EFEO embarked on an ethnolinguistic survey soon after becoming operational. In 1903 it sent questionnaires to local colonial administrators, the design of which had been inspired by Marcel Mauss, one of the participants in the opening conference of the EFEO in Hanoi. The results of the *Enquête ethno-linguistique* were never published, however, and can still be consulted in the manuscripts division of the EFEO in Paris. This marked a lull in the ethnographic interest of the EFEO that would last until the establishment of an ethnographic branch in 1937 under the ethnologist Paul Lévy.

Léopold Sabatier became known for his protection of one highland group, the Rhadé (or Edê), and his attempts to base development of Darlac province on (his version of) their culture through the codification of customary law (*coutumier*) and the establishment of a *tribunal coutumier* as the basis for law enforcement in the province; the codification of Rhadé script and the establishment of a *Franco-Rhadé* school; the use of local chiefs and locally recruited soldiers; and the institution of the *palabre du serment*, a ritual oath-swearing ceremony of local big men and village headmen to the French Resident. From an administrative point of view, his work was seen as very successful in policing the tribes. As early as 1923, the colonial administration instructed the Residents to see to it that coutumiers were compiled for every ethnic group in the Central Highlands, in collaboration with the EFEO. Sabatier failed, however, in protecting the traditional land rights of "his" Rhadé not only against Vietnamese "encroachment" but also against French plantation interests. By antagonizing these powerful interests at the height of the rubber boom of the 1920s, Sabatier created a colonial scandal by attempting to stop the arrival of settlers in the fertile Plateau of Darlac. In 1926 he was forced to step down as Resident of Darlac and was refused further access to the Central Highlands. All the copies of his Coutumier Rhadé (in the Rhadé language) were confiscated by the colonial administration, and he returned to France an embittered man. The famous ethnologist Lucien Lévy-Bruhl, cofounder of the *Institut d'Ethnologie* in Paris, tried to encourage him to continue his ethnographic writing in order to chart the Rhadé "primitive mentality." At the same time, Lévy-Bruhl lobbied with the colonial administration for Sabatier's continued access to the field. Sabatier himself, however, had lost interest now that his ethnography no longer served the practical purposes of protecting and perfecting the Rhadé. When finally he was officially rehabilitated by French President Doumergue in the 1930s, his health had already deteriorated too much.

The EFEO did not actively pursue Sabatier's line of ethnographic work during the adverse political and economic circumstances of the late 1920s and early 1930s, which for the Central Highlands were dominated by plantation interests. The prevailing ethnographic discourse during that period was a brand of evolutionism that denied indigenous minorities any value, rights, or even any future in the sense that they were seen as headed for extinction. Sabatier's work was a radical departure from that evolutionism, in that he showed the cultural values underlying Montagnard life-styles and mentality (their "primitive logic," in Lévy Bruhl's terms) and also showed that development based on these cultural values was possible. By publishing their oral history, he drew attention to the capacity of Rhadé people to create beautiful poetry. In this sense, Sabatier's representation of Rhadé culture was imbued with cultural relativism. And, insofar as he was aware of the functional relations between land rights (keeping French and Vietnamese settlers out), the legal system (coutumier), religion (keeping missionaries out), language (through education in the vernacular language), and administration and development, his work may even be interpreted as functionalist. His awareness of these functional linkages was clearly brought out in his (published) speech to the chiefs during the 1926 palabre du serment, in which he linked Rhadé obedience to (his version of) their coutumier and their loyalty to the French administration to their ability to retain their land rights. In French Indochina during the 1920s, the times were not yet ripe for such a perspective, but this would change in the late 1930s with the institutionalization of ethnography in the EFEO and other institutes.

With the rise of nationalism, fascism, and communism in Asia during the 1930s, the French colonial regime in Indochina felt increasingly threatened from abroad, and the French colonial government took measures to defend the colony. The growing concern with security and strategic affairs channeled official attention to the Central Highlands, which were of strategic importance in any scheme for the defense and control of the colony. In the late 1930s, the French colonial regime in Indochina felt increasingly threatened from abroad, first of all by Japan, which sought to expand its empire in East Asia, starting with China. In the west, the new military government of Siam had expansionist ambitions, aspiring to incorporate all Tai-speaking nations, like Laos, and to reconquer territories that it had been forced to cede to France around the turn of the century. Since the densely populated areas (the deltas, the coastal strip, and the Mekong Valley) were narrow and vulnerable in case of attack or uprising, the colonial government and army turned their attention to the strategic Central Highlands, from which most of Indochina could be controlled. When in 1935 the possible merits of an administrative reorganization of the Central Highlands began to be debated in French administrative and military circles, with the military pleading for the "creation of an autonomous Moï territory" to be administered directly by military officers, the Governor-General still decided in favor of a continuation of the civil administration from the different "countries" involved, because of the expertise of the administrators. This policy was reconsidered after 1937, when the Montagnards' supposed need for protection seemed to justify direct French administration of the Montagnards in a secluded area, which was presented as "autonomy."

As increasing political tension highlighted the political and military value of the area, the colonial administration became concerned with the effects of unfettered colonization on the political attitude of the indigenous population of the Central Highlands and began once again to encourage ethnographic work. This was a double-edged sword, as ethnographers usually stressed the necessity of a special ethnic policy vis-à-vis the Montagnards, while protagonists of an ethnic policy emphasized the relevance of ethnographic knowledge. Practiced mostly by colonial officials, ethnographic practice concentrated on the possibilities of political management of the ethnic groups, viewed from the perspective of direct rule. There was an attempt to combine a policy of economic development with a conservative indigenous policy that played on ethnic sentiments in order to exclude Vietnamese influence. This ethnographic practice was increasingly institutionalized, notably within the framework of the *Ecole Française d'Extrême-Orient.* The EFEO became more active in the discipline of ethnography since the founding in 1937 of an ethnographic branch headed by the respected French ethnologist Paul Lévy. For an Orientalist institute with mainly historical interests, this was a major step toward the study of contemporary social issues (Boudarel 1976:147). Besides the EFEO, the *Société des Etudes Indochinoises* (SEI) in Saigon was turning again to ethnography after an earlier interest around 1880, and the *Institute Indochinois de l'Etude de l'Homme* (IIEH), a "joint venture" of the EFEO and the medical faculty of the University of Hanoi, was founded to cover research in the fields of ethnography and physical anthropology. All these institutions, knit closely together through personal networks, had their own scientific journals (*bulletins*) or publication series (*cahiers*), and exercised editorial control over ethnographic publications. Moreover, the EFEO exercised supervision over ethnographic research, through its attempts at ethnographic standardization in the fields of ethnolinguistic classification, linguistic notation, and customary law (coutumier).

The renewed ethnographic appreciation of Montagnard culture necessitated a new attempt at ethnographic classification and mapping. In 1935 and 1936 the province chiefs of Indochina were requested to turn in exact ethnolinguistic maps of their provinces for the benefit of the *Ecole Française d'Extrême-Orient* (cf. BEFEO XXXVI-2, 1936:598). On the basis of these maps, Georges Taboulet charted a *Carte Ethnographique*, which found a place in *Groupes Ethniques de l'Indochine Française* (1937), a semiofficial publication of the *Société des Études Indochinoises* (with official sanction by the *Gouvernement Général*, the *Gouvernement de la Cochinchine*, the Protectorate of Annam, and the *Direction Générale de l'Instruction Publique en Indochine*). Louis Malleret, conservator of the Museum of Saigon and member of the EFEO, wrote the text for the album, which consisted furthermore of 100 photographs. In 1949 the mapping exercise would be repeated, this time directly under the auspices of the EFEO. That *Carte ethnolinguistique*, dressed by the *Service Géographique de l'Indochine*, was very detailed indeed and would for some time be considered *the* ethnographic map of Indochina; the considerable population movements of the years to come were obviously not anticipated.

The ethnic classification arrived at by Malleret and Taboulet (1937), however, was far less detailed than an earlier ethnographic classification by the military explorer Henri Maitre (1912) or the later, official *Carte ethnolinguistique* (1949). On the one hand, this was due to the popular character of the book, which discouraged a too rigid, "scientific" classification. On the other hand, this reflected a trend toward the identification of larger units, partly on the basis of linguistic similarities, but also motivated by administrative exigencies, as the provincial administrations were based on the largest or dominant groups within the province, which in turn would subsume the smaller "ethnic groups" previously identified. This process was most evident in Haut-Donnai, where groups like the Sre, Çop, Cil, and Lat, were increasingly identified as Koho (with the former name sometimes as affix, e.g., Koho Sre). This debouched into a situation where the provinces were more or less identified with the main constituting group: Kontum: Bahnar; Pleiku: Jarai; Darlac: Rhadé; Haut-Donnaï: Koho. In a situation where ethnic and linguistic differences tended to be gradual and fluid, such administrative divisions tended to become ethnic boundaries, resulting in an administrative process of tribalization. The coutumiers, compiled for the major groups only, would also be validated for the smaller groups, as was the case with Sabatier's coutumier Rhadé, which was made to apply to Darlac's Mnong population, too. Resident Guilleminet of Kontum province went as far as to declare his coutumier

Bahnar valid for the Sedang and Jarai groups in Kontum province as well, even though Jarai kinship and linguistic affiliation is very different from those of Bahnar and Sedang (Guilleminet 1952a).

The differences in kinship systems in particular resulted in much confusion among French ethnographers, and interventions based on misconceptions regarding the role of women contributed to a process of gender transformation (cf. Risseeuw 1988:14) that was detrimental for women's position in society. Among the two major matrilineal, matrilocal Austronesian language groups in the Highlands, Rhadé and Jarai, women traditionally played an important position in society because they controlled access to land and assets through the inheritance system that largely excluded in-marrying males. Villagewide periodic reallocation of land in the rotational shifting cultivation system, and continuous redistribution of food within clans or extended families (traditionally living together in longhouses) or through feasting, all combined to ensure women and their families of more or less secure livelihoods. This security was upheld by practices concerning adoption, taking domestic servants or "slaves" (for indebtedness), and by marriage rules that proscribed marriage with partners from clans belonging to the same phratrie (considered incest) while prescribing preferential partners from certain other clans (real or classificatory cross-cousins). While courting was initiated by the girl or her family, there were certain rules about replacement of a deceased husband by his younger brother in order to ensure the alliance between the two families and in order not to upset the economic exchanges between the two families—to the advantage of the wife and her family (Dournes 1972; De Hautecloque-Howe 1985).

Considered "matriarchal" and hence "archaic" societies by the French (cf. Condominas 1955:555), colonial administrators tended to exclusively listen to male informants—though simultaneously often practicing "ethnography on the pillow" by taking local concubines—because elderly males assumed the authority of representing the clan or community to outside visitors. Missionaries, administrators, military officers, teachers, and medical personnel condemned and combated precisely those practices as "savage" that provided support for women's access to assets and resources within this agricultural and kinship system. Shifting cultivation was seen as a waste of forest resources, and communal land rights, periodically ritually affirmed by a (female) guardian of the land (*pô lan*) in Rhadé society, were not recognized by the colonial administration. "Slavery" and domestic service for indebtedness—often confused and misunderstood—were actively repressed, depriving poor people from a secure livelihood by becoming part of the creditor's household. Also, colonial administrators discouraged the custom of substituting deceased husbands by their younger brothers as "tyrannical," thereby not simply reflecting their male bias, but in practice eroding the livelihoods of widows and their offspring.

In order to be able to govern the disparate and diverse Montagnard populations, the colonial administration appointed village headmen early on and invested these headmen with a degree of authority that village elders had never had before. In a 1937 report to the Minister of Colonies, then Governor-General Brévié linked the question of village headmen to the administrative circumscription of ethnic groups and the codification of customary law.

> It will be essential to determine the groupings that could be constituted, and that will be encompassed in distinct administrative circumscriptions. We shall re-create the ancient tribes, and we shall give each village a chief whom we will support with all our authority. We shall create chiefs where we need. [. . .] It will therefore be all-important to codify these oral arrangements [coutumiers—OS] while making, with caution, the necessary modifications.[2]

References to the "re-creation" of the "old tribes" by appointing village heads in an effort to strengthen Montagnard society against the putative onslaught by Kinh colonizers have dotted French administrative/ethnographic narratives ever since Sabatier's *Palabre du serment* (1930; see also Guilleminet 1952a:394). By instituting male village headmen and codifying/modifying customary law as part of colonial administrative practice, ethnographic occasions became institutionalized as an exclusively male interaction between native chiefs and colonial administrators from which women were systematically excluded. The *palabre du serment*, the oath-swearing ceremony of (male) Montagnard "chiefs" to the French administration is a case in point. Thus, the space for women to represent themselves in their own societies and to protect their interests was effectively curtailed. This process was noted and commented upon by some contemporary ethnographers. Marcel Ner, who in the 1930s was ethnographic correspondent for the EFEO, and after World War II became professor of the ethnography of Indochina in France's colonial institute, argued that the prominent position of women—in harmony with nature and with the community—had better not be undermined.

> It appears serious to us to break that equilibrium while we are not capable of reestablishing it on a new level. (Ner 1952:177)

---

2. Brévié, "Inspection Générale des Pays Moïs en Indochine" [ANSOM 137.1240].

Others, however, like the military ethnographer Albert Maurice, spoke favorably of the weakening of the position of women in matrilineal Rhadé society, which was often labeled "matriarchal." Writing in retrospect, he termed this process, brought about by Western colonization, "male emancipation" (Maurice 1956:11).

Belatedly, then, the EFEO started to actively implement the colonial government's circular of 1923 that instructed it to work with local administrators to codify coutumiers for every ethnic group in the Central Highlands. In this atmosphere the composition of a coutumier was to be the aspiring ethnographer's test of ability. Next to the coutumiers, ethnolinguistic research was being promoted, intended to result in transcriptions of the various Montagnard languages and, eventually, in school primers. In 1935, the EFEO established a commission to supervise and coordinate the linguistic notations. Thus, under the auspices of the *Ecole Française d'Extrême-Orient* the privileged ethnographic research topics were the codification of Montagnard customary law for reasons of policing and administration, and the transcription of Montagnard languages for educational policies. Even contemporary ethnographers observed that the convergence of ethnography and administration, most notable in the collusion of linguistics and education and of customary law and policing, resulted in a practical reduction of the number of tribes for administrative purposes by the identification of four "major tribes" dominating the four Highland provinces of Vietnam (Guilleminet 1952a:8, 91). As this type of tribal classification would be pursued through three decades of colonial warfare, when the French and later the Americans sought the support of the Montagnards against the nationalist movements of the Vietnamese, this tribalization was increasingly reflected in Montagnard consciousness and self-organization. During the 1930s, however, the tribal classification realized in ethnographic and administrative practice was reflected in a French classificatory grid distinguishing tribal groups rather than in "real" ethnic boundaries.

In the late 1930s and through World War II, this tribalizing classificatory grid yielded to a discourse that construed the Highland peoples as a separate ethnic group, distinct from the other "nations" of French Indochina, in a process of *ethnicization* (see Salemink 1994; 1995). In the 1930s, the tribalizing classificatory grid still seemed to preclude the possibility of a "pan-tribal" movement emerging in the Highlands. Yet this is what happened in 1937/38 with the *Dieu Python* movement (see Salemink 1994). The immediate political consequence of the politicized construction of the *Dieu Python* movement was an acceleration of the implementation of a special ethnic policy concerning the Montagnards.³ This coincided with a brief, more lenient policy of the colonial administration during the "Popular Front" era in France (1936–37), resulting in a growing humanitarian concern with the "social question," both in France and in the French colonies. The installation of a Commission of Inquiry into the Overseas Territories (the *Commission Guernut*) in 1937, with which the newly elected Popular Front government in France responded to left-wing criticisms of French colonial rule, sped up the process of assessing the consequences of the *Dieu Python*, and of formulating a "racial policy" with respect to the Montagnard population. One report for the Commission Guernut was a plea against the old "divide and rule" formula, because "it appears to be superfluous to maintain among the moï populations the tribal rivalries which have kept them in a deplorable state of stagnation [. . .] in order to be able to repress more quickly those among them who might one day rise against our authority."⁴

Thus, with respect to Montagnard policies, the humanitarian concerns professed during the Popular Front era converged with the strategic preoccupations of the times. A *politique d'apprivoisement* (policy of domestication) was attempted, which combined seduction—medical services (campaigns against smallpox and malaria) and educational facilities in the vernacular languages—with coercion, as embodied in the French monopolization of the scarce product salt—the so-called salt policy. One of the professed aims of this policy was to increase the number of Montagnard recruits for the *Bataillon des tirailleurs montagnards du Sud-Annam* (BTMSA) from 1938 onward.⁵ In June 1938 a "Commission charged with the Establishment of a general Action Programme in Moï country" was established in Annam, which promoted "the vigilant protection of the natural qualities of the Moï races" for both human and strategic reasons. This resulted in a "Plan of penetration and organization of the Moï Regions," based on the principles of "evolution of the Moï in his natural environment and direct administration." In July 1938, the Governor-General of French Indochina sent his study of the *Pays Moï* to the Minister of Colonies, arguing that the Moï—despite their differences—constitute one racial group, distinct from the other Indochinese races. Referring to the danger of revolt, in particular "the incidents recently provoked by the sorcerer Sam Bram" (i.e., the *Dieu Python* movement), he pleaded for a direct French

---

3. For a more detailed analysis of that millenarian movement and its aftermath, see Salemink 1994.
4. [AOM Gougal 53.647; ANSOM Commission Guernut Be-Bf] M. d'Hugues, Commission d'Enquête, Cochinchine, Questions Sociales/Minorités ethniques, 1937.
5. Programme de recrutement en pays moï, 1937–38 [RSA, box 3996].

administration in all the area and for a central coordinating body. In October 1939, the Minister of Colonies and the French president officially established the *Inspection Générale des Pays Moïs*, which was largely grounded in strategic arguments (recruitment of Montagnards, construction of strategic roads), as the increasing political tension highlighted the political and military value of the area. In his first report, the new High-Commissioner of the Pays Moïs emphasized the ethnic and geographic unity of the area, which would justify its territorial detachment from the constituent states of French Indochina. He found in the Moï a number of virtues that "differentiate him [*sic!*] enough from the other peoples of the peninsula, which make him closer to our mentality and whose management should make him into a first rate auxiliary" (3). In this context, their much-ridiculed credulity was a major advantage, as it "transforms, upon contact with us, very often in trust, a bit childlike, but total" (5).[6]

The Inspection Générale of the Pays Moïs was also financially responsible for ethnographic research—notably on language and customary law—executed in collaboration with the EFEO, thus directly stimulating the institutionalization of ethnographic practice in French Indochina.[7] The themes of an essential Montagnard unity, their difference from the other nations, their amenability and similarity to the French, and their need to be protected by France were constantly echoed in French ethnographic writing. This is most evident in the work by Guilleminet, who in an article on the "economy of the Moï tribes" stated that despite ethnic diversity, the Moï share a fundamental cultural unity (Guilleminet 1943:82–86). In the conclusion to this article, Guilleminet even claims that French administrative activity led to the formation of one group—"ethnographically speaking"—which made it imperative for the French to suppress ethnic rivalries (1943:124). With reference to such themes, the Central Highlands were turned into a military base during World War II. In this context, ethnographic and administrative constructions that applied to individual tribes only—like the coutumier Rhadé—were now oriented toward the construction of a separate Montagnard ethnic identity and territory.

Simultaneously with this process of ethnicization, French strategists contemplated the detachment of a separate Montagnard territory from what was then known as Annam. Annam was the middle part of present-day Vietnam, which together with Tonkin, Cochinchina, Laos, and Cambodia made up French Indochina. Although Tonkin, Annam, and Cochinchina were all predominantly inhabited by *Annamites* (ethnic Vietnamese), Annam was the seat and symbol of Vietnamese sovereignty:

---

6. [ANSOM 137.1240] Rapport du lieutenant Omer Sarraut, 1940.

7. [ANSOM 137.1240] Procès-verbal de la commission, 2/3-6-1938; Lignes générales du lan de pénétration; [ANSOM 370.1240] Brévié 21-7-1938; Pays Moï 1938–40.

l'Empire d'Annam (Goscha 1996). From the late 1930s onward, a series of French moves attempted to circumscribe a separate Montagnard (Moï) territory and to gradually detach that territory from Vietnam. After France's defeat by Germany and its concessions to Japan, the new Governor-General Decoux both ritually and administratively reaffirmed the special status of the Pays Moï repeatedly throughout World War II, while the essential cultural unity of the Montagnards and their alleged fundamental antagonism to the lowlander Vietnamese were celebrated in an increasingly institutionalized ethnographic discourse. Against the backdrop of a militarization of the Central Highlands during World War II, the myth of a special relationship between the Montagnards and their French protectors was loudly proclaimed. Governor-General Decoux himself, Marshall Pétain's confidant in Indochina since the defeat of France by Nazi Germany in spring 1940 took a personal interest in policy planning for the Central Highlands. He often toured the Highlands himself to preside over the *palabre du serment*, which was widely publicized in semiofficial, Pétainist periodicals like *Indochine* as the culmination of France's *mission civilisatrice* (Decoux 1950:281–83). In this view, the Montagnards needed protection from the neighboring nations, which would justify direct French administration in a secluded area, presented as Montagnard "autonomy." With reference to the Montagnards' essential unity, their difference from the other Indochinese nations, their amenability and "similarity" to the French, and their need to be protected by France—themes that were constantly echoed in French ethnographic writing—the Central Highlands were turned into a military base area under the governorship of Admiral Decoux.

The ethnographic practice not only facilitated French rule in the Highlands, but also put the Montagnards and their relations with the French and the Vietnamese in a different light. Sanctioned by the political developments, the theme of an "essential cultural unity" of the Montagnards began to dominate ethnographic writing. These discursive changes provided the administration both with tools for cultural management and with an appropriate ideological legitimation for their direct-rule policy, aimed at keeping ethnic Vietnamese influence out. Under French protection Montagnard culture would be protected, meaning "respected" and even "perfected" by means of an appropriate development policy, a *politique d'égards*, termed *faire du Moï* after the populist slogan *faire de l'ouvrier*.[8] In other words, just as populist policies in Europe played on workers' sentiments, colonial policies could play on ethnic sentiments of a particular indigenous ethnic group. In the ethnographic discourse that

---

8. Governor-General to Resident-Superior of Annam, 1940 [ANSOM 370.1240].

attended ethnic policy an image of the Montagnards was constructed that sought to legitimize direct French rule in the Central Highlands, officially an integral part of the protectorate of Annam. The ethnographic discourse provided the arguments to exclude the ethnic Vietnamese from the region, to counter Vietnamese claims of the Highlands, and even to separate the Highlands from Annam. The French ethnographic interest seemed enough evidence of their concern for the local populations, as opposed to the ethnic Vietnamese who would only be concerned with cheating and landgrabbing. The usual metaphor was of a benevolent father (France) who had to be stern to the elder son (Vietnam) because he intimidates the little kid (Montagnards). The Montagnards were often likened to children, labeled credulous, naive, sometimes violent, but very loyal if one knew how to handle them; they needed the firm but just guidance from France into the twentieth century.

Despite major cultural differences, Montagnards were increasingly seen as one group, to be opposed to the ethnic Vietnamese. Their languages, belonging to the Malayo-Polynesian (Austronesian) and Mon-Khmer (Austroasiatic) language groups, were seen as fundamentally opposed to the Vietnamese tonal language.[9] Their coutumiers, although varying considerably, made them comparable to each other to the exclusion of the Vietnamese (who, of course, have their own village-based customary law). Their cultural identity was symbolized by certain cultural features like the coutumiers, the *palabres du serment*, and rituals like the buffalo sacrifice, redefined as a folkloric spectacle to be gazed at by outsiders. Put in the terms used by Miles and Eipper (1985), Montagnard cultural identity was reified and bureaucratically prescribed by the colonial state, and the Montagnards were made to conform to this image of their culture insofar as it suited the colonial administration. The French claimed that Montagnard culture was valuable in itself and had no need for assimilation to Vietnamese culture. However, it was the French who defined what constituted Montagnard culture, which aspects of it were to be preserved, and which aspects were to be changed. Cultural expressions that did not suit the colonial administration were not recognized as valuable or even authentic. For example, the Montagnards had to give up shifting cultivation, allegedly because it would destroy the forest, but in reality because it did not suit French economic interests. And the *Dieu-Python* movement, which could hardly be a more authentic cultural expression, was conveniently reinterpreted as organized by Vietnamese communists, and participants in this millenarian movement were sentenced by customary law courts (Salemink 1994).

---

9. Ironically, the Vietnamese and Muong languages have in recent years been grouped with the Austroasiatic language family.

This representation was very persistent. It was loudly proclaimed during World War II when the colonial administration considered the oeuvre by Sabatier as being a model to follow. Publications by Antomarchi (1941), Boudet (1942), and Ner (1943) in *Indochine* glorified Sabatier's oeuvre, after the translation (by Antomarchi) and publication (by the EFEO) in 1940 of his *coutumier rhadé* as *Recueil des coutumes rhadées du Darlac*. There was one important difference from Sabatier's ethnographic and administrative oeuvre of the 1920s, though. Sabatier was exclusively interested in the Rhadé group, which he constituted as a separate tribe with a bounded culture and territory; he was not interested in other groups in the Central Highlands. The ethnographic discourse of the 1940s, on the other hand, constituted the Rhadé group as part of a larger unit of Montagnards, and the ethnographic studies were not meant to set Rhadé apart from other groups in the Highlands, but from lowlanders. Coutumiers, palabres, and other ethnographic genres came to signify a separate Montagnard identity. The culmination of this was the *Conférence des Pays Moïs,* held in 1942 in the presence of Admiral Decoux, where the ethnographic and administrative oeuvre of Sabatier was celebrated, with this crucial difference: that his most famous creations—the coutumier, the *palabre du serment* (oathswearing ceremony of tribal chiefs to French representatives), the franco-rhadé school—which were intended for the reconstruction and defense of the Rhadé tribe only, were now oriented toward the construction of a separate Montagnard identity and territory. Simultaneously, the good relationship between the French and the Montagnards, and France's accomplishments in the development of the Montagnards region, were celebrated as well. In this context, Guilleminet (1942:26–27) stated that nobody would then repeat the words by Lavallée, that the Montagnards would "remain a useless force for the civilizing action" of France (Lavallée 1901:291), a stark example of an earlier evolutionist representation of Montagnard culture.

In this section, I have argued that French ethnographic practice was institutionalized in the context of mounting political tension in the region just before and during World War II. The resulting ethnographic discourse, which harked back to the early relativist oeuvre by Léopold Sabatier, no longer applied to a wide variety of disparate tribes, but to a separate ethnic group of Moï or Montagnards who were seen as having a common identity, fundamentally opposed to the other nations in French Indochina. Through this process of ethnicization the Montagnards were—culturally, if not politically—construed as one of the constituent "nations" of French Indochina, to be treated equally with the other groups. As in other colonial contexts, this resulted in an ethnographic discourse characterized by a brand of cultural relativism that aimed to preserve a distinct

Montagnard identity and tradition, governed by customary law insofar as it did not harm French interests. The logical corollary of this process of ethnicization was the increased territorialization of French rule, as evidenced in attempts at ethnographic classification, mapping, and the linking of populations to bureaucratically prescribed territories.[10] The French preferred to call the cultural and political separation of Montagnards from Vietnam the "autonomy" of the Pays Moï. This "autonomy" acquired definite contours in the light of competing claims to the Highlands during the Vietnamese War for Independence, setting the stage for the professionalization of ethnographic practice.

The Ethnography of a Montagnard Homeland

After World War II, the French colonial administration attempted to preempt any Vietnamese claims over the upland parts of the protectorate of Annam and to counter any Vietnamese influence in that area by establishing the *Pays Montagnard du Sud-Indochinois* (PMSI) and detaching that territory from Vietnam. The establishment of the PMSI by the new High-Commissioner Thierry D'Argenlieu, grounded in military and political motives in the struggle against the Viêt-Minh, was the logical outcome of earlier developments in the area. Although based on a recently constructed Montagnard ethnic identity, this move in fact created a "homeland" for a Montagnard ethnic nation, distinct and detached from a Vietnamese nation-state. Although, due to Vietnamese pressure, the PMSI was in 1949 transformed in the Vietnamese emperor's "Crown Domain," with a *statut particulier* (special status) for the Montagnards, the PMSI remained detached from Vietnam throughout the First Indochina War (1945–54), its inhabitants enjoying "autonomy" under French tutelage.[11]

This resulted in a rare mix of indirect and direct rule with respect to the Montagnards. The French themselves called their policy *administration directe*, as opposed to the "indirect" administrative system that had been in place in the protectorates of Annam, Tonkin, Cambodia, and Laos, where the French—at least in theory—governed through intermediary strata of indigenous rulers, mandarins, and other dignitaries. If compared with British forms of colonial rule in Africa and Malaya, however, the

---

10. For other examples of the use of the concept of territorialization in the Thai case, see Thongchai 1994 and Vandergeest and Peluso 1995.

11. The political processes leading to the establishment of a separate Montagnard territory are described in more detail in Salemink 1995. The attainment of a common Highlander identity is also the main theme of Hickey's two-volume *Ethnohistory of the Vietnamese Central Highlands* (1982a, b).

French administrative system in the PMSI might be termed *indirect*, insofar as it claimed to respect and protect local cultural forms. The French view was that in wartime conditions, this administrative system needed a heavy French presence in the area, militarily, politically, and economically. Though that particular combination of tactics turned out to be largely contradictory and therefore self-defeating, it proved fertile ground for a surge in ethnographic research and writing. Even contemporary observers, like Georges Hardy of the *Bureau Scientifique de l'Armée*, noted in a review of scientific articles on Asia that "the prolonged drama of which the Indochinese peninsula is the theatre seems to have spurred on the ethnographic research, especially concerning the Moï populations" (Hardy 1951:300). In this section, I shall describe how this battleground formed a préterrain that proved fertile ground for a particular form of ethnographic practice, which was increasingly professionalized in the wake of the earlier process of ethnographic institutionalization before 1945.

When in 1946 the Central Highlands, formerly known as the Pays moï, was rebaptized as *Pays Montagnard du Sud-Indochinois* (PMSI), the indigenous populations underwent a few name changes.

> The administration and the ethnographers abandoned the term "savages," which was considered vague and insulting. First, they adopted the term "Moï" which they borrowed from the Vietnamese, while specifying it and stripping it from its pejorative connotations. More recently, the "policy of consideration" [*politique d'égards*] was prescribed. One tried "Indomalais," and then "populations montagnardes du Sud-Indochinois," whose initials produced "Pemsiens." (Ner 1952:45)

The term *Pemsien* was enthusiastically embraced by some influential ethnographers, like the missionary Jacques Dournes. Although Dournes claimed that this label had no political connotations, he stressed that it would symbolize Montagnard unity as opposed to the Vietnamese. For Dournes, the "Indonesian race" was as different from the "yellow race" as from the "white race" (Dam Bo 1950:5–6, 19). With the abolition of the PMSI, the term *Pemsien* was soon replaced by *Proto-indochinois*, which is still being used in French scientific circles. The most enduring label, however, would be *Montagnard*, which seemed less offensive than *Moï*, less politicized than *Pemsien*, and less scientistic than *Proto-indochinois*, while being sufficiently vague to encompass a wide variety of groups or tribes and being sufficiently French to hint at that "special relationship" between France and Montagnards. The anthropologist Condominas (1953:658) reported that "developed Moï reject this offensive label and prefer the French word 'Montagnard' which [Condominas] often heard often in the middle of a conversation in vernacular dialect." Ironically, the use of the gallicism *Montagnard* would become most widespread during the era of American involvement in Vietnam.

The theme of a special relationship between France and the Montagnards was constantly reaffirmed—in ethnographic or popular publications, at conferences, in political statements, and on other occasions. While the Montagnards were effectively reduced to the status of "ethnic minorities" with the rise of Vietnamese sovereignty, the French claimed the protection of minorities as their exclusive responsibility, as an integral part of their *mission civilisatrice*. Often, the French used Montagnards willing to give voice to this "special relationship" in public forums. Malleable Montagnards, demanding autonomy, or a *statut particulier* under French protection, could always be found among the French-appointed chiefs, as was evident during the Dalat Conference of August 1946. At that occasion, the French claims were supported by a "PMSI delegation" that the French had summoned up. The head of the delegation was Ma Krong, president of the customary law court of Darlac province, and the nephew of and successor to the *Khun Jonob*, once a close collaborator of Sabatier. While their first "wish" (*voeu*) was that the Vietnamese delegation at the Fontainebleau Conference not speak for other "member states" of the Federation (in this case for the PMSI), their second wish was that "all the individuals wearing loincloths"—who in one sentence were reduced to the five provinces making up the PMSI—be protected directly by France and acquire independence—from Vietnam, that is. The motive was that the Montagnards had no resemblance whatsoever to the other Indochinese—a strange argument for Ma Krong, who derived his authority from his uncle whose descent was mixed Lao-Mnong. While two "motions" entailed the preservation of minority education in French and of Montagnard customary law, a third motion presented on August 6 concerned the incorporation of Montagnard soldiers in the French colonial army. The keyword here was Montagnard *loyalty* to the French, which may be contrasted with the *solidarity* propagated by the Viêt Minh. For the French and the PMSI delegation, this loyalty was symbolized by the odyssey of a Rhadé battalion that followed their French officer through Laos to China after the Japanese takeover in Indochina. Loyalty was also the symbolic substance of the *palabres du serment* that were immediately organized in the newly "liberated" towns in the presence of High Commissioner D'Argenlieu. The Montagnard "chiefs" who spoke out against "Annamese tutelage" were rewarded with medals, guns, and occasionally a *Légion d'Honneur*.[12]

This conceptualization of the upland populations as a separate ethnic group that had a special relationship with the French and that would become extinct under Vietnamese sovereignty provided the conceptual context for the ethnographic writing after 1945—both by amateur ethnographers working and publishing under the supervision of special ethnographic institutes, and also by professional ethnographers working under the auspices of mostly the same institutions: in Indochina, the EFEO and the SEI; in the metropole, the *Institut d'Ethnologie*, the *Office de la Recherche Scientifique Coloniale*, and the *Centre de Formation aux Recherches Ethnologiques*, partly financed by the colonies or "associated states" of the French Union. The first serious ethnographic publication after the world war was a detailed description of Rhadé funerary rituals by the medical doctor of Ban Me Thuot, Bernard Jouin, a "veteran" of the Highlands. Jouin's monograph, claiming academic status, was published by the prestigious *Institut d'Ethnologie* of the University of Paris. Cofounded by the famous ethnologists Marcel Mauss, Lucien Lévy-Bruhl, and Paul Rivet in 1926, the *Institut d'Ethnologie* published works by such renowned ethnologists as Henri Labouret, Marcel Griaule, André Leroi-Gourhan, Georges Dumézil, and Maurice Leenhardt. In his conclusion, Jouin denied any historical relationship of the Rhadé with the Vietnamese, as he failed to detect a similarity between Rhadé funerary practices and rituals and those of the Viêt, whereas he could detect "traces" of Cham, Khmer, and Lao influences in Rhadé funerary customs (Jouin 1949:207). It was customary for French ethnographers to stress French concern for the Montagnards, and to deny any legitimacy of Vietnamese claims to the Highlands. Jouin concluded from his description of the funerary rituals that the French had to save the Montagnards from extinction caused by economic, political, and demographic factors, even though there does not seem to be a logical connection between this political conclusion and the ethnographic narrative. In order to save the rich Montagnard culture that Jouin had just described, the French had to change it by fighting diseases, laziness, carelessness, and superstition. Only by developing to the same level as the neighboring nations would the Montagnards be able to resist their "invasions."

Other publications in the context of the EFEO and the SEI by "ama-

---

12. Visite de D'Argenlieu en Pays Moï, serment Ban Me Thuot (17-5-'46, again 11-8-'46), Kontum (12 August), Pleiku (13 August) [ANSOM, box 137.1241]; Conférence franco-vietnamienne de Dalat, notes sur les minorités ethniques, août 1946 [ANSOM, box 56PA6]. On the Khun Jonob and Ma Krong, see Botreau-Roussel and Jouin 1943:377.

teur" ethnographers who had held positions with the colonial administration or the colonial army before 1945 were a *Coutumier Stieng* by Théophile Gerber (1951–52); a *Coutumier Bahnar* (1952a) and a study of Bahnar worldview and religion (1952b) by the erstwhile Resident of Kontum province, Paul Guilleminet, all published under the auspices of the EFEO; an "ethnopsychological" study of the "archaic Moï populations" in the *Revue de Psychologie des Peuples* by Marcel Ner (1952); and studies of Rhadé agricultural rituals and Rhadé society by the military officer Maurice (1947, 1951, 1956) and Maurice with Proux (1954). Military officer Albert-Marie Maurice was an old hand in the Central Highlands. Involved in the suppression of the "Mnong revolt" of the 1930s, he had copublished (with Paul Huard) a study on "Les Mnong du Plateau central indochinois" in the *Travaux de l'Institut Indochinois pour l'Etude de l'Homme* (Huard and Maurice 1939).[13] After 1945, Maurice became involved in the reconquest of the Central Highlands and again commanded Rhadé *Tirailleurs*, hence his ethnographic writing on the Rhadé. In several post-1945 publications, Maurice tended to focus on Montagnard warfare and the utilization of their warrior instinct in the *bataillons montagnards*—against the Vietnamese. Maurice became more critical of French rule in the Highlands as their position became weaker. After their retreat from Vietnam in 1955, Maurice even wrote critically of Sabatier, whom he had praised before, for distorting authentic cultural traditions in the interest of colonial administration. He gave the examples of the modification of the *mnam thun ian prong* Rhadé New Year celebration into the *palabre du serment* and the modifications to the *coutumier rhadé* (Maurice 1956:11). Marcel Ner, a former civil servant and ethnographer of the Montagnards as correspondent of the EFEO who had played a role during the 1946 negotiations with the Viêt Minh, was after World War II appointed professor of ethnology of Indochina at the *Ecole Nationale de la France d'Outre-Mer*, which trained future colonial administrators. His "ethnopsychological" analysis, aiming at the instruction of aspiring colonial administrators, was depressingly chaotic, with streaks of racism, like in his psychological assessment that "[t]he Moï is not entirely free from the fear that fire instills in the animal" (Ner 1952:163). Nevertheless, Ner contended that even these creatures could be led into civilization, as they were being forged into one nation by the evolution that was brought toward them by French rule.

One of the most prolific ethnographers after 1945 was Paul Guilleminet, the former resident of Kontum province, who had dealt with the Dieu-Python movement in 1937 and had analyzed it in detail in 1941. He

---

13. In 1993, Albert-Marie Maurice would rework his and Paul Huard's work in the Mnong in a two-volume study on the Mnong, encouraged by Georges Condominas. For a critique of this work, see my review in *Anthropos* (1996:278–79).

published a *Coutumier de la tribu Bahnar, des Sedang et des Jarai de la province de Kontum* (1952a) that is significant in many different ways, because it was quite frank about the rationale and the method of codification.

> The customary law [*coutumier*] ... can be defined as the totality of rules that the authority now has respected, basing itself on the juridical customs of Kontum, in order to avoid that anyone trouble public order or the peaceful life of the community, harm or bring material, ritual or moral damage to others. The principles stated at each article express the state of affairs in 1941. They are the result of a slow and progressive modification of customs [*coutumes*] that adapt by themselves, or by decision of the chiefs and assessors, to the evolution of practices [*moeurs*], to the new needs of the era, to the desire that the political Administration has to reform them without shocks. (Guilleminet 1952a:101)

While orally transmitted customary law by its very nature tends to be flexible and adaptable—until it is codified in writing—Guilleminet's version was excessively adapted to the new colonial context, containing numerous "articles" that refer to the colonial administration. Obedience to (appointed) headmen and other colonial officials, punishment of resistance, corvee labor, regulation of travel, and prohibition of relocation of villages may be expedient for the colonial authorities but can hardly be construed as in line with tradition. While the establishment of statutory law requires a redefinition and circumscription of customary law, it is useful to see this as an essentially political process. The coutumiers that were invariably presented as the embodiment of Montagnard tradition, meticulously recorded by careful ethnographers eager to preserve that tradition, were the outcome of that political process at a certain point in time.

One striking example of "reinterpretation" of custom is discernible in those "articles" (the format follows French legalistic traditions rather than the poetic tradition of Montagnards) that deal with land rights. Bahnar society traditionally assigned land use rights through an institution called *to'ring*. However, in his coutumier Guilleminet does not wish to call these land use rights *property rights*, and he assigns the exclusive ownership over all lands and assets that are not the object of private property to the colonial state (Guilleminet 1952a:459–63). In the rotational shifting cultivation systems common among many highland communities, only a small portion of the land needed for its sustainable use was actually cleared and in use; the remainder was left to fallow by allowing the forest to regenerate. The appropriation of the latter plots would contribute to the degeneration of the forest and the soil, and in time rendered the indigenous agricultural systems unsustainable. Thus, though all the land was communally owned or at least claimed, by disavowing all land rights that did not fit the Western category of private property (which meant almost all the land) and proclaiming the state sole proprietor of these lands, Guilleminet could legally appropriate lands for plantations and other uses. By the legalistic reasoning of Guilleminet and others, Bahnar, Sedang, and Jarai communities of Kontum could be legally alienated from their lands in the name of their own custom. Small wonder, then, that this part of "their" customary law was unpopular among Montagnards themselves, as Guilleminet was well aware.

> But nothing has justified (in the eyes of the Moï, of course) the installation of French or Vietnamese colonists; the licensing of group privileges to individuals; nor the installation of fishermen or hunters under the conditions that this was done ... The Moï was in fact forced to bow, and has accepted this situation because he could not do otherwise. (1952a:464–65)

Obviously, such tactics of dispossession were in the interest of (aspiring) plantation owners, who of course had more means to claim land as private property. But even these tactics were presented as not only conforming to the letter of the customary law, but as beneficial for the Moï who would be lifted up from their backward, primitive, and destructive agricultural condition—combining *mission civilisatrice* with *mise en valeur*.

The influential ethnographic publications by Ner, Jouin, Maurice, and Guilleminet had explicit scientific pretensions and were all intended to provide the French administration with a framework for action in the Central Highlands, by representing Montagnard culture as valuable enough to protect against the Vietnamese, while simultaneously in need of development for economic, social, demographic or political reasons. As early as 1942, in an article in the *Cahiers de l'Ecole Française d'Extrême-Orient* entitled "Recherches ethnologiques en pays moï," Paul Guilleminet gave a frank statement about the objectives of ethnography in the Highlands.

> The ethnographic researches in the highlands have for objective to make known the tribes that the planters, the Administration, as well as the Army employ more and more regularly; to contribute to the establishment of an inventory of the races that populate the Indochinese Peninsula, but also and mainly to give to ethnographers precise

information on human groupings that have, in contact with neighbouring civilizations, evolved without disappearing. (1942:21)

Guilleminet was right that the work of amateur ethnographers like himself would inform and contextualize the narratives of ethnologists and professional anthropologists. Even in 1960, Claude Lévi-Strauss upheld Guilleminet's work as a model to follow and as an ethnographic gold mine in a conference paper entitled "Méthode et conditions de la recherche ethnologique en Asie." The interplay between amateur ethnography practiced under the auspices of scholarly institutions and professional ethnography in the context of war forms the subject of the next section.

The Politics of Ethnographic Professionalization

Montagnard culture was represented in rather similar ways by a new generation of young, aspiring ethnographers, who conducted fieldwork in the Central Highlands, applying the methods of participant observation. This new generation of French ethnographers of the Montagnards started off either as professional anthropologists conducting fieldwork (Georges Condominas, Pierre-Bernard Lafont) or as amateur ethnographers who gradually moved into the profession of anthropologist by applying the research methods of modern ethnographic fieldwork (the missionary Jacques Dournes, the settler Jean Boulbet). Thus, the process of institutionalization of ethnographic practice, starting with the foundation of the EFEO and receiving a new impetus in the 1930s, converged with a process of professionalization of ethnographic practice. The new professional anthropologists referred to anthropological theory and followed the ethnographic instructions that had been given from 1926 to 1939 by (again) Marcel Mauss at the *Institut d'Ethnologie*—posthumously published as *Manuel d'Ethnographie* (1947)—which became the basis of anthropological instruction at the newly founded *Centre de Formation aux Recherches Ethnologiques* (1946).

In prewar France, a distinction had been maintained between academic ethnologists and local ethnographers. The latter would provide the former with research data, which could be used then for scientific abstraction. There were, of course, ethnologists who did fieldwork themselves, but fieldwork as a scientific method did not receive the attention it got in the Anglo-Saxon part of the world. In French Indochina, for example, the composition of a coutumier played a role similar to that of fieldwork elsewhere. As late as the 1960s, French anthropologists were still publishing coutumiers, often complete with the jurisprudence of the colonial court

(Boulbet 1957; Lafont 1963). Since there was no tradition of fieldwork in France, the *Centre de Formation* had to cross the Channel, even the Atlantic, to find the model of participant observation and the ideas of functionalism, structuralism, and cultural relativism that permeated research praxis there. Directly or indirectly, the courses taught at this institute made aspiring French anthropologists aware of the theories that attended fieldwork in the Anglo-Saxon part of the world. The *Centre de Formation* was sponsored by different parts of the "Union Française," the postwar name of the former "Empire Française," and its graduates were employed in the "associate state" (read: colony) that needed research.

The most productive ethnographer before 1954 was Jacques Dournes. Dournes was a Catholic missionary of the *Missions Etrangères de Paris* who was sent to the Central Highlands immediately after World War II and soon found himself engaged in all kinds of ethnographic work, including, of course, the composition of a coutumier (1951) and ethnolinguistic research (1950). He was well aware of anthropological theory and practice, and he gradually shifted away from the church into the anthropological profession, becoming a professional anthropologist in the 1970s. Dournes loved the Montagnards, most of all their Tradition (which he would write with a capital *T*) and their oral literature, and he was concerned about the eventual disappearance of their culture (significantly, he would use the singular). From this perspective, Dournes could be critical about French policies that seemed detrimental to the preservation of traditional society and culture. In several publications he wrote disapprovingly about the use of straw men as village heads who started to form a separate, corrupt class propped up by colonial rule, undermining the real, spiritual authority of the village elders. Though he underscored the need for education, he was wary about its effects in terms of Westernization and hence the cultural uprooting of Montagnard children. He saw the latter process even more strongly represented among the Montagnard soldiers fighting for the French (Dournes 1955:72; see also Dournes 1948, 1949). Moreover, Dournes commented that the French administration built too few schools and hospitals, while simultaneously allowing Montagnard land and labor to be appropriated by plantations.

> It is not unfounded to conclude that in the economic domain the *Pémsiens* have not gained from the change in domination, as the European wave has reduced their circulation, slowed down the streams of exchange, and diminished their ancient prosperity. (Dam Bo 1950:47)

Nevertheless, he did not distance himself from French rule, which he saw as the best guarantee against a Vietnamese "invasion" of the Highlands.

On the contrary, he promoted direct rule and was the one of the major proponents of the "one Montagnard nation" thesis.

Dournes invented the term *Pémsiens*, "these poor relatives among the Nations, these men of another race and another time" (Dam Bo 1950:5–6). The term *Pémsien* should express Montagnard unity, as opposed to the Vietnamese nation. Thus, his major monograph pretended to describe all the *Pémsiens*, although it was based solely on research among the Koho Sré of the province of Haut-Donnaï. Dournes justified this *Pémsien* unity on geographical, ethnic and racial grounds, specifying that the Montagnards belonged to the "Indonesian race," which would be as different from the "Yellow" as from the "White Race." He denied that the term *Pémsien* had any political connotation, despite the contested character of the PMSI (5–6, 19). Yet, in that same publication, he acknowledged the largely fictional character of this eternal antagonism between Montagnards and Viêt by describing the happy memories that the "Elders" had of their relations with the Vietnamese administration before the arrival of the French (25). Despite his acknowledgment that Montagnard-Vietnamese relations had not always been antagonistic, and that French rule had not always been beneficial for Montagnard society, Dournes apparently found it expedient to reinscribe the prevailing discourse about their need for protection by the French against the Vietnamese onslaught—which after all was the rationale for his own presence in the Central Highlands. This trope in the ethnographic narratives was premised on the conception of the Montagnards as one nation comparable to the other nations making up French Indochina. The cultural relativism that was the most convincing perspective to bolster such claims was expressed most forcefully by those who applied the anthropological method of ethnographic fieldwork to which Dournes also subscribed, based on "human contact [and] observations and personal conversations, obtained during several years of life in common with these people, thus excluding fantasy and gratuitousness" (6).

The first professionally trained anthropologist after World War II to conduct modern fieldwork in the Central Highlands was Georges Condominas. His research, commissioned in 1947 by the Office of Colonial Scientific Research in France, was carried out in 1948–49. In Indochina, supervision was exerted by the director of the EFEO, the ethnologist Paul Lévy. In accordance with colonial officials, the isolated Mnong Gar village of Sar Luk was chosen as the location for the research, which was meant to be a study of acculturation.

> We think that the study of the contacts [with Western and Vietnamese civilization] and of the transformations which they produce

in the autochthonous society, must be the main concern of the "colonial" anthropologist because it allows for a practical and efficient extension of the ethnographic work. (Condominas 1952:305)

In other words, Condominas positioned his ethnographic work firmly in colonial governmentality, conceived as the scientifically informed management of native populations.

This opinion about the use of ethnography was typical of postwar French anthropology, which had been profoundly reformed to be able to meet the demands of the newly formed "Union Française," successor of the former "Empire Française." In the two volumes of the *Ethnologie de l'Union Française* (1953), to which Condominas contributed an article on the ethnology of Indochina, a kind of applied anthropology was proposed.

> Only anthropology can form a valid basis for a policy. It would be vain to pretend to advise and direct an indigenous society without proceeding with the methodical study of its habits and mentality [. . .] French anthropological research, then, seems to be of national interest; formerly, colonization could not do without it, and now it is one of the vital conditions of the Union. (Leroi-Gourhan and Poirier 1953:897)

This anthropology, practiced within the framework of new institutes like the *Office de la Recherche Scientifique Coloniale* and the *Centre de Formation aux Recherches Ethnologiques* and financed by the colonies or associated states, could only be of value on the basis of fieldwork by professional anthropologists. Two decades earlier, Malinowski had made a similar argument and claim for funding for a "practical anthropology" based on professional field research. Much later, Condominas would note in retrospect that "certain ethnologists, and not the lowliest, wanted to be taken seriously by the colonial environment. Hence the creation of 'applied anthropology,' a good deal of which is used as an instrument of government, that is, government of colonial oppression" (Condominas 1980:125).

The new brand of professional anthropology, encompassing ethnographic research, writing, and theory within a colonial context, stressed problems of acculturation, education, and economic development (Leroi-Gourhan and Poirier 1953:898). The research by Condominas, however, did not produce the desired results, since he became aware early of the less positive effects of colonial rule on the local populations, notably the recruitment for the army, the plantation regime, and the exploitation by French-appointed chiefs (Condominas 1977:459). In the context of emerging anticolonial critique in the metropole by prominent anthropologists like Michel Leiris and Georges Balandier, he started to doubt the value of the opinion of the colonial environment as a favorable context for ethnographic field research, for which he coined the term *préterrain*. Condominas gave *préterrain* a more restricted meaning than Pels and I did in the introduction to this volume, namely as the local colonial milieu from which the academic ethnographer departed and to which he returned for comfort or need (1973:9–10). It was problematic insofar as it detracted from the academic nature of the fieldwork. The use of that term in front of his students in courses he gave back in Paris prompted the French colonial administration of Madagascar to deny him permission to enter that colony for research (Condominas, personal communication). His newly acquired political sensitivity did not prevent Condominas from contributing to the *Ethnologie de l'Union Française* (1953). There, rejecting the neologism *Pémsien* as too politicized, the term *Moï* as pejorative, and the term *Montagnard* as vague, he proposed the term *tribus proto-indochinoises* as a scientific alternative. He designated the *Proto-indochinois* as the oldest, if not the aboriginal, population of Indochina—thereby confirming tribalizing classifications that he would denounce in later writings (1953:658).

When Condominas published his ethnographic monograph of the Mnong Gar in 1957, after the French military withdrawal from Indochina, it was in the form of a highly influential and innovative ethnographic experiment—an ethnographic diary, which included conflicts in Mnong Gar society, aggravated by the colonial presence, as well as his own role in the society under study. A book of a highly literary quality, the scientific value of this classic was safeguarded by the elaborate analytical indexes, which allowed for topical reading and analysis as well. This is well in line with a French ethnographic tradition that values the combination of ethnographic experiment with literary presentation—a genre that emphasizes ethnography as text, a genre whose audience allows itself to be convinced by an impressive style or by the simplistic beauty of a theoretical model of reality rather than by claims to direct empirical representation of reality. The popularity of structuralists like Claude Lévi-Strauss (*Tristes Tropiques*) and neo-Marxists like Maurice Godelier or Claude Meillassoux are cases in point; but it was, of course, already evident in the prewar work by Marcel Mauss, Lucien Lévy-Bruhl, Marcel Griaule, and Michel Leiris, who tried to capture underlying structures by (physically or discursively) traveling through cultures.

A similar preoccupation with ethnography as text is evident in the high tolerance in France for the integral publication of translations of indigenous texts like coutumiers, epics, or other narratives. Like Condominas, other professional ethnographers like Pierre-Bernard Lafont and Jean Boulbet also published after the end of the First Indochina War. Though their work reinscribed the dominant French discourse, for instance by presenting the minutes of the colonial customary law court as authentic indigenous texts, their research results could not be used for the *Action Psychologique* and *Maquis* counterinsurgency programs against the Viêt Minh combining military and political tactics that the French military developed and applied from the late 1940s onward (which will be dealt with in the next section). The same is not true for some of the ethnographic work that had preceded them, like that by Dournes. In 1950, the Haut-Commissariat des PMS gave Dournes a subvention to have his *Dictionnaire Sre (Koho)-Français* published by the official *Imprimerie d'Extrême-Orient*. Just one year later, Gilbert Bochet of the *Service Géographique de l'Indochine* published *Eléments de conversation Franco-Koho: Us et coutumes des Montagnards de la province du Haut-Donnai* (1951), mainly intended as a practical guide for the military traveler in that area. According to the reviewer Groslier (1952), the main source must have been Dournes's publications and those of his predecessor, Mgr. Cassaigne of the Dalat diocese. The first part of the booklet was a sort of Koho phrase book complete with cultural dos and don'ts, including attention for matrilinearity. The second part contained an introduction to Koho culture and social organization, including psychological warfare tips. Bochet argued for a sort of "localized" propaganda to counter Viêt Minh propaganda, but warned that "the Montagnards have heard many discourses . . . to the extent that though they may be satisfied that one addresses them, they will in the final analysis judge their interlocutor, whoever he may be, by his practical achievements" (Bochet 1951:82). In other words, insofar as the French military needed the support of local populations, these needed to be taken seriously. It is this realization that contextualized the ethnographic practice after World War II, especially its institutionalization and professionalization.

The processes of institutionalization and professionalization of ethnographic practice did not necessarily mean that ethnography acquired a more scientific or scientistic character. Inserting themselves into a more encompassing ethnographic discourse, "serious" ethnographers had to come to terms with more politicized or popular ethnographic statements and often contributed to such publications. Before 1945 EFEO members had already contributed articles to the Pétainist weekly *Indochine*, which had also published and propagated the anti-Jew decrees promulgated by the Decoux regime in French Indochina. After 1945, serious ethnographers, often administrators themselves, would lend their names and their writing to publications with an overt propagandistic character.

The most striking example is *Revue Education* no. 16 (1949). The *Revue Education*, a semiofficial "popular scientific" journal published by the *Rectorat d'Académie* in Saigon, devoted a special ethnographic issue to the PMSI even though by then the PMSI had been officially abolished and the territory was formally reattached to Vietnam as the Emperor's Crown Domain. Edited by the *Inspection des Colonies* and with articles contributed by ethnographers like Guilleminet, Dournes, and Jouin as well as administrators, school teachers, and missionaries, the *action civilisatrice* of France was glorified and contrasted with the barbarism that allegedly characterized the Viêt Minh, falsely represented as a Japanese war ally. *Inspecteur général des Colonies* Gayet self-complacently proclaimed the beneficial effects of French policies on the Montagnards' development, and hence France's right and responsibility in terms of protection of their traditional culture by safeguarding their "autonomy." The *statut particulier* provided for a "free evolution of these populations while respecting their traditions and their customs. The road to development consisted of the imposition of a social and political organization by the Administration on the one hand, and the establishment of plantations coupled with suppression of the shifting cultivation system that formed the economic basis for Montagnard society and culture" (Gayet 1949:78–79). The need for suppression of shifting cultivation was reiterated by many other contributors to *Revue Education*. In retrospect, it seems ironic that the "free evolution" of these groups apparently necessitated the suppression of indigenous land rights, part and parcel of traditional custom and culture. But perhaps "free evolution" referred to the freedom to establish plantations on appropriated Montagnard lands, thus demonstrating the inherent ambiguity of the French economic and politico-military interests in the Central Highlands.

The volume contained a novelty, namely ethnographic articles written by Montagnard (mostly Rhadé) intellectuals. Montagnards who contributed articles wrote how happy they were to eat French food, wear Western clothes, to have acquired qualities like obedience, loyalty, and respect taught at school, in short, to enjoy the benefactions of civilization.

> This quick overview allows already the appreciation of the benefactions of France in the Montagnard region. From plundering and warring tribes, without laws or beliefs, France has made them [. . .] a race which is almost ready for modern civilization. But in many respects, the Montagnards lag behind, and their evolution remains incomplete. If the realizations continue, the Montagnards will not be destined for extinction, but on the contrary will become a strong and beautiful race, worthy of its educators. (Y Bih Nie-Kdam 1949:90)

Of course, such attempts at self-representation were only acceptable insofar as these narratives supported French direct rule in the PMSI. The irony of this is that, in spite of other, more relativist French narratives, Montagnards like Y Bih Nie-Kdam basically disavowed their own culture as primitive and backward, hence in need of "improvement." Other—mostly French—authors in the *Revue Education* also stressed the blessings of French administration in the Highlands, while at the same time depicting the Montagnards as destitute, due to the shifting cultivation that they generally practiced. They needed guidance and development, which only France could bring them, as protector of minorities.

The ethnographic descriptions in *Education* had the effect of legitimating direct French rule in the Highlands at a time when there were competitors for power and sovereignty. The ethnographic narratives, written by serious ethnographers including Guilleminet, Jouin, and Dournes, were intended for a popular audience and were meant to serve educational purposes, as indicated in the title of the journal. Even though the descriptions were rather shallow, they realized two goals. First, the overall message was communicated that the Montagnards were different from the Viêt people, indeed closer to the French than to the Viêt. This rendered them sufficiently valuable in French eyes to protect them from the "imperialist" Vietnamese civilization, considered an aberration from Chinese civilization and a "swallowing monster" in the context of Indochina. Second, the massive French ethnographic interest in the Montagnards seemed to indicate French concern with the Montagnards, regardless of the effects of actual policies on the ground. The only critical notes in *Revue Education* (1949) could be found in Jacques Dournes's contributions, which expressed doubts about the effects of Western-style development on Montagnards, especially Montagnard youth.

The French Indochina War proved to be fertile ground for the emergence of professional ethnographic fieldwork, resulting in cumulative and mutually influencing processes of institutionalization and professionalization of ethnographic practice. Thus, despite occasional professional doubts about the legitimacy and the morality of the colonial préterrain, the war itself turned out to be a favorable ethnographic occasion for professional ethnographic fieldwork. Concerned with funding and the usefulness of the research, professional anthropologists by and large operated within the boundaries of established colonial discourse. Locally working in the framework of the very same institutions as the amateur ethnographers before, during, and after them, the new professional anthropology was part and parcel of the same ethnographic tradition that shifted the locus of research from individual "tribes" to the "Montagnards" as an ethnic category. Focusing on the same genres of ethnolinguistic research and customary law, professional anthropologists carried on an ethnographic tradition started by Léopold Sabatier thirty years before, with the one major difference that they made statements not just about one tribe, but about the Montagnards as a separate ethnic group and hence ethnographic unit. The major conceptual innovation that professional anthropologists promised—the study of "acculturation"—was meant to insert it more firmly into a colonial governmentality that had caused the surge in ethnographic practice in the first place.

Yet, the *methodological* ethnographic innovations implied in professional anthropology—the immersion in a different culture through prolonged fieldwork—would lead to a reconceptualization of self as the subject of research and to the (temporary) adoption of a new identity by the new generation of professional researchers. This is best brought out by the late Jacques Dournes who published his major pre-1954 monograph under the pseudonym Dam Bo, which was the name given to him by the "Koho Sré" group. In this way he tried to convince his audience of the degree of his integration into Montagnard society. This adoption of indigenous names was typical of the new generation of anthropologists after World War II, who conducted fieldwork among the Montagnards. Writing in hindsight (1977), Dournes would analyze this pose of himself (Dam Bo), Condominas (Yo Sar Luk), and Boulbet (Dam Böt) in romantic terms.

> Yo Sar Luk, Dam Böt [. . .] and myself, Dam Bo at the time, publicized our "savage" names as the program of our dreams: This was the integration into a people, quite different from our community of origin, knowing well that we remained Whites in the eyes of those who, we pretended, had adopted us—although we had been imposed upon them—and for whom our strangeness excused our marginal lives and our privileges, within a context of colonization. (Dournes 1977:76)

Alternatively, we could analyze this pose from the perspective of the triangular relationship between "colonial subjects" conceived as the universalizing subject of colonialism; as the subjects of colonial rule; and as the substantive topics of colonial discourse. Where earlier claims to ethnographic authority would be derived from the identification of the ethnographer with the universalizing colonial subject, professional anthropologists would try to distance themselves from that governmental identity by assuming an identity as part of the community where they did their field research—those who can be defined as the subjects of colonial rule. Positioning themselves in a mediating role between colonial subjects in the first and second senses, they thus enhanced claims to ethnographic authority when making statements on topics of colonial discourse. In this sense Condominas's distancing himself from the colonial préterrain is not contradictory to but rather a necessary part of his effort to make anthropological knowledge (e.g., of acculturation) useful for colonial rule. The adoption of local names, intended to sanction professional anthropologists' claim to expert status in cultural brokerage and cultural management, had a similar discursive effect as those French-sanctioned forums where Montagnards were allowed to represent themselves, like at the Dalat Conference of 1946, or in the special issue of *Revue Education* (1949). This effect was to emphasize the empathetic proximity of French and Montagnard mentalities and the appropriateness of direct French rule in the Central Highlands, while subverting other (read: Vietnamese) claims to ethnographic authority concerning the Montagnards. This assertion of ethnographic authority by the adoption of local names as a sign of their insertion into native society and culture on the part of professional anthropologists implied a cultural relativism that saw a generic Montagnard culture as on a par with the cultures and civilizations of the majority nations in Indochina (Viêt, Khmer, Lao). This cultural relativism was conditioned by the renewed appreciation and celebration of Montagnard culture by amateur ethnographers and the colonial administration alike during a period of heightened strategic interest in the Central Highlands. It was this brand of cultural relativism that allowed the French to arrogate the responsibility for the protection and perfection of the Montagnards, conveniently coinciding with the military defense of the Central Highlands. In the next section I shall argue that this cultural relativism was a precondition for the military relationships characterizing two innovative paramilitary programs in the Central Highlands during the First Indochina War.

Cultural Relativism as Martial Art

In the previous section, we have seen that despite the formal reattachment of the Pays Moï to the Vietnamese state, French ethnographic discourse continued to emphasize the essential cultural unity of the Montagnards as fundamentally opposed to Vietnamese identity, both in ethnographic writing and in military propaganda. It was implied that the French not only bore the responsibility to protect the Montagnards from the Vietnamese, but they even saw themselves as "closer" to the Montagnards than the Kinh (ethnic Vietnamese). Consequently, French ethnic policy was glorified as the "salvation" of the Montagnards, both physically and culturally, who were depicted as loyal to the French. In this section I briefly describe three French counterinsurgency programs, the *Bataillons montagnards*, the *Action Psychologique*, and the *Maquis*, that attempted to draw Montagnards into the French war effort by adapting to some degree to local culture and society. These programs were prompted by Viêt Minh military successes in the Highlands that effectively subverted a self-complacent French ethnographic discourse on mutual Kinh-Montagnard antagonism. On the other hand, these programs could only be implemented in the context of this powerful discourse, and they were conditioned by constant reference to the cumulative discursive effect of decades of ethnographic research.

In French military strategy, this colonial discourse had specific gender effects in the groups targeted for military recruitment into the *Bataillons montagnards*, which provided new career opportunities for young men outside of the confines of village society. Many ethnographic narratives hinted at the appetite for adventure among younger Rhadé and Jarai males, as evidenced in epics (*khan*) and other forms of oral literature. Condominas, for instance, interpreted the Rhadé *Chant épique de Kdam Yi* as "revenge by the man [the hero of the epic] for the grip by the clan dominated by the women: 'Superman' in revolt against almighty 'Mom'" (1980:228). In his "Observations sociologiques sur deux chants épiques rhadés" of 1955 (reprinted in 1980), Condominas considered the exploits and adventures of the (male) heroes of the epics as an escape from female predominance in Rhadé society, and therefore as revolt against the authority of mothers, sisters, and/or wives—even though the most famous culture hero, Dam San, ultimately conforms to matrilineal custom (for Jarai epics, see Dournes 1972:257). Writing about changing male and female identities in Jarai society, Dournes described the male tendency to escape their customary responsibilities by resorting to adventurism—war, vagabondage, and peddling. In the context of the French colonial presence and the Indochina War, Dournes observed "at present an alarming number of youngsters that are recruited as mercenaries in this foreign war, which interests them only as a convenient life-style" (1972:262).

Not surprisingly, then, both the French colonial army and the Viêt Minh were able to recruit the largest number of Montagnard youngsters among the matrilineal Rhadé and Jarai groups, providing these young men with new (military) career and life-style options reminiscent of the adventures of their culture heroes—warriors from a mythical era. In the words of the military ethnographer Captain Maurice (1947), the French "presence has established peace and put an end to the political anarchy that still reigned at the beginning of the century and, undoubtedly, for millennia. Today, the warrior instincts of the [Rhadé] tribe bloom within our *bataillons montagnards*." Perhaps Maurice was too optimistic about that peace, but he was right about the military career opportunities for Montagnards. One consequence of the military recruitment in matrilocal societies was a change in residence patterns when wives followed their husbands in their pursuit of new careers as soldiers (but oftentimes also as clerks, teachers, plantation workers, etc.). This definitely meant a break with tradition, even if it did not constitute a move to a patrilocal residence system. More often than not, the wife would follow her husband to a new location altogether, wherever he made his living; this could be a town or a military camp. For the women, the result was that she would be physically separated from her clan and from the family assets, while becoming dependent on her husband's income and her own labor (if she continued to grow food) for a livelihood. While she would perhaps have a better income this way and derive some indirect prestige from her husband's position, she would become more vulnerable as she would no longer have easy access to the security provided by an extended family—a badly needed asset during the vagaries of war. Thus, war accelerated a process of gender transformation in the two main matrilineal societies of Vietnam, leading to a redefinition of gender roles and identities in changing circumstances, fueled by men's monopolization of the ethnographic occasions that fed ethnographic discourse and by women's exclusion from representing their interests. In a situation where ethnographic discourse claimed to protect Montagnard tradition from outside corruption, this may be an ironic observation. On the other hand, insofar as this ethnographic discourse was part and parcel of a colonial tactics aiming at controlling the strategic Central Highlands area and its population militarily, this observation is not very surprising, because, during wartime, ethnography is contextualized by male camaraderie in the colonial army.

In the course of the French Indochina War, the image of a "natural" Franco-Montagnard alliance became increasingly marred by the political and military developments in the Highlands. The French separatist aspirations for the Highlands proved to be formally untenable, while the burdens that their demand for manpower for the army, for corvee, and for the plantations imposed on Montagnard society had the effect of alienating the Montagnards from the French. But the image was marred not only because of the failure of French ethnic policy in the Highlands, but also because of an apparent rapprochement between Montagnards and Viêt Minh. The steady military advance of the Viêt Minh in the Highlands was often attributed to their accommodation to Montagnard culture. The guerrilla tactics employed by the Viêt Minh could only be successful if they heeded Mao Tse-Tung's adage that the guerrilla must move among the local population like a fish in the water. In this respect, the training of communist cadres was increasingly geared to the exigencies of life among

Ethnography as Martial Art 317

non-Viêt peoples in the jungle. The famous "eight orders" given by Hô Chí Minh, which amounted to professing respect for the local population and their culture, were important guidelines for establishing good working relations with local populations, including Montagnards. There were also stories of Viêt Minh cadres who totally immersed in local Montagnard societies by learning the language, dressing in loincloth, marrying a local woman, and even filing their teeth. Undoubtedly, such stories were exaggerated, but the importance of such rumors lay in the fact that they were believed, and therefore stirred the French into action. In an intelligence report on the rapid Viêt Minh advance in Darlac province in 1951, it is observed that "The Viet-Minh has a Moï policy, too," which necessitated political action by the French military.[14]

The Viêt Minh successes on the battlefield, which by 1950 could no longer be denied, prompted a reassessment of the military tactics employed by the French military. In general, this entailed a move away from conventional warfare tactics to guerrilla tactics. This was not only a tacit acknowledgment of the Viêt Minh military successes in the Highlands, but entailed an awareness that the war between the French and the Viêt Minh was as much a political as a military struggle. In fact, the French attempted an adaptation to the Viêt Minh strategy of incorporation of the local population in the war effort by responding to local aspirations on a more basic level than promising some sort of abstract autonomy in a fictional homeland. The new tactics employed by the French were the *Action Psychologique* and the *Maquis*, which were both initiated in the Highlands in 1950.

The *Action Psychologique* was set up by Jean Le Pichon, who had been commanding Montagnard militia for twenty years. The psychological action was an integral part of the military effort and consisted of three coordinated elements: propaganda, social action, and military action. Schools that had been set up in response to literacy campaigns mounted by the Viêt Minh were transformed into formation centres of Montagnard propagandists. These *propagateurs* took care of the political training of village headmen, who were informed about the dubious character of Viêt Minh promises of autonomy, and of the Viêt in general. From 1953 on, a propaganda journal, *Le Petit Montagnard*, was available in four languages (Koho, Bahnar, Sedang, and Rhadé/Jarai, which were close anyway) and distributed among Montagnard soldiers and other Montagnard "brothers" [*sic!*]. The social action, which was coordinated with the Catholic mission, consisted of the distribution of salt (a scarce product in the Highlands) and of medical care, in an effort to win the Montagnards over to the

---

14. 2me Bureau, Fiche critique a/s d'une Etude sur la Situation Militaire des Plateaux, 13 Mars 1951 [SHAT, box 10H917]; also Chesneaux 1955:285; Viet Chung 1967.

French side. For the military action the Viêt Minh concept of the "fighting village" was adopted and changed to suit French objectives. Characteristically, the French resettled the population of a number of scattered hamlets into one big agglomeration (*regroupement des villages*), which would then be defended by armed youths from the village, trained and led by French soldiers (*organismes d'autodéfense*). These small-scale resettlement schemes, aimed at preventing Viêt Minh guerrillas from contacting village populations, heralded later, more massive American attempts to concentrate the rural population in strategic hamlets.[15]

The Maquis were commandos who tried to set up counterguerrilla groups in enemy territory and thus went much further in adapting to local cultures than the *Action Psychologique*. Colonel Trinquier, the genius behind the Maquis in Indochina (*Maquis* was also the name of the anti-Nazi resistance in France during World War II), stated that it would be in vain to try to interest half-savage peoples with a limited horizon in the complexity of the Indochina War, and that the only way to reach them was to play on their immediate interests and ambitions, and to revive old antagonisms, in particular against the ethnic Vietnamese. The idea was to parachute one or more French commandos of the *Groupes de Commandos Mixtes Aeroportés* (GCMA) among such groups to set up a self-defense system and to train recruits. Most of the ten Maquis were in the northern mountains, where most of the fighting took place; in the Central Highlands the French capitalized on a revolt against the Viêt Minh by the Hrê "tribe" in Quang Ngai. Among the Hrê, the Viêt Minh had felt sufficiently safe to step up their exactions in terms of taxes in foodstuff and labor, and to settle thousands of Viêt migrants in Hrê territory, in a way making the same political mistake as the French with their plantations. When the Hrê revolted against this regime, reportedly killing hundreds of ethnic Vietnamese in their midst, the French immediately sent Captain Hentic to try to turn the Hrê, who feared a Viêt Minh retaliation, into "partisans." In 1955, Hentic published his experiences among the Hrê under the pseudonym René Riesen, relating how he learned the language and adopted their life-style in order to win their confidence; how he married a Hrê girl in order to ally himself to a Hrê leader; and how he baptized his partisans *ôc Lâp Hrê* ("Hrê Independence" in Vietnamese), for they fought only for

---

15. Direction de l'Action Psychologique, Cap. Caniot, "Stage de Guerre Psychologique"; Chef de Bataillon Fossey-François, "Historique de l'Action Psychologique en Indochine de 1945 au 20 juillet 1954" [SHAT, box 10H346]; Action Psychologique, Plateau du Centre, "tracts" comptes-rendus des activités de propagande, 1953–54 [SHAT, box 10H433]; see also Bochet 1951:64; Nguyên Dê 1953:5–22; Pagniez 1954:135–42; and Hickey 1982a:409–13.

themselves—albeit against the same enemy as France, as Trinquier aptly noted.[16]

Even when the Hrê Maquis was initially successful, Hentic's eight battalions were no match for the regular Viêt Minh units supported by Montagnard guerrillas from 1951 onward. Although the *Action Hrê* lasted until 1954, the French military efforts were not successful, as was shown in the steady deterioration of their position in the Highlands since 1950. This culminated in the annihilation of the elite *Groupe Mobile 100* near An Khê in June 1954. By that time—during the Geneva Conference of 1954— only Ban Me Thuot and Dalat were still in French hands. According to Bernard Fall, "whatever tribesmen had remained loyal to the French were now in the posts and camps, and the remainder retreated with the Viêt into the inaccessible hills a few miles off the paths and roads." This may be explained by the fact that the Viêt Minh had an overall strategy of combining political and military struggle while avoiding disruptive factors. The example of the revolt of the Hrê shows also that the Viêt Minh paid dearly when they broke their own code. However, the combination of political and military struggle remained a tactical ploy for the French, whose strategy was complicated by a continued reliance on conventional warfare tactics and undermined by the economic interests of the plantations. But even the political struggle was waged clumsily, if we may believe the British journalist Norman Lewis when he described the arrest of eighty inhabitants of a village who did not wish to inform on the Viêt Minh; twenty were hanged right away, and the others were tortured and kept in prison for at least another three months. It is hard to imagine what propaganda could undo the effects of such action (Lewis 1951:140; Fall 1963:195–96).

The French counterinsurgency programs attempted to draw the Montagnards into the French war effort by adapting in some degree to local culture and society. These programs were prompted by Viêt Minh military successes in the Highlands that effectively subverted a self-complacent French ethnographic discourse on mutual Kinh-Montagnard antagonism. On the other hand, these programs could only be implemented in the context of this powerful discourse and were conditioned by constant reference to the cumulative discursive effect of decades of ethnographic practice: ethnicization, territorialization, and cultural relativism. From 1953 on, the magazine *Le Petit Montagnard* (available in French, Bah-

---

16. Plan de stationnement des troupes, no. 341/FTPM/3S, Décembre 1951; Plan de stationnement des troupes, no. 341/FTPM/3S, 10 août 1953, [SHAT, box 10H3734]; 2me Bureau, télégrammes officiels (1951–53) [SHAT, box 10H3677]; see also Bodard 1950:16–33; Riesen 1955; Trinquier 1976.

nar, Sedang, Rhadé/Jarai, and Koho) was distributed among Montagnard soldiers and other Montagnard "brothers." This French propaganda journal tried to convince Montagnards that they really were one ethnic group in a separate territory with a *statut spécial*, and that they were fighting for the defense of their own culture in their own homeland.[17] This became very graphic in the Maquis fighting for Hrê independence (which they nevertheless spelled in Vietnamese), in which Hrê culture and identity were territorialized. Cultural relativism was brought out in the increasingly horizontal relations between French military officers and their Montagnard recruits/informants on whom they depended for survival and military success. The immersion in local cultures, the adoption of local identities, the celebration of local culture thus became the prerogative not only of professional anthropologists, but increasingly of military officers fighting side by side with Montagnards.

But even that position became politically untenable as the nominally independent Vietnamese state under Emperor Bao Dai asserted sovereignty over the *"Pays Montagnard du Sud"* with its own *Plan de Développement économique pour les PMS du Domaine de la Couronne* drafted by Bao Dai's *Chef de cabinet* Nguyên Dê (1953). Like the French, Nguyên Dê wished to fix the "primitive and nomadic" Montagnard populations to the soil by introducing modern agricultural techniques, but the main difference from French programs was that he wished to promote the migration of lowlanders into the Central Highlands (1953:5–6). Though conceived too late to be implemented before 1954, Nguyên Dê's plans heralded later, massive internal colonization schemes by the Diêm regime and the Socialist Republic of Vietnam. Even so, the ethnographic discourse and ethnic policies with respect to the Central Highlands would deeply influence relations of Montagnards with outsiders for times to come. During the Second and Third Indochina Wars it would become impossible for any outside force to coopt the Montagnards for their own purposes without coming to terms with the notion of a Montagnard *statut particulier*. In that context, it is not surprising that American interventions in the Central Highlands would be couched in the same discourses and would employ most of the same tactics as the French before them (even if they did not always realize it), albeit on a grander scale. But like the French before them, American ethnographic discourses with respect to the Montagnards were both politically untenable and riddled with contradictions that could only result in political failure.

---

17. Action Psychologique, Plateau du Centre, "tracts" comptes-rendus des activités de propagande, 1953–54 [SHAT, box 10H433].

Conclusion

Although the French lost the First Indochina War and Vietnam gained independence temporarily divided into two separate states, the effects of the war—both as préterrain and as ethnographic occasion—on ethnographic discourse regarding Montagnards remained very real. Intertwined processes of tribalization, ethnicization, and territorialization, spurred on by changing political perceptions about the strategic importance of the Central Highlands and its inhabitants, contextualized the institutionalization and the professionalization of ethnography. But, reciprocally, the institutionalization and consequent professionalization tended to harden an ethnographic discourse imbued with notions of cultural relativism into a hegemonic ethnographic tradition. This resulted in new forms of cultural relativism, linked to the new method of ethnographic fieldwork and a redefinition of self by researchers as mediators between the subjects of colonial rule and the universalizing colonial subject, thus assuming an authority that in the particular context of war went beyond the ethnographic. Yet the discursive effect of the new, professional anthropology was similar to that of the "relativist" amateur ethnography, in that it construed the Montagnards as fundamentally different from and antagonistic to the lowland Vietnamese. This hegemonic ethnographic narrative formed the discursive context for French counterinsurgency programs, which inserted themselves in this discourse, although they were more directly motivated by military and political developments on the battlefield that seemed to negate and subvert this discourse of Franco-Montagnard closeness and Montagnard-Viêt antagonism. War proved a special préterrain as well as a special ethnographic occasion, resulting in a proliferation of an ethnographic discourse that fundamentally changed the political equation in the Central Highlands for decades to come. After the Geneva Agreements of 1954 that effectively divided the country, and even after the reunification in 1975, most non-Vietnamese ethnographies continued to reinscribe this ethnographic discourse that tended to harden into reality. The rise and demise of a Montagnard ethnonationalism aiming to revive the *statut particulier* complete with customary law courts in the Central Highlands testify to both the power and the political failure of this ethnographic discourse.

REFERENCES

Manuscript Sources

ANSOM   Archives Nationales, Section d'Outre-Mer (now Centre des Archives d'Outre-Mer, Aix-en-Provence)
AOM   Archives d'Outre-Mer (now Centre des Archives d'Outre-Mer, Aix-en-Provence)
RSA   Résidence Supérieure d'Annam (Vietnam National Archives #2, Ho Chi Minh City)
SHAT   Service Historique de l'Armée de Terre (Vincennes)

Published Sources

Antomarchi, Dominique. 1941. "Le 'Bi-Duê,' recueil des coutumes rhadées." *Indochine Hebdomaire illustrée* 2 (25): 5–10.
Bochet, Gilbert. 1951. *Eléments de conversation Franco-Koho. Us et coutumes des Montagnards de la Province du Haut-Donnai*. Dalat: Service Géographique de l'Indochine.
Bodard, Lucien. 1950. "La révolte des Rhés." *Sud-Est Asiatique* 17:16–33.
Boteau-Roussel Jules, and Yves Jouin. 1943. "Un sacrifice au génie des éléphants à Bandon chez l'héritière de Kundjonob." *Travaux de l'Institut Indochinoise de l'Etude de l'Homme* 7:375–86.
Boudarel, Georges. 1976. "Sciences sociales et contre-insurrection au Vietnam." In H. Moniot, ed., *Le mal du voir*. Paris: Cahiers Jussieu.
Boudet, Paul. 1942. "Léopold Sabatier, Apôtre des Rhadés." *Indochine Hebdomaire illustrée* III (113): I–VII.
Boulbet, Jean. 1957. "Quelques aspects du coutumier (N'dri) des Cau Maa." *Bulletin de la Société des Etudes Indochinoises* 32:110–78.
Chesneaux, Jean. 1955. *Contribution à l'histoire de la nation vietnamienne*. Paris: Editions Social.
Clifford, James. 1982. *Person and Myth: Maurice Leenhardt in the Melanesian World*. Berkeley and Los Angeles: University of California Press.
———. 1983. "Power and Dialogue in Ethnography: Marcel Griaule's Initiation." In G. Stocking, ed., *Observers Observed. History of Anthropology*, vol. 1, 121–56. Madison: University of Wisconsin Press.
Condominas, Georges. 1952. "Rapport d'une mission en pays Mnong Gar (PMSI)." *Bulletin de l'Ecole Française d'Extrême-Orient* 46:303–13.
———. 1953. "Ethnologie de l'Indochine et bibliographie ethnographique." In André Leroi-Gourhan and Jean Poirier, eds., *Ethnologie de l'Union Française*. 2 vols. Paris: Presses Universitaires de France.
———. 1955. "Observations sociologiques sur deux chants épiques Rhadés." *Bulletin de l'Ecole Française d'Extrême-Orient* 47:555–68.
———. 1957. *Nous avons mangé la forêt de la Pierre-Génie Gôo*. Paris: Mercure.
———. 1965. *L'exotique est quotidien: Sar Luk, Viet-nam central*. Paris: Plon.
———. 1966. "Classes sociales et groupes tribaux au Sud-Vietnam." *Cahiers Internationaux de la Sociologie* 40:161–70.
———. 1973. "Ethics and Comfort: An Ethnographer's View of His Profession." *Annual Report 1972, American Anthropological Association*, 1–17.

———. 1977. *We Have Eaten the Forest: The Story of a Montagnard Village in the Central Highlands of Vietnam* (with new Preface to the English language edition). New York: Hill and Wang.
———. 1980. *L'espace social à propos de l'Asie du Sud-Est.* Paris: Flammarion.
Copans, Jean. 1975. *Anthropologie et Impérialisme.* Paris: Maspéro.
Dam Bo. 1950. "Les Populations Montagnardes du Sud-Indochinois." *France-Asie* 49–50. (numéro spécial).
De Hautecloque-Howe, Anne. 1985. *Les Rhadés: une société de droit maternel.* Paris: Editions du CNRS.
Decoux, Amiral. 1950. *A la barre de l'Indochine.* Paris: Plon.
Dournes, Jacques. 1948. "Structure social des Montagnards du Haut-Donnai. Tribu des riziculteurs." *Bulletin de la Société des Etudes Indochinoises* 24 (3): 9–111.
———. 1949. "L'âme et les songes. Etude Moï pour servir à la philosophie des primitifs." *France-Asie* 55:1107–23.
———. 1951. "Nri (coutumier Srê; extraits)." *France-Asie* 60:1232–41.
———. 1955. *En suivant la piste des hommes sur les Hauts-Plateaux de Viet-Nam.* Paris: Julliard.
———. 1972. *Coordonnées: Structures Jörai familiales et sociales.* Paris: Institut d'Ethnologie.
———. 1977. *Pötao: Une théorie de pouvoir chez les Indochinois Jörai.* Paris: Flammarion.
Fall, Bernard. 1963. *Street Without Joy: Insurgency in Indochina, 1946–1963.* London: Pall Mall Press.
Galliéni, J. 1941. *Galliéni au Tonkin, 1892–1896, pax lui mème.* Paris: Berger-Levrault [orig. 1913].
Gayet, Inspecteur des Colonies, ed. 1949. Numéro spécial consacré aux Populations Montagnardes de Sud-Indochinois. *Revue Education* 16. Saigon: Rectorat d'Académie.
Gerber, Théophile. 1951–52. "Coutumier Stieng." *Bulletin de l'Ecole Française d'Extrême-Orient* 45:227–73.
Goscha, Christopher. 1996. "Annam and Vietnam in the New Indochinese Space, 1887–1945." In Stein Tønnesson and Hans Antlöv, eds., *Asian Forms of the Nation,* 93–130. London: Curzon Press.
Groshier, B. P. 1952. "Commentaire de Gilbert Bochet, *Eléments de conversations franco-koho,*" *Bulletin de la Société des Etudes Indochinoises* 27:333–42.
Guilleminet, Paul. 1942. "Recherches ethnologiques in pays moï: But, résultats, difficultés." *Cahiers de l'Ecole Française d'Extrême-Orient* 33:21.
———. 1952a. *Coutumier de la Tribu Bahnar, des Sedang at des Jarai de la Province de Kontum.* Hanoi: Ecole Française d'Extrême-Orient.
———. 1952b. "La tribu Bahnar du Kontum. Contribution à l'étude de la société montagnarde du Sud-Indochinois." *Bulletin de l'Ecole Française d'Extrême-Orient* 45:393–561.
Hardy, Georges. 1951. "A travers les revues qui nous parlent de l'Asie." *Revue de Psychologie des Peuples* 3:289–303.
Hickey, Gerald. 1982a. *Sons of the Mountains: Ethnohistory of the Vietnamese Central Highlands to 1954.* New Haven: Yale University Press.
———. 1982b. *Free in the Forest: Ethnohistory of the Vietnamese Central Highlands to 1954–1976.* New Haven: Yale University Press.
Huard, Paul, and Albert-Marie Maurice. 1939. "Les Mnong du Plateau central indochinois." *Travaux de l'Institut Indochinoise de l'Etude de l'Homme* 2:27–148.

Jouin, Bernard. 1949. *La mort et la tombe.* Paris: Institut d'Ethnologie.
Lafont, Pierre-Bernard. 1963. *Toloi Djuat: Coutumier de la tribu jarai.* Paris: Publications de l'Ecole Française d'Extrême-Orient.
Lavallée, A. 1901. "Notes ethnographiques sur diverses tribus du Sud-Est de l'Indochine." *Bulletin de l'Ecole François d'Extrême-Orient I*: 291–311.
Leroi-Gourhan, André, and Jean Poirier, eds. 1953. *Ethnologie de l'Union Française* (2 vols.). Paris: Presses Universitaires de France.
Lévi-Strauss, Claude. 1960. "Méthode et conditions de la recherche ethnologique en Asie." In *Actes du VIe Congrès Internationales des Sciences anthropologiques et ethnologiques.* Paris: Lahure.
Lewis, Norman. 1951. *A Dragon Apparent.* London: Jonathan Cape.
Maitre, Henri. 1912. *Les Jungles Moï.* Paris: Larose.
Malleret, Louis (text) and Georges Taboulet (map). 1937. *Groupes ethniques de l'Indochine française.* Saigon: Société des Études Indochinoises.
Marr, David. 1995. *Vietnam 1945: The Quest for Power.* Berkeley: University of California Press.
Maurice, Albert-Marie. 1947. "Croquis rhadé." *Revue des Troupes Coloniales* 292 (October).
———. 1951. "Trois fêtes agraires rhadé." *Bulletin de l'Ecole Française d'Extrême-Orient* 45:158–207.
———. 1956. *La société rhadé.* Algiers: Centre des Hautes Etudes d'Administration Musulmane.
———. 1993. *Les Mnong des Hauts-Plateaux (Centre-Vietnam).* 2 vols. Paris: L'Harmattan.
Maurice, Albert-Marie, and Georges Proux. 1954. "L'âme du riz." *Bulletin de la Société des Etudes Indochinoises* 29:129–258.
Mauss, Marcel. 1967. *Manuel d'Ethnographie.* Paris: Payot.
Miles, Douglas, and C. Eipper. 1985. Introduction to the special volume *Minorities and the State. Canberra Anthropology* 8 (1/2): 1–3.
Ner, Marcel. 1943. "La France en Pays Moï: Humbles constructeurs de l'Empire." *Indochine Hebdomaire illustrée* 4 (143): 7–9; (144): I–VII.
———. 1952. "Psychologie des populations archaïques (Moï) du Sud de l'Indochine." *Revue de Psychologie des Peuples* 1:44–61; 157–77.
Nguyên Dê. 1953. *Plan d'Action Sociale pour les Pays Montagnard du Sud du Domaine de la Couronne.* Saigon: Editions de la Délégation Impériale de la Domaine de la Couronne.
Pagniez, F. P. 1954. "Sur les Plateaux d'Indochine, guerre psychologique." *Revue des Deux Mondes* 1954:135–42.
Pagniez, Y. 1954. *Le Viet Minh et la Guerre Psychologique.* Paris: La Colombe.
Pels, Peter. 1994. "The Construction of Ethnographic Occasions in Late Colonial Uluguru." *History and Anthropology* 8 (1–4): 321–51.
Pels, Peter, and Oscar Salemink. 1994. "Introduction: Five Theses on Ethnography as Colonial Practice." In Peter Pels and Oscar Salemink, eds., *Colonial Ethnographies,* special issue of *History and Anthropology* 8 (1–4): 1–34.
Riesen, René. 1955. *Mission spéciale en forêt moï.* Paris: France-Empire.
Risseeuw, Carla. 1988. *The Fish Don't Talk About The Water. Gender Transformation and Resistance among Women in Sri Lanka.* Leiden: Brill.
Sabatier, Léopold. 1930. *Palabre du serment au Darlac.* Hanoi: Imprimerie d'Extrême-Orient.

Sabatier, Léopold, and Dominique Antomarchi. 1940. *Recueil des coutumes rhadées du Darlac*. Hanoi: Ecole Française d'Extrême-Orient.
Salemink, Oscar. 1987. *Ethnografie en kolonialisme: Minderheden in Vietnam, 1850–1954*. Amsterdam: Universiteit van Amsterdam.
———. 1991. "Mois and Maquis: The Invention and Appropriation of Vietnam's Montagnards from Sabatier to the CIA." In George W. Stocking, ed., *Colonial Situations: Essays on the Contextualization of Ethnographic Knowledge* (*History of Anthropology*, vol. 7), 243–84. Madison: University of Wisconsin Press.
———. 1994. "The Return of the Python God: Multiple Interpretations of a Millenarian Movement in Colonial Vietnam." *History and Anthropology* 8 (1–4): 129–64.
———. 1995. "Primitive Partisans: French Strategy and the Construction of a Montagnard Ethnic Identity in Indochina." In Hans Antlöv and Stein Tønnesson, eds., *Imperial Policy and South East Asian Nationalism*, 261–93. Richmond, Surrey: Curzon Press.
Thongchai Winichakul. 1994. *Siam Mapped: A History of the Geo-Body of a Nation*. Honolulu: University of Hawaii Press.
———. 1996. "Maps and the Formation of the Geo-Body of Siam." In Stein Tønnesson and Hans Antlöv, eds., *Asian Forms of the Nation*, 67–92. London: Curzon Press.
Trinquier, Colonel. 1976 [1952]. *Les maquis d'Indochine. Les missions spéciales de service action*. Paris: Ed. Albatros.
Vandergeest, Peter, and Nancy Peluso. 1995. "Territorialization and State Power in Thailand." *Theory and Society* 24:385–426.
Viet Chung. 1967. "Minorités Nationales et politiques des nationalités en R.D. du Vietnam." *Etudes Vietnamiennes* 15:3–24.
Y Bi Nie-Kdam. 1949. "Notice sommaire sur le Darlac." *Revue Education* 16:31–32.

Constructing Racial Landscapes
Africans, Administrators, and Anthropologists in Northern Rhodesia

Lyn Schumaker

Introduction

In the colonial period, anthropologists, their African research assistants, and colonial administrators had differing views of the field—the physical space in which they carried out their work. These differences depended to a large extent on how each group constructed racial landscapes and placed themselves and others in them. The word *constructed* is used deliberately here to place emphasis upon the materials and labor processes used to shape the landscape, to move through it, or to build a place from which to view it. The same physical space could have a different meaning depending on how the viewer came to see it—through what processes and practices the view was achieved.

When anthropologists arrived in late colonial Northern Rhodesia, they did research in a place that had already been shaped to a great extent by the activities of previous whites, including settlers, missionaries, and administrators. Along with building roads and towns and altering African settlement and labor patterns, missionaries and administrators had determined the basic landmarks on the ethnographic map well before professional anthropologists arrived.

Thus, anthropologists had to work within a field already partly defined by those who preceded them, and they often relied on practices developed by their predecessors for living in and moving through that field. This article examines this sharing of spaces and practices by anthropologists and administrators, while seeking to understand the different racial landscapes that each group saw in the field. A number of factors contributed to these differing landscapes, but two are of key importance. One was the existence of an urban field in southern and central Africa that became a focus for anthropological study; the other was the urban African perspective, influencing anthropology through the work of African research assistants.

The methods used in this article come from the history of the field sciences—those sciences that rely on fieldwork instead of or in addition to laboratory work. This theoretical perspective has been developed by historians of science and technology who have used it to analyze fieldwork styles from the natural sciences as well as the social sciences. This approach draws attention to the field itself; the material side of fieldwork; and the infrastructure, equipment, and work organization necessary to conduct scientific work in a particular field site. It also allows one to relate scientific practices to nonscientific practices occurring in the same field site, such as the sharing of practices between colonial administrators and anthropologists considered in this study. For example, historians of the field sciences have shown how the practices associated with tourism partly formed the basis of astronomers' solar eclipse expeditions in the late Victorian period and, in the early Victorian period, how the practices of painters, mining engineers, and prospectors came to be employed by geologists (Pang 1991; Rudwick 1976).

A field science approach allows one to examine the relationship between the technology of a science and the view of the field that informs its daily practice and that makes the field what it is for a particular science. The history of colonial science in Africa has suffered from too sharp a dichotomy between the external and the indigenous, with science often being viewed as a European import more or less successfully transferred into a hostile environment. What a field science perspective brings to the history of anthropology, as a colonial science in Africa, is the ability to ground it in its African context and thus to understand what is African about anthropology in Africa. Its method—to focus on equipment, housing, transport, and the practical and political strategies anthropologists must use in order to do their research on a daily basis—makes a field science approach ideal for highlighting the *preterrain* of anthropology, as defined in the introduction to this book.

Since at least the 1920s fieldwork has held a special place in anthropology, both as a scientific method and as a central tenet of its professional ethos. As part of that ethos, fieldwork functions as the essential rite of passage that any student of anthropology must endure before aspiring to an academic career. Some historians of anthropology have focused on the place of fieldwork in the rhetoric of the discipline, analyzing anthropologists' textual use of the image of the tent to establish ethnographic authority by emphasizing the anthropologist's field experience (Stocking 1983:70–120; Clifford 1988). In this article I will shift the focus from anthropologists' use of fieldwork to establish textual authority, to a focus on their strategic choice of practices and equipment to establish their authority to others in the field—to administrators, to Africans, and to each other.

The Rhodes-Livingstone Institute

The fieldwork of anthropologists at the Rhodes-Livingstone Institute (RLI) in Northern Rhodesia (now Zambia) provides a good case study for this field science approach to the history of anthropology. The RLI served as the institutional focus for a large group of anthropologists who accomplished pathbreaking work after World War II. They later became known as the Manchester School anthropologists, after Max Gluckman, the second director of the RLI, founded social anthropology at the University of Manchester in 1949 and brought many of the RLI anthropologists there to lecture and write up their research.

The research at the RLI was based not only on fieldwork in the usual rural setting for anthropology but also in an urban field new to professional anthropology. In the 1930s the governor of Northern Rhodesia, keen on the potential uses of anthropology for solving problems of social change in the colony, pushed for the founding of an anthropological institute and garnered support for it from local sources such as the mining companies (Brown 1973). After World War II, this institute became part of the British government's postwar colonial development effort and was lavishly funded by the Colonial Social Science Research Council. This enabled the RLI to recruit a team of talented young anthropologists.

The RLI's first directors set out to create a coordinated program of applied anthropology useful for colonial development. They trained teams of researchers specifically for that purpose, attempting to achieve comparability of data on a range of topics studied in different field sites. This extended to the collection of demographic statistics that RLI researchers used for comparative analysis of a number of local societies and their adaptation to changes brought about by urbanization, industrialization, and labor migration. As a group the RLI anthropologists developed new methods of fieldwork and analysis, including the case method, situational analysis, and network theory, to name but a few. They produced studies that engaged with problems of contemporary African life rather than producing retrospective descriptions of precolonial social systems. They also broke down the dichotomy previously drawn between urban and rural societies.

They accomplished this in a difficult social and political environment. The political context of Northern Rhodesia in the 1940s and 1950s formed a watershed between decolonization in the more northern British colonies and greater segregation and apartheid to the south in Southern Rhodesia and South Africa. The black majority expressed its aspirations for political and economic self-determination through the growth of political parties such as the Northern Rhodesian African National Congress and other organizations such as the African Mine Workers Union.

A second wave of European colonialism also swept the country in this period with an influx of white settlers and mine workers attracted by Northern Rhodesia's copper boom. Many of these immigrants came from the so-called white South—Southern Rhodesia and South Africa—where Europeans earlier had settled in large numbers. Whites similarly pressed for self-determination and an end to British colonial rule. In response, in 1953 Britain created the Central African Federation—Northern and Southern Rhodesia, joined together with Nyasaland—as a step toward a future settler-dominated dominion that would help maintain a balance of power against an increasingly segregationist and nationalistic South Africa. The African fight against Federation boosted the development of black nationalist parties, and the late 1950s saw a militant and increasingly well-organized drive for majority rule, which led to Zambian independence in 1964.

To understand how the RLI's field methods evolved in the context of late colonial Northern Rhodesia, one must focus on two crucial factors: first, the sharing of field practices with colonial administrators in the rural research of the 1940s, when the Institute was especially vulnerable to government pressure; and second, the importance that anthropologists increasingly placed on differentiating their practices from those of administrators. The latter was partly a response to political pressure from the researchers' African informants and assistants, pressure that shaped their practices. But it also derived from the RLI anthropologists' different construction of the racial landscape of Northern Rhodesia, incorporating the urban environment, the urban African, and even the colonial administrator into that landscape.

Anthropology, Administration, and the Picturesque

Accounts given in interviews and memoirs by administrators and anthropologists often include an evaluation of the landscape in the places where they worked. For example, Max Marwick of the RLI mentioned the "great view" at 5,000 feet, from a wattle-and-daub house where he and his wife lived while doing a short period of fieldwork in Dedza, Nyasaland, on the Mozambique border (Max and Joan Marwick, interview, November 1992). A government administrator had chosen the site for them. Similarly, when Marwick first began his fieldwork in Northern Rhodesia in 1946, the district commissioner, Sir Douglas Hall, suggested a site near a place called Chenjela Mountain (Max Marwick, personal communication). According to J. A. Barnes—who came to do his research there when

Marwick left soon after—Hall had suggested the site and provided concrete for the foundation on the understanding that it would later become a government rest house for touring administrators. Barnes built the house on a slope of Chenjela with a view of the bush and scattered villages below, using bricks scavenged from the ruined administrative center, Fort Young. He cut down several trees to improve the view, an enterprise his research assistant thought a bit peculiar, perhaps not sharing the European evaluation of the view (Barnes, interview, August 1993; M. B. Lukhero, interview, May 1991).

Although both anthropologists and administrators often appreciated the same view of the landscape, as in the preceding examples, they constructed these views rather differently. This came about both in terms of the way they shaped the view—Barnes cut down the trees himself, something an administrator would be unlikely to do—and in the way they placed themselves and others in the landscapes that they viewed. The practices involved in administrative and anthropological fieldwork differed in crucial ways, though anthropologists initially relied on emulating administrative practices. This section will describe the style of administrative fieldwork in Northern Rhodesia, and the following section will discuss anthropologists' sharing in those practices.

Northern Rhodesia's large rural areas were administered through a system of provincial and district headquarters called *bomas* (a term taken from Swahili, referring originally to a brush stockade built for security), from which government officers carried out regular tours to the surrounding villages, collecting taxes, settling disputes, and encouraging local development. The views and practices associated with this style of administrative fieldwork were what the first RLI anthropologists, Godfrey Wilson (director, 1938–41) and Max Gluckman (director, 1942–47), found when they arrived just prior to World War II.

The administrator's tour of the rural areas demonstrated the relationship of the government to the people and the land, providing an opportunity for tax collection, the hearing of local disputes, and surveillance of local compliance with conservation measures. Depending on cost and availability of transport, as well as local conditions, touring officers walked, rode bicycles or horses, traveled by boat, or were sometimes carried in hammocks accompanied by an entourage of porters and assistants. Chief among the assistants were the district messengers, the unarmed African enforcement wing of the local administration. In a few places the government built rest houses for touring officers, but in most places officers used tents and camped outside, rather than within, the villages. They did this primarily for reasons of health, associating African villages with increased exposure to mosquitoes, vermin, and human carriers of disease.

Constructing Racial Landscapes

Administrators referred to touring as "getting under canvas," and colonial officers rose in the esteem of their colleagues according to the amount of time they had spent touring. This suggests the importance of the experience of camping in the rural areas for shaping the colonial officer's ethic of administrative fieldwork, his view of Africa, and his vision of its proper development. The fieldwork ethic involving camping may have originated from precedents in colonial India as well as in the hunting expeditions of the early colonial period in Africa (Mackenzie 1987). The colonial officer selected a tent site using a number of criteria combining the practical and the aesthetic. The aesthetic elements, in particular, reveal the development vision of Africa that colonial administrators saw in the raw material of the landscape and the human societies that they administered. Looking at the colonial "technical imagination," as William Beinart calls it, is useful because "[p]lanning was an imaginative task; it explored the realms of what could be and indeed was often engaged in with very limited attention to what was." The commitment and "zeal" of technical officers was "part of a colonial vision of the future," a vision with "almost pictorial content" (Beinart 1984b:95–96).

As District Officer Kenneth Bradley observed of a less-than-desirable tent site in Northern Rhodesia in 1938:

> We found an uninspiring camp, set in small, shadeless scrub against a kopje which radiated heat like an electric stove. The view was entirely shut off by a mat of small bushes and one dead tree. (Bradley 1947:16)

Situated near a heat-radiating kopje, this camp lacked human comforts (85). Moreover, the dead and suffocating foliage completely blocked any view. In contrast, the qualities of a tent site and its view that Bradley found inspiring can be detected in the following description.

> I am camped tonight on the slope of . . . a valley under a grove of tall, thin trees. Across the valley a great precipice rises a thousand feet or more. . . . I like the precipice opposite my camp. . . . Maize gardens lie thick along the valley floor. Perhaps that is why I feel affection for my precipice. If its foot were shod in dark and ancient forest or had a scree of shattered boulders where leopards den, it would be sinister. Instead, at its foot is a tiny golden square, where an old man and his wife have cut their precious garden out from among the trees. (85)

What Bradley found inspiring was a view of a wild African scene—a "precipice" (escarpment) rising dramatically from a valley floor. But the scene was not too wild, for at the foot of the escarpment a husband and wife cultivated a small, "precious" garden. In contrast, the uninspiring camp had no view and gave Bradley an impression opposite that of the Eden-like scene of the man and woman in their maize garden. Bradley also took possession of the more pleasing view when he said that he felt affection for his precipice—and perhaps also for his people, the villagers he administered while on tour.

Bradley expressed values similar to those found in the early Victorian view of the "picturesque" tropical landscape, a view that expressed a compromise between Romanticism's admiration of the sublime, fearsome, and often barren wilderness, and Utilitarianism's emphasis on usefulness and order. The compromise resulted in an ideal landscape, wild and productive, so productive that it overflowed the boundaries of human cultivation. An implicit ownership by the viewer also featured in the Victorian appreciation of such landscapes. In both England and the tropics, British landscape gardeners planted trees or trimmed existing ones in order to frame the view in such a way that the distant fields and villages looked to be part of a manorial estate, with the villagers unconsciously playing the role of serfs for the lord of the manor (Schumaker 1988; Liu 1989; Barrell 1980; Smith 1985; Bermingham 1986). Whether or not individual touring officers in the colonial period felt the same sense of possession of the land and the people in it, the best view from the tent combined wildness and human productivity—open bush land dotted with villages or a valley decorated with scattered gardens of maize.

Notions of the picturesque vary with time and place, and Bradley's view, though it contains elements of the Victorian picturesque, also expressed the mid-twentieth-century values of the colonial service in Africa. Experiences of both the changing British landscape and of the changing landscape in southern Africa contributed to the colonial administrator's aesthetics. The urbanization and industrialization of Britain during the nineteenth century stimulated fears of degeneration of the English race and, especially, the emasculation of British men, fears that were strongest around the turn of the century. Colonial service, along with hunting and sports, was one way to escape those influences and lead a more vigorous and masculine life. Middle-class aspirations also contributed to nostalgia for the life of the upper-class rural gentry, set in an idealized manorial landscape. Africa promised a setting where such rural elite ways of life might still be attained.

Nevertheless, settlers and administrators did not simply apply the aesthetics of the rural British picturesque landscape to the African land. The history of their own exploration and settlement of Africa shaped particular ways of seeing the land based on its cultural, social, and economic associations. By Bradley's day, the European view of Africa was considerably tamer than that of the eighteenth century and earlier, discussed by Philip Curtin under the rubric of "the myth of tropical exuberance" (Curtin 1964:60). In southern Africa, as Terence Ranger observes, painters, prospectors, and priests had applied their imagination to the view and constructed the landscape according to the values appropriate to their different activities (Ranger n.d.). As early as the 1880s, professional hunting guides and the developers associated with the British South Africa Company had begun to shape a tourist view of Victoria Falls and the lands lying beyond it in Northern Rhodesia (Husbands n.d.). And in the new copper-mining towns of Northern Rhodesia, whites with previous experience of urban environments in South Africa built segregated cityscapes with luxurious low-density white areas. These featured swimming pools and expansive houses set in huge plots, allowing for gardens and relatively distant servants' quarters within the grounds.

The picturesque view of landscapes implied neither passivity on the part of the viewer nor the static condition of the landscape itself. In late colonial British Africa, as well as in Britain during the age of industrialization and enclosure, the idea of an active viewer and an evolving—or even degenerating—landscape became part of the colonial vision of rural development. In the period immediately preceding the arrival of the RLI anthropologists, the colonial government introduced the policy of indirect rule to Northern Rhodesia, a policy that required administrators to stimulate the supposedly natural evolution of African societies toward higher levels of civilization, while depending primarily on local rulers rather than on their own direct administration.

Indirect rule philosophy espoused giving more responsibility to chiefs, but the government's development goals, especially after World War II, demanded greater activity by both administrators and technical officers in the areas of housing, health, and agriculture. A sense of urgency motivated colonial intervention in a landscape that, far from being static, seemed to be degenerating from the impact of rapid social change. Laws concerning African agricultural practices, intended to prevent the erosion and deforestation of land under population pressure, stood as one example of this type of colonial intervention—and one that rural Africans deeply resented (Anderson 1984; Anderson and Grove 1987; McCracken 1982; Beinart 1984a; Ranger 1985; Beinart and Bundy 1987).

In the area of African political development, however, administrators in Northern Rhodesia in the 1940s and 1950s did not feel the same sense of urgency that motivated regulation of land use. Administrators assumed that African political development would be gradual and based on hierarchical chieftainship and cooperative village communities, forms of organization they believed to be appropriate to primitive peoples slowly evolving toward civilization. A not uncommon form of this evolutionary view of African political development is revealed in one of the questions a provincial administrator felt that the RLI anthropologists should investigate—the African's potential for responsibility and whether he would "become a 'first class Britisher' or a 'third class Italian' when left on his own." (DC Petauke, 19 October, 1944; SEC 1/131, National Archives of Zambia [NAZ]). The comparison the administrator made was to the racial landscape of Europe and its familiar gradient—from the nineteenth century and earlier—of racial degeneration from north to south, of the superior Anglo-Saxon to the inferior Mediterranean type.

Although in more northerly parts of British Africa, the postwar period saw an increasing tempo in colonial efforts to stimulate African political development in anticipation of decolonization, in Northern Rhodesia, Southern Rhodesia, and Nyasaland, the creation of the Federation led to stagnation in policies advocating devolution of power to Africans. The strong white settler community in Northern Rhodesia also influenced the attitudes of some, though not all, administrators posted there, for administrators participated in local white social networks and so were familiar with the prevailing settler views of Africans, perhaps more so than in colonies where settlers were fewer in number. Because of their ties with South Africa, many settlers saw in Northern Rhodesia a racial landscape that they hoped would evolve toward that which had developed in the south in the years leading up to apartheid. This was a landscape in which both industry and commercial farming would be dominated by whites, with Africans segregated to ever-diminishing rural reserves and kept out of the cities except when their labor was temporarily required. The RLI anthropologists who, like many of the settlers, came from South Africa, saw a similar landscape evolving in Northern Rhodesia, but took a very different message from the view.

"Like Switzerland, the Africans Should Export Their Picturesqueness"

The first two RLI anthropologists arrived in Northern Rhodesia just prior to World War II. Because of the war, only one or two anthropologists worked at the Institute until 1946. During the period between 1938 and 1946, however, these director/researchers established precedents for fieldwork and negotiated with the government for the resources necessary to conduct research.

Although officially an independent research institute, the RLI was controlled by a board of trustees comprised of members of government and representatives of the mining companies and white settler communities (Brown 1973:185–86). In the field as well as when dealing with the board of trustees, RLI anthropologists found themselves in an environment strongly influenced by the colonial civil service, for Northern Rhodesia had the highest proportion of administrators to population in British Africa (Apthorpe 1961). This high proportion may have been due to the necessity to cover the large but sparsely populated area of Northern Rhodesia and to the importance of the colony's copper. Moreover, the RLI anthropologists as individuals may have felt these colonial civil service influences more than was ordinarily the case for anthropologists, because many of them were born in Africa and/or educated in anthropology in courses also attended by trainees for the colonial civil service. Of the first six directors of the Institute, three had family connections or were born in Africa (Godfrey Wilson, Max Gluckman, and J. Clyde Mitchell) and two others were civil servants themselves (Henry Fosbrooke and C. M. N. White).

The influence of the civil service on RLI anthropologists also formed part of the more extensive contact developing between colonial governments and anthropologists of the functionalist school that had emerged between the two world wars. Functionalists studied societies as organic wholes characterized by harmonious systems of relationships and institutions that could be elucidated through scientific methods of observation based on fieldwork. The first group of anthropologists "to make field research an indispensable feature of anthropological inquiry," they gained acceptance by colonial governments partly because their "descriptions of their research methods were very like [colonial] political officers' accounts of their administrative procedures." These procedures included the district officer's immersion in the life of his subjects, which was supposed to lead to an intuitive understanding similar to the "nearly mystical communion" that the anthropologists claimed they also could achieve with their subjects. Both anthropologist and district officer spent considerable time in the field, both learned African languages and customs, and both often came to identify with the interests of "their people" (Kuklick 1991:190).

They also suffered from similar occupational hazards. District officers sometimes became "bushed"—a malady characterized by lethargy, inability to maintain European standards of dress and behavior, and failure to follow government directives and policies. Although medical and psychological explanations were given for these symptoms, the political dimensions of this "disease" are apparent. The fear of becoming bushed, and the accusation that one had become bushed, made erring civil servants adhere to government policy. The government gave leave privileges and moved administrators to new areas partly to prevent this malady, keeping the civil servant from developing too great an identification with a particular area or people. Anthropologists could also "go native" in this way, though by the late colonial period, other factors such as the anthropologist's political or social behavior with respect to educated members of native societies caused more irritation than imitating traditional dress or behavior did. An important precedent for the RLI was the case of its own first director, Godfrey Wilson. Local mining companies cited his conscientious objector status as one of the reasons for banning Wilson from his urban research site at the beginning of World War II.

But in the early days of the RLI, the directors set out to establish a good working relationship with the government and to prove the usefulness of social research for the government's development plans. Through this they hoped to gain favorable conditions for their research. Wilson and Gluckman, the first two directors, negotiated terms for research officers that were similar to those for civil servants. Wilson was hired under the usual civil service conditions, with traveling allowances and transport similar to those of general orders for district officers. The differences in the ways that anthropologists and district officers traveled, however, caused some difficulty. In negotiating for the best possible allowances, both Wilson and, later, Gluckman used civil service language to express the similarity of their work to that of civil servants. Where they admitted to differences, the directors stressed the greater difficulty of anthropological fieldwork. Wilson, when asked to suggest a basis for the amount of traveling allowance for an anthropologist in the field, spoke of the "officers" of the Institute being "encamped in rural districts"—language that suggests their similarities to district officers. "District officers on tour" were allowed 22 carriers if alone and 28 if accompanied by their wives. Anthropologists, Wilson felt, needed 30 and 40 carriers respectively, because a "longer stay in camp necessitates more baggage." The longer stay in camp meant that the anthropologist must also spend more money on "presents to natives" than the district officer who was just passing through (RC 1385: September 3, 1937; July 18, 1938; March 11, 1939 [correspondence between Wilson and the board of trustees], National Archives of Zambia [NAZ]).

Wilson's use of phrases such as "on tour," "in camp," and "presents to natives" played down important differences between anthropologists and district officers. Anthropologists may have moved from one village to another in the course of fieldwork, but not in the manner of the visiting delegation of the district officer. "In camp" was appropriate terminology for the district officer's temporary sleeping arrangements. Anthropologists, however, needed more permanent accommodation for their longer stays—larger tents or even houses, as Gluckman argued when asking for fixed field allowances for periods when the anthropologist was not on the move. Moreover, the allowance for "presents to natives" was larger than that of the district officer, he argued, because the anthropologist remained a long time in a particular village (RC 1385:minutes of the board of trustees meeting, August 1, 1941, NAZ). This revealed an important difference in the anthropologist's relations with the local people. The district officer's "presents" did, indeed, function as gifts, designed to buy the favor of chiefs and offset the cost of local provisioning of food for the officer and his carriers. The anthropologist's presents functioned more as wages paid to informants for their cooperation over the considerable period of time that he or she lived with them.

A visible dimension of identification with government accompanied this verbal identification. When in the field, some male RLI anthropologists wore *kabadula* or "khaki"—long, baggy shorts similar to those worn by colonial civil servants. At least in the early days, anthropologists did not attract criticism from the African population for this overtly colonial style of dress. Other anthropologists, however, may have been critical of those who wore what they called "Pommie Pants" instead of the briefer style of shorts more commonly worn in southern Africa by men who were not members of the civil service (Marwick, interview, November 1992).

RLI anthropologists followed the model of the colonial administrator in more than dress, talk, and negotiation for similar conditions of service. Government patterns of work and movement in the field influenced anthropological activity, and Africans sometimes perceived anthropologists to be following those patterns. Touring government officers conducted simple village censuses for tax purposes and rough surveys of agricultural production. An anthropologist collecting data for a quantitative survey also moved from village to village asking similar, though more extensive, questions on local populations, and mapping gardens in the manner of a government surveyor. A man from the Luapula province of Zambia who, as a boy of seven, had seen the RLI researcher Ian Cunnison at work in his village, remembered him as "some kind of census taker" because of the questions he asked about marriage, family size, and clan affiliation (M., Luapula, interview, July 1992). African perceptions of whites in the field depended on their previous experience of white activities in rural areas. For most Africans, this experience was limited to their contacts with administrators, missionaries, and, perhaps, a few farmers or traders, though the most frequent contacts would usually have been with administrators.

Another pattern of behavior shared with colonial administrators expressed the RLI researchers' development orientation. Both colonial officers and anthropologists engaged in the cultural promotion of the people they worked with in Northern Rhodesia—that is, they employed arguments based upon supposedly ethnically based cultural traits to argue for appropriate kinds of development for their favorite tribes. Colonial officers often put forward the particular characteristics of their people that suited them for progress. Bradley, for example, evaluated the various tribes he toured among according to their industry and ambition. Nevertheless, only those kinds of ambition that fit with a people's appropriate place on an implicit evolutionary scale of development met with his approval. Bradley admired the Kunda people, who had responded enthusiastically to a cotton-growing scheme, but criticized a Chewa chief who bought a motorcar for being a fool (Bradley 1947:75–78, 65–66). By becoming better farmers, the Kunda were responding in an appropriate way. The chief, on the other hand, had developed a craving for European luxuries beyond his appropriate level of development—and his pocketbook.

Because African political development was intended to advance gradually along "traditional" lines, the government showed considerable interest in discovering the traditional political structures of the various tribes in order to stimulate them to evolve appropriately. For example, the government commissioned Gluckman to report on the Lozi political structure, including his recommendations for reforming it. His report, however, carried his cultural promotion of the Lozi too far for the government, which refused to implement the reforms he recommended because of the high expense of paying the numerous traditional officeholders who he thought should be maintained (Brown 1979:536–37).

The Institute's link with the Rhodes-Livingstone Museum fostered other opportunities for cultural promotion. The museum, conveniently located near the major tourist attraction of Victoria Falls, provided a connection with the white public, who may not have had a clear idea of what an anthropologist was, but who understood the value of collections of African curios. RLI anthropologists collected cultural artifacts for the museum and wrote essays for a "material culture" series of booklets for tourists. Indeed, the potential of Northern Rhodesia for tourism led Gluckman to make some of the most imaginative moves in the area of cultural promotion. In 1944, he suggested to the provincial commissioner a scheme for promoting tourism in Barotseland, the home of the Lozi people, his research subjects.

> Like Switzerland, the Africans should export their picturesqueness. Again, Barotse is most suitable here, though I speak without knowledge of other areas. I can see rich tourists being prepared to pay to fly to Mongu for the barge-trip down river with some hunting and fishing. . . . They would enjoy buying curios in situ . . . A levy for the

Native Treasury could be made on each tourist . . . (RLI Manuscripts File: "Gluckman"; Letter from Gluckman to PC Southern Province, March 15, 1944, Institute for African Studies [IAS], Lusaka, Zambia)

In this plan, Gluckman shared something of the development vision of the colonial officer—the Lozi should prosper through culturally appropriate activities such as local crafts and their own "picturesqueness," an approach that Bradley, with his love of Kunda cotton-growing and dislike of chiefs in motorcars, would have understood. The anthropologist, however, gave a contemporary European example for the Lozi to emulate: Swiss exploitation of their own picturesqueness. This perhaps suggests a difference between the colonial officer's development vision and that of the RLI. Bradley's approval was based on the Kunda fitting into the idyllic agrarian type of development vision, coinciding with his favorite view of the landscape. The Chewa chief's mistake, therefore, was to import into the African rural landscape a product of the European city and its advanced civilization—a motorcar. Administrators often laid blame on the city for contaminating the natural course of African evolution. An administrative practice that reflected this view was "rustication," the practice of sending political activists to rural areas as a punishment, and perhaps also as a form of purification.

Although it is not expressed in the preceding quotation, Gluckman's larger view of the Lozi allowed for contemporary urban development. He did no urban research aside from a brief visit to Lozi workers in the gold mines of the South African Rand, but Gluckman always placed rural Barotseland in the context of southern African urbanization and industrialization. He applied to Northern Rhodesia the ideas of the South African historian William Macmillan, who held that South Africa was a single society, racially diverse but economically and socially interdependent (Marks and Macmillan 1989; Saunders 1988). South African anthropologist Isaac Schapera also gave inspiration to Gluckman's view, when he wrote that "the missionary, administrator, trader and labour recruiter must be regarded as factors in the tribal life in the same way as are the chief and the magician." Gluckman quoted this passage in an article based on his earlier fieldwork among the Zulu in South Africa, "Analysis of a Social Situation in Modern Zululand," and he interpreted Schapera to mean that "White personalities have to be studied *in the same way* as Black" in anthropological fieldwork (Gluckman 1940; Gluckman 1968:5–6, emphasis in original).

Indeed, the field that Gluckman studied in his Zulu research included Africans, administrators, and himself as anthropologist, all of whom appear and are analyzed in the resulting article. In the article he also paid close attention to the relative placement of each of these groups during a ceremony for the opening of a new bridge in Zululand, looking at how they defined racial, class, and religiously demarcated spaces and at how individuals moved across the resulting boundaries. It was this South African racial landscape that underlay his view of Northern Rhodesia. And the urban was not far away in this landscape, either in South Africa or in Northern Rhodesia. Gluckman gave urban research a prominent place in the research plans he drew up for the RLI. He perceived Northern Rhodesia as developing toward a situation similar to that in South Africa, in terms of urbanization, industrialization, and segregation. With this in mind he trained the first team of researchers who arrived after World War II, arranging for them to have experiences in South Africa that would prime them to see similar factors at work in Northern Rhodesia. Most of them took courses at the University of Cape Town and met or studied with prominent interpreters of the South African situation—including Schapera. They also visited the African township of Langa with Jack Simons, the first sociologist to do urban research in South Africa. In addition they visited the vibrant, racially mixed Johannesburg suburb of Sophiatown, and some of them had a tour of a gold mine.

Although Gluckman used administrative talk and wore *kabadula*, in the end his analysis of administrators as part of the landscape of Northern Rhodesia caused problems with the colonial government that contributed to his reasons for leaving the field for a university career. Although friction with the administration was an important factor in Gluckman's decision to leave Northern Rhodesia, more important was the opportunity for an academic career—the offer of an Oxford lectureship in 1947. Perhaps his most irritating behavior from the perspective of colonial administrators was revealing that Africans might have a view of administrators and their work. In an article for the South African magazine *Libertas*, Gluckman included a photograph of a Lozi man beside a small wicker tent, with the caption:

> Prefabrication: The tent of the touring official, so important a figure in African life, has inspired this Lozi imitation, decorated in many-coloured designs. (1946:42)

The crucial element in Gluckman's vision of Africa indicating the difference between his view and that of colonial administrators was the presence of the administrator himself in the African field that the anthropologist studied.

It is not pleasant to be made an object of study, and I can only urge District Officers to appreciate that when they say they are more interested in, and do more for, the welfare of the people than the chiefs they must allow themselves to be studied in their role as a most important part of the modern political administration. (Gluckman to Beresford Stooke, Chief Secretary to the Northern Rhodesia Government, "Memorandum on Co-operation between Government and the Rhodes-Livingstone Institute," April 18, 1944 [1/1, SEC 1/126; ANT 4, 16, 19:"Rhodes-Livingstone Institute General, Plan of Research, Minutes of Meetings, 1944–1947," NAZ])

This must have been particularly disturbing to administrators who considered themselves to be the experts on African societies and who now found themselves included with Africans within the scope of another professional group's expertise. Moreover, Gluckman remarked in the same memorandum that the administration should welcome the possibility that the African "should begin to feel that he can use the expert" and cite the "sociologist's knowledge" in arguments with the administration.

Thus, the dislike of being observed and the possibility that Africans might use anthropologists' expert knowledge contributed to the hostility many administrators felt toward the RLI. A hint of this administrative perspective can be found in another RLI anthropologist's observation: "I well remember the surprise with which a District Officer greeted my naive remark that I was studying him too, and I think I was more circumspect thereafter" (Barnes 1967:200).

Landscaping the RLI

By the 1950s, the changing political situation and the RLI's move toward urban research led to still greater differences between administrative and anthropological practice. The difference between administrators' and anthropologists' field practices—as perceived by Africans—became the key factor contributing to a researcher's success or failure in the field. Even in rural fieldwork anthropologists had to distance themselves from colonial practices. Arriving in the 1950s, Ian Cunnison could not imagine any way that being like an administrator would have helped with fieldwork, since at that point it would have involved seeming to take the government's side in relation to the people he was studying (Ian Cunnison, interview, August 1993). In urban fieldwork, the demonstration of difference helped to mold new field practices and create a very different kind of anthropological field.

In the late colonial period, urbanization had gained "at least partial official acceptance." The 1935 strike by Northern Rhodesia's African miners and the general strike wave that hit Africa in the mid-1930s and continued into the 1940s led to dramatic changes in labor and urban policies on the part of the British government (Cooper 1987:250). The mines fluctuated in their commitment to the creation of a permanent urban labor force, with the high price of copper in the postwar period generally leading them to encourage long-term "stabilisation" if not permanent urbanization (Parpart 1983).

Administrative practices, however, changed more slowly than policy. The government maintained a form of the district officers' tour in the cities on the grounds that it was familiar to Africans from village life. When things went wrong, as in the 1935 strike, colonial administrators cited as the "central problem" the lack of personal administrative contact with Africans in the mine compounds of the kind familiar from the rural areas (Epstein 1958:22, 30).

In the wake of the unrest, the colonial government also considered the possibility that social research might be useful for solving urban problems and supported the establishment of an anthropological institute in central Africa. Governor Hubert Young had long wanted to establish a museum for archeological and anthropological exhibits. After the 1935 strike the governor used the argument that societies undergoing rapid social change needed study (Cooper 1987:255). It is possible the strike wave also strengthened the arguments of technocrats within government who, unlike the provincial administrators based in the rural areas, may have looked favorably on the employment of experts like themselves to study these problems. The postwar period was generally a time of experimentation by local governments and the Colonial Office in the use of expert knowledge and the different ways of employing it. This experimentation extended to anthropology and sociology both in the greater numbers of their personnel deployed in Africa relative to other social sciences and in the variety of positions supported—from government sociologists to social science institute researchers to individuals working directly under the Colonial Research Committee.

As scholars have noted, "The success of anthropology in securing CSSRC and other funding during this period may be gauged from any list of the personnel of the institutes, and may be seen in figures for 1956 that show that of 214 British and Commonwealth social scientists then working in Africa, 90 were anthropologists or sociologists" (Lee, cited in Grillo and Rew 1985:13). This must be qualified by the fact that other social scientists, such as economists, were not as easy to attract to these relatively low-paid positions, nor to the hardships of fieldwork and life in the colonies, as were anthropologists. This was partly due to better opportunities for economists in Great Britain and the lower prestige of fieldwork in their profession (Phyllis Deane, interview, December 1990). Externally based economists may have also not been in as much demand by colonial governments, because the Colonial Office provided economic advice and the colonial governments themselves employed agricultural economists. The RLI was unable to recruit an economist, because the person they had in mind received a higher paying job elsewhere (J. Clyde Mitchell, interview, October 1993).

The Colonial Office and the colonial governments carried out their experiments with professional experts cautiously, however, fearing the political implications of the use of expert knowledge. For example, the Colonial Office's plan for a labor department in Northern Rhodesia met with considerable opposition from the government's provincial (mostly rurally based) administrators, though the strike of 1940 finally forced the issue. Even then the administrators and mining companies severely restricted the scope and independence of the new labor officers. The first officers were seconded from the provincial administration itself, and the new department had to agree that these officers would not discuss labor policy with African workers or "become intermediaries between workers and the mines" (Parpart 1983:100).

The treatment of the RLI's urban anthropologists—another potentially troublesome group of experts—paralleled this case in some respects. Like labor experts, anthropologists had developed expertise on another aspect of African life—social organization and culture, areas where their views might clash with those of the administration. Administrators, along with missionaries, were the chief group of experts on African life, with ethnographic study, at least at the level of reports on local customs, being one of the administrator's usual tasks. Thus, anthropologists represented a rival group of experts claiming greater professional credentials for the task and, perhaps even more alarming, the right to look at administration itself as part of the relevant social situation. And, as in the case of the labor officers, Africans might use the results of expert study to challenge government policy, following the anthropologists' example. Despite the anthropologists' sharing of practices with administrators in the early years of the RLI, the rivalry between them as experts on African culture would come to dominate the relationship.

The practices of anthropologists, like those of administrators, had been shaped by the conditions of the rural field. The move to an urban field site brought a number of new forces to bear upon them. From the beginning of urban research, RLI anthropologists felt even greater pressure to conform to local European standards of behavior. With Federation, anthropologists and their African assistants were also subjected to growing pressure from African nationalists and intellectuals.

The urban work began during the directorship of Elizabeth Colson (1948–51). At that time the RLI headquarters moved from Livingstone to Lusaka, within range of the Copperbelt towns that became the main focus of the urban research. Before he left Northern Rhodesia in 1947, Gluckman had ensured that the RLI had a mandate for urban research from the CSSRC and the Northern Rhodesia government. Some of the funding from the CSSRC was earmarked for urban research, and the mining companies—through the urging of the prominent South African liberal, Rheinalt Jones—had also contributed to this project and, thus, had a stake in its success (Board of Trustees Minutes for the meeting on August 25, 1947:CO 927/64/2; PRO). The chief problem that remained was to find an anthropologist or sociologist willing and able to do urban fieldwork.

In 1950, A. L. Epstein received a Colonial Research Fellowship to conduct a study of African urban courts in Northern Rhodesia, which he carried out in the Copperbelt town of Ndola. This fellowship meant that he was directly responsible to the CSSRC, but he also associated with researchers at the RLI, sometimes attending their conferences. After his court study he became a research officer at the Institute and began a study of African urban organization in Luanshya, another Copperbelt town. J. Clyde Mitchell, who had already done a rural study for the RLI in Nyasaland, agreed to put off his plans for an academic career to become senior sociologist of the RLI in 1950 and mount the social survey of the Copperbelt, which he started in 1951. He continued the work while director of the Institute from 1952 to 1955. Mitchell lived in Lusaka during his directorship, but visited the Copperbelt regularly to direct the survey. Epstein lived in Luanshya for the duration of his study there. After Mitchell left in 1956, urban research of various kinds continued under the later directors.

RLI researchers had few concrete precedents to follow for adapting rural research practices to an urban setting. For example, the status of the participant-observer method customarily employed by functionalists came into question in racially segregated urban areas. Researchers could not simply join in the activities of their subjects in places where their behavior could be observed by other whites. Neither could they hope to blend into the background and watch the natural functioning of urban black society when their very presence violated the strictures of segregation and constituted a political stand in the eyes of local whites. Language presented another difficulty unfamiliar in rural areas, where research was usually restricted to a single ethnic group. RLI anthropologists chose "town Bemba" for the Copperbelt research, but the choice of any particular language would have placed them in a position of greater distance from speakers of other languages. Moreover, their proficiency in any local language might also have been resented by whites in positions of authority in the mines, most of whom used "Fanagalo" (also called "Chilapalapa"), a "patois of Zulu and English evolved in South Africa [that] had become the language of the mines in Southern Africa" and that was comprised mainly of commands (Parpart 1983:62). Part of the difficulty of speaking a single language in a town setting could be overcome through the employment of African research assistants from different tribes.

Other things besides language differences contributed to making the researcher's dependence on local assistants greater in towns than in rural areas. The RLI also supported two different approaches to urban research: individual qualitative studies focusing on single themes and large quantitative social surveys. The latter required a team of African assistants trained in survey methods and often working autonomously.

African nationalists and intellectuals during the Federation period applied pressure on the Institute through these assistants. Africans on the RLI survey team found research at times involved harassment, when their research subjects accused them of being "Federal agentsi" and threatened to beat them (J. C. Chiwale, interview, January 1992). As intellectuals with political beliefs of their own, the African assistants also applied pressure on the Institute. The Institute found itself in a difficult position during the two days of prayer called by Congress to protest the coming of Federation in 1953. Assistants in the field working on the urban surveys participated in this strike without repercussion, arguing that for reasons of statistical accuracy working on the survey on those days would be counterproductive. As the head of the team, Simon Katilungu, explained, "it should be noted that the leading Congress members and a number of followers did not go to work on the 'Two Days of Prayer.' We refrained from conducting interviews on these two days at Bwacha as this would prejudice our survey" (Report on Work Done During Period 23rd March to 17th April, 1953; The Rhodes-Livingstone Institute, Broken Hill, 28th April, 1953:JCM 24/3).

At the RLI headquarters, however, the situation was different. Government informed the administrative secretary that it was planning to dismiss African employees who failed to come to work on the days of prayer and implied that she should follow the same policy. To back this up, they planned an official visit to the Institute during the strike (RLI Management File: "Mitchell"—Letter from M. McCulloch to Mitchell, April 17, 1953).

The assistants' political loyalties, however, more often helped the Institute to continue its research in the urban areas. Assistants went in first to talk to nationalist or union groups about the proposed research, smoothing the way for the survey teams. RLI researchers were careful to obtain formal permission for their activities from these groups. And despite the efforts of government security to clean out activists from the RLI staff, most research assistants actually carried on political work while employed by the Institute, sometimes with the help of the researchers (Chiwale, interview, January 1992; A. L. Epstein, interview, December 1990). Ultimately, pressures from both sides transformed RLI fieldwork practices. In response to the color bar, anthropologists grew more dependent on African assistants for fieldwork in urban areas. Nationalist pressures also led to greater dependence on assistants who were themselves political activists, giving legitimacy to the research in the eyes of other Africans.

But in terms of fieldwork the research assistants did not share the mystique of "getting under canvas" that anthropologists and colonial officers shared. For urban Africans, fastidious standards of dress and behavior indicated status in the "smart" 1950s and were incompatible with many aspects of the anthropologists' rural field practice. As part of an emerging group of African intellectuals, the assistants often dressed in suits in contrast to the anthropologists' more casual appearance; and shorts, much less administrative-style *kabadula,* were out of the question for political reasons, particularly for urban work.

Indeed, the friction between urban and rural styles of fieldwork and views of the field that existed among research assistants, administrators, and anthropologists came into particularly sharp focus at the RLI headquarters in Lusaka. Here were located the Institute's offices and library, plus houses for researchers, assistants, and African clerks and cleaners, built on the outskirts of Lusaka near the African secondary school at Munali. As a cost-cutting measure the government had insisted the main building follow the blueprints standardly used for *boma* construction. The researchers' and director's houses stretched in two arcs out from the front of the main building, while research assistants' and African staff quarters occupied the rear.

Tensions over the physical—and racial—landscape of the RLI headquarters arose during the directorship of Henry Fosbrooke (1956–60), who irritated many of the white researchers and black assistants with his administrative mannerisms and practices. Although Fosbrooke had favored African majority rule and eventually resigned over a disagreement with the colonial government, he was always seen by government administrators and the mining companies as someone they could work with. This was because he was an administrator-ethnographer, and he had been employed both as a government sociologist and colonial officer in Tanganyika (Henry Fosbrooke, interview, January 1992). There he worked in soil conservation, an activity that involved reshaping the landscape and its use, and that could also stir up local resentment.

Early in his career in Tanganyika he had "caught the Maasai bug" and had identified closely with the people he administered (Peter Rigby, interview, March 1993). But his social habits in Lusaka were staunchly European, and when he entertained Africans at the RLI's headquarters, it was in formal European style—inviting African secondary school boys for tea and allowing his children to play tennis with them—though these, too, were controversial actions at the time (Fosbrooke, interview, January 1992; C, Lusaka, interview, August 1991). Activities such as these, however, fitted well with the civilizing mission of the colonial administration. Its practices focused on the maintenance of authority and the training of youth to fit into a hierarchical system, and their roots can be found in the British public school on which the early colonial service was partly modeled (Kirk-Greene 1987:81–113). An evolutionary model with implications for racial discrimination underlay the hierarchical structure of the public school as well as the colonial administration's paternalistic practices.

This administrative style, however, offended some at the RLI—both black and white—who were accustomed to the more collegial, informal, and egalitarian style of earlier directors, such as Mitchell and Colson. Anthropologists sometimes referred to him disparagingly as a mere "ethnographer," indicating that their differences with him were part of the more general struggle over the use of expertise in the late colonial period. And his work policy of "interchangeability without loss of status" was deeply resented by the research assistants. It meant that they had to take on nonresearch jobs—including gardening tasks—which represented a loss of professional self-esteem, even though it did not involve a lowering of pay. A white anthropologist, who had just returned from research in Nyasaland at the time, understood this resentment and would stalk about the Institute grounds observing in a loud voice that "Bwana DC says you must be his garden boys!" (Lukhero, interview, October 1991). It is ironic that these landscaping duties were intended to change the Institute's appearance so that visiting Africans would not be offended by its colonial-style architecture (Henry Fosbrooke 1977:320; Fosbrooke, interview, January 1992).

The researchers were even more critical of Fosbrooke's decision to allocate funds to build a large new director's house at the back of the Institute, which some of them referred to as "Fosbrooke's Palace." Along with a tennis court, the house had a garden in the back and a Scottish-type upstairs sitting room with a view of the nearby bush. The garden had an African-style thatched summerhouse framed by large trees, which was used for outdoor entertaining.

The director's house and garden expressed several themes of colonial landscape aesthetics. The inclusion of elements of rural landscape within an urban setting was typical of European housing styles in Africa, and the views from the house resonated with those rural views described by Bradley. The view of the still-wild bush surrounding Lusaka would have been reminiscent of the view from an administrator's *boma* in a rural district. The thatched summerhouse framed by trees in the garden echoed the wild yet productive scenes described by Bradley, with a picturesque African dwelling standing in for the village framed—and, in a sense, possessed—by the manorial viewer. Even the tennis court spoke of colonial administrative values, for rough packed earth tennis courts could sometimes be found at the remotest *bomas,* as well as in the more spacious European gardens in the cities. The tropical hygiene of the time recommended that Europeans participate in tennis or other vigorous sports on a daily basis in order to maintain health in the debilitating climate, and this activity played an important role in Europeans' distinctive placement with respect to Africans in the tropical landscape.

Conclusion

Anthropologists, administrators, and African research assistants held contradictory—as well as overlapping—views of fieldwork and the field in Northern Rhodesia. The differences and the similarities in their views depended on how they were themselves placed in the racial landscape and how they chose to place others. Administrators saw a landscape of large rural areas in need of development but in danger of contamination from the towns, and even when recognizing the unavoidable effects of rapid change, they idealized a more natural and slower evolution for their African subjects. African research assistants moved through an urbanized and politicized landscape, recognizing and pressing for change even while working for white employers and facilitating fieldwork that shared practices with colonial administration. They often saw and explained that fieldwork as part of a modernizing and improving project and certainly used their own African nationalist political connections to get the work done. Anthropologists also moved in this difficult landscape, adapting the practices of rural fieldwork—if not always its ethos—to an urban environment with the considerable help of their assistants.

For each group the shape of the landscape depended on the practices that went into constructing it. Crucial to differences between anthropologists and administrators were their different relations with their African assistants. At the RLI headquarters, anthropologists had fostered relatively collegial relations with the research assistants, while Fosbrooke attempted a return to a more colonial administrative pattern. Indeed, the landscape of the Institute headquarters itself revealed the contradictions that existed in colonial anthropology in Northern Rhodesia, balanced between the larger forces of African nationalism and apartheid. Smartly dressed assistants engaged in noisy discussions about the implications of social research presented a striking picture of the breakdown of colonial relations. But despite the landscaping that softened the edges of the *boma* design of the Institute's main building, the windows of the director's house framed a nostalgic view of the colonial landscape.

REFERENCES

Anderson, David. 1984. "Depression, Dust Bowl, Demography and Drought: The Colonial State and Soil Conservation in East Africa during the 1930s." *African Affairs* 83 (332): 321–43.

Anderson, David, and Richard Grove, eds. 1987. *Conservation in Africa: People, Policies, and Practice.* Cambridge: Cambridge University Press.

Apthorpe, Raymond, ed. 1961. *Social Research and Community Development.* Based on the 15th Conference of the Rhodes-Livingstone Institute for Social Research, Lusaka, Northern Rhodesia.

Barnes, J. A. 1967. "Some Ethical Problems of Modern Fieldwork." In D. G. Jongmans and P. C. W. Gutkind, eds., *Anthropologists in the Field.* Assen, The Netherlands: Van Gorcum.

Barrell, John. 1980. *The Dark Side of the Landscape: The Rural Poor in English Painting, 1730–1840.* Cambridge: Cambridge University Press.

Beinart, William. 1984a. "Soil Erosion, Conservationism and Ideas about Development: A Southern African Exploration, 1900–1960." *Journal of Southern African Studies* 11 (1): 52–83.

———. 1984b. "Agricultural Planning and the Late Colonial Technical Imagination: The Lower Shire Valley in Malawi, 1940–1960." In *Malawi: An Alternative Pattern of Development*, 93–148. Edinburgh: University of Edinburgh Centre of African Studies.

Beinart, William, and Colin Bundy. 1987. *Hidden Struggles in Rural South Africa: Politics and Popular Movements in the Transkei and Eastern Cape, 1890–1930.* London: James Currey.

Bermingham, Ann. 1986. *Landscape and Ideology: The English Rustic Tradition, 1740–1860.* Berkeley: University of California Press.

Bradley, Kenneth. 1947 [1943]. *The Diary of a District Officer.* New York: St. Martin's Press.

Brown, Richard. 1973. "Anthropology and Colonial Rule: Godfrey Wilson and the Rhodes-Livingstone Institute, Northern Rhodesia." In Talal Asad, ed., *Anthropology and the Colonial Encounter*, 173–92. London: Ithaca Press.

———. 1979. "Passages in the Life of a White Anthropologist: Max Gluckman in Northern Rhodesia." *Journal of African History* 20:525–41.

Clifford, James. 1988. "On Ethnographic Authority." In *The Predicament of Culture: Twentieth-Century Ethnography, Literature and Art.* Cambridge, MA: Harvard University Press.

Cooper, Frederick. 1987. *On the African Waterfront: Urban Disorder and the Transformation of Work in Colonial Mombasa.* New Haven: Yale University Press.

Curtin, Philip. 1964. *The Image of Africa: British Ideas and Action, 1790–1850.* Madison: University of Wisconsin Press.
Epstein, A. L. 1958. *Politics in an Urban African Community.* Manchester: Manchester University Press.
Fosbrooke, Henry. 1977. "From Lusaka to Salisbury, 1956–60." *African Social Research* 24:319–25.
Gluckman, Max. 1940. "Analysis of a Social Situation in Modern Zululand." *Bantu Studies* 14:1–30.
———. 1946. "Human Laboratory across the Zambesi." *Libertas* 6 (4) (March): 38–49.
———. 1968 [1949]. "Malinowski's Sociological Theories." *Rhodes-Livingstone Papers* 16:1–28.
Grillo, Ralph. 1985. "Applied Anthropology in the 1980s: Retrospect and Prospect." In *Social Anthropology and Development Policy,* ed. Ralph Grillo and Alan Rew. ASA Monographs 23. London: Tavistock Publications.
Grillo, Ralph, and Alan Rew, eds. 1985. *Social Anthropology and Development Policy.* London: Tavistock Publications (ASA Monographs 23).
Husbands, Winston. n.d.. "Nature, Society and the Origin of Tourism at Victoria Falls (Zambia)." Ryerson Polytechnic University, Ontario, Canada.
Kirk-Greene, Anthony. 1987. "Imperial Administration and the Athletic Imperative: The Case of the District Officer in Africa." In William J. Baker and James A. Mangan, eds., *Sport in Africa: Essays in Social History.* New York: Africana Publishing Company.
Kuklick, Henrika. 1989. *The Imperial Bureaucrat: The Colonial Administrative Service in the Gold Coast, 1920–1939.* Stanford: The Hoover Institution.
———. 1991. *The Savage Within: The Social History of British Anthropology, 1885–1945.* Cambridge: Cambridge University Press.
Liu, Alan. 1989. *Wordsworth: The Sense of History.* Stanford: Stanford University Press.
Mackenzie, John M. 1987. "Hunting in Eastern and Central Africa in the Late Nineteenth Century, with Special Reference to Zimbabwe." In William J. Baker and James A. Mangan, eds., *Sport in Africa: Essays in Social History.* New York: Africana Publishing Company.
Marks, Shula, and Hugh Macmillan, eds. 1989. *Africa and Empire: W.M. Macmillan, Historian and Social Critic.* London: Temple Smith.
McCracken, John. 1982. "Experts and Expertise in Colonial Malawi." *African Affairs* 81:101–16.
Mitchell, J. Clyde. 1956. "The Kalela Dance." *Rhodes-Livingstone Papers* 27.
Pang, Alex Soojung-Kim. 1991. "Spheres of Interest: Imperialism, Culture, and Practice in British Solar Eclipse Expeditions, 1860–1914." Ph.D. dissertation, University of Pennsylvania.
Parpart, Jane. 1983. *Labor and Capital on the African Copperbelt.* Philadelphia: Temple University Press.
Ranger, Terence. n.d. "Making Zimbabwean Landscapes: Painters, Prospectors and Priests." National Gallery of Zimbabwe Lecture, St. Antony's College, Oxford, Great Britain.
———. 1985. *Peasant Consciousness and Guerrilla War in Zimbabwe.* London: James Curry.
Rudwick, Martin J. S. 1976. "The Emergence of a Visual Language for Geological Science, 1760–1830." *History of Science* 14:149–95.

Saunders, Christopher. 1988. *The Making of the South African Past: Major Historians on Race and Class.* Cape Town: David Philip.

Schumaker, Lynette. 1988. "Tropical Garden and Ocean Waste: Darwin's View of Tropical Landscapes on the Voyage of the H.M.S. Beagle." M.A. thesis, Michigan State University.

Smith, Bernard. 1985. *European Vision and the South Pacific.* New Haven: Yale University Press.

Stocking, George W., Jr. 1983. "The Ethnographer's Magic: Fieldwork in British Social Anthropology from Tylor to Malinowski." In George W. Stocking Jr., ed., *Observers Observed: Essays on Ethnographic Fieldwork (History of Anthropology,* vol. 1), 70–120.

Contributors

Nicholas B. Dirks is Professor of Anthropology and History at Columbia University in New York. He is the author of *The Hollow Crown: Ethnohistory of an Indian Kingdom* (1987) and the editor of *Colonialism and Culture* (1992) and has written numerous articles on the history of anthropology of India. He is currently completing a manuscript to be entitled *Castes of Mind: Colonial History and Postcolonial Society in India.*

Curtis M. Hinsley is Regents' Professor of History at Northern Arizona University. He has written widely on the history of American anthropology, including *From Site to Sight: Anthropology, Photography, and the Power of Imagery* (1986), and *The Smithsonian and the American Indian: Making a Moral Anthropology in Victorian America* (1995). With archaeologist David R. Wilcox, he is currently writing a multivolume history of the Hemenway Southwestern Archaeological Expedition (1886–89); the first volume, *The Southwest in the American Imagination,* appeared in 1996. He lives in Flagstaff, Arizona, with his wife, historian Victoria L. Enders.

Peter Pels lectures at the Research Centre for Religion and Society, University of Amsterdam, and is a research fellow of the Department of Anthropology, University of Leiden. He edited, with Lorraine Nencel, *Constructing Knowledge: Authority and Critique in Social Science* (1991) and, with Oscar Salemink, a special issue of *History and Anthropology* (1994) entitled *Colonial Ethnographies.* Further, he is the author of *A Politics of Presence: Contacts between Missionaries and Waluguru in Late Colonial Tanganyika* (1999) and "The Pidginization of Luguru Politics" (*American Ethnologist* 24, 1996). He is currently working on the anthropology and history of elections in 1950s Tanganyika and the history of anthropology and occultism in nineteenth-century Britain.

William Pietz is coeditor with Emily Apter of *Fetishism as Cultural Discourse* (1993) and has written essays on the history of the idea of fetishism. He lives in Los Angeles.

Gloria Goodwin Raheja teaches in the Department of Anthropology at the University of Minnesota. Her publications include *The Poison in the Gift: Ritual, Prestation and the Dominant Caste in a North Indian Village*

(1988) and *Listen to the Heron's Words: Reimagining Gender and Kinship in North India* (with Ann Grodzins Gold; 1994). She is currently writing a book on the politics of colonial ethnography in nineteenth-century India.

Oscar Salemink studied anthropology at the University of Nijmegen, doing Ph.D. research on the highland minorities of Vietnam. He has been attached to various Dutch universities since, besides working as a consultant for international organizations and NGOs. His publications include "Mois and Maquis" (*History of Anthropology* 1991) and "The King of Fire and Vietnamese Ethnic Policy in the Central Highlands" (in Kampe and McCaskill, eds., *Development of Domestication?* 1997), and he edited a special issue of *History and Anthropology* with Peter Pels entitled *Colonial Ethnographies* (1994). He currently works with the Ford Foundation in Vietnam as program officer for social sciences and humanities.

Henk Schulte Nordholt is assistant professor in the Departments of Anthropology and Modern Asian History at the University of Amsterdam. His major interests are Indonesian history, the interplay between local history and larger processes of (colonial) state formation, and the anthropology of colonial rule. His publications include *State, Village, and Ritual in Bali: A Historical Perspective* (1991), "Leadership and the Limits of Political Control: A Balinese 'Response' to Clifford Geertz," *Social Anthropology* 1 (1993), *The Spell of Power: A History of Balinese Politics, 1650–1940* (1996), and an edited volume, *Outward Appearances: Dressing State and Society in Indonesia* (1997).

Lyn Schumaker is a lecturer at the Wellcome Unit for the History of Medicine, Centre for the History of Science, Technology and Medicine, University of Manchester. Her background is interdisciplinary in anthropology and history of science. She recently completed her first book, *Africanizing Anthropology: Fieldwork, Networks, and the Making of Cultural Knowledge in Central Africa* (forthcoming).

Patrick Wolfe is Victoria Research Fellow in the Europe-Australia Institute at Victoria University of Technology. He has lectured and published on race and colonialism, the history of anthropology, and Aboriginal-European encounters. He is a council member of the Institute of Postcolonial Studies, 78–80 Curzon Street, North Melbourne, Victoria 3051, Australia, and one of the editors of its monograph series, "Writing Past Colonialism." Wolfe's book *Settler Colonialism and the Transformation of Anthropology: The Politics and Poetics of an Ethnographic Event* develops and extends the present article. He is currently working on a history of colonial discourse, to be entitled "Deep Genealogies."

Name Index

Aborigines Protection Society, 31, 32, 33, 42, 67, 109
Asante kingdom, 65, 66, 71, 72, 73, 75. *See also* Gold Coast (Ghana)
Asiatic Society of Bengal, 27, 36, 84, 85, 86, 92, 93, 103, 104, 105, 106, 109

Bachofen, Johann Jakob, 201, 226
Bali, 1, 14, 27, 44, 241, 243, 244, 247, 248, 252, 254, 274, 277
Bateson, Gregory, 27, 44, 241, 269, 270, 272, 275, 276
Belo, Jane, 241, 269, 270, 275
Benin (City), 53, 68, 72, 73, 75
Bentham, Jeremy, 90, 100
Bertillon, Alphonse, 165, 166
Bingley, A. H., 139, 140, 147
Boas, Franz, 3, 38, 188
Bosman, Willem, 9, 10, 11, 12, 15, 16, 35, 60, 61, 69
Boulbet, Jean, 305, 306, 310, 313
Bourke, John Gregory, 44, 181, 182, 183, 184, 185, 186, 187, 189, 193, 194
Briggs, John, 98, 99, 100, 103, 109
Brosses, Charles de, 11, 12, 15, 57, 58, 59, 60
Buchanan, Francis Hamilton, 88, 89, 91, 102
Bureau of American Ethnology, 26, 36, 38, 184, 188, 189
Burton, Sir Richard, 21, 26, 54, 66, 70
Buxton, Thomas Fowell, 42, 67, 68

Caldwell, Rev. Robert, 98, 99, 100, 105, 106, 107
Campbell, Sir George, 82, 83, 84, 99, 100–107, 108, 109, 110
Chaube, Ram Gharib, 126, 127, 130, 131

Colonial Social Science Research Council (CSSRC), 342, 344
Colson, Elizabeth, 344, 347
Comte, Auguste, 11, 12, 59, 60
Condominas, George, 13, 34, 44, 284, 286, 290, 300, 302, 305, 307, 308, 309, 313, 314, 315
Cook, Captain James, 18, 23, 200, 217, 278
Crawfurd, John, 23, 110, 243
Crooke, William, 43, 122, 123, 125, 126, 127, 130, 131, 132, 133, 138, 140, 143, 145, 146
Cushing, Frank Hamilton, 44, 184, 188, 189, 190, 192, 193, 194
Cuvier, Baron Georges, 88, 96

Dalton, Colonel Edward, 104, 105
Dalzel, Archibald, 59, 64
Damsté, H. T., 243, 258, 268
D'Argenlieu, High Commissioner Thierry, 298, 300
Darwin, Charles, 98, 202
Decoux, Gouverneur-General, 295, 297, 310
Dournes, Jacques, 290, 299, 305, 306, 307, 310, 311, 312, 313, 315
Durkheim, Emile, 38, 205

East India Company, 23, 24, 86, 89, 140, 144, 176
Ecole Française d'Extrême-Orient (EFEO), 37, 286, 287, 288, 289, 291, 292, 294, 297, 301, 302, 304, 305, 307, 310
Ethnological Society of London, 32, 42, 82, 98, 105, 107, 108, 109

Fison, Lorimer, 36, 204
Folk-Lore Society, 122, 135, 210

355

Fort William College, 36, 91, 140, 143, 144
Fosbrooke, Henry, 335, 346, 347, 348
Frazer, Sir James, 36, 170, 172, 207, 211, 212, 214, 215, 231
Friederich, R. T., 243, 244, 247, 248, 249, 251

Galliéni, Marshall Joseph, 282, 283
Galton, Sir Francis, 29, 105, 168
Geertz, Clifford, 27, 44, 241, 242
Ghana. *See* Gold Coast (Ghana)
Gilchrist, John Borthwick, 141, 142, 143, 144, 145, 146, 148
Gillen, Francis James, 36, 196, 197, 198, 202–4, 208–16, 224, 226–31
Gluckman, Max, 5, 328, 330, 335, 336, 337, 338, 339, 340, 341, 344
Gold Coast (Ghana), 66, 67, 69, 71, 76, 77
Griaule, Marcel, 283, 284, 301, 309
Guilleminet, Paul, 289, 291, 292, 297, 302, 303, 304, 305, 311, 312

Haddon, Alfred Cort, 35, 36, 37, 163
Haileybury College, 36, 87, 91, 100
Hartland, Edwin Sydney, 206, 207, 208, 209, 210, 211, 212, 214, 215, 226
Hodgson, Brian Houghton, 84, 91–100, 101, 103, 104, 106, 107, 109, 110
Hooker, Joseph, 92, 98
Hunter, William Wilson, 98, 100, 106, 143
Huxley, Thomas Henry, 82, 84, 98, 108, 109, 110

Ibbetson, Denzil, 117, 123, 132, 133, 134, 137, 138, 140
Institut d'Ethnologie, 286, 301, 305
International African Institute, 31, 38

Jones, Sir William, 27, 82, 84, 85, 86, 104, 108
Jouin, Bernard, 301, 304, 311, 312

Kingsley, Mary, 12, 13, 14
Korn, Victor, 242, 249, 251, 259, 262, 263, 264, 268, 269, 272, 273, 274, 275, 276, 277

Lafont, Pierre-Bernard, 305, 306, 309
Leenhardt, Maurice, 283, 284, 301
Leroi-Gourhan, André, 301, 308
Lévi-Strauss, Claude, 188, 227, 305, 309
Lévy, Paul, 286, 288, 307
Lévy-Bruhl, Lucien, 197, 284, 286, 287, 301, 309
Liefrinck, F. A., 244, 245, 246, 247, 248, 249, 251, 252, 254, 256, 262, 268
Luard, Charles Eckford, 123, 146
Lubbock, Sir John, 59, 201

Macaulay, Sir Thomas Babington, 87, 94, 97
MacCarthy, Sir Charles, 65, 66, 67, 71, 72
MacKenzie, Colin, 24, 25, 89
Madras, 98, 99, 108, 159, 160, 161, 162, 164, 165, 167, 170, 172
Maine, Sir Henry Sumner, 28, 57, 102, 104
Malinowski, Bronislaw, 2, 6, 7, 23, 31, 36, 38, 39, 40, 43, 197, 227, 308
Malthus, Thomas, 89, 91, 94, 202, 203
Marees, Pieter de, 9, 10, 12, 16
Marx, Karl, 12, 60, 61, 62, 70, 230
Maurice, Albert-Marie, 292, 302, 304, 315
Mauss, Marcel, 37, 38, 286, 301, 305, 309
McLennan, John, 201, 202, 203, 205, 208, 226
Mead, Margaret, 27, 36, 44, 241, 267, 269, 270, 271, 275, 276, 277
Mill, James, 85, 86, 87, 88, 90, 102
Millar, John, 200, 201, 202, 216
Mitchell, J. Clyde, 335, 343, 344, 345, 347
Morgan, Lewis Henry, 201, 226
Mullaly, Frederick S., 159, 160, 161, 162, 167, 172
Müller, Friedrich Max, 59, 84, 95, 96, 104

Nepal, 92, 93, 94, 95, 97, 99, 100, 106, 108
Ner, Marcel, 291, 297, 299, 302, 304
Nigeria, 63, 64, 66, 69, 77, 79

Oldham, C.E.A.W., 124, 125, 135, 136, 137, 138, 142, 145

Powell, John Wesley, 36, 183, 184, 188, 189
Prichard, James Cowles, 58, 96, 109
Punjab, 90, 101, 102, 104, 107, 117, 118, 122, 133, 138, 143

Radcliffe-Brown, Alred Reginald, 6, 37, 40
Raffles, Sir Thomas Stamford, 23, 243
Rattray, Richard Sutherland, 72, 73
Rhodes-Livingstone Institute (RLI), 45, 328, 329–30, 333–38, 340–48
Risley, Herbert Hope, 35, 36, 43, 100, 106–7, 122–23, 128–32, 136, 161, 163, 166, 170, 175
Rivers, William Halse, 7, 36, 37, 38, 162, 172
Rockefeller Foundation, 7, 31, 38
Roebuck, Captain Thomas, 143, 144, 145, 146, 148
Royal Anthropological Institute, 107, 122

Sabatier, Leopold, 284, 286, 287, 289, 291, 297, 300, 302, 313

Sierra Leone, 61, 65, 67
Sikkim, 95, 98, 108
Sinclair, Sir John, 19, 89, 90
Smithsonian Institution, 183, 188, 190
Spencer, Herbert, 204, 205, 208
Spencer, William Baldwin, 36, 196–99, 202–3, 209–16, 223–24, 226–32
Spies, Walter, 266, 270, 271, 273, 275
Stirling, Edward Charles, 212, 213, 214, 215, 229, 230, 231, 232

Temple, Richard Carnac, 36, 37, 43, 102, 104, 122, 124, 125, 127, 128, 143, 145
Thomason, Sir James, 100, 101, 102
Thurston, Edgar, 157, 162–77
Traill, George William, 91, 92, 93, 94, 98, 100
Tylor, Edward Burnett, 11, 12, 36, 185, 201, 204, 205, 206, 212, 226

Vollenhoven, Cornelis van, 245, 246

Williams, Sir Monier, 142, 144
Wilson, Godfrey, 330, 335, 336
Wilson, Horace Hayman, 85, 86, 87, 143, 144, 145, 146, 148

Subject Index

aboriginal, 32, 103, 106, 181, 182, 183, 193, 198, 221, 223, 229, 231, 309
   tribes of Australia, 200, 202, 208, 209, 219
   tribes of India, 100, 105, 110
aboriginality, 83, 84, 96, 99–100, 105–6, 224, 227, 230
   politics of, 96, 97, 99, 108–11
aborigine(s), 82, 92, 93, 94, 95, 97, 98, 99, 102, 109, 110, 204, 212, 213, 222, 224, 225, 226, 228, 230
academic. *See* anthropology (-ical)
adat, 23, 27, 246, 248, 252, 253, 259, 262, 267–69, 276, 277
administration (-ive), 7, 21, 22, 26–29, 37, 86, 90, 97, 110, 138, 244, 251, 255, 260, 262, 263, 264, 268, 283, 286, 288, 291, 293, 296, 297, 298, 303, 331, 347, 348
administrators, 2, 8, 12–14, 33, 37–38, 76, 77, 119, 120, 122, 124, 125, 131, 134, 157, 181, 242, 244–48, 254, 257, 261, 265, 266, 269, 272, 274, 275, 278, 290, 302, 326, 327, 331–32, 337, 339, 340, 342–43
advocacy, 96, 110, 335
American Civil War, 32, 181, 182, 184
Andaman(ese), 37, 122
anglicism, 31, 84, 87, 94, 95, 99, 101
animism, 12, 60, 130, 204–7, 215, 216
anthropology (-ical), 9, 16, 37, 122, 342
   academic, 5, 7, 9, 241 (*see also* professional(ism))
   applied, 2, 6, 37–39, 328
   armchair, 34, 108
   of colonialism, vii, 40
   complicity with colonialism, 5, 6, 45, 199
   evolutionary, 197–200, 202, 203, 205–6, 208, 211, 216, 220, 225–28, 287, 297, 334
   history of, vii, 1–7, 14, 22, 24, 39, 40–45, 84, 174–76, 197, 283, 284, 327, 328
   practical, 40, 41, 45, 163, 308
   pure, 2–9, 34–39, 40
Anthropology and the Colonial Encounter, vii, 5, 6
anthropometry, 1, 15, 21, 29, 35, 98, 162–68, 176, 177
archive, 173–77
ars apodemica. *See* art, of travel
art, 264, 265, 266, 275, 282
   of government, 15–17, 41, 45
   of travel, 15–17, 41, 89
Arunta tribe (Australia), 196, 197, 198, 210–16, 226–29
Aryan, 82, 88, 95–96, 98–99, 103, 107, 110, 126, 164
assimilation, 199, 222, 223, 225–26, 227–28, 230–31
authentic, 128, 131, 227, 302

Bhil tribe (India), 94, 96, 99, 106
biopolitics, 29, 111
body (-ies), 29, 35, 83, 84–90, 96, 101, 106, 110, 168, 169, 173, 177
Brahman(ism), 91, 93, 94, 107, 118, 126, 130, 132, 138, 139, 140, 164
bureaucratic, 246, 249, 251, 263, 276, 277, 278, 296, 298
   reproduction, 44, 176, 241, 242, 246, 268, 275, 296

caste, 15, 22, 43, 83, 99, 102, 103–7, 110, 117–48, 157–58, 159, 160, 161, 162, 163, 164, 166, 167, 168, 169, 171, 173–74, 175, 176, 177, 247, 248–51, 252, 258, 268, 277

census, 18, 26, 27, 32, 58, 89, 101, 102, 119, 122, 128, 133, 143, 252, 337
Christian(ity), 11, 22, 187, 230, 263, 267
citizen(ship), 3, 29, 30, 84, 99, 100, 222, 225
civilization, 42, 55–57, 63, 67–68, 83, 87, 88, 102, 106, 107, 110, 185, 209, 224, 334
classification, 15, 17–19, 25, 26, 83, 88, 90, 93, 97, 99, 101, 102, 105, 106, 107, 108, 123, 146, 168, 174, 176, 225, 228, 283, 285, 286, 289, 292, 298, 309. *See also* ethnicization; tribal(ization)
coevalness, 4, 17, 227
colonial administration(s). *See* administration (-ive)
colonial administrator(s). *See* administrators
colonial(ism), 6, 7, 20, 28, 36, 43, 215, 241
   discourse, 20, 24, 26, 27, 181
   modern, 15, 16, 27, 29, 30, 31
commodity (form), 10, 11, 61, 66, 71, 155, 194. *See also* fetishism
commonplace(s), rethorical, 3, 13, 14, 15, 20, 22, 23, 25, 28, 41, 44, 83, 158
communism, 287, 296, 316
complicity. *See* anthropology (-ical)
conquest, 4, 24, 57, 68, 71, 72, 174, 176, 282
contact, 4, 13, 22, 27, 227, 229, 230
conversion, 4, 77, 83, 99, 100, 106, 108, 226, 227, 243
coproduction, 3, 4, 13, 20, 34. *See also* coevalness
counterinsurgency, 5, 6, 26, 39, 41, 310, 315, 319, 321
coutumier. *See* law
crime, 90, 134, 168, 173
criminal castes and tribes, 29, 43, 120, 133, 135, 158, 159–61, 165, 167, 168
cultural, 156, 190, 192, 225, 228. *See also* relativism
culturalism, 38, 177
culture, 19, 154, 157, 158, 178, 222, 243, 306

debt, 60, 61, 63, 69, 70, 72, 76, 77, 78, 79
   monetary, 56, 57, 61, 62, 63, 70, 74, 78
decolonization, 3, 328, 334. *See also* national (-ism, -ity)
degeneration, 204, 243, 266
development, 31, 33, 38, 39, 40, 41, 45, 328, 331, 333, 334, 337, 338, 339, 348
discipline, 24, 25, 31, 32, 85
   academic, 2, 5–8, 23, 24, 34, 39, 40, 41, 45, 156, 174–76 (*see also* anthropology (-ical), history of)
   colonial, 29, 31, 118, 119, 121, 122, 135, 137, 140
   military, 25, 93, 131, 285
Dravidian, 99, 106, 109. *See also* Kolarian; Tamulian
dualism, 27, 28, 76, 253
Dutch (Leiden) Indology, 36, 38, 269
dyadic, 3, 7, 40, 41

education, 30, 31, 83, 87, 90, 94, 95, 98, 100, 101, 109, 183, 263, 264, 287, 292
empiricism, 35, 85, 86, 88
Enlightenment, 11, 16, 18, 59, 60, 174
entextualization. *See* textualization
essence, 8, 9, 11, 13, 15, 27, 28, 160, 252, 254, 295
essentialization, 4, 5, 9–15, 30, 32, 39, 93, 103, 105, 132, 137, 140, 143, 144, 177
ethnicization, 31, 93, 285, 292, 294, 297, 298, 320, 321
ethnocide, 32, 33, 198, 199, 220, 223, 225, 230
ethnographic, 8, 14, 19, 20, 32, 35, 118, 227, 284, 305, 309
   occasion, 12–15, 20, 21, 22, 24, 27, 41, 44, 45, 109, 262, 282, 283, 284, 285, 291, 312, 316, 321
   tradition, 7, 9, 12–15, 20, 21, 22, 24, 27, 28, 29, 31, 32, 39, 43, 44, 82, 283, 284, 312
ethnography, 2, 12–15, 18, 21, 23, 24, 29, 33, 36, 68, 89, 109, 199, 214, 215, 226, 228, 229, 230, 231, 242, 309

Subject Index

ethnology, 21, 25, 31, 32, 42, 82, 85, 92, 95, 96, 97, 98, 100, 102, 103, 104, 105, 107, 111, 158
  of India, 43, 82–107, 108, 109, 110
eugenic(s), 32, 38, 105, 199
Evangelical(s), 86, 87, 90, 101, 104, 109
evolutionary. *See* anthropology (-ical)
expeditions, 24, 72. *See also* art, of travel
expert(ise), 37, 39, 41, 341–43, 347. *See also* welfare (state)
extinction, 32, 183, 193, 220–24, 311. *See also* salvage

fetish(es), 9–15, 21, 35, 54, 55, 61, 65, 66, 70, 71, 72, 76, 77, 155
fetishism, 1, 9–15, 25, 32, 42, 54, 55, 56, 57–63, 64, 65, 68, 70, 71, 72, 77, 155, 176, 205
field(work), 1, 14, 21, 22, 27, 30, 33, 34, 36, 43, 45, 153, 154, 157, 177, 184, 197, 212, 213, 283, 284, 305, 307, 309, 312, 321, 326–31, 334–37, 339–43, 346, 348
  field science(s), 34, 45, 109, 327, 328
  intensive work, 37–38
fingerprinting, 29, 35, 166
folklore, 43, 110, 119, 121–25, 127, 148, 211, 215, 226, 296
functionalism, 38, 40, 85, 269, 270, 287, 306, 335, 344

gazetteer, 90, 146, 176
gender (transformation), 203, 285, 290, 315, 316
  masculine, 22, 292, 332
genealogical(ly), 156, 157, 170, 173, 176
genealogy (-ies), 20, 88, 109, 158, 159, 161, 169, 177, 197, 199, 225
Ghorka. *See* Gurkha
governmental, 18, 24, 62, 63, 170, 263
governmentality, 16–17, 19–20, 26–27, 32, 40, 43, 171, 174–76, 308, 313. *See also* art, of government
Gurkha, 25, 93, 94, 109

Hindu(ism), 83, 85–88, 92, 96–97, 102, 106, 107, 110, 130, 136, 163, 243, 244, 249. *See also* Brahman(ism)

history, 39, 40, 171, 174, 176, 193, 225, 232. *See also* anthropology (-ical), history of; archive of the present, 39–40, 156–57
holism, 30, 34–36, 38
home, 21, 33, 34, 38, 45, 175, 221, 227

ignorance of paternity. *See* nescience
improvement, 28, 33, 90, 91, 97, 99, 100, 101, 204, 217, 231, 312
indigenous authorities, 1, 14, 25, 28, 33, 91, 126, 168, 169, 257, 298, 333
  zamindar(s), 136, 137, 141, 142, 161
indigenous elite, 21, 27, 101, 126, 131, 134, 135, 147, 253, 258, 277
indirect rule, 25, 27, 33, 38, 76, 77, 246, 260, 262, 298, 333
informants, 1, 3, 20, 21, 24, 74, 88, 90, 92, 97, 121, 127, 128, 134, 147, 248, 277, 290, 329, 337
intelligence, colonial, 23, 24, 25, 26, 32, 39, 83, 84, 85, 87, 88, 89, 317
Islam, 86, 230, 243, 258, 263, 267

Kolarian, 105, 106, 107, 109. *See also* Dravidian; Tamulian

labor, 31–33, 56, 66, 69, 78, 83, 97, 99, 103, 105–6, 218, 221, 249, 255, 285, 303, 326, 328, 339, 342–43
laboratory, 166, 210, 241
land, 29, 31, 100, 101, 107, 109, 120, 137, 176, 181, 218. See also *terra nullius*
language, 21, 31, 35, 65, 85, 88, 92, 94, 95, 99, 103, 104, 119, 123, 144, 189, 190, 292, 344, 345. *See also* linguistic(s)
  of command, 123, 345
  speech, 118, 119, 121, 123, 131, 145
law, 26, 28, 29, 56, 76, 79, 86, 90, 110, 158, 169, 249
  adat, 23, 246, 262, 268, 276
  colonial, 70, 76, 77
  coutumier, 27, 28, 286, 287, 289, 291, 292, 294, 296, 297, 302, 303, 305, 306, 309
  custom(ary), 27, 76, 124, 129, 135, 286, 289, 291, 292, 296, 298, 303, 304, 310

legal, 27, 28, 55, 57, 63, 70, 71, 72, 77, 78, 86, 107, 171, 177, 245, 251, 268, 269, 304
Leiden Indology. *See* Dutch (Leiden) Indology
liberal(ism), 57, 67, 68, 69, 77, 78
linguistic(s), 1, 97, 228
location(s), 4, 7, 8, 9, 12, 19, 20, 24, 29, 40, 94

magic(al), 11, 94, 97, 207, 208, 339. *See also* superstition; witchcraft
martial (races, tribes, castes), 25, 94, 97, 99, 135, 139, 158, 160, 282, 283, 285. *See also* criminal castes and tribes; turbulent (castes, tribes)
material(ity), 9, 10, 11, 60, 156, 173, 326, 327, 338
medical (science), 29, 78, 90, 104
mercantile, 11, 13, 16, 17, 60, 61
method(ology), 8, 12, 17, 25, 35, 36, 37, 56, 57, 77, 83, 84, 85, 86, 89, 90, 91, 188, 189, 313, 327, 328, 329, 335
metropolitan, 35, 44, 63, 166, 175, 181, 182, 194, 283, 285
middleman, 1, 10, 12, 13, 21, 64, 65, 67, 141, 228, 253
  tangomao(s), 10, 13, 14, 15
military, 15, 24–26, 29, 37, 44, 45, 63, 72, 83, 93, 97, 99, 109, 131, 137, 180, 181, 182, 184, 282, 283, 285, 290, 310, 314
  recruitment, 97, 99, 139, 140, 158, 285, 293, 294, 302, 315, 316
  tribes (*see* martial (races, tribes, castes))
mission, 16, 17, 22, 59, 68, 87, 180, 283
missionary, 1, 8, 12, 13, 15, 29–31, 37, 43, 66, 67, 69, 77, 83, 87, 95, 99, 100, 104, 109, 169, 170, 175, 181, 221, 263, 287, 290, 299, 305, 306, 326, 337, 339, 343
money, 61, 62, 75, 76, 78. *See also* debt, monetary
monogenists, 32, 204
Montagnards, Vietnamese, 44, 282–321
  Rhadé, 25, 283, 286, 287, 289, 290, 292, 294, 297, 300, 301, 302, 311, 315

mother-right, 200, 201, 203, 209, 210, 216
museum (anthropology), 8, 9, 17, 162, 164, 165, 181, 188, 212, 338, 342
Mutiny of 1857, Indian, 94, 98, 103, 106, 120, 132, 133, 137, 139, 140, 249

nation(s), 102, 110, 174, 175, 180, 182, 216, 297, 307, 314
national (-ism, -ity), 16, 21, 23, 40, 45, 84, 119, 120, 187, 221, 222, 223, 225, 247, 259, 260, 263, 264, 267, 277, 284, 285, 287, 292, 296, 308, 329, 344, 345, 346, 348, 349
native point of view, 1, 21, 43, 120, 122, 123, 131, 135, 137, 143, 146
nescience, 198, 199, 203, 207, 209, 210, 211, 212, 213, 214, 215, 216, 226, 228, 229, 230, 231. *See also* virgin birth
  insemination, ignorance of, 202, 203, 204, 208
  paternity, ignorance of, 15, 196, 202, 203, 204, 210, 228, 230, 231, 232
  two forms of, 204, 205, 208

observation, 18, 19, 35
  personal, 21, 35, 88, 90, 92, 93, 97, 108, 159
observer(s), 3, 4, 8, 22, 35, 90, 167
oriental(ism), 4, 21, 23, 26, 27, 37, 40, 83, 84, 88, 90, 95, 98, 101, 111, 260
orientalist(s), 23, 25, 28, 42, 43, 85, 86, 87, 91, 93, 94, 99, 100, 107, 108, 110, 243, 244, 286, 288
origin(s), 88, 90, 92, 93, 95, 101, 156, 158, 226, 242
original, 247, 248, 252, 254, 258, 266, 276

pacification, 25, 29, 99, 105, 172, 282, 283
palabre du serment, 286, 291, 295, 296, 297, 300, 302
panoptic(ism), 24, 25, 90, 282
peasant(s), 28, 101, 117, 118, 125, 131
picturesque, 25, 187, 329–39, 348
pidgin, 10, 64, 228, 232

police, 26, 65, 157, 159, 160, 161, 163, 165, 166, 171, 176
policing, 28, 29, 35, 43, 110, 168, 286, 292
polygenism, 32, 110, 204
population(s), 18, 19, 26, 31, 71, 83, 89, 90, 91, 92, 94, 96, 99, 100, 102, 109, 203, 217, 223
préterrain, 12–15, 19–22, 24, 27, 34, 36, 41–45, 109, 283, 284, 299, 309, 312, 314, 321, 327
primitive, 200, 206, 286, 287. *See also* savagery
professional(ism), 1–3, 6–8, 13–14, 22, 34, 38, 40, 44, 45, 188, 189, 284, 306–8, 313, 314, 320, 326–28, 341, 343, 347
 anthropology, 3, 13, 14, 31, 45, 188, 284, 299, 306, 308, 310, 313, 314, 320, 321, 326, 328
 ethnography, 1, 26, 27, 193, 301, 305, 312
progress. *See* improvement
promiscuity, 200, 202, 203, 204, 209
proverb(ial), 21, 35, 43, 117–48

quantification, 19, 57, 90
questionnaire, 17, 34, 89, 90. *See also* statistics

race, 19, 21, 26, 32, 34, 38, 43, 69, 83, 95, 96, 98, 100, 101, 102, 104, 107, 326, 332, 334, 340, 344, 346, 347, 348
 racialization of caste, 100, 103–7, 110
railroad, 182, 185, 187
Rajputs (India), 118, 132, 133, 137, 138, 139, 140
relativism, 34, 44, 45, 197, 232, 285
 cultural, 283, 287, 297, 306, 307, 314, 320, 321
religion, 58, 252, 253, 256, 258, 259, 263. *See also* Christian(ity); fetishism; Hindu(ism); Islam; secular; theology (-igical)
representation(s), 4, 8, 14, 26, 35, 61, 62, 84, 86, 88, 90, 93, 100, 108, 118, 170, 180

research, 104. *See also* field(work); method(ology)
 assistants, 21, 126, 127, 130, 131, 229, 277, 329
resistance, 19, 20, 22, 33, 63, 136, 182, 220, 242, 246
revenue (settlement), 35, 90, 91, 100, 101, 103, 109, 119, 120, 126, 127, 131, 132, 137, 138, 157, 171, 172, 176, 255, 274
Rhadé. *See* Montagnards, Vietnamese

sacrifice, 71, 74, 75, 78, 79
 blood, 15, 42, 56, 63, 70–76, 79
 human, 53, 54, 57, 63, 64, 65, 67, 68, 69, 72, 73, 75, 170, 172
salvage, 32, 109, 183, 193, 227, 228, 229, 230, 231. *See also* extinction
savage(s), 42, 30, 54, 56, 82, 100, 103, 182, 187, 192, 193, 202, 203, 205, 206, 209, 210, 228, 271, 283, 290, 299, 313
savagery, 44, 63, 126, 197, 227
schakel-society, 271, 272, 275
secular, 87, 99, 253
settler colonialism, 33, 44, 143, 196–232, 283
settler(s), 1, 31, 32, 61, 109, 182, 196–232, 286, 326, 329, 332, 334, 335
slavery, 4, 31, 32, 33, 42, 55, 61, 67, 68, 69, 73, 109, 168, 169, 204, 242
sovereign(ty), 17, 76, 77, 177
speech. *See* language
state, 44, 174, 224, 225, 226, 228, 230, 252, 261
statecraft, 17, 18, 89. *See also* statistics, *Statistik*
statistical, 19, 24, 25, 26, 35, 83, 89, 92, 102, 345
statistics, 17, 18, 29, 35, 38, 85, 87, 89–91, 93, 95, 100, 101, 105, 164, 166, 167, 328
Statistik, 23, 89
strategic, 24, 121, 293, 294, 316, 321, 327
strategy (-ies), 3, 4, 19, 20, 22, 24, 33, 129, 131, 137, 140, 155, 185, 197, 198, 223, 228, 319
subaltern, 20, 27

subject(s), 4, 5, 16, 35, 174. *See also* universal (subject)
  colonial, 3, 5, 15, 20, 22, 24, 26, 41, 313, 321
  European or Western, 16, 19
  peoples, 3, 7, 22, 26, 37, 73
  position, 27, 35, 42, 39
superstition, 127, 208. *See also* magic(al); witchcraft
survey(s), 25, 26, 29, 89, 92, 102, 118, 286, 337. *See also* statistics
  ethnographic, 35, 100, 162, 167, 168, 169, 170
  (pan-) Indian, 36, 89, 100, 102, 103, 106, 107
survivals, 129, 130, 131, 136, 187, 208
sympathy, 37, 124, 192
synecdoche, 27, 28, 34, 35

tact(ics), 3, 4, 19, 20, 24, 25, 26, 37, 126, 299, 304, 310, 316, 317, 319, 320. *See also* sympathy
Tamulian, 95, 96, 105. *See also* Dravidian; Kolarian
taxation. *See* revenue (settlement)
technology, 10, 11, 17, 18, 66
terra nullius, 31, 32, 109, 217, 218. *See also* land
territory (-ialization), 17, 24, 29, 92, 106, 180, 198, 218, 221, 225, 246, 282, 285, 294, 295, 298, 320–21
text, 12, 14, 20, 29, 35, 71, 83, 86, 84–90, 91, 94, 110, 125, 154, 168, 172, 175, 176, 177, 181, 189, 197, 226, 228, 230, 243, 309
textualization, 20, 21, 27, 28, 43, 120–23, 128, 129, 131, 137, 140, 147, 148, 153
theology (-ical), 10, 59, 174
Toda tribe (India), 162, 164
topos. *See* commonplace(s), rhetorical
torture, 170, 171, 172, 175
totemism, 60, 205, 206, 207, 215, 228, 231
tourist (-ism), 172, 182, 185, 187, 194, 266, 267, 275, 327, 333, 338, 339

trade, 1, 4, 10, 11, 12–15, 16, 17, 18, 35, 37, 42, 55, 56, 60, 64, 65, 68, 71, 72, 76, 110, 180, 190, 222, 337, 339
tradition(s), 73, 86, 87, 92, 124, 167, 173, 174, 177, 268, 269, 270, 298, 338
  invention of, 21, 28, 119, 121, 123, 125, 126, 131, 246, 250, 252, 253, 257, 261, 265, 273, 278, 303, 306 (*see also* ethnographic, tradition)
travel writing, 184–85. *See also* art, of travel
tribal(ization), 21, 26, 27, 118, 126, 285, 286, 289, 292, 309, 321, 339
tribe, 22, 25, 40, 83, 93, 101, 107, 162, 164, 166, 167, 169, 173
trifle, 11, 12, 59, 61, 64
turbulent (castes, tribes), 132, 133, 134, 135, 137, 139, 140

universal (subject), 3, 9, 16, 19, 56, 60, 67
urban, 326, 328, 340, 341, 343, 344, 348
utilitarian(ism), 86, 87, 90, 101, 332

Viêt Minh, 284, 285, 298, 300, 302, 310, 311, 315, 316, 317, 318, 319
village (community, republic), 28, 35, 99, 101, 102, 103, 104, 110, 147, 242, 244, 245, 247, 248, 252, 253, 254, 260, 268, 274, 333
virgin birth, 1, 15, 44, 197, 225, 226. *See also* nescience

war, 24, 26, 45, 56, 61, 71, 194, 282, 284, 285, 299, 315, 316, 321
welfare (state), 22, 36, 39, 40, 41, 45, 341. *See also* expert(ise)
Whiggish interpretation, 1, 39, 69, 91. *See also* anthropology (-ical), history of
witchcraft, 10, 64, 77, 78, 206. *See also* magic(al); superstition

zamindar(s). *See* indigenous authorities